D1409388

Structural Hearing

TONAL COHERENCE IN MUSIC

Structural Hearing

TONAL COHERENCE IN MUSIC

VOLUME TWO

BY FELIX SALZER

WITH A FOREWORD BY LEOPOLD MANNES

DOVER PUBLICATIONS, INC. • NEW YORK

Published in Canada by General Publishing Company, Ltd., 30 Lesmill Road, Don Mills, Toronto, Ontario.
Published in the United Kingdom by Constable and Company, Ltd., 10 Orange Street, London WC 2.

This Dover edition, first published in 1962, is an unabridged and corrected republication of the work originally published by Charles Boni in 1952, to which has been added a new Preface by the author.

Standard Book Number: 486-22276-4

Manufactured in the United States of America
Dover Publications, Inc.
180 Varick Street
New York, N. Y. 10014

Acknowledgments

Grateful acknowledgment is made to the following publishers for permission to use copyrighted material:
Associated Music Publishers, Inc. (Ex. X, 410, 411, 445, 453).
Boosey & Hawkes, Inc. (Ex. 239, 241, 377, 386, 406, 407, 412, 416, 419, 452).
Elkan-Vogel Co., Inc. for Durand et Cie. (Ex. 290).
Leeds Music Corp. (Ex. 380, 451).
E. B. Marks Music Corp. (Ex. 413).
Oxford University Press, Ltd. (Ex. 319, 331).
Salabert, Inc. (Ex. 414).

I wish, furthermore, to thank the following for permission to reprint material from their publications:
Harvard University Press, for various quotations from *Historical Anthology of Music; Oriental, Medieval and Renaissance*, Vol. I, Revised edition, 1949 (Ex. 184, 185, 510, 513, 515, 524, 525).
E. B. Marks Music Corp. for Ex. 415.
Oxford University Press, Ltd. for Ex. 209.
G. Schirmer, Inc. for Ex. 418 and for the excerpts from Ruth and Thomas Martin's translation of *The Magic Flute* (Ex. 483).

F.S.

Contents

Musical Illustrations

Notes to the Reader

Ideally, a book of this type would present every musical quotation discussed, along with its voice-leading graphs. This proved impractical for reasons of space; therefore, the following plan has been adopted. With very few exceptions the examples in Part I, Part II through Chapter Six and in Part III appear in complete form (music and graphs). In Chapter Seven the music has been omitted for most quotations from standard literature and for the quotations of large excerpts. Chapter Eight, which deals with complete compositions, offers exclusively voice-leading graphs without the music. Since all the music omitted is from available editions, it is hoped that this procedure will not be disadvantageous to the reader.

It has been found practical to print many examples and their graphs (especially the larger ones) running across facing pages, in order to make the course of voice leading clearer for the eye, and to avoid awkward turning of pages as much as possible. The first such example is Ex. X. If there is doubt about the continuity, the reader is advised to orient himself by means of the measure numbers.

In the quotations from music of earlier times, treble and bass clefs have been consistently used, even if the transcriptions in the indicated sources do not follow this procedure. Furthermore, in some compositions, transpositions and change of note-values have been carried out, thus reverting to the readings of earlier sources.

List of Musical Illustrations

Notes and Glossary for the Voice-Leading Graphs

1. The note-values indicate the structural value and significance of tones and chords; they do not indicate rhythmic values.

2. The difference in structural significance is given in four different note-values: half-notes, quarter-notes, notes without stem and occasionally eighth-notes. The latter are used to indicate embellishments and appoggiaturas. The highest note-values in a graph represent tones or chords of the highest structural order. Among notes of equal value, those whose stems reach the same level are of the same structural order.

3. The relation between identical and different tones or chords, and specifically their structural connection, is indicated by dotted or solid slurs and lines, curved or horizontal arrows or by beams.

4. Horizontal, solid arrows (used mostly in regard to bass motions) indicate the direction or driving tendency of the music in general, or passing motions in particular.

5. A note in parenthesis with or without a dotted stem means a note expected on the basis of direct voice leading, but omitted or substituted for in the composition.

6. Brackets of various kinds indicate either chord prolongations ⏟ or melodic parallelisms ⌐¬ .

7. Roman numerals are assigned to harmonic chords only; the relative size of these numerals corresponds to their structural value.

8. A small Roman numeral in parenthesis indicates the chord of harmonic emphasis.

Glossary of Symbols

P	Passing tone or passing chord
N	Neighbor note or neighbor-note chord
UN and LN	Upper and lower neighbor note
IN	Incomplete neighbor note
N P	Neighbor-passing chord
Em	Embellishing chord
CS	Contrapuntal-structural chord
DF	Double function chord
M	Mixture
||	Interruption
D	Dividing dominant
A B or A B A^1	Indication of form

List of Sources (*Abbreviations*)

AM *Altniederländische Motetten*, ed. by W. Braunfels. Oratoriumsverlag, Köln.

AMI *L'Arte musicale in Italia*, ed. by L. Torchi. G. Ricordi e C., Milano.

AUDM *Aufführungspraxis der Musik*, by R. Haas. Akademische Verlagsgesellschaft Athenaion, Potsdam.

CM *Cent Motets du XIIIe Siècle*, transcribed by P. Aubry. Rouart, Lerolle & Cie., Paris.

DAS CHORWERK *Das Chorwerk*, ed. by F. Blume. G. Kallmeyer Verlag, Wolfenbüttel.

DTOE *Denkmäler der Tonkunst in Oesterreich*. Artaria & Co., Wien.

HAM *Historical Anthology of Music; Oriental, Medieval and Renaissance Music*, ed. by A. T. Davison and W. Apel, Vol. I. Rev. ed. Harvard University Press, Cambridge, Mass.

HDM *Handbuch der Musikgeschichte*, ed. by G. Adler, 2nd ed. Heinrich Keller, Berlin.

EPM *The Evolution of Piano Music (1350–1700)*, ed. by C. Sachs. E. B. Marks Music Corp., N. Y.

MET *Music of Earlier Times (13th Century to Bach)*, ed. by J. Wolf. Broude Bros., N. Y.

MMA *Music in the Middle Ages*, by G. Reese. W. W. Norton & Co., N. Y.

MW Guillaume de Machaut, *Musikalische Werke*, ed. by F. Ludwig. Breitkopf & Härtel, Leipzig.

OHM *The Oxford History of Music*. Oxford University Press, Ltd., London.

OL Orlando di Lasso, *Sämtliche Werke*. Breitkopf & Härtel, Leipzig.

SHM *A Short History of Music*, by A. Einstein. 2nd ed. Alfred A. Knopf, N. Y.

TC *Sechs Trienter Codices*, ed. by G. Adler. In DTOE.

VDO *Studien zur Vorgeschichte der Orchestersuite im 15. und 16. Jahrhundert*, by F. Blume. Kistner & Siegel, Leipzig.

WJO Jacob Obrecht, *Werken*, ed. by J. Wolf. Johannes Müller, Amsterdam.

WJP Josquin des Prés, *Werken*, ed. by A. Smijers. G. Alsbach & Co., Amsterdam.

Note: Sources for the quotations from English virginal compositions, which have been repeatedly reprinted, are omitted.

Musical Illustrations

I BACH Prelude No. 21 (Well-Tempered Clavier, Bk I)

III BACH Chorale (No. 23)

V SCHUBERT Waltz, Op 18, No. 10

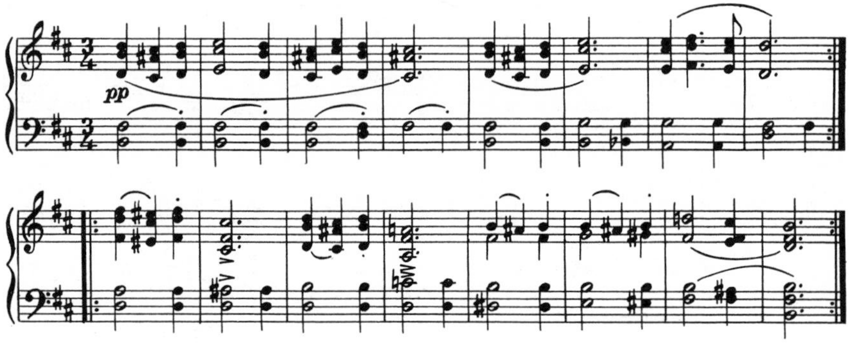
pp

a

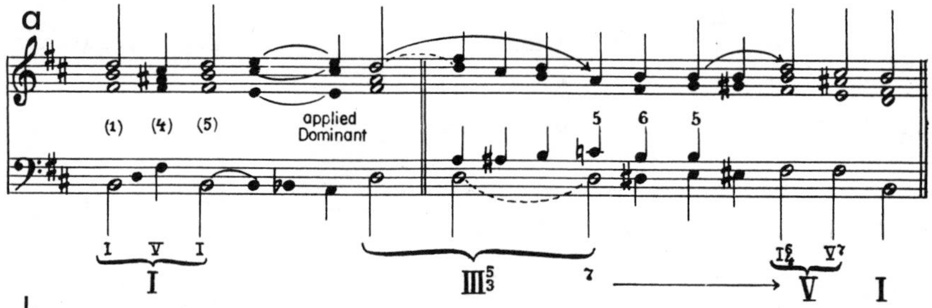
(1) (4) (5)
applied Dominant
5 6 5
I V I
I
III 5/3
7
I 6/4 V7
V I

b

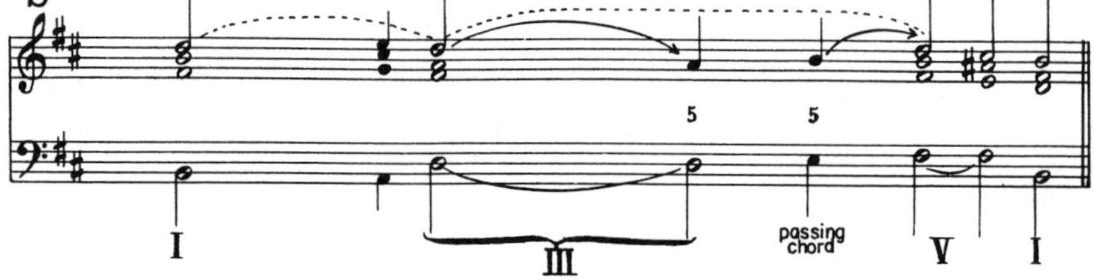
5 5
I
III
passing chord
V I

c

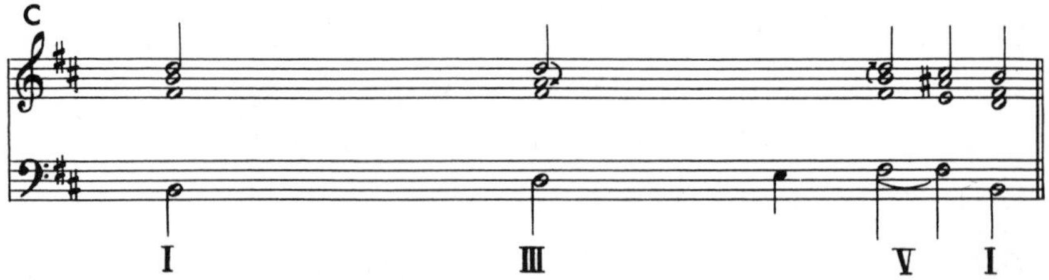
I
III
V I

VI

horizontalization of

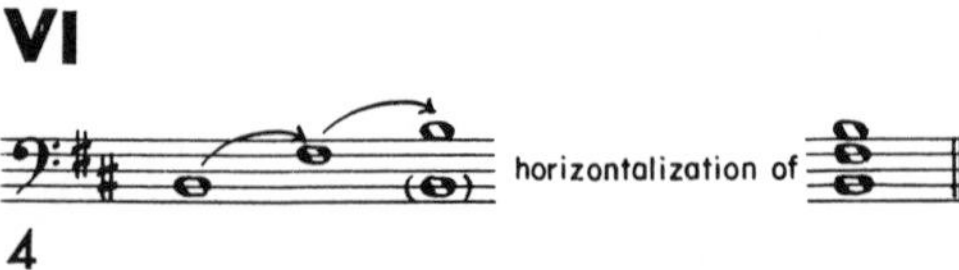

VII
or
I V I I V I
I
VIII
MOZART Piano Sonata, A minor, K. 310
Exp.
Dev.
Rec.
a
1st subject
2nd subject
(50)
(58)
(66)
(70)
(74–79)
(80)
applied Dominant
applied Dominant
P
I
III
III
V
I
b
8
8
8
P
III
V
c
P
III
V

IX

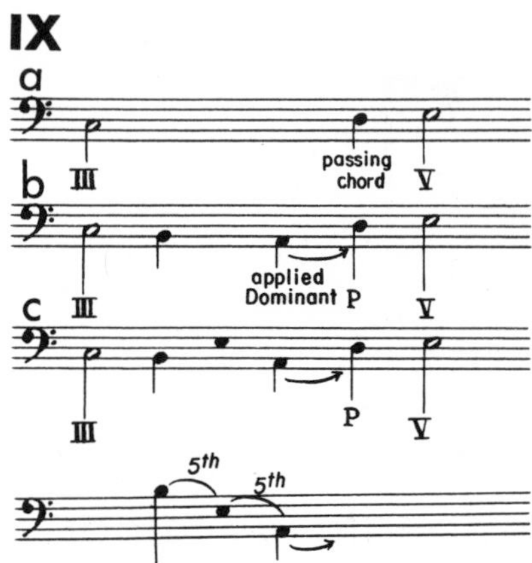

X HINDEMITH Piano Sonata No. 3

With quiet motion

mp

(4)

p

a

I

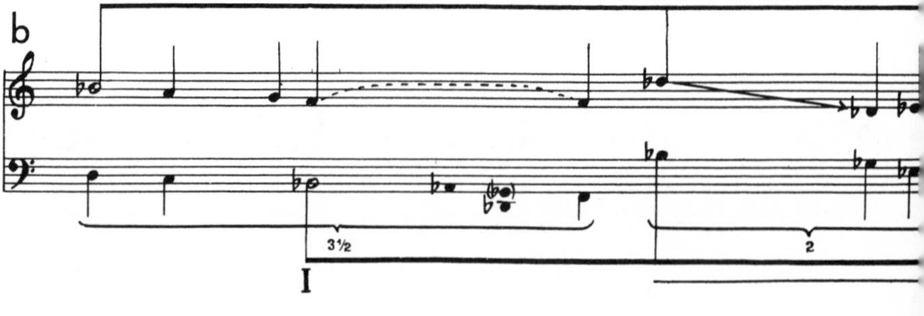

b

3½

2

I

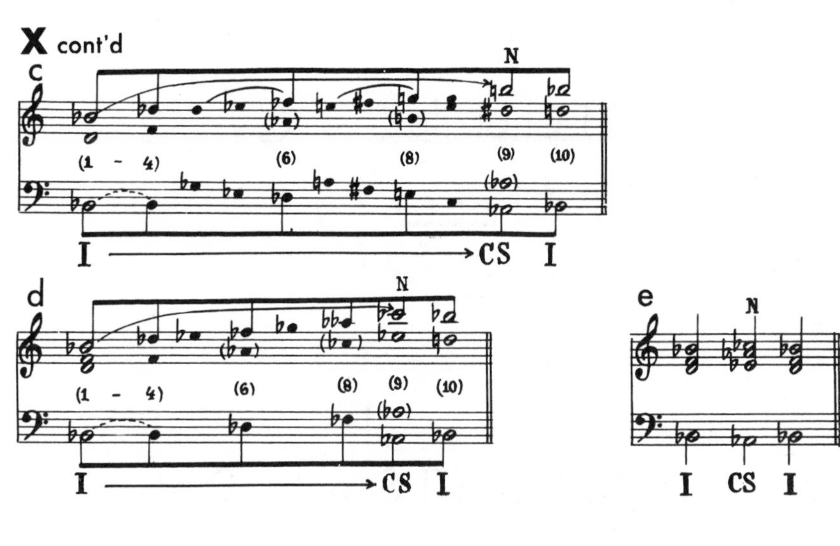
X cont'd
c
N
(1 - 4)
(6)
(8)
(9)
(10)
I → CS I
d
N
(1 - 4)
(6)
(8)
(9)
(10)
I → CS I
e
N
I CS I

ont'd
(6)
(8)
(10)
mp
mf

cont'd
N
→ CS I
cont'd
N
2
1
½
→ CS I

1 BACH Chorale (No. 6)

2 D. SCARLATTI Sonata, D minor, L. 413

3 BEETHOVEN Bagatelle, Op 119, No. 11

4

5 SCHUMANN Little Piece (Album for the Young)

6 SCHUBERT Waltz, Op 9, No. 8

7 HAYDN Minuet

8 FOLK TUNE

9 SCHUMANN Album-Leaves, Op 124 No. 16

10 BEETHOVEN Piano Sonata, A Major, Op 2, No. 2

10 cont'd

a

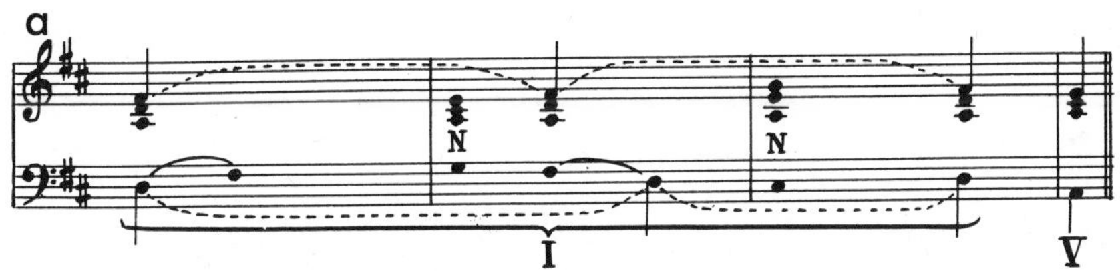

11 BACH Chorale (No. 7)

a

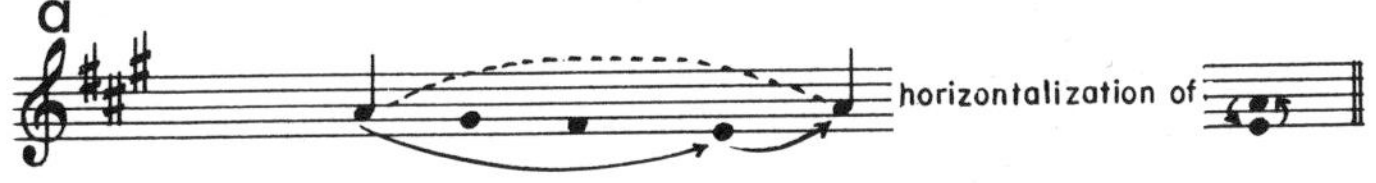

b

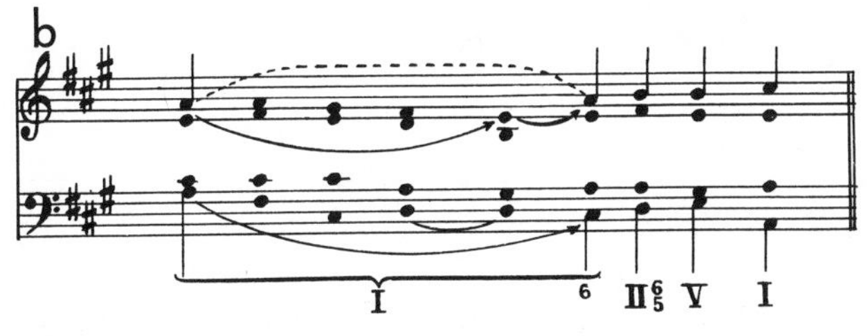

c

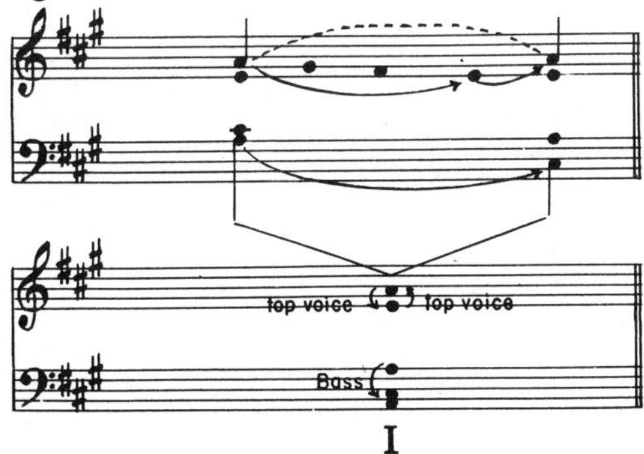

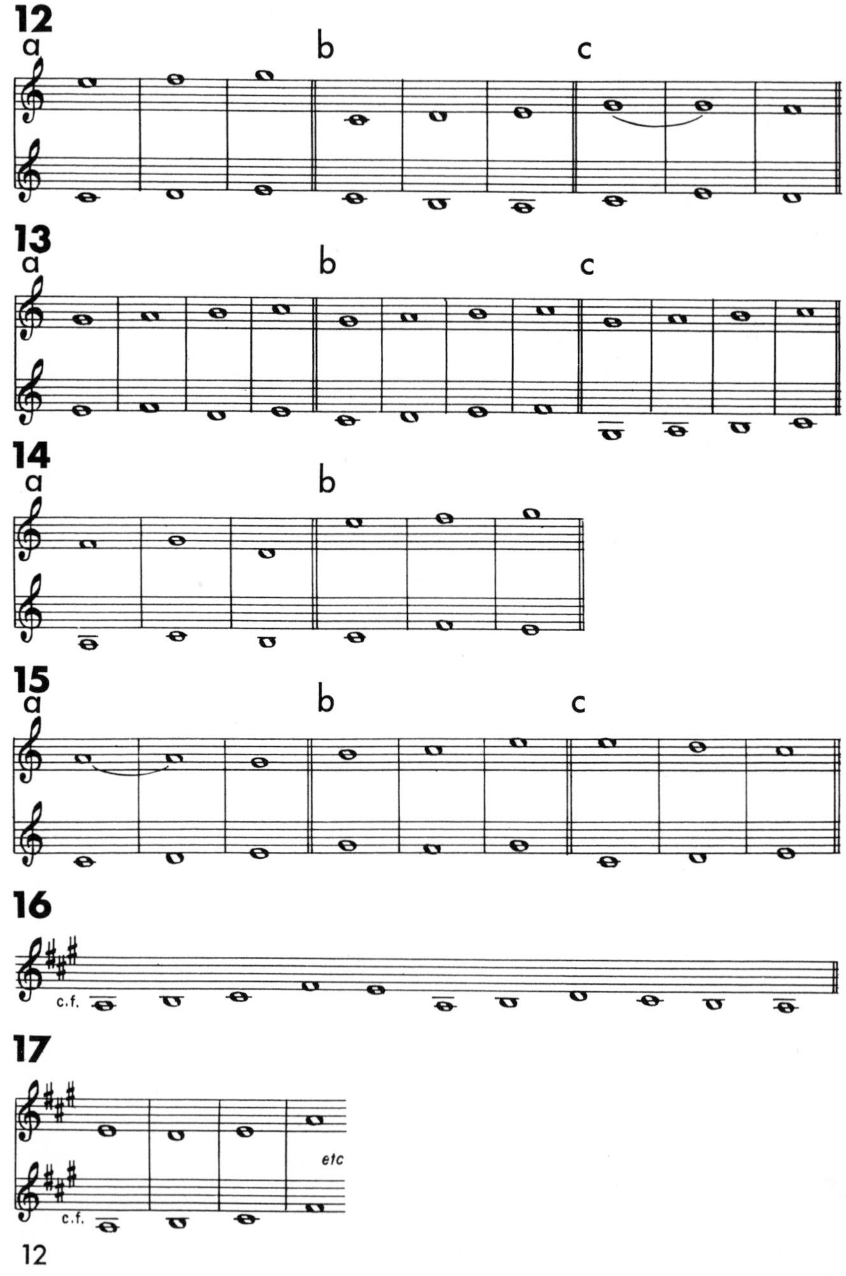
12
a
b
c
13
a
b
c
14
a
b
15
a
b
c
16
c.f.
17
etc
c.f.

18

19

20

21

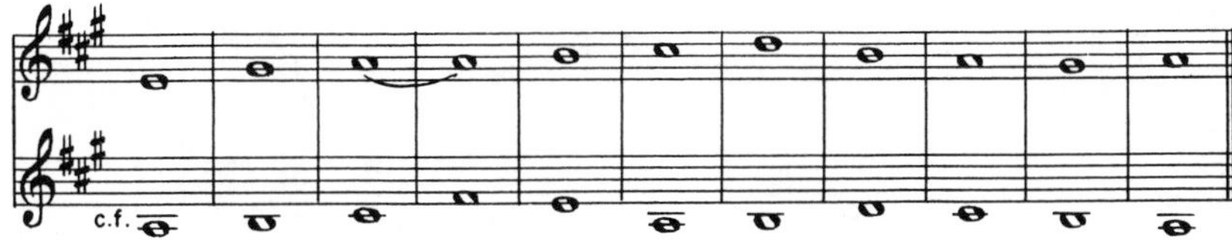

22

23

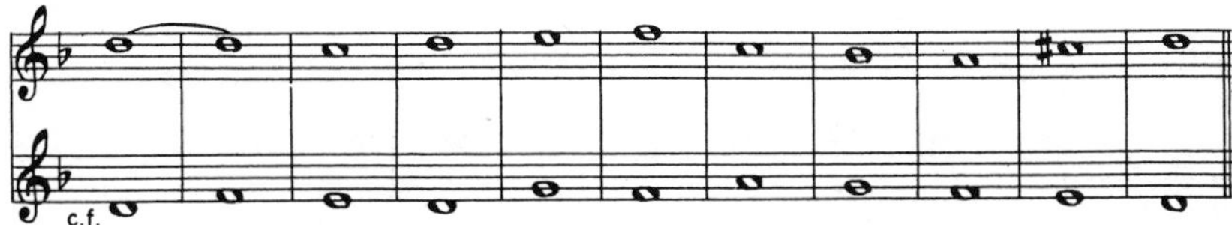

24

a

b

25 a b

26 a b

27 a b

28

29

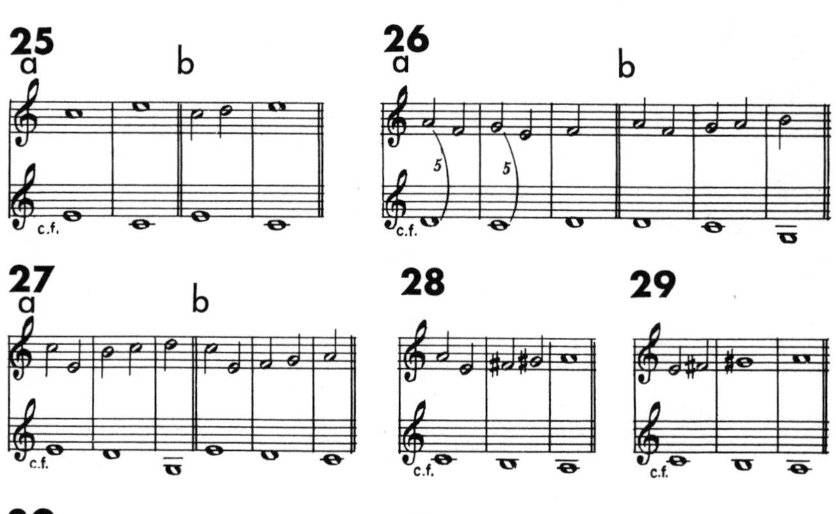

30

31

32

c.f. from

33

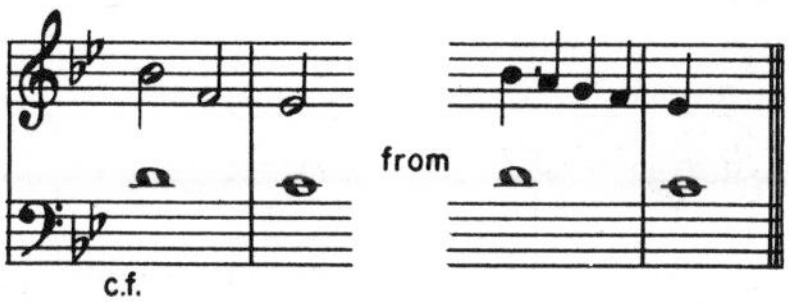

c.f. from

34

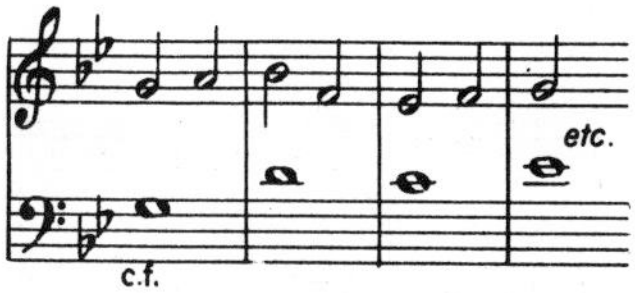

c.f. *etc.*

35

not good good not good good

c.f.

36

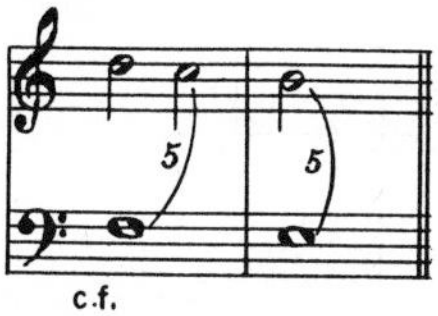

5 5

c.f.

37

c.f.

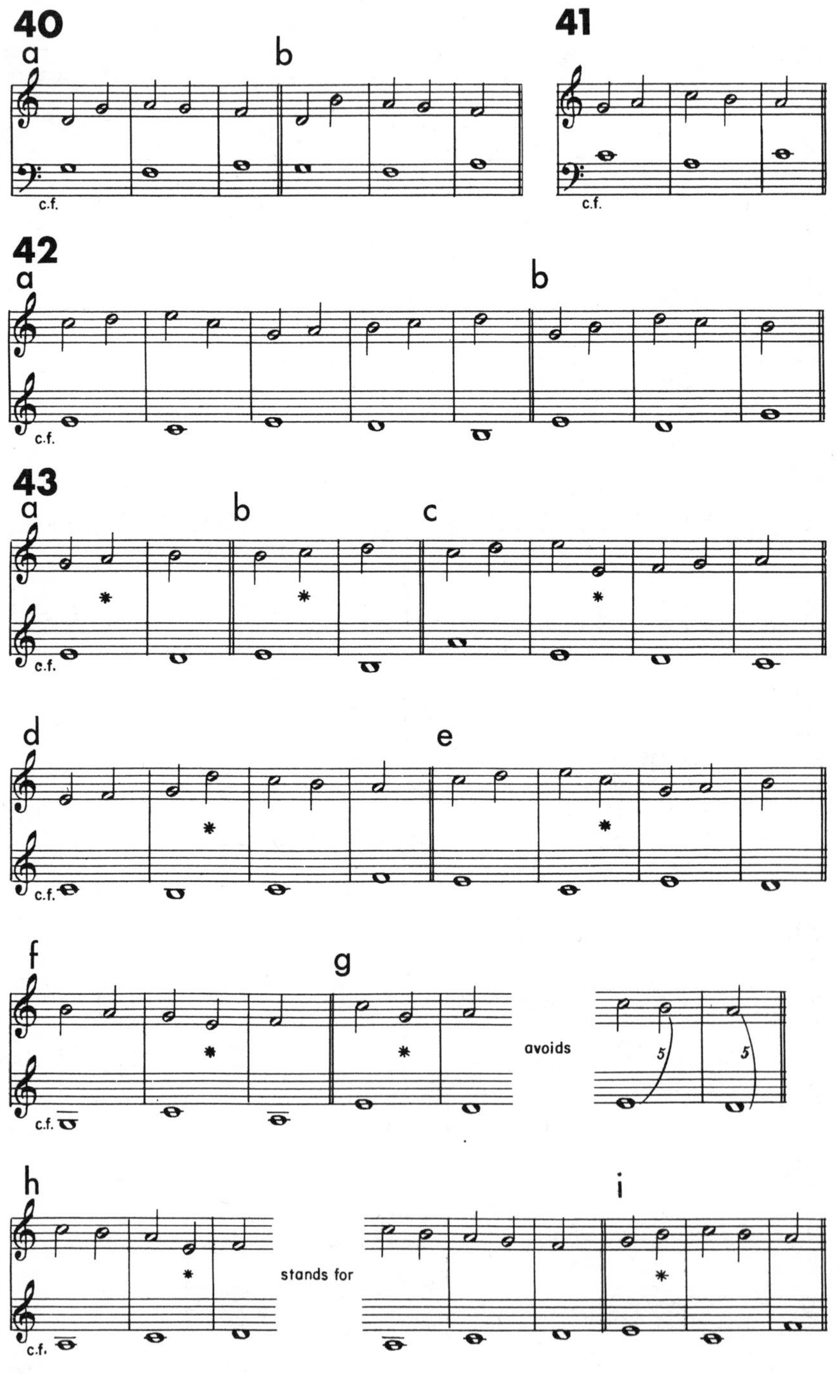
40
a
b
c.f.
41
c.f.
42
a
b
c.f.
43
a
b
c
c.f.
d
e
c.f.
f
g
c.f.
avoids
5
5
h
i
c.f.
stands for

44

45

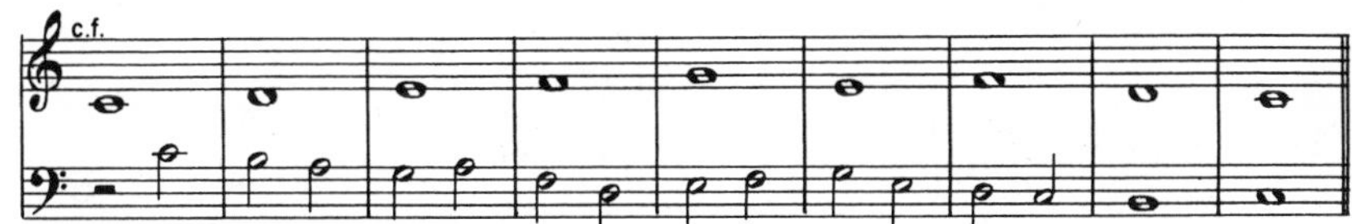

46

47

48

49

50

51 **52**

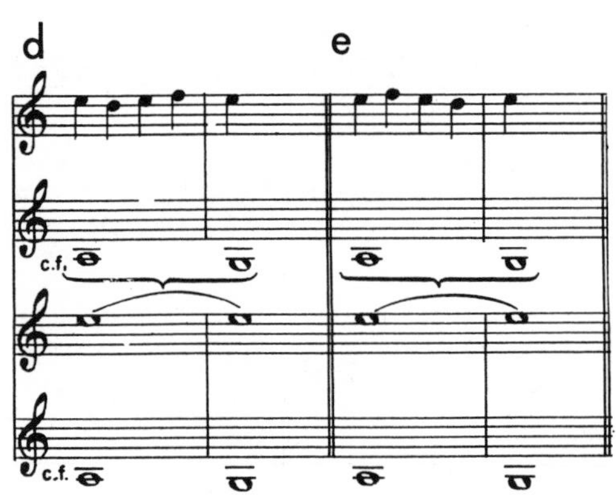

53 **54**

55

58

59

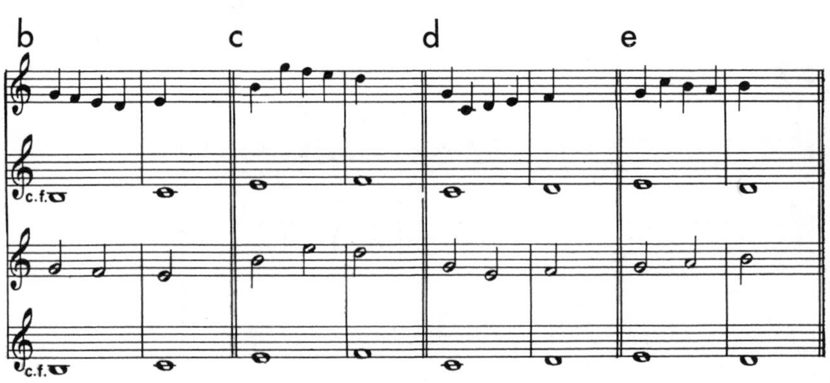

60

61
c.f.
62
a
7 - 6
7 - 6
7 - 6
c.f.
b
4 - 3
4 - 3
4 - 3
c.f.
c
c.f.
9 - 10
9 - 10
9 - 10
63
a
9 - 10
9 - 10
9 - 10
c.f.
b
c.f.
7 - 6
7 - 6
7 - 6
64
a
c.f.
5 - 6
5 - 6
5 - 6
b
6 - 5
6 - 5
6 - 5
c.f.
65
a
c.f.

65 cont'd
b
c.f.
66
a
good
b
c
d
a
not good
b
c
d
67
a
b
c
d
e
f
g
h
68
c.f.
69
a
b
c
c.f.
70
a
b
c
c.f.
71
c.f.
72
c.f.

73

75

76

c.f.

77

78

79

80

81

82

83

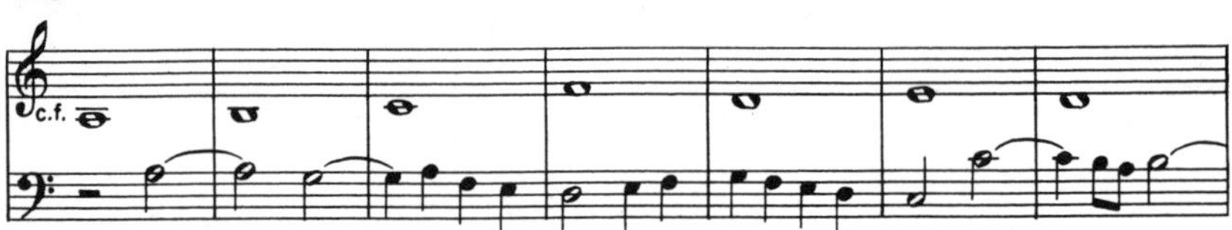

84

85

86

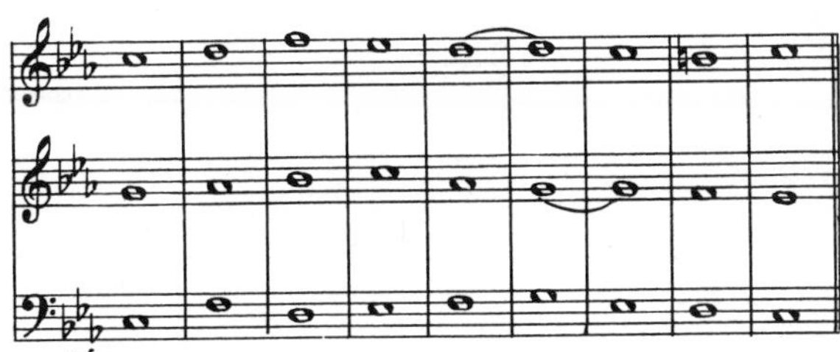

87

88

89

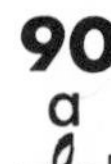

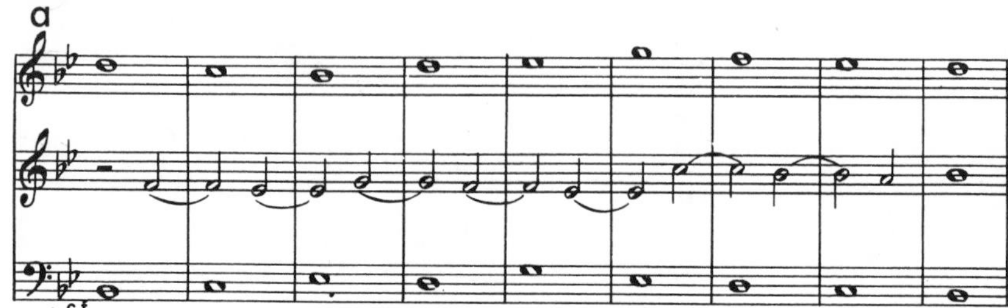

91

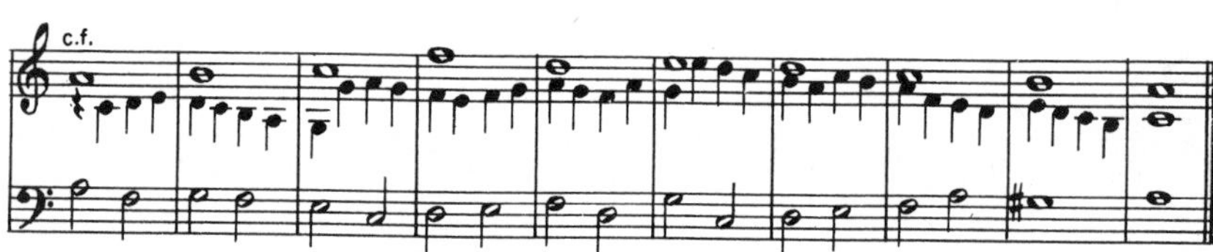

92

93

94

a b

c.f.

95

c.f.

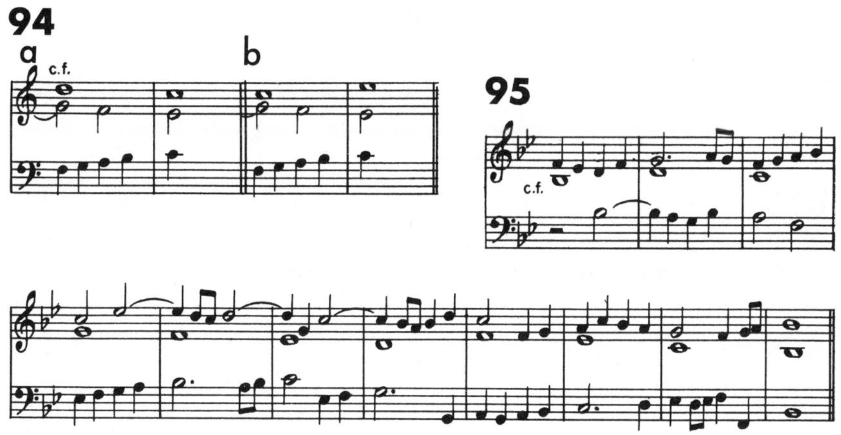

Part II Chapter Four

96

a b

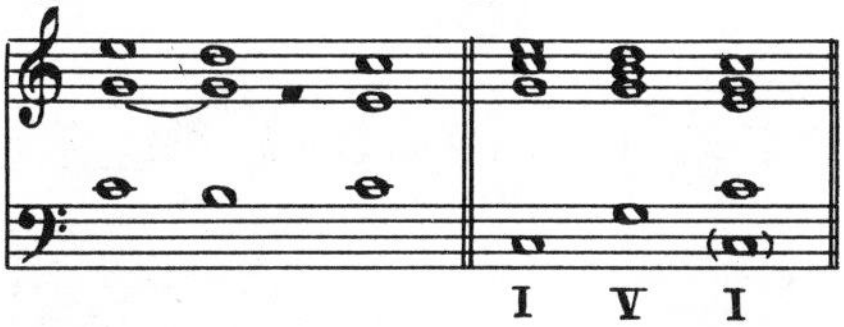
I V I

97

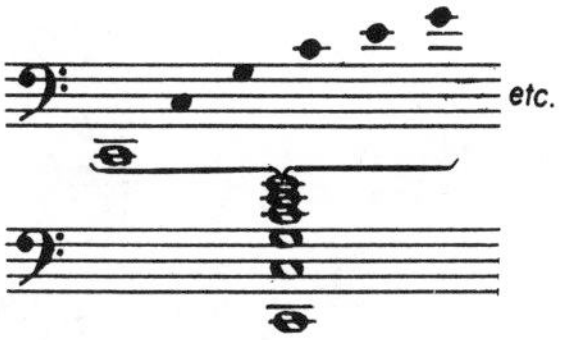
etc.

98

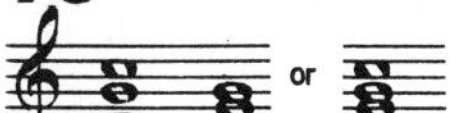
or

99

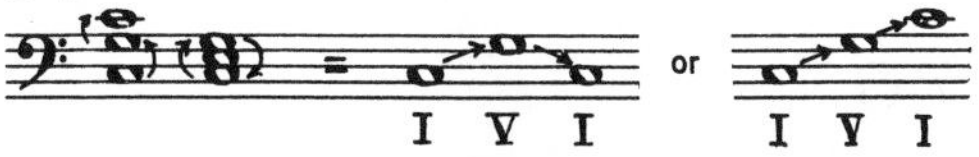
=
or
I V I
I V I

100

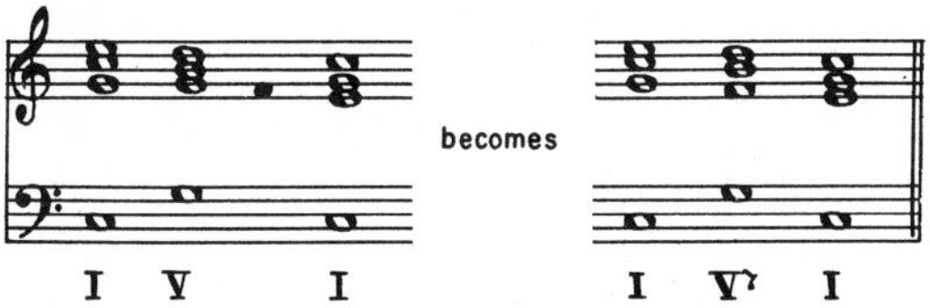
becomes
I V I
I V7 I

101

a

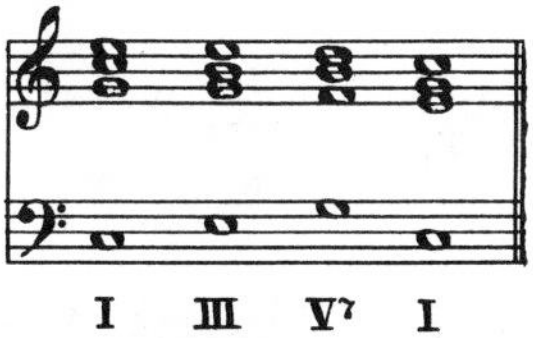
I III V7 I

b

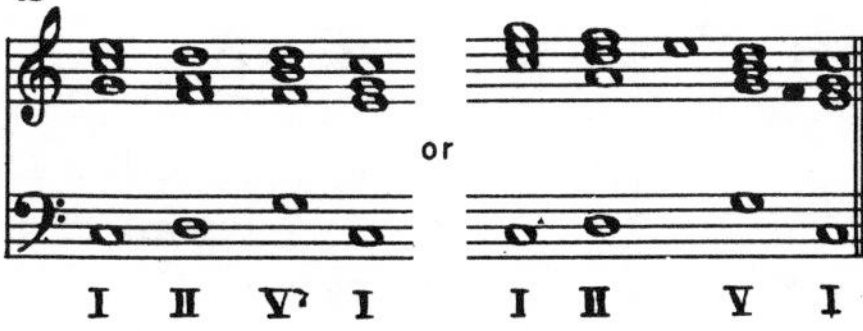
or
I II V7 I
I II V I

c

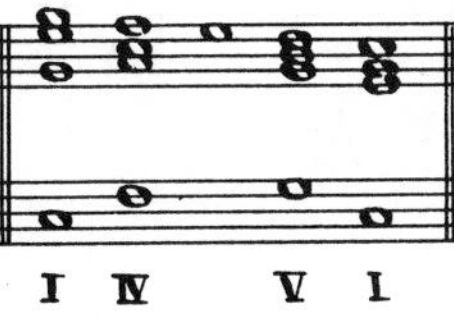
I IV V I

102

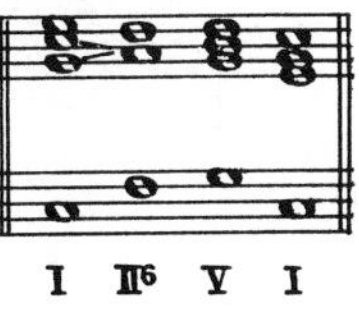
I II6 V I

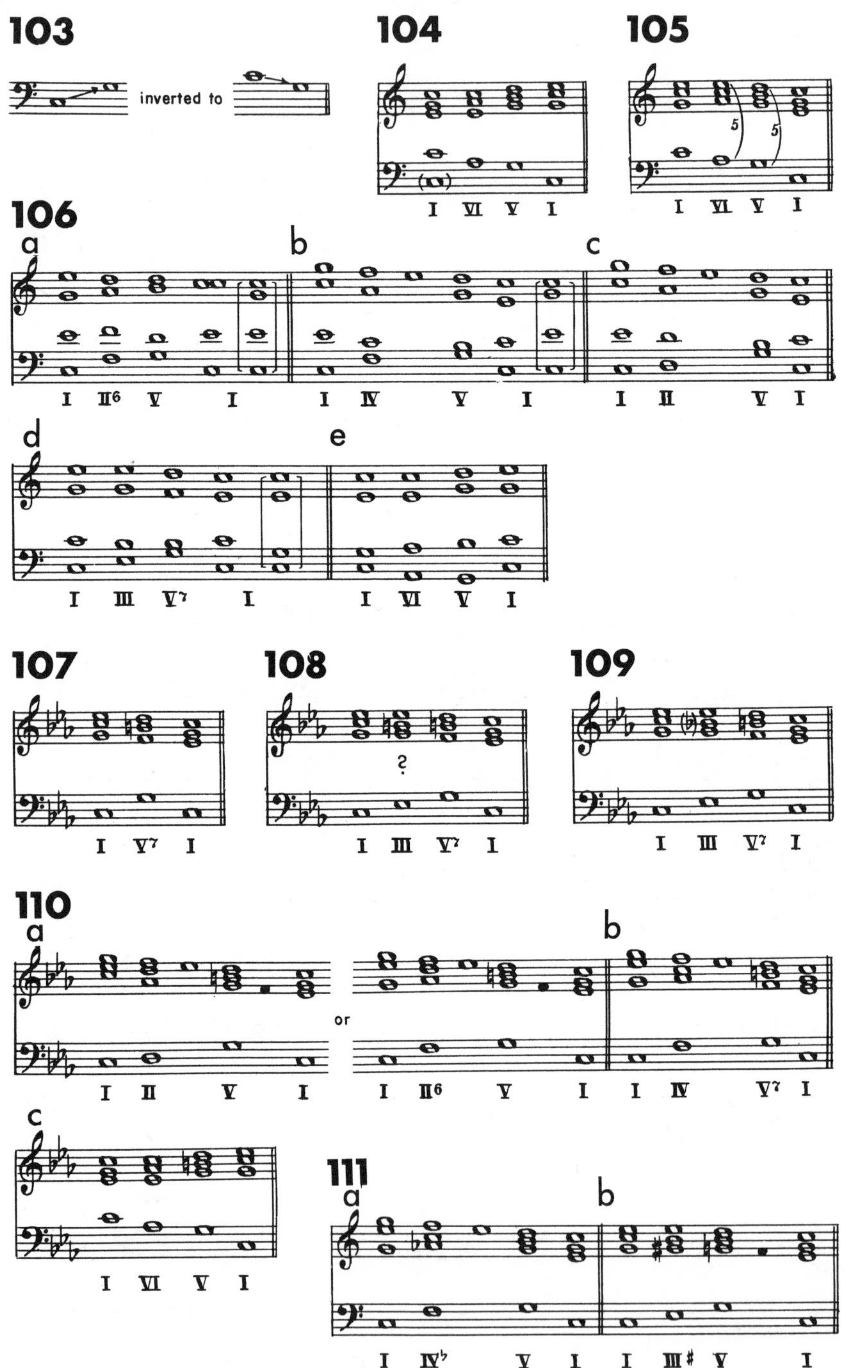
103
inverted to
104
I VI V I
105
5
5
I VI V I
106
a
I II6 V I
b
I IV V I
c
I II V I
d
I III V7 I
e
I VI V I
107
I V7 I
108
?
I III V7 I
109
I III V7 I
110
a
I II V I
or
I II6 V I
b
I IV V7 I
c
I VI V I
111
a
I IV♭ V I
b
I III♯ V I

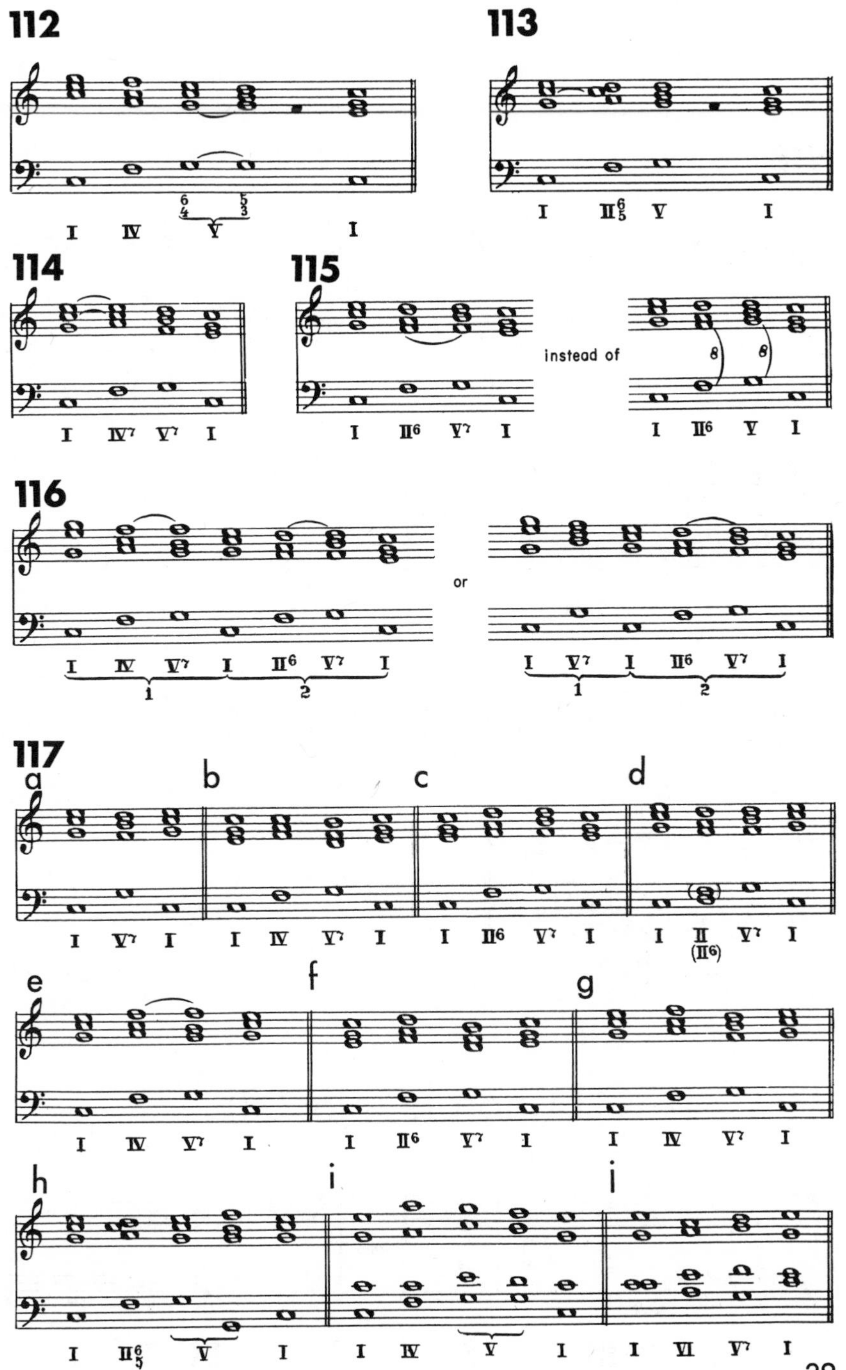
112
I IV V I
113
I II6/5 V I
114
I IV7 V7 I
115
I II6 V7 I
instead of
I II6 V I
116
I IV V7 I II6 V7 I
1 2
or
I V7 I II6 V7 I
1 2
117
a
I V7 I
b
I IV V7 I
c
I II6 V7 I
d
I II (II6) V7 I
e
I IV V7 I
f
I II6 V7 I
g
I IV V7 I
h
I II6/5 V I
i
I IV V I
j
I VI V7 I

118

119 BACH Chorale (No. 337)

120 BACH Chorale (No. 88)

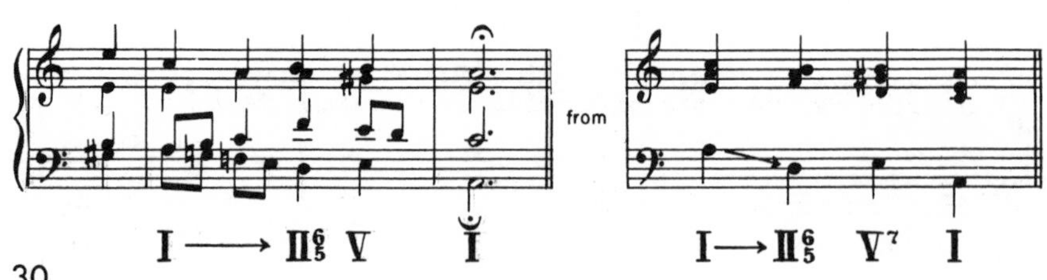

121

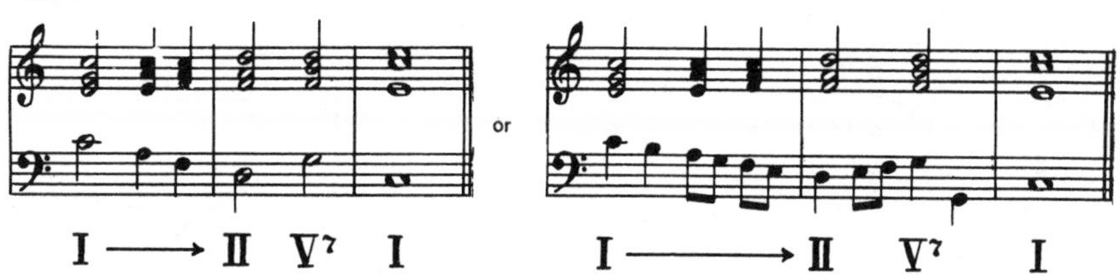

122 BACH Chorale (No. 348)

123

BACH Chorale (No. 246)

124

125

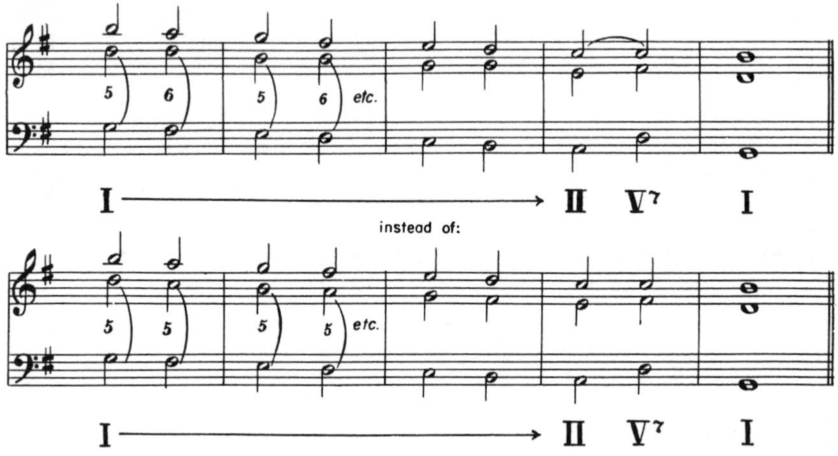
5 6 5 6 etc.
I → II V7 I
instead of:
5 5 5 5 etc.
I → II V7 I

126

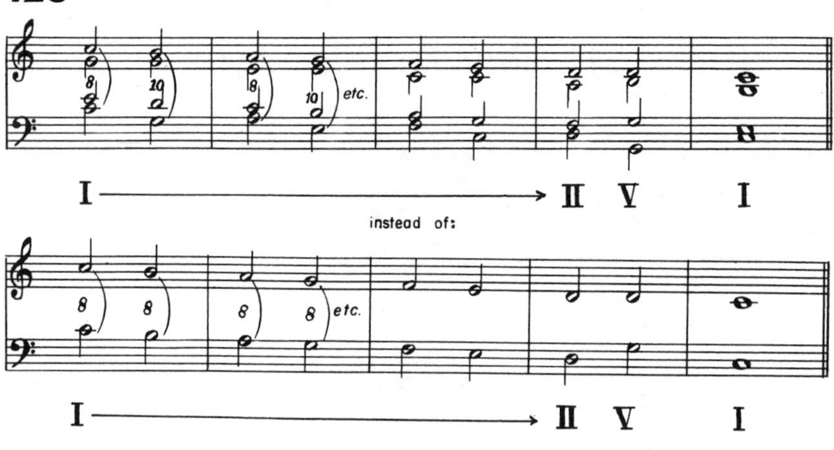
8 10 8 10 etc.
I → II V I
instead of:
8 8 8 8 etc.
I → II V I

127

a
I → II7 V I

127 cont'd
b
I → III6/5 or II6 V I
128
from
I → II V I
I II V7 I
129
a
I II V7 I
b
I II V I
c
I → V I
d
I → V I

130

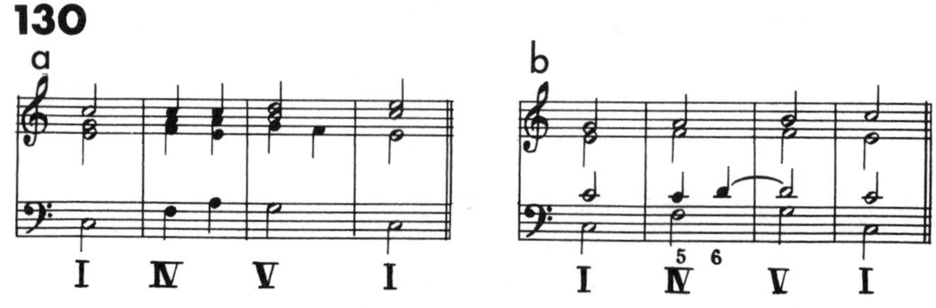

131 CHOPIN Waltz, Op 34, No. 2

132 BACH Gavotte (French Suite No. 5)

133 BRAHMS Piano Sonata, F minor, Op 5

136 cont'd
f
g
137
a
b
c
d
e
138
a
b
c
d
139
a
b
c
140 BACH Chorale (No. 330)
141 SCHUBERT Waltz, Op 50, No. 1
p

142 CHOPIN Waltz, E Major (Posth.)

143 MOZART Piano Sonata, C Major, K. 545

144 SCHUBERT Ländler Op 67 No. 5

145 BACH Chorale (No. 346)

146

a

b

147 BACH Little Prelude, C minor

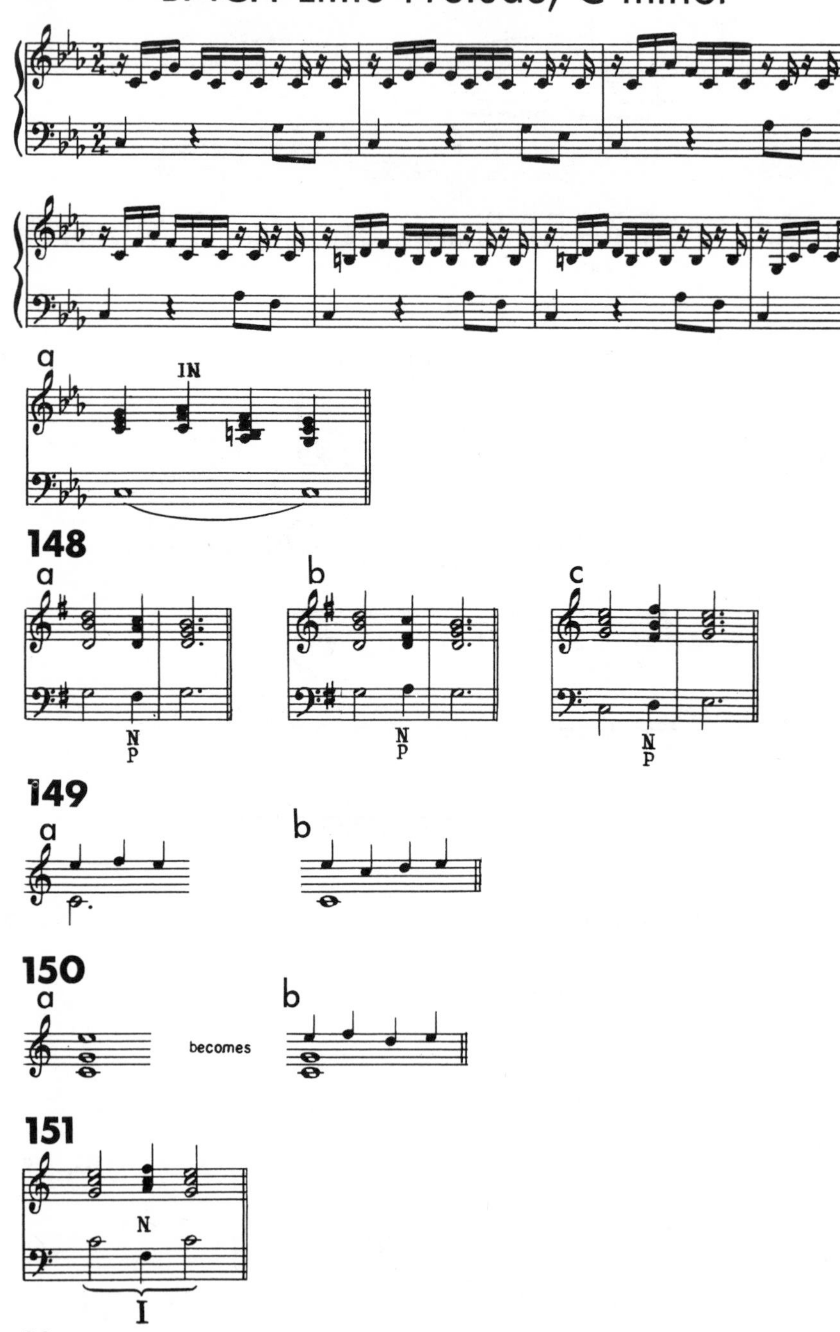

152 BACH Prelude No. 1 (Well-Tempered Clavier, Bk I)

a

153

a

b

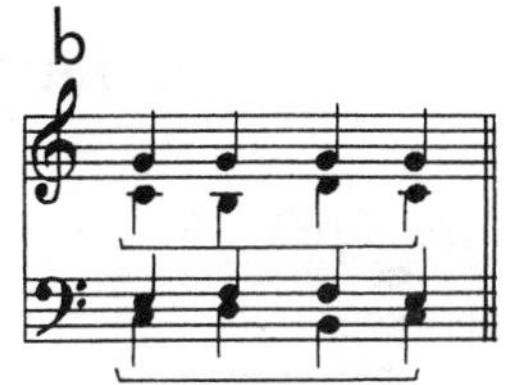

c

154 C. P. E. BACH Minuetto

155 CHOPIN Waltz, Op 69, No. 2

156 JOSQUIN Missa: Pange lingua

Et in - car - na - tus est

Et in - car - na - tus est

Et in - car - na - tus est

Et in - car - na - tus est

[From *DAS CHORWERK*, Vol. I]

157

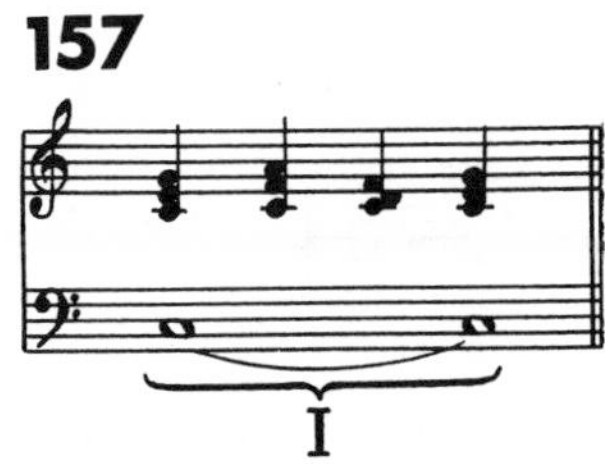

158 BACH Prelude No. 6 (Well-Tempered Clavier, Bk I)

159

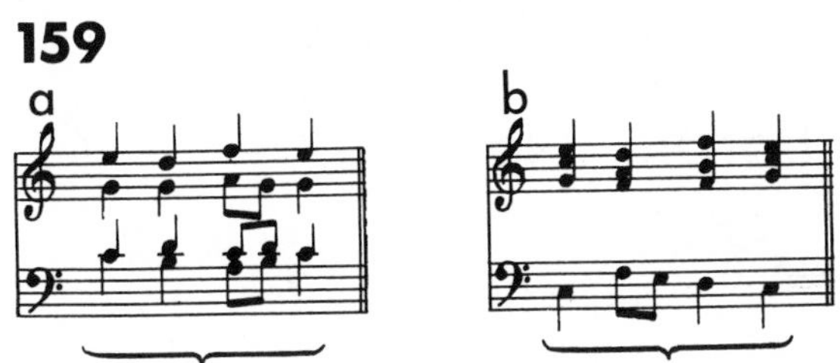

160 BACH Chorale (No. 11)

160 cont'd
a
I
161
a
b
c
d
e
f
g
162 BACH Chorale (No. 366)
163 BACH Chorale (No. 367)

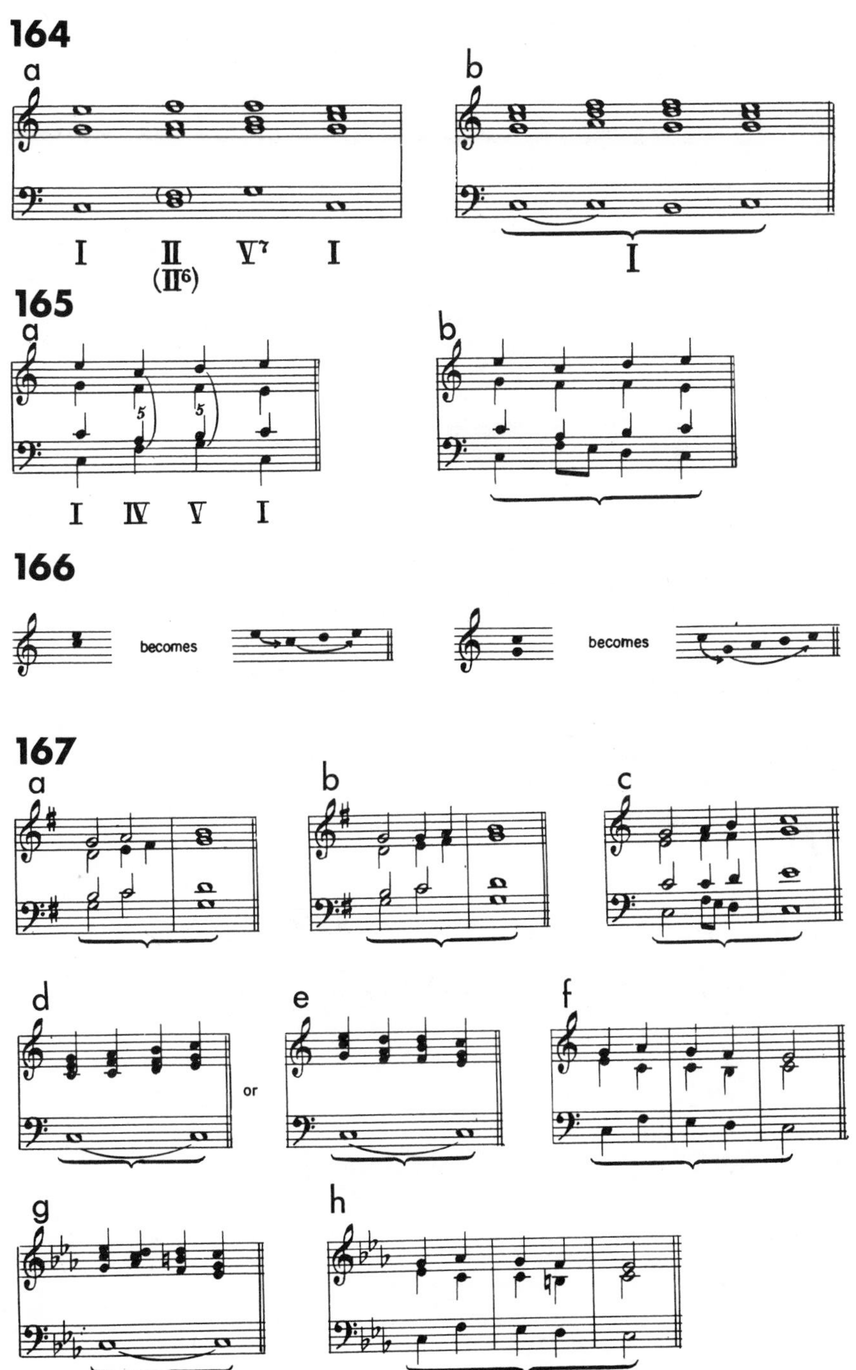
164
a
b
I
II
(II6)
V7
I
I
165
a
b
5
5
I
IV
V
I
166
becomes
becomes
167
a
b
c
d
or
e
f
g
h

168 BACH Chorale (No. 24)

169 BACH Prelude No. 2 (Well-Tempered Clavier, Bk II)

170 BACH Little Prelude, F Major

171

171 cont'd
c
172
a
6
b
6
4
c
4
3
or
4
3
173
174
BACH Chorale (No. 233)
a
b
5
4
7
I
V
I

175 BACH Chorale (No. 367)

176 BACH Chorale (No. 362)

177 BACH Chorale (Peters No. 118)

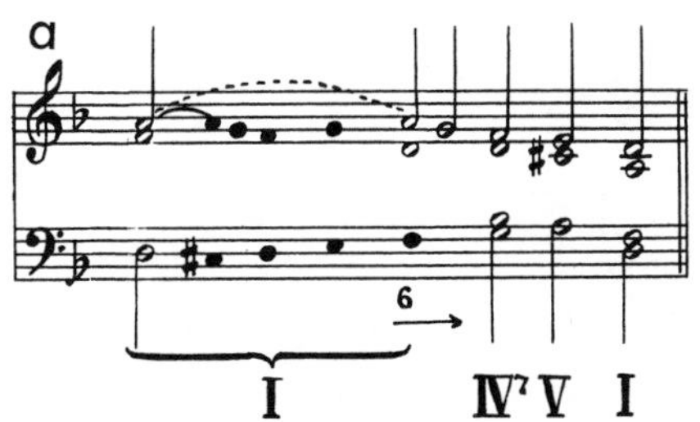

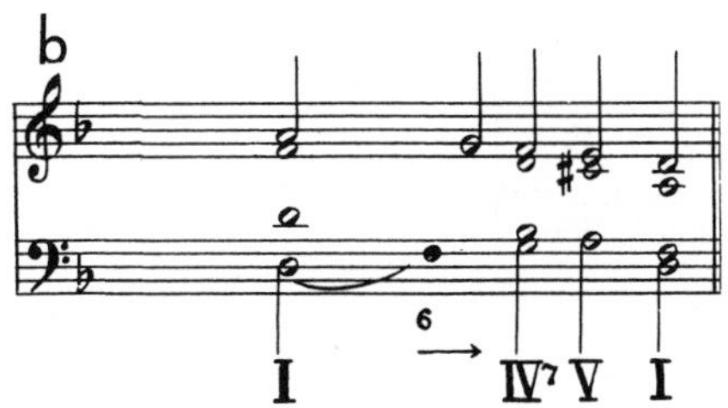

178

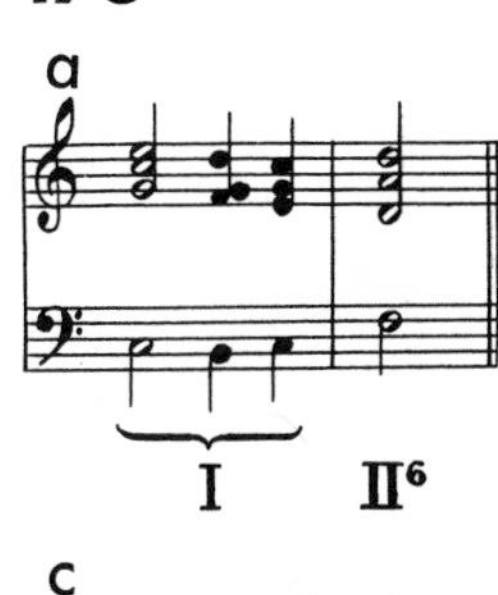

179 BACH Chorale (No. 110)

180

181

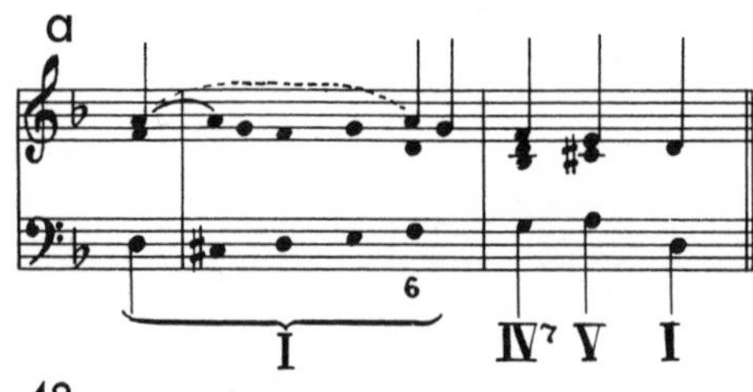

181 cont'd

b

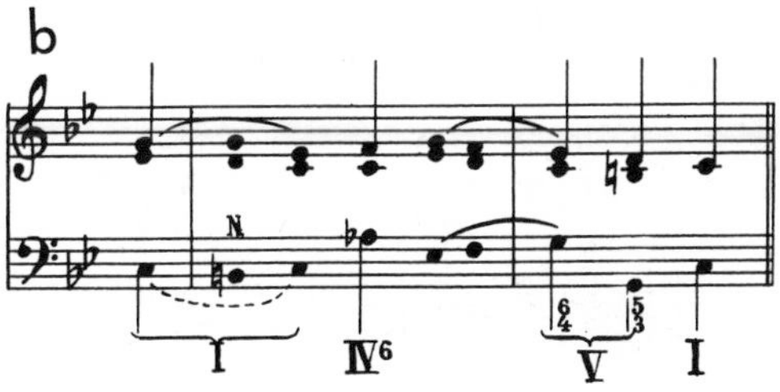

182 BACH Chorale (No. 42)

a

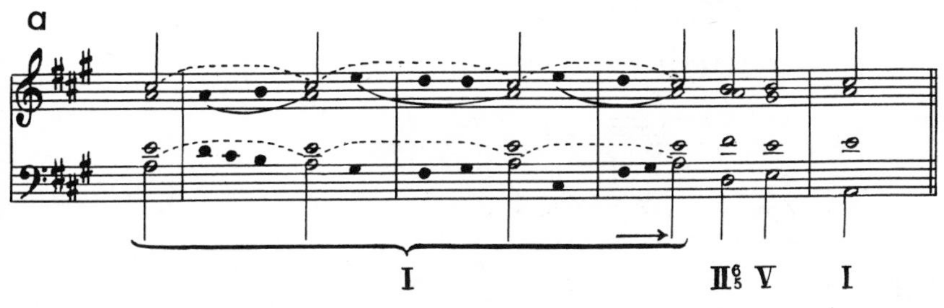

b

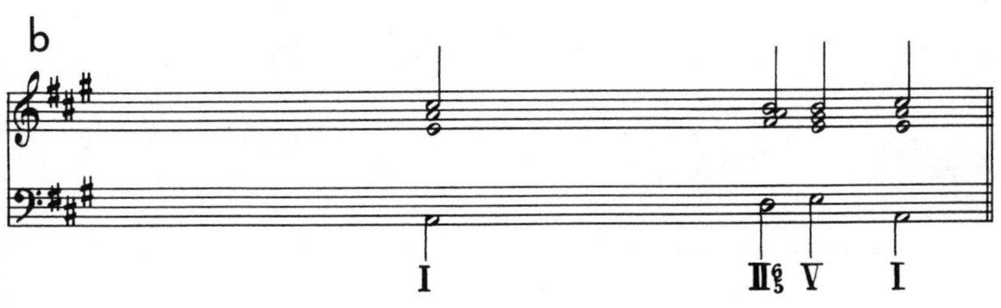

183 MOZART Piano Sonata, D Major, K. 311.

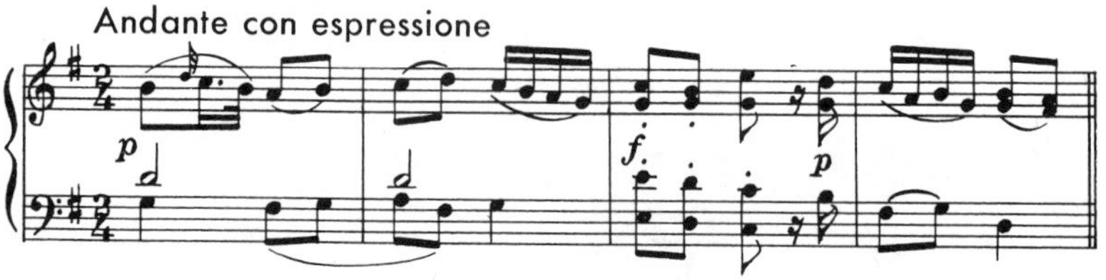

Andante con espressione
p
f.
p

a

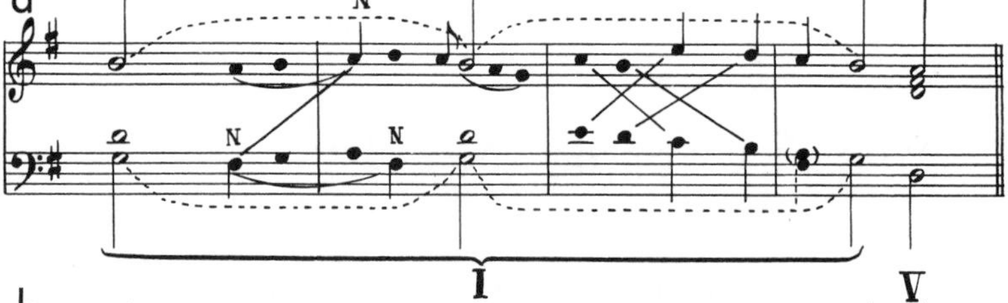

N
N
N
I
V

b

N
I
V

184 JOSQUIN Motet: Tu pauperum refugium

Tu pau - pe - rum re - fu - gi - um,

[From *HAM*, Vol. I, No. 90]

a

N
N

b

N

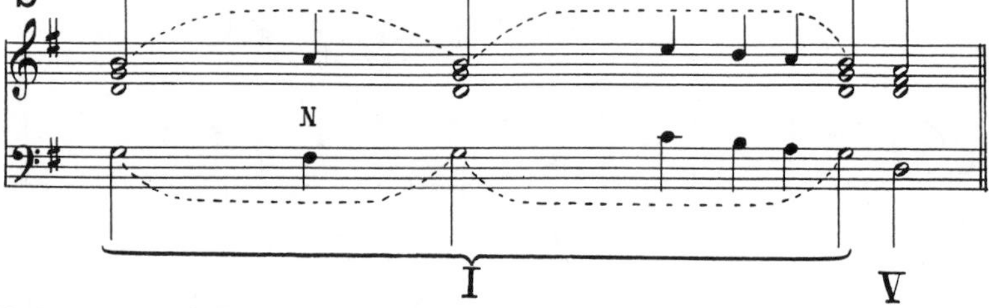

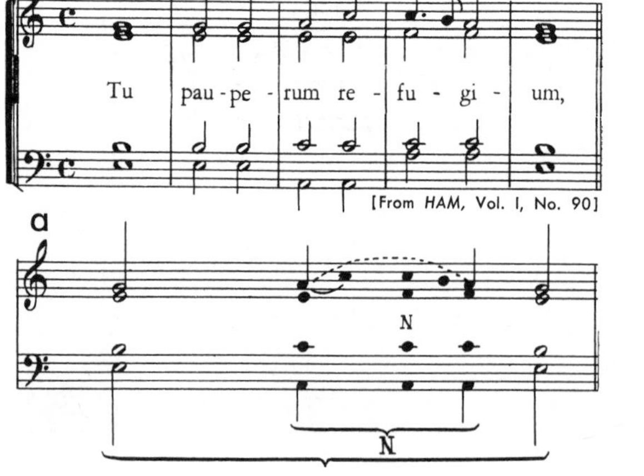

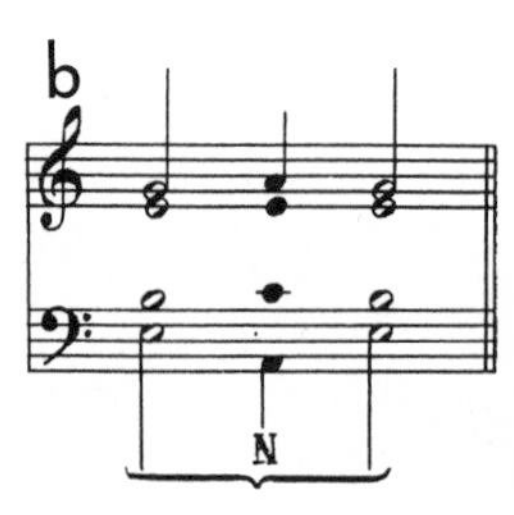

185 GIACOMO FOGLIANO Ave Maria

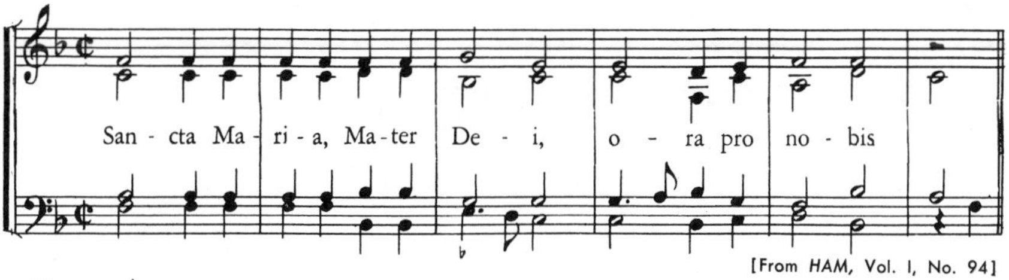
San - cta Ma - ri - a, Ma - ter De - i, o - ra pro no - bis

[From *HAM*, Vol. I, No. 94]

a

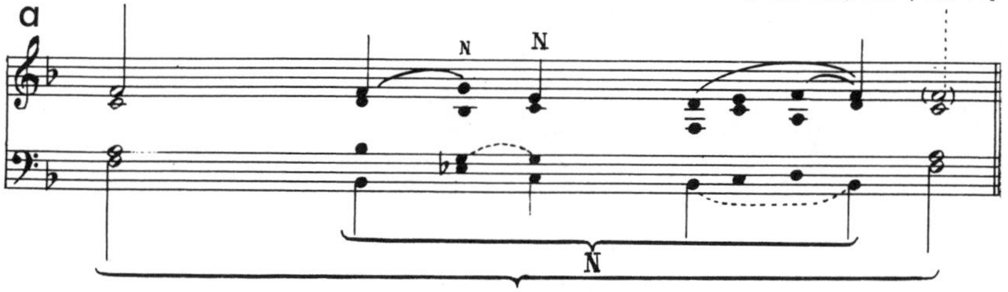
N
N
N

b

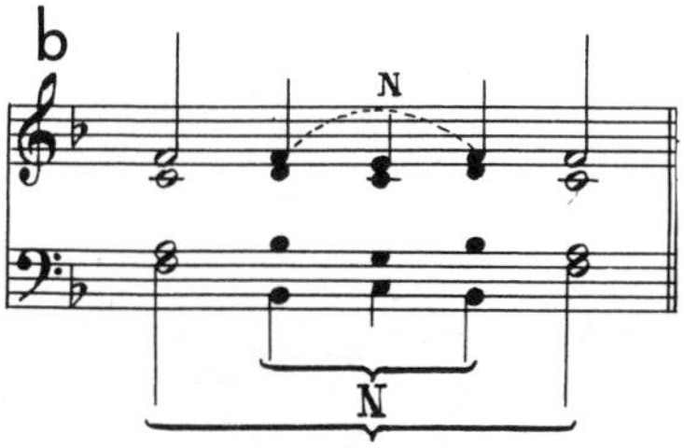
N
N

c

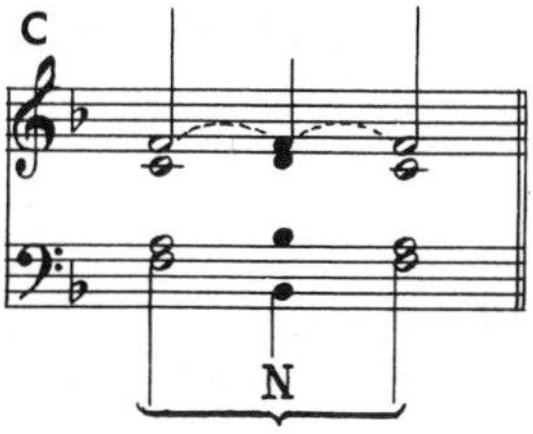
N

186 BARTÓK Piano Pieces for Children, No. 32

Allegro ironico

f

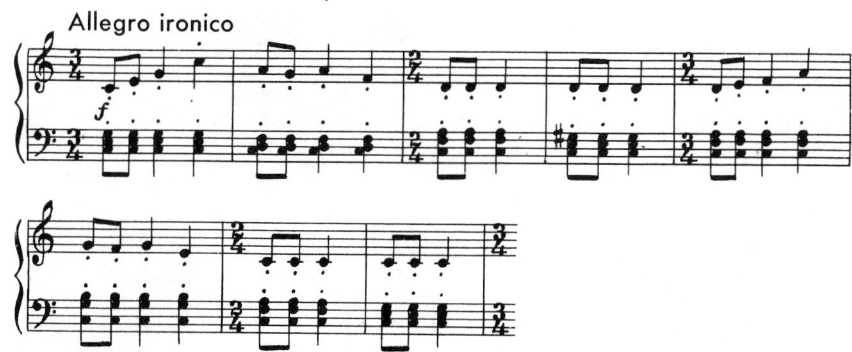

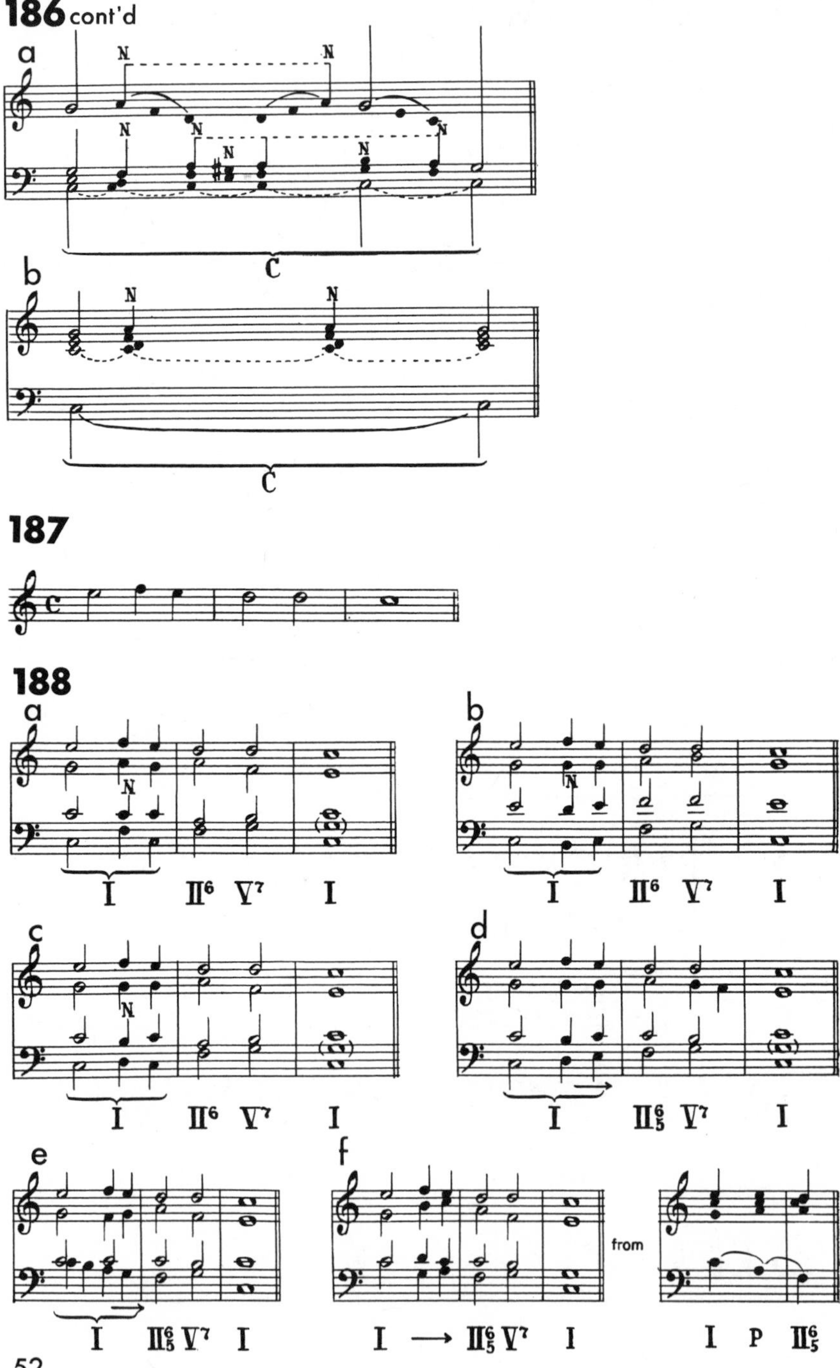
186 cont'd
a
N
N
N
N
N
N
N
C
b
N
N
C
187
188
a
N
I II6 V7 I
b
N
I II6 V7 I
c
N
I II6 V7 I
d
I II6/5 V7 I
e
I II6/5 V7 I
f
I → II6/5 V7 I
from
I P II6/5

189

a

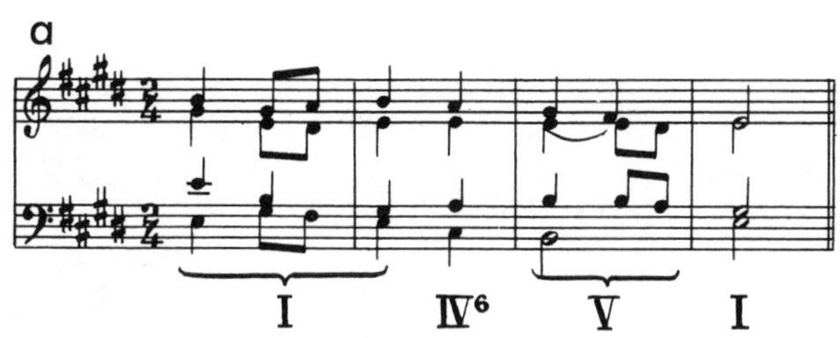

b

190

a

b

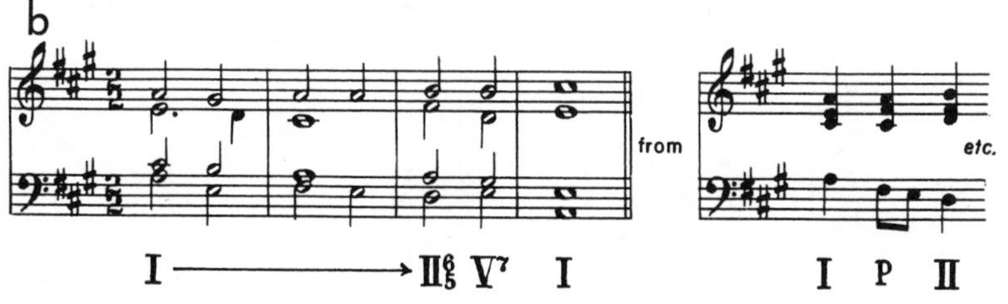

191

192

193

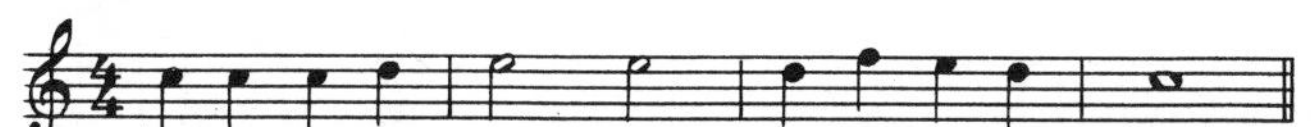

a

b

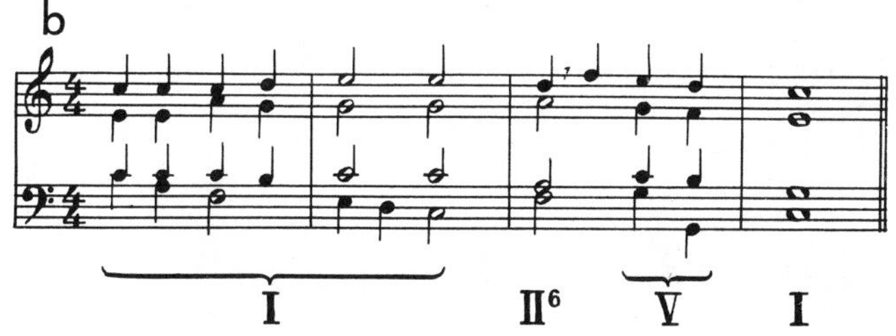

194

a

b

c

194 cont'd

d

I ——→ II^6_5 V I from I → II^6_5 V I

195

a

b

c

d

196

a Interval-filling

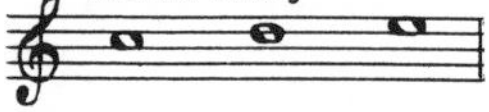

b Interval-outlining

c ornamental

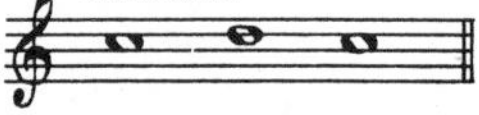

197

a

b

198 MOZART Piano Sonata, F Major, K. 280

199 MOZART Piano Sonata, C Major, K. 279

200 BACH Courante (Partita No. 5)

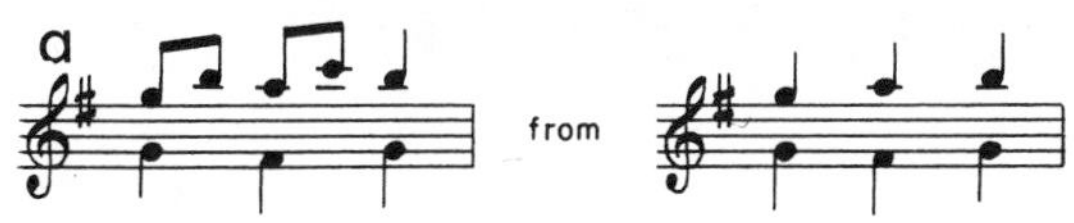

201 MOZART Piano Sonata, C Major, K. 279

202 HANDEL Double

a

203 MOZART Rondo, A minor, K. 511

Andante

p

cresc.

p

p

a

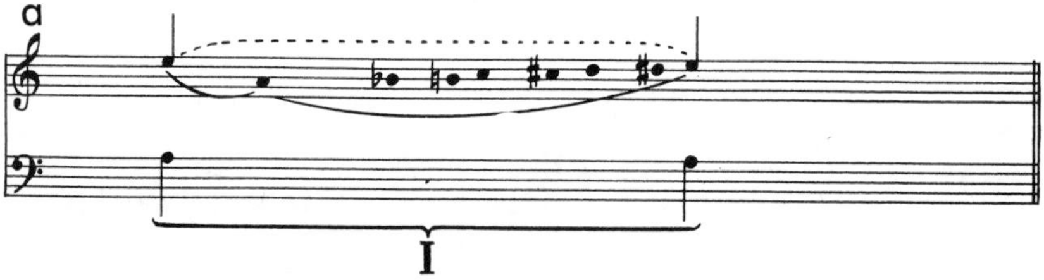

I

204

a

b

or

c

205 MENDELSSOHN Song Without Words, Op 62, No. 1

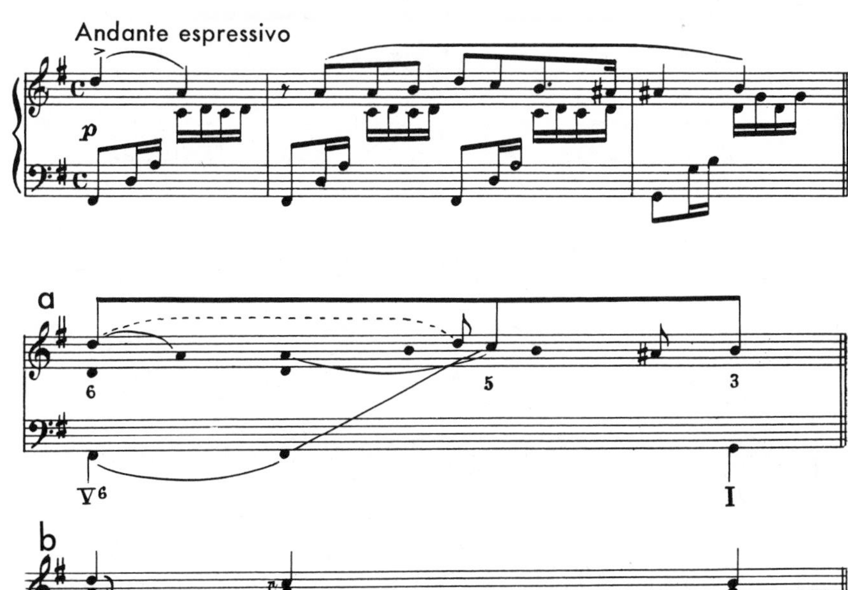

206 BEETHOVEN Piano Sonata, F minor, Op 2, No. 1

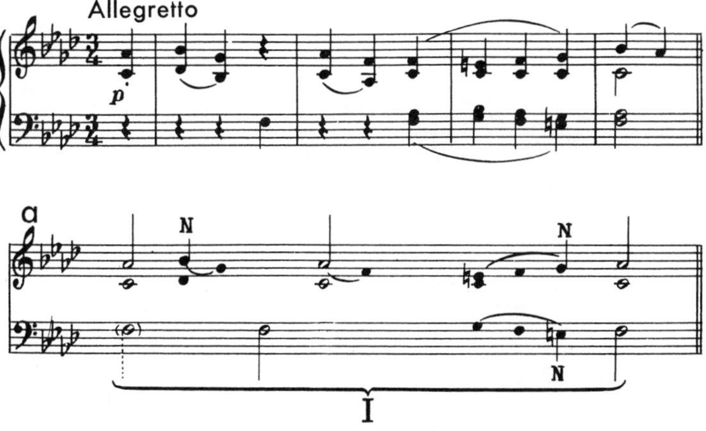

207 MOZART Fantasia, D minor, K. 397

208 MOZART Piano Sonata, C minor, K. 457

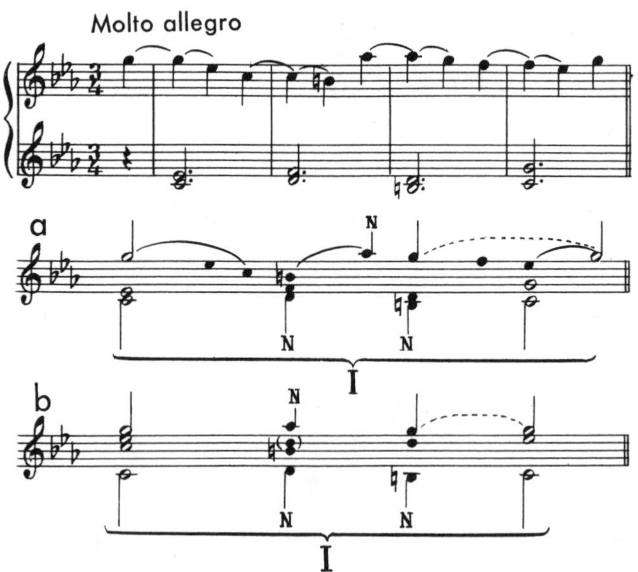

209 CARISSIMI Cantata: Mary Stuart

210 HAYDN Piano Sonata, C Major, No. 35

Allegro con brio

p

fz

a

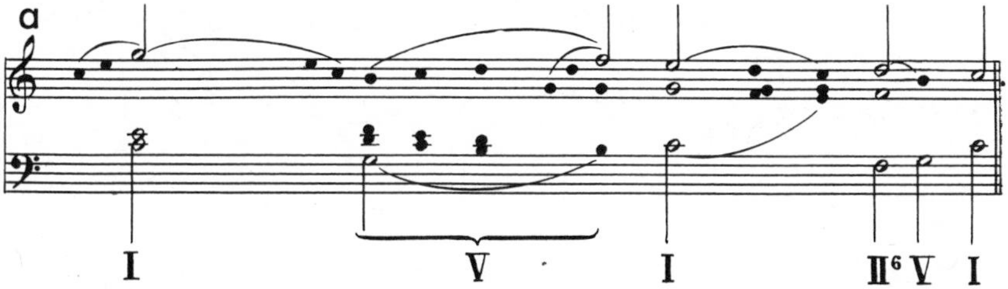

I V I II⁶ V I

b

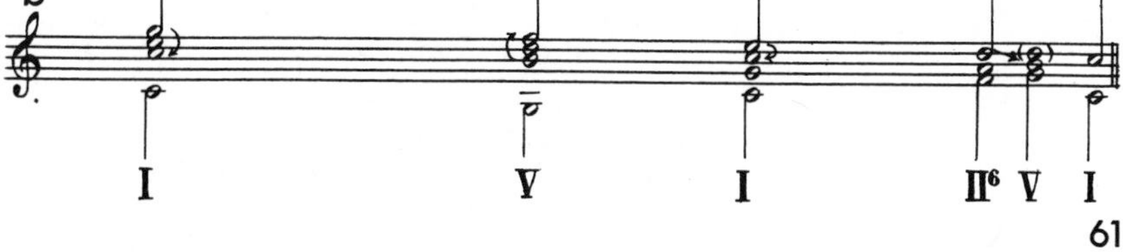

I V I II⁶ V I

210 cont'd

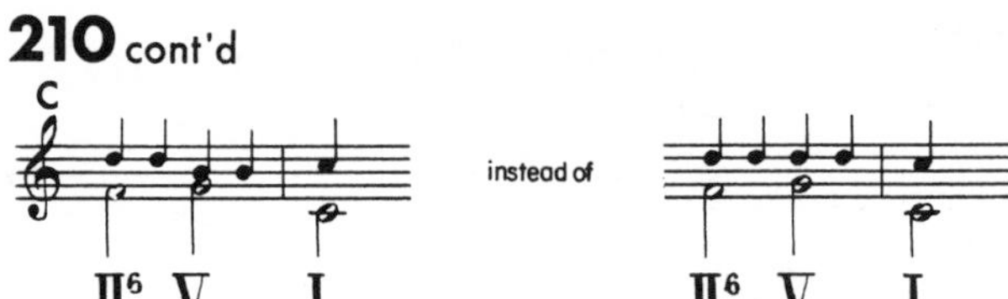

211 HAYDN Piano Sonata, D Major, No. 19

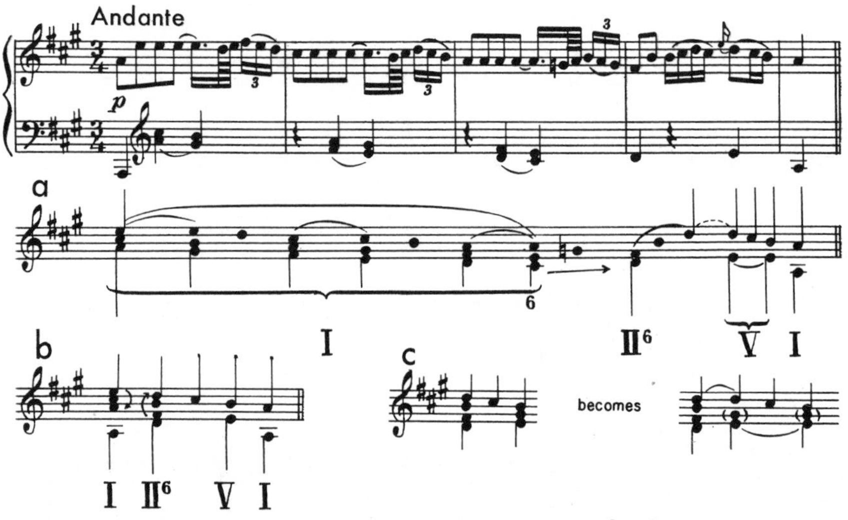

212 FROBERGER Suite: "Auf die Mayerin"

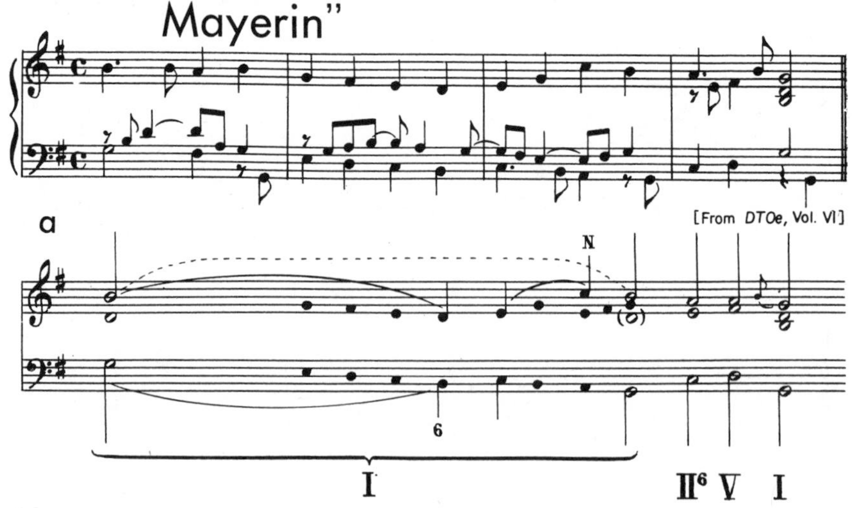

213 MOZART Courante (Suite, K. 399)
Allegretto
p
a
I II V I II6 → V I
I II6→V I
214 HAYDN Piano Sonata, G Major, No. 27
a
I II6 V I
215 FOLK TUNE
a
I II6 V I

216 CHOPIN Nocturne, Op 32, No. 1

217 MOZART Piano Sonata, F Major, K. 280

Allegro assai

tr

p

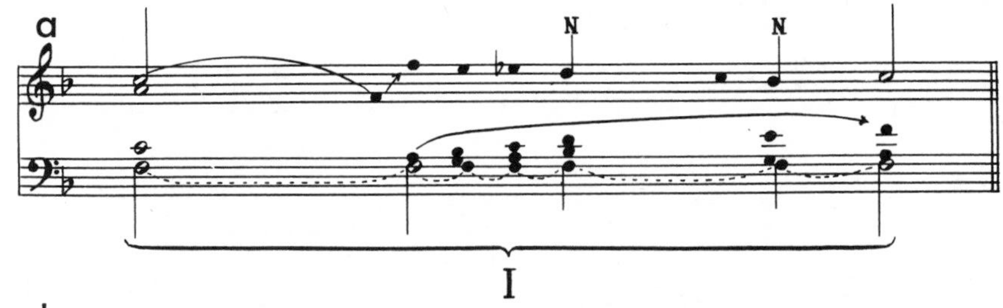

a

N

N

I

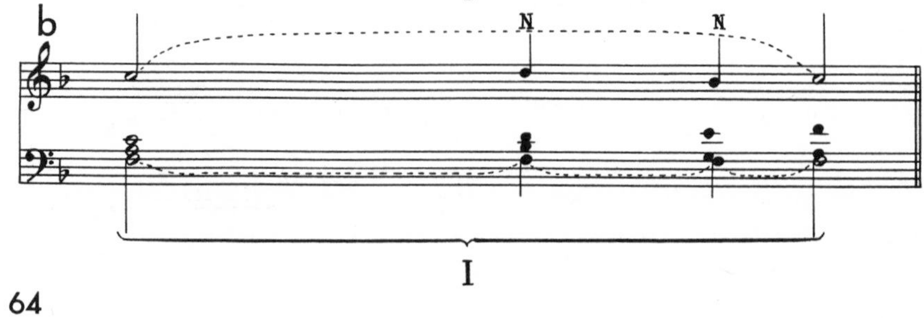

b

N

N

I

218 MENDELSSOHN Song Without Words, Op 102, No. 2

Adagio

mf *p*

a

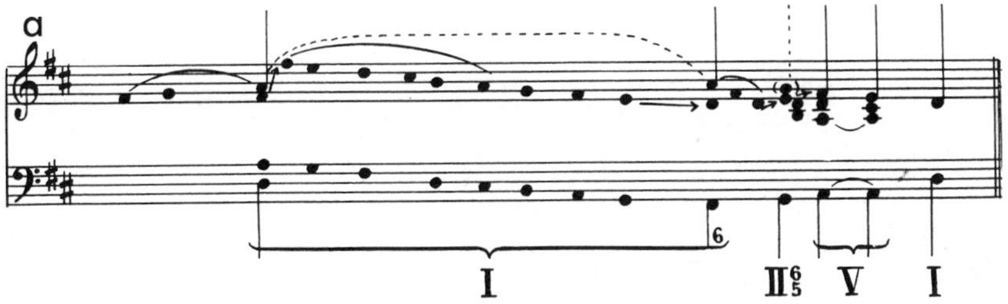

6

I II$^6_5$ V I

b

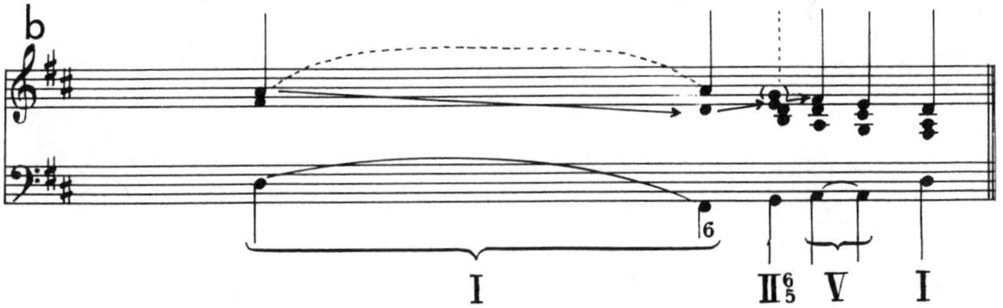

6

I II$^6_5$ V I

219 MOZART Aria ("Don Giovanni")

219 cont'd

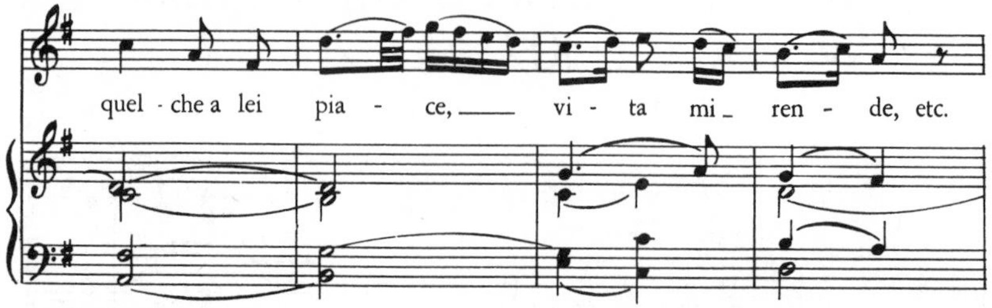
quel - che a lei pia - ce, vi - ta mi - ren - de, etc.

a

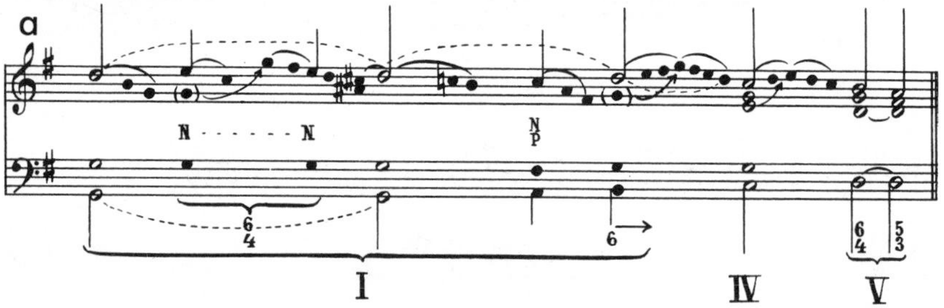
N N
N
P
6
4
6
6 5
4 3
I
IV
V

b

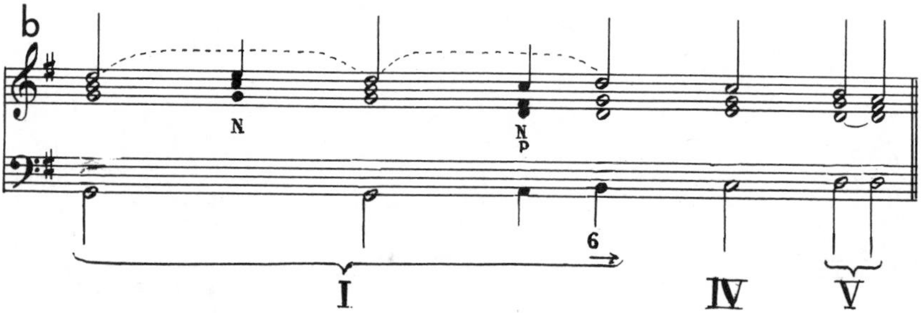
N
N
P
6
I
IV
V

220 CLEMENTI Sonatina, G Major, Op 36, No. 2

a

N N
I
II6 V I

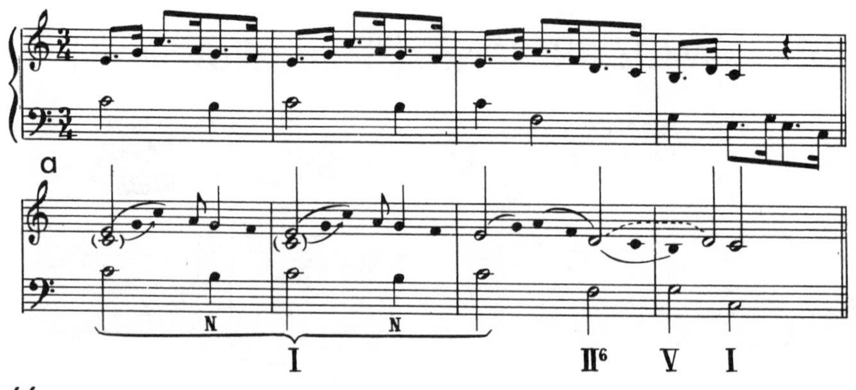

221 BEETHOVEN Piano Sonata, E Major, Op 109

a

b

c

222 BEETHOVEN Symphony No. 9

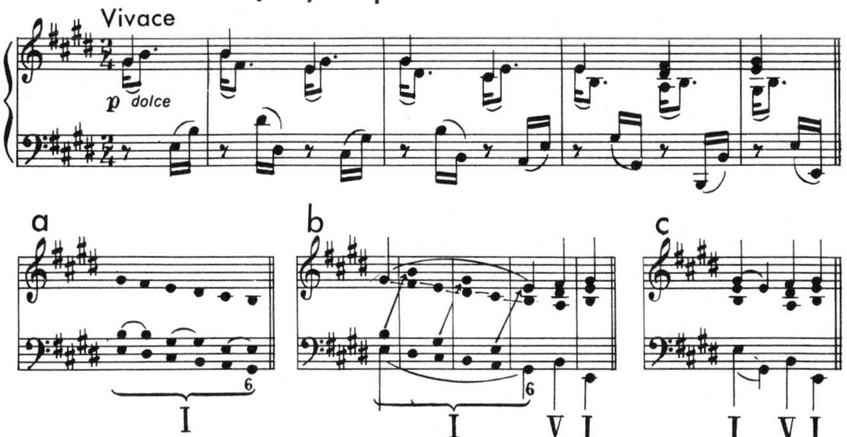

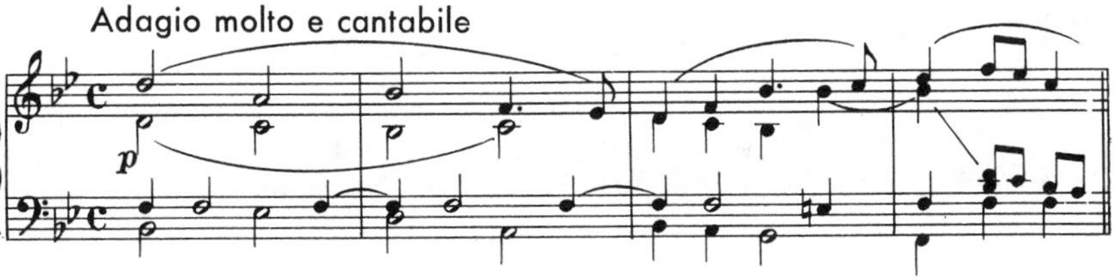

a

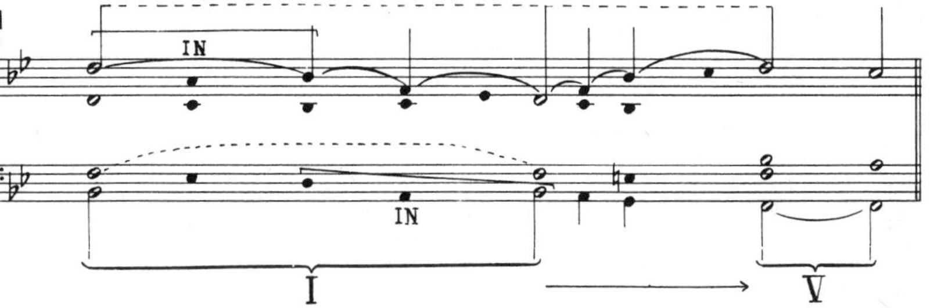

b

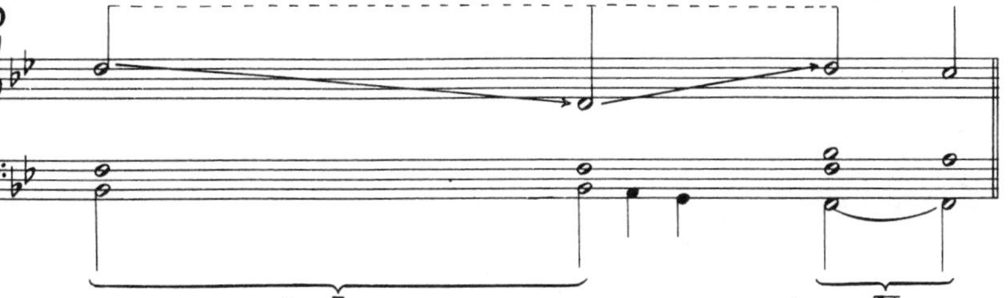

223 SCHUBERT Ländler, Op 18, No. 2

224 C. P. E. BACH Fantasia

225 BACH Praeludium (Partita No. 1)

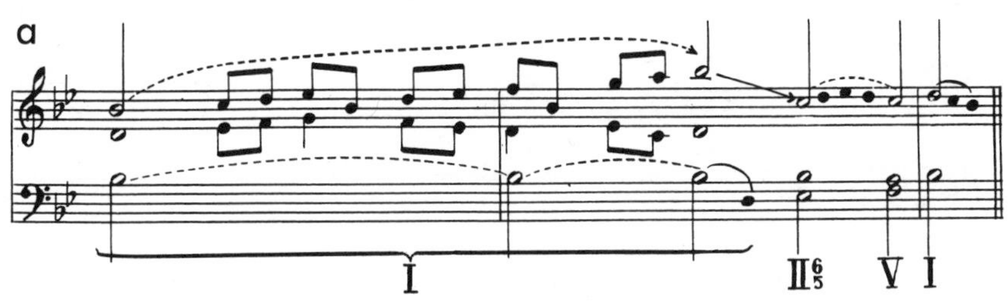

226 BEETHOVEN Piano Sonata, G Major, Op 79

226 cont'd

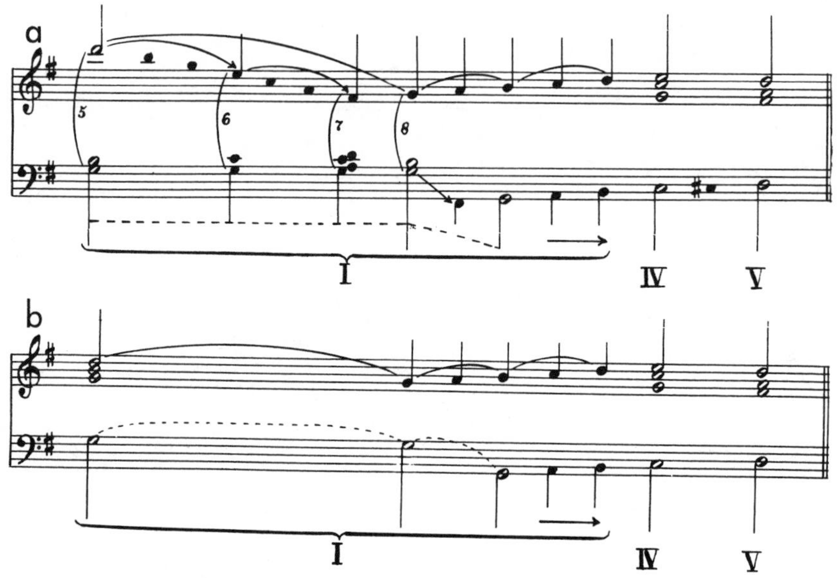

227 HANDEL Variation 1 (Air from Suite No. 3)

228 BACH Courante (Suite pour le clavecin, E♭ Major)

229 BEETHOVEN Piano Sonata, E Major, Op 14, No. 1

229 cont'd

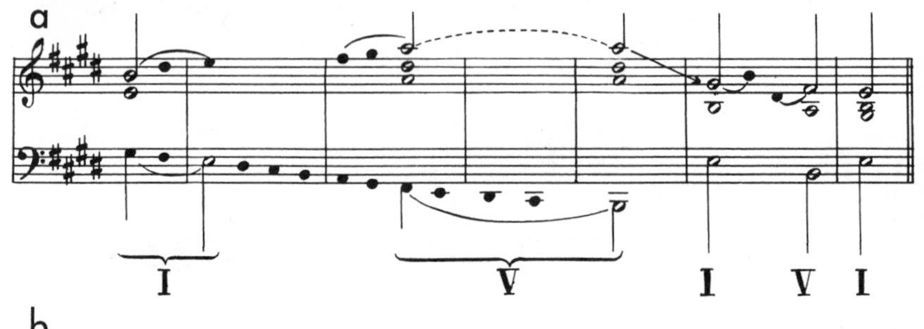

230 MOZART Trio, E♭ Major, K. 498

231 BACH Praeambulum (Partita No. 5)

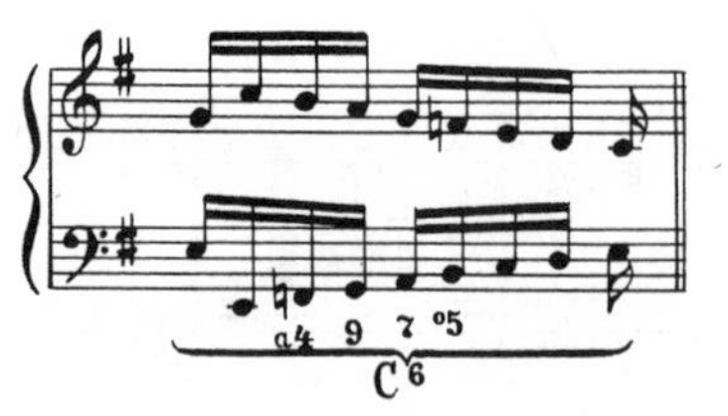

a

232 BACH Aria variata

233 MOZART Piano Sonata, C Major, K 545

234 SCHUMANN Melody (Album for the Young)

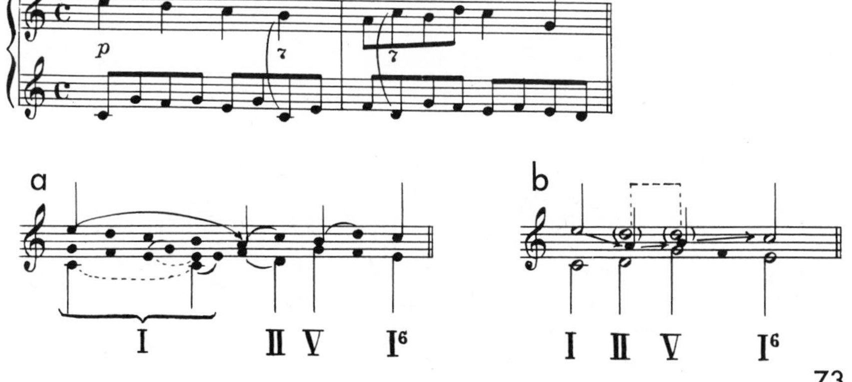

235 MOZART Fugue, C Major (Fantasia, K. 394)

236 BACH Chorale (No. 64)

237 BACH Chorale (Peters No. 43)

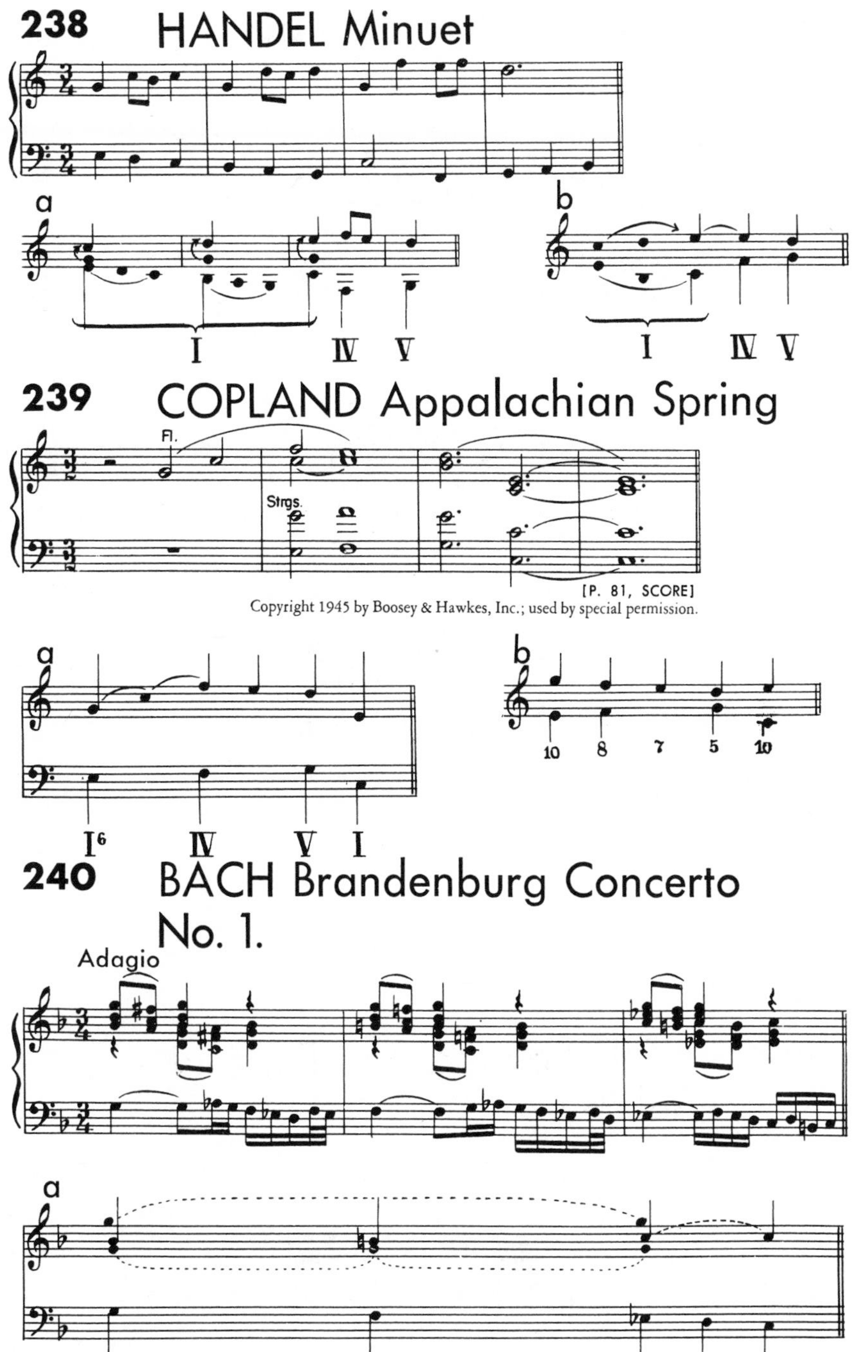
238 HANDEL Minuet
a
I IV V
b
I IV V
239 COPLAND Appalachian Spring
Fl.
Strgs.
[P. 81, SCORE]
Copyright 1945 by Boosey & Hawkes, Inc.; used by special permission.
a
I6 IV V I
b
10 8 7 5 10
240 BACH Brandenburg Concerto No. 1.
Adagio
a

241 BARTOK Ukrainian Song (Petite Suite)

243 BYRD Pavane: The Earle of Salisbury

244 MOZART Piano Sonata, G Major, K. 283

245 GOTTLIEB MUFFAT Air (Suite, B♭ Major)

246 BACH Prelude No. 10 (Well-Tempered Clavier, Bk I)

246 cont'd

a

9 10 9 10 9 10 9 10 10

247 HAYDN Piano Sonata, C Major, No. 21

248 MOZART Piano Sonata, G Major, K. 283

249 BACH Little Prelude, C minor

250 CHOPIN Mazurka, Op 41, No. 4

252 SCHUMANN Kreisleriana, Op 16, No. 8

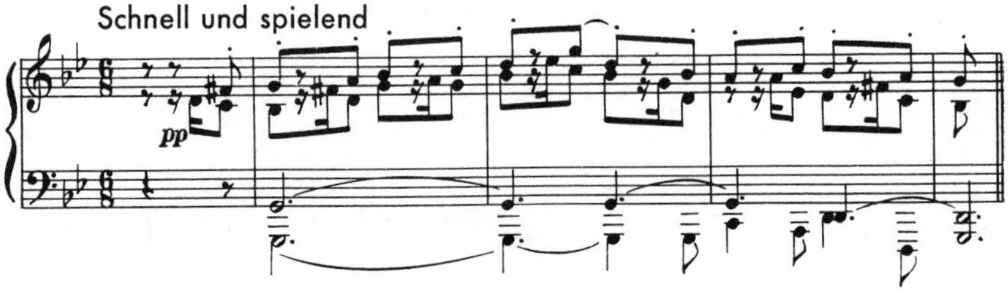
Schnell und spielend
pp

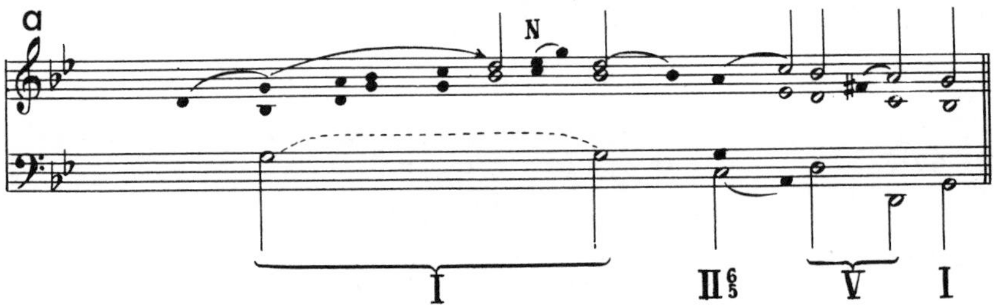
a
N
I
II 6 5
V
I

253

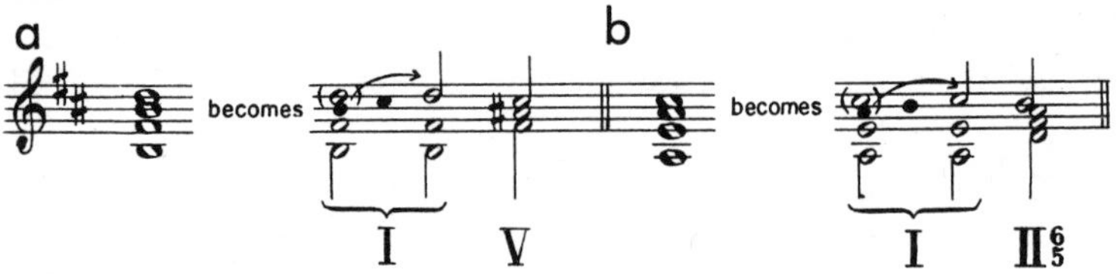
a
becomes
I
V
b
becomes
I
II 6 5

254 BEETHOVEN Piano Sonata, G Major, Op 14, No. 2

Allegro
p

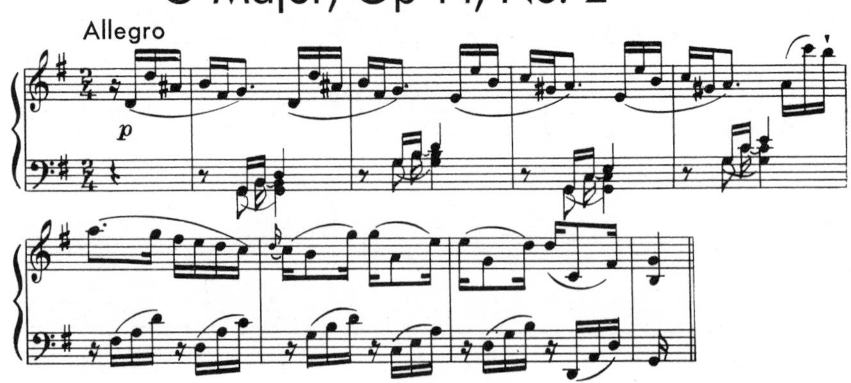

a

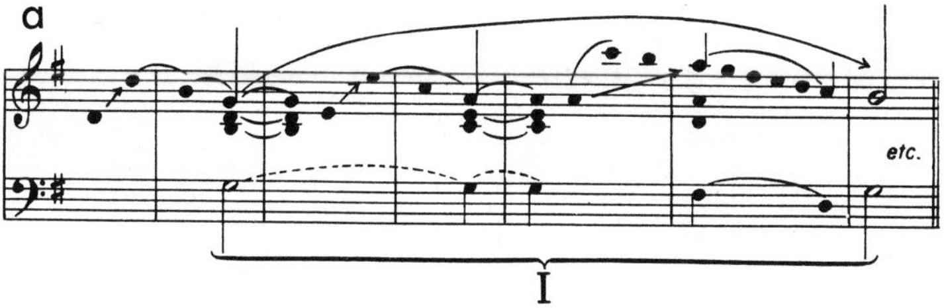

etc.

I

b

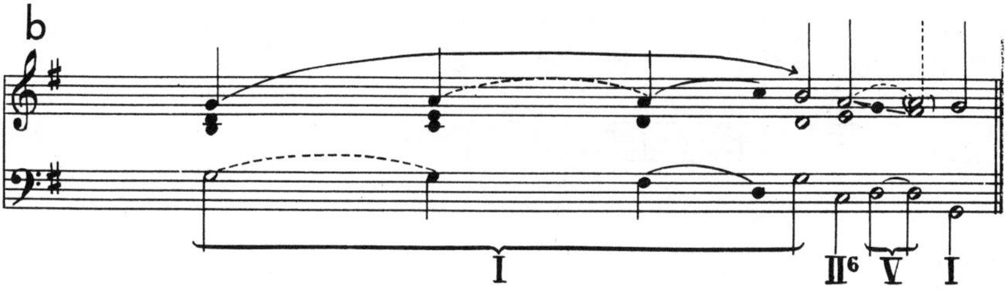

I

II⁶ V I

c

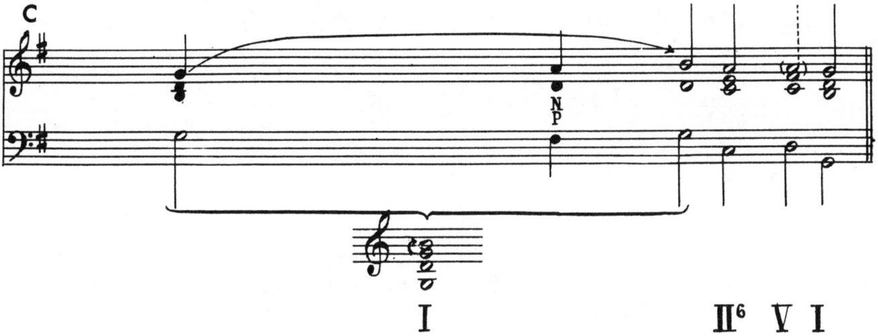

NP

I

II⁶ V I

d

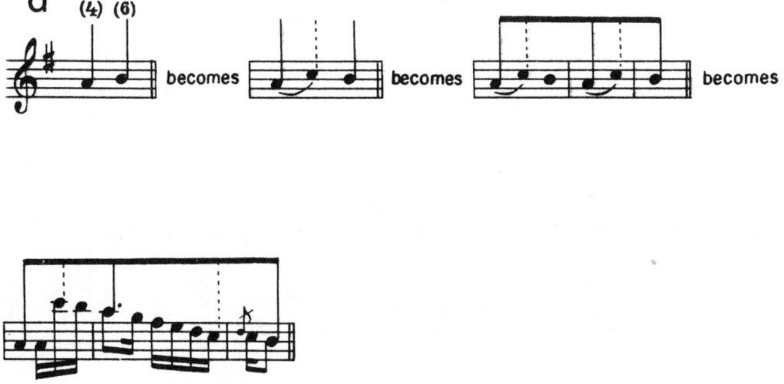

(4) (6)

becomes

becomes

becomes

255

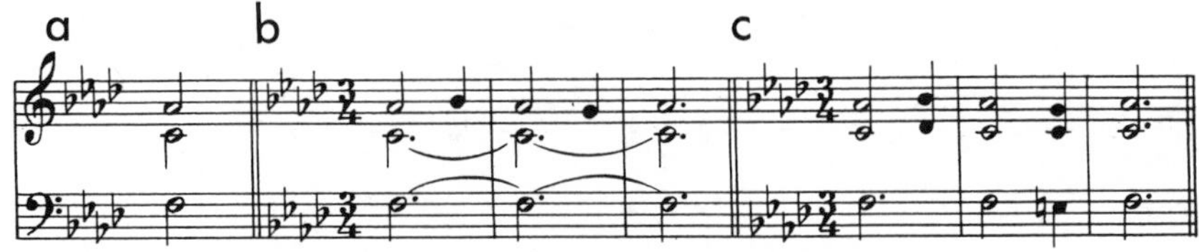

256

257

258

259

260

261

262

263

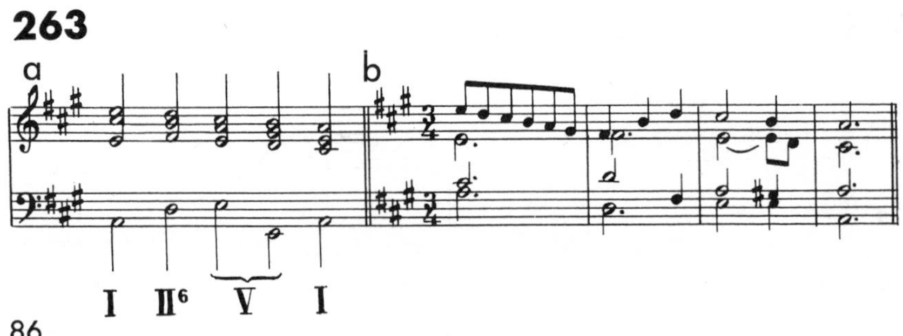

263 cont'd

c

264

a

3 2 1
I V I

divided through interruption (||)

b

3 2 || 3 2 1
I V || I V I
(D)

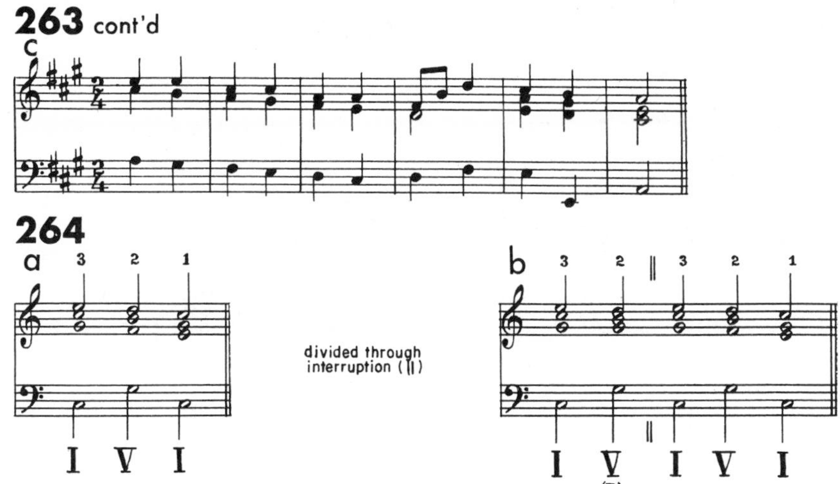

265 BEETHOVEN Piano Sonata, E Major, Op 14, No. 1

Allegretto
p
sf
p
cresc.
sf

a

see meas. 1-6
I
V
(D)
I V I

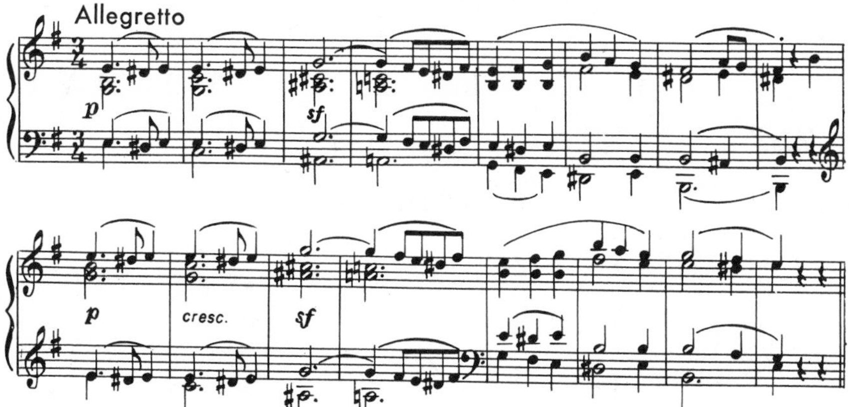

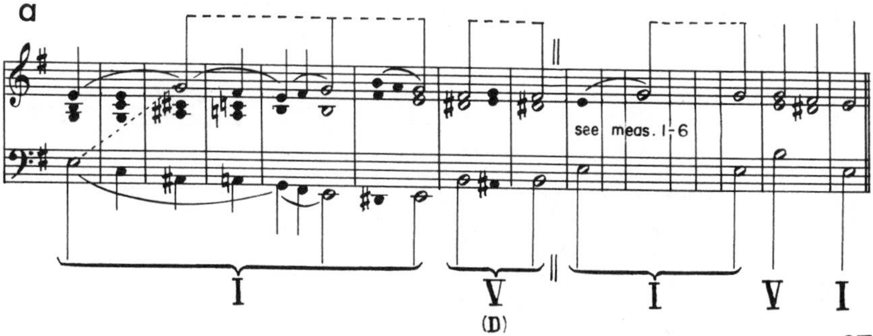

266 HAYDN Symphony, G Major, No. 100

Presto

p

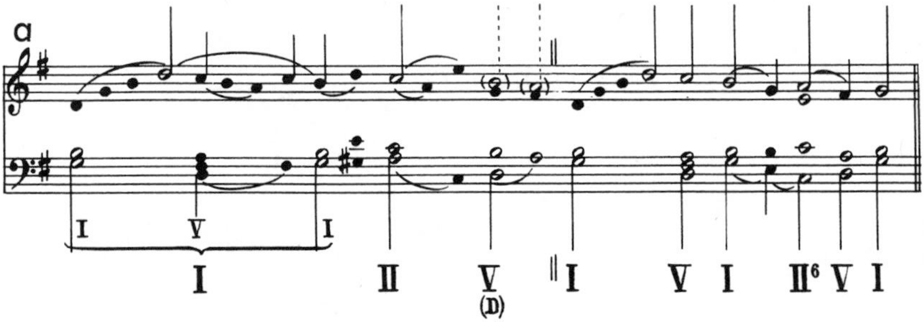

a

I V I

I II V (D) I V I II⁶ V I

267 MOZART Quartet ("Don Giovanni")

267 cont'd

268 BASSE DANSE

[From *VDO*, App. P. 35]

269 BACH Chorale (No. 192)

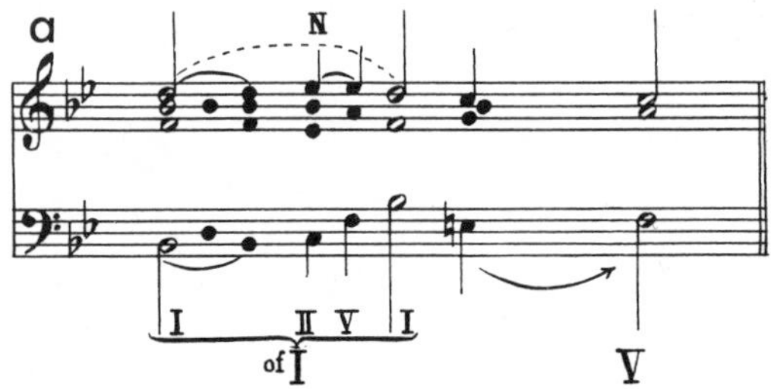

270

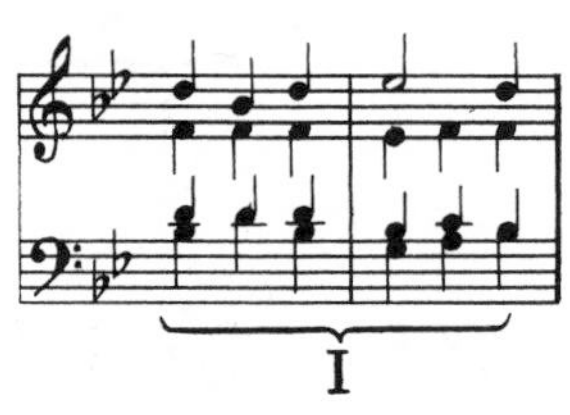

271 GIBBONS The Queene's Command

272 HAYDN Piano Sonata, E^b Major, No. 52

273 JOSQUIN Motet: Ave Maria

[From AM, P. 9]

273 cont'd

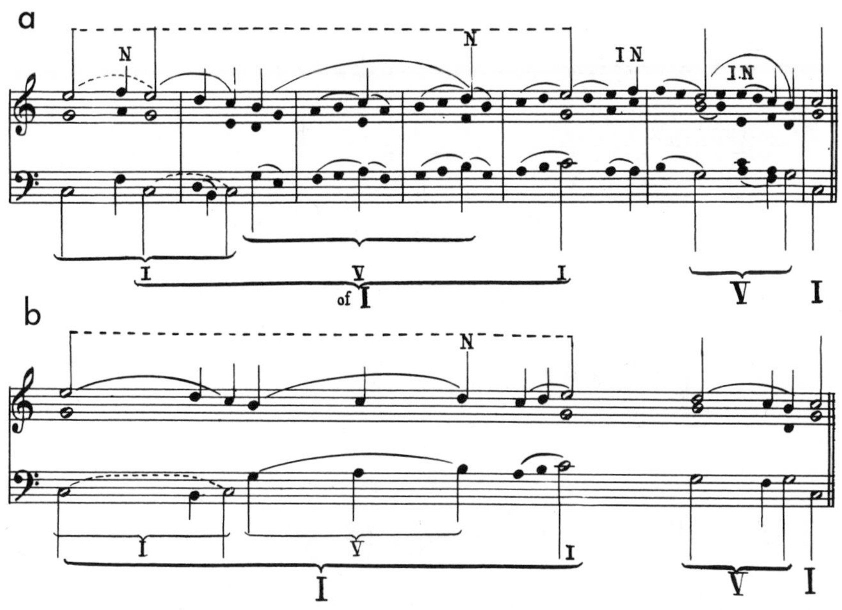

274 CLÉREAU Missa: In me transierunt

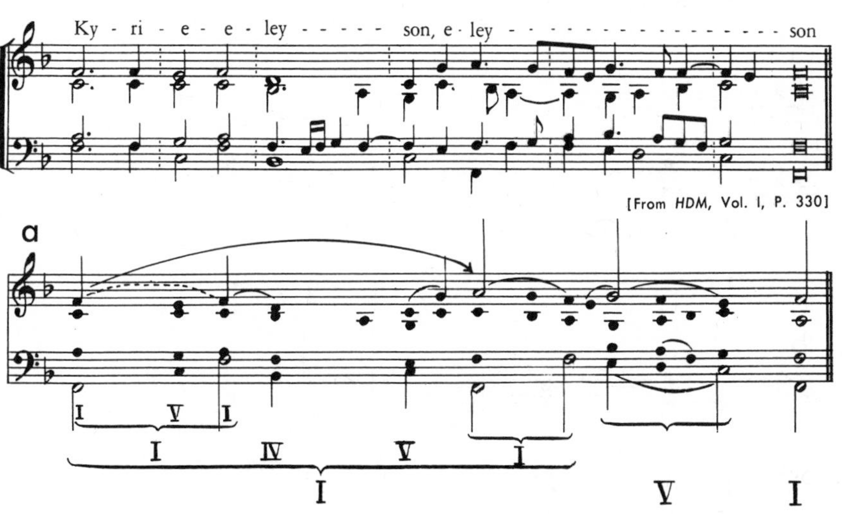

275
a
I II V I
I
II6 V I
b
I V I
of I N I
of I
IV6 V I
276 BACH Chorale (No. 5)
a
IV
V
I
II V I
b
IV V
I
II V I

277 MOZART Piano Sonata, D Major, K. 576

278

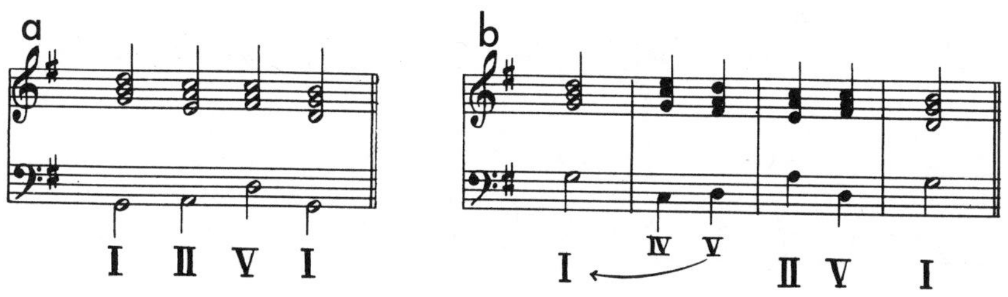

279 SCHUMANN Bunte Blätter, Op 99

280 BACH Prelude No. 7 (Well-Tempered Clavier, Bk II)

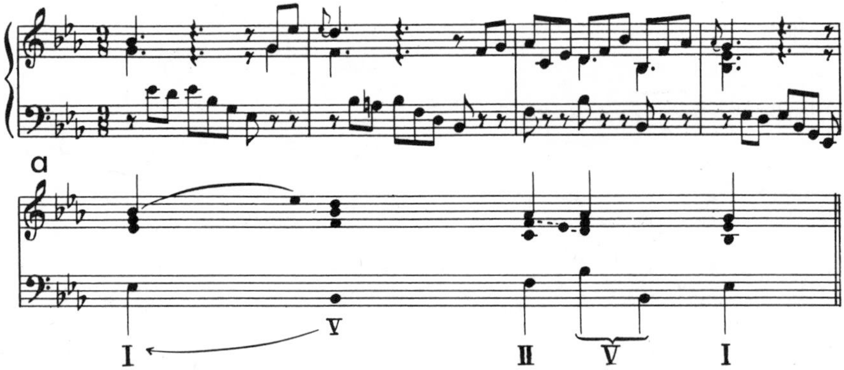
a
V
I
II
V
I

281

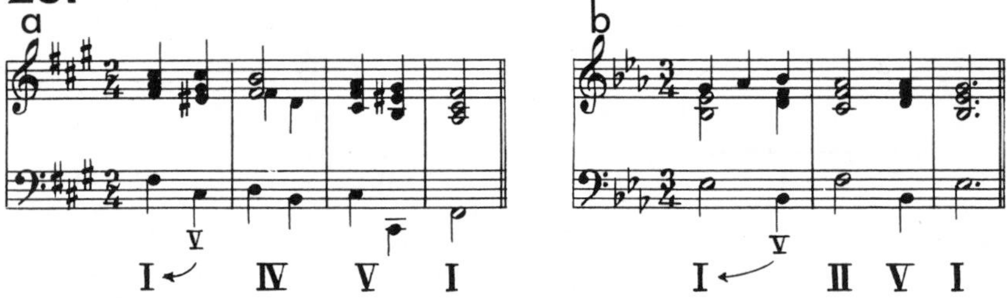
a
V
I
IV
V
I
b
V
I
II
V
I

282 SCHUBERT Ländler, Op 18, No. 10

3
3
V
I

283 CHOPIN Etude, Op 10, No. 4

Presto
f
V
I

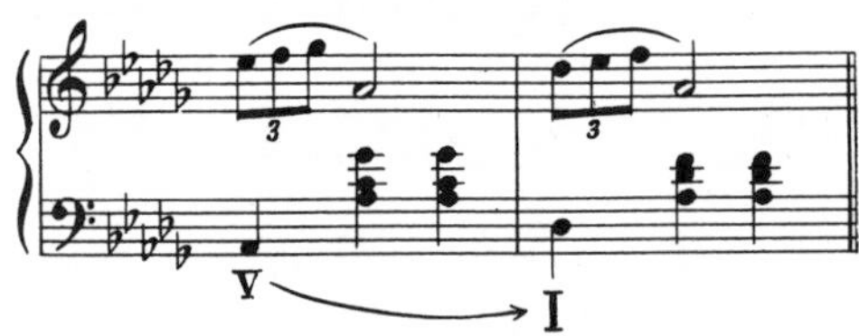

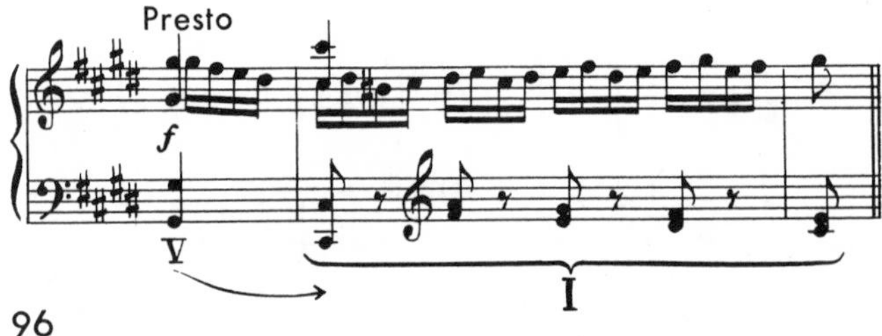

284 CHOPIN Mazurka, Op 63, No. 2

285 CHOPIN Mazurka, Op 24, No. 3

286 SCHUMANN Der Nussbaum

287 SCHUMANN Dichterliebe, No. 5

288 BEETHOVEN Piano Sonata, E♭ Major, Op 31, No. 3

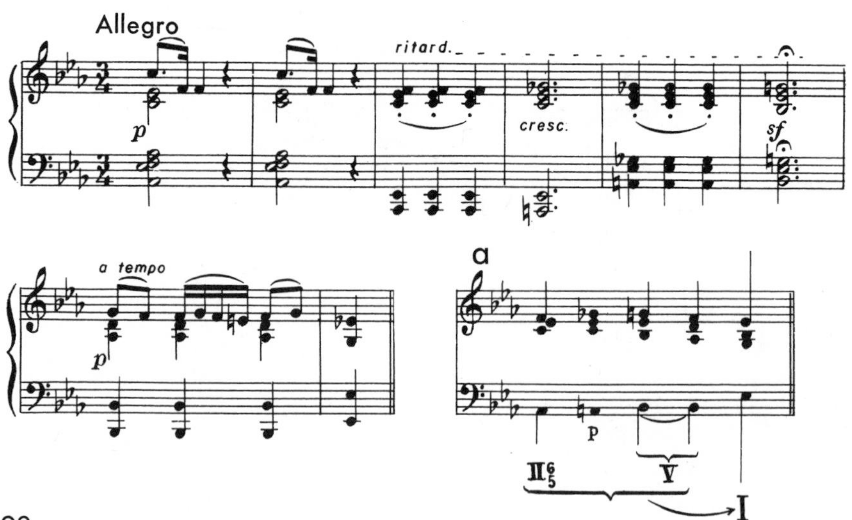

289 BEETHOVEN Piano Sonata, E♭ Major, Op 81a

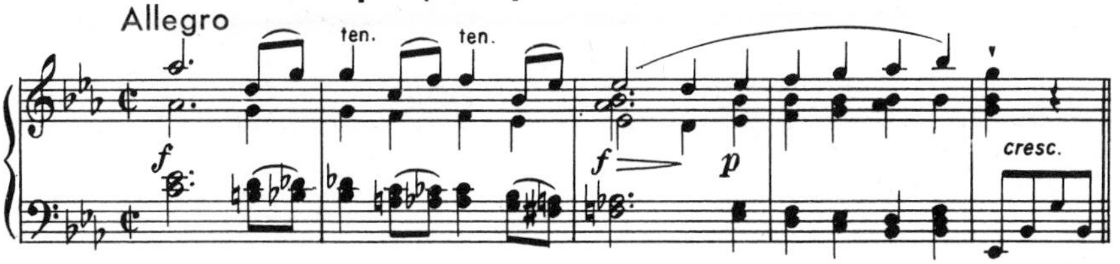

Allegro
ten.
ten.
f
f
p
cresc.

a

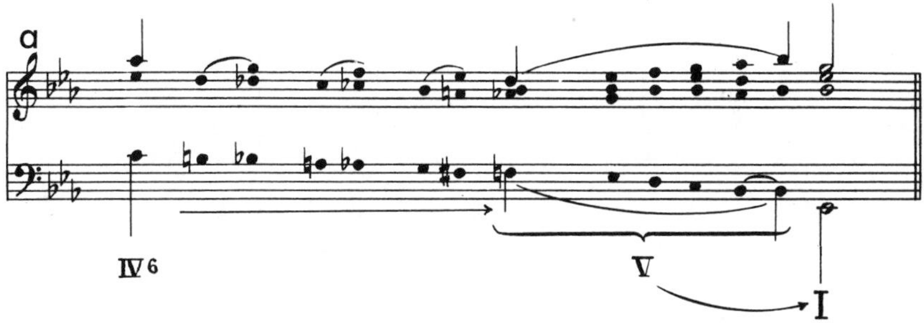

IV6
V
I

b

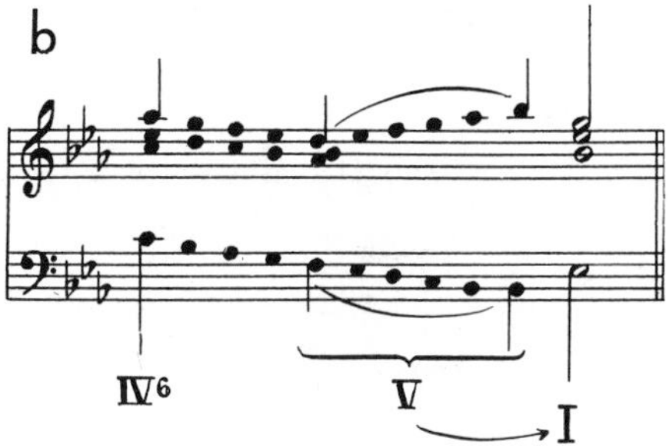

IV6
V
I

c

IV6
V
I

290 RAVEL Rigaudon (Tombeau de Couperin)

Assez vif
ff

a

IV7
(II11)
V13
I

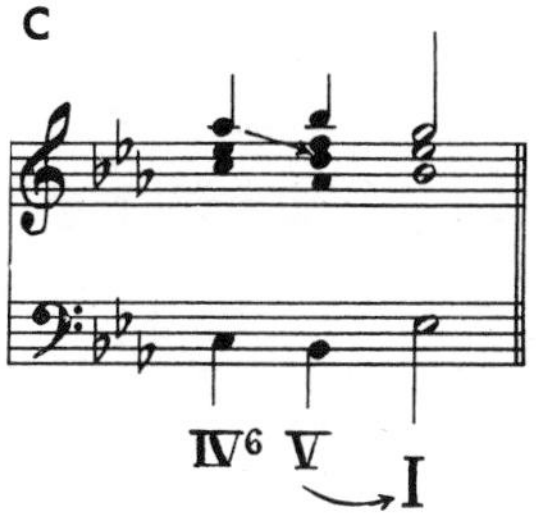

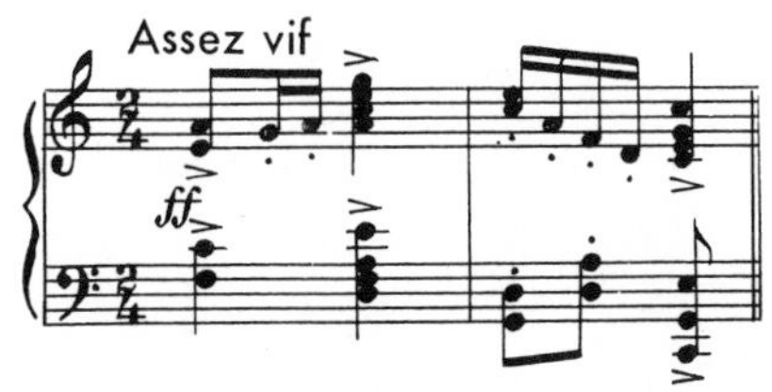

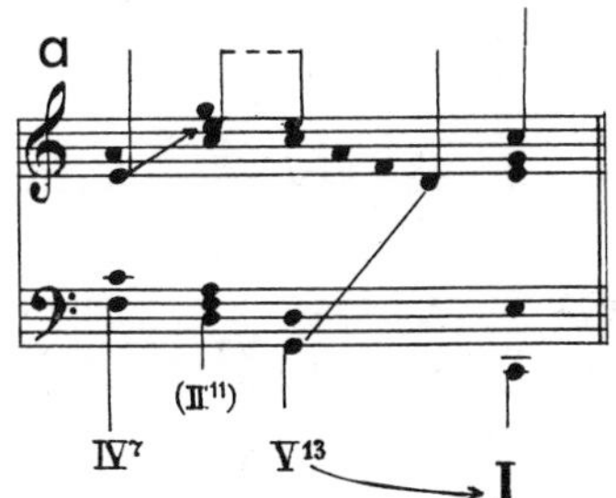

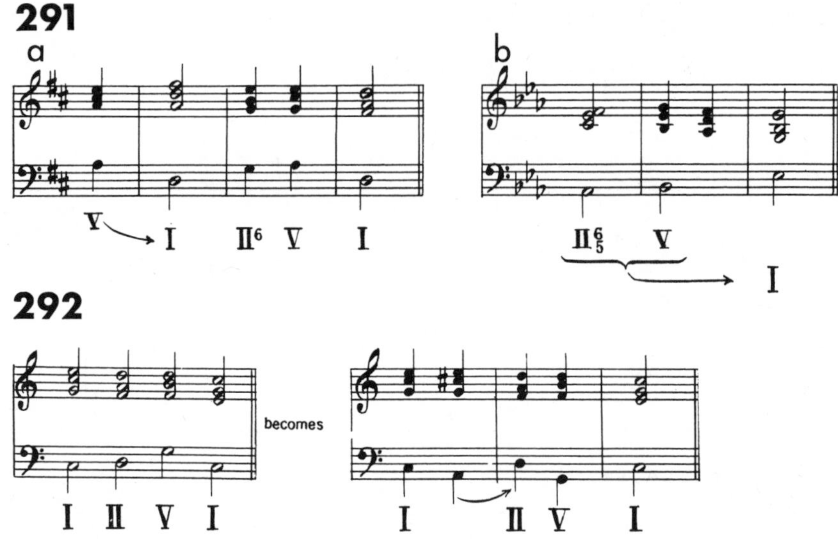

293 SCHUBERT Waltz Op 127, No. 3

f

sf

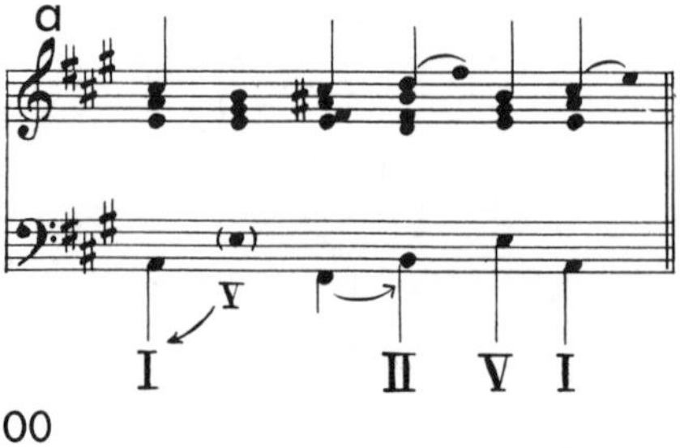

a

V

I II V I

Steve Garner

294 SCHUBERT Piano Sonata, D Major,

295 SCHUBERT Waltz, Op 10, No. 6

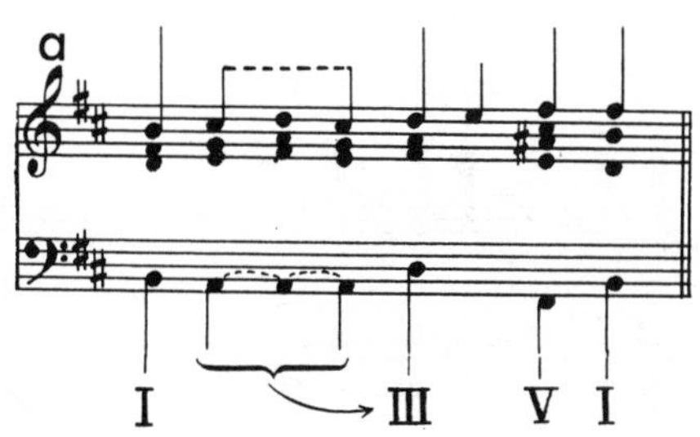

296 SCHUMANN Humoreske, Op 20

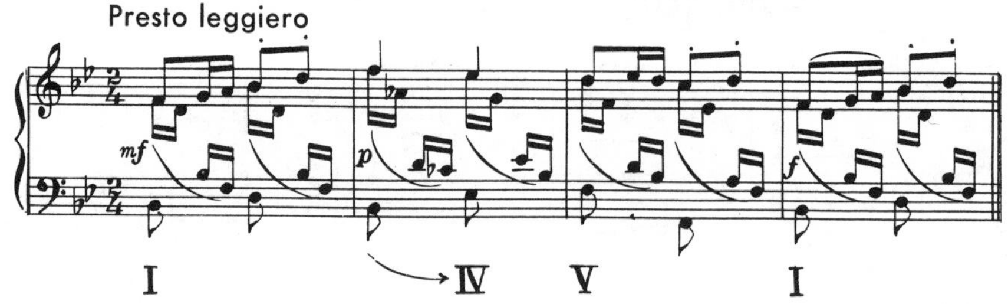

297 CHOPIN Waltz, Op 64, No. 2

298 BEETHOVEN Piano Sonata, C Major, Op 2, No. 3

298 cont'd

a

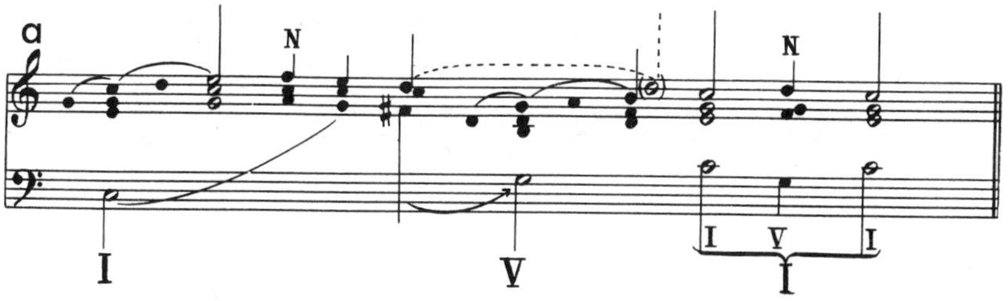

N N

I V I V I

I

b

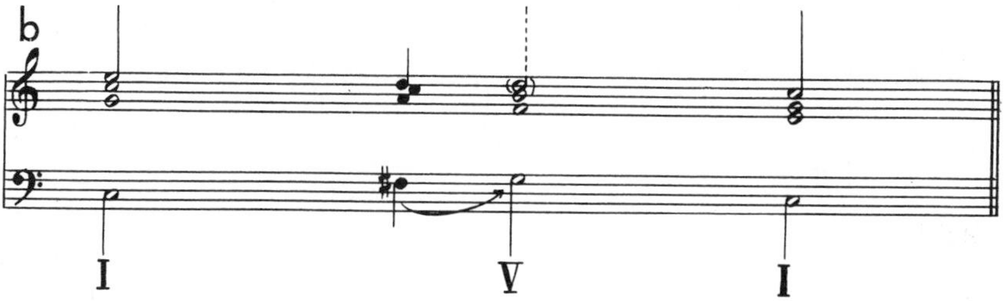

I V I

299 SCHUMANN Fantasiestücke, Op 12, No. 3

300 LISZT Liebestraum (Nocturne No. 3)

302

303 SCHUMANN Scenes from Childhood, Op 15, No. 1

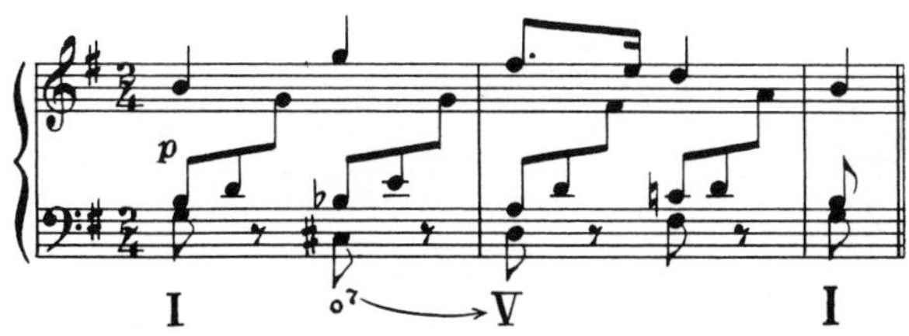

304 CHOPIN Mazurka, Op 17, No. 2

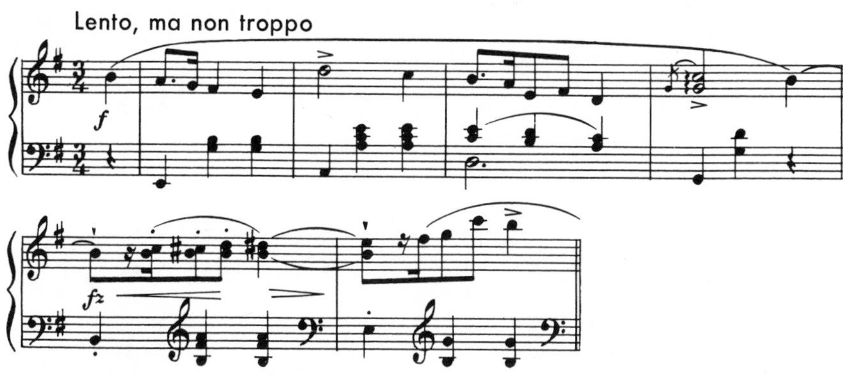

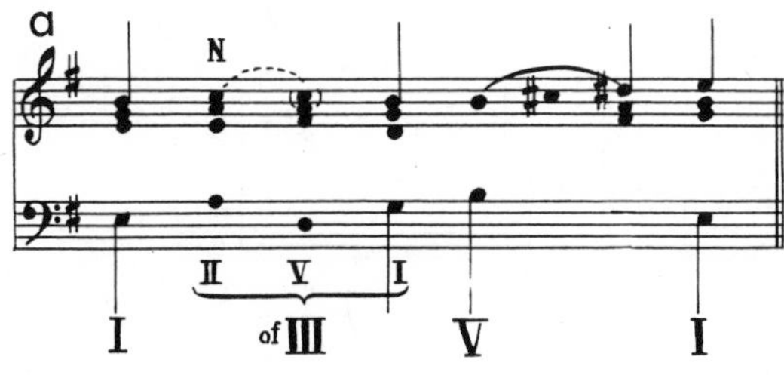

305 SCHUMANN Album-Leaves, Op 124, No. 10

307 SCHUMANN Album-Leaves, Op 124, No. 5

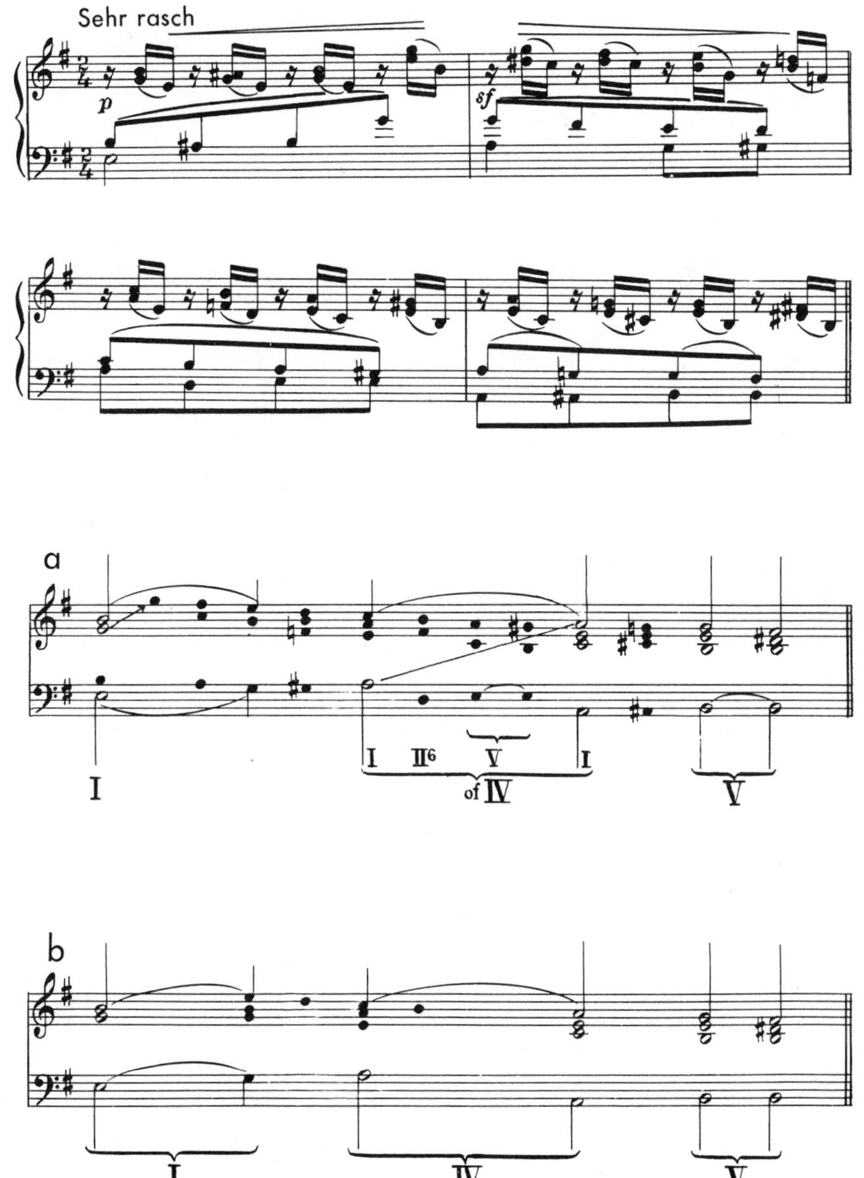

308 BRAHMS Intermezzo, Op 118, No. 2

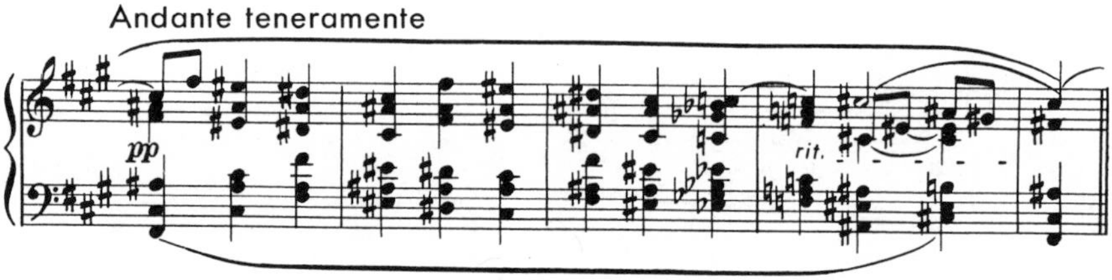

Andante teneramente
pp
rit.

a
I⁶
II⁶₅
V
I
I
of III
V
I

b
I
III
V
I

309

a
I
II
V
I
becomes
I
II⁶
V
I
I
of II
V
I

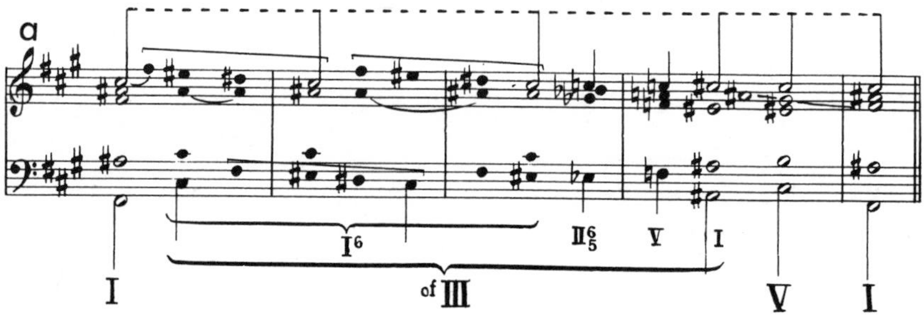

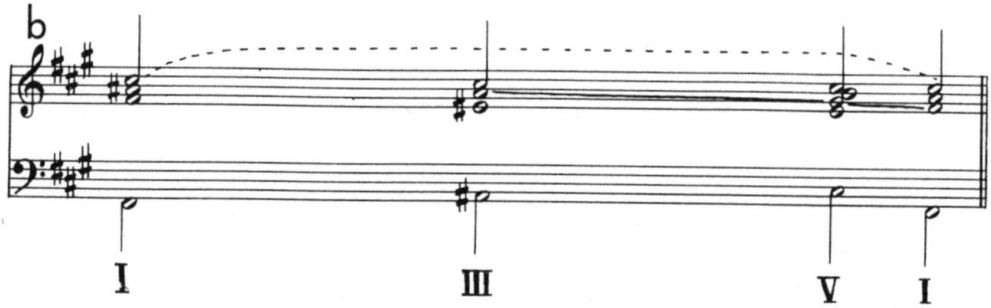

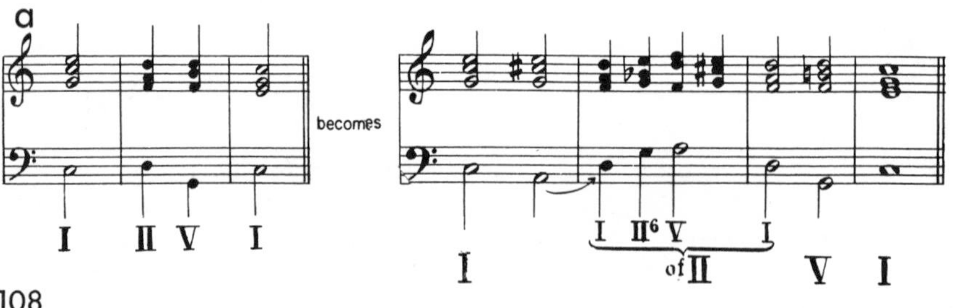

309 cont'd

b

I IV V I
becomes
I
I II6 V I
of IV
V I

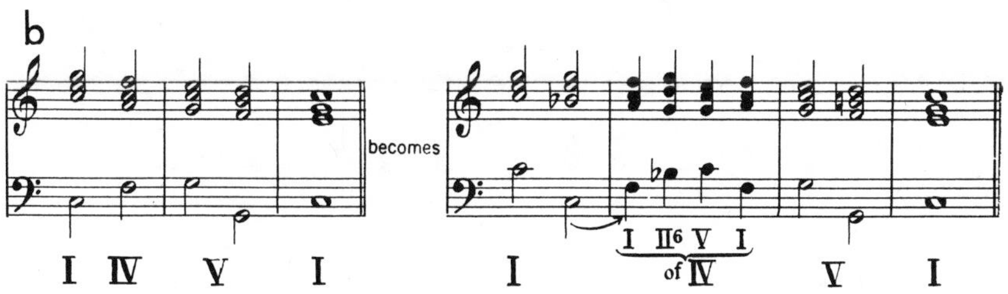

310 SCHUMANN Auf dem Rhein

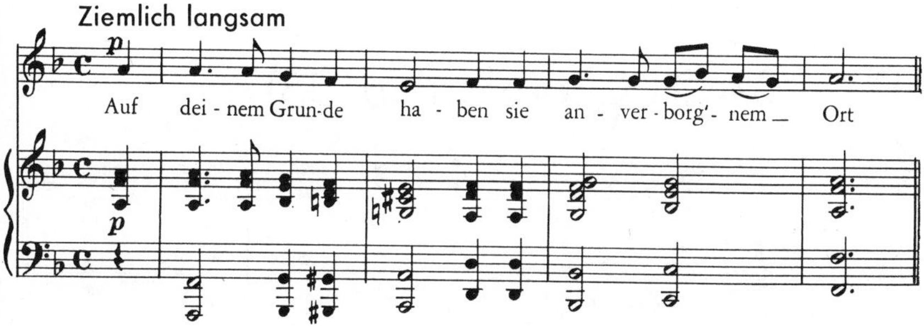

Ziemlich langsam
p
Auf dei-nem Grun-de ha-ben sie an-ver-borg'-nem — Ort
p

a

II6 V I
I
of P
II 6/5
V
I

b

I
P
II 6/5
V
I

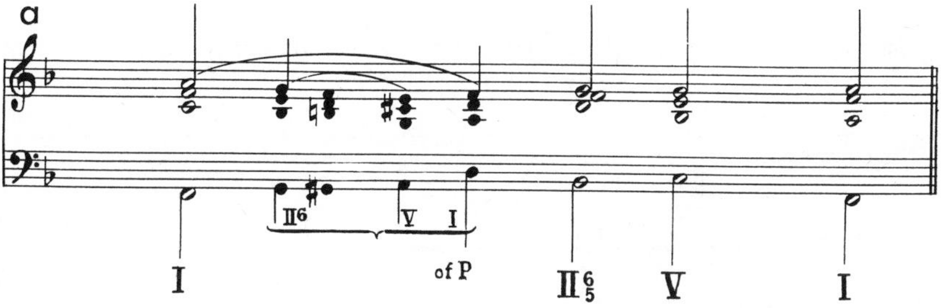

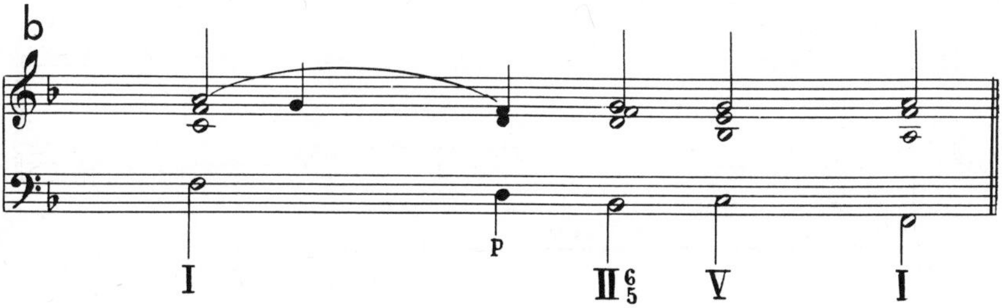

311 CHOPIN Mazurka, Op 59, No. 2

312 BACH Chorale (No. 55)

313 BACH Chorale (No. 177)

a

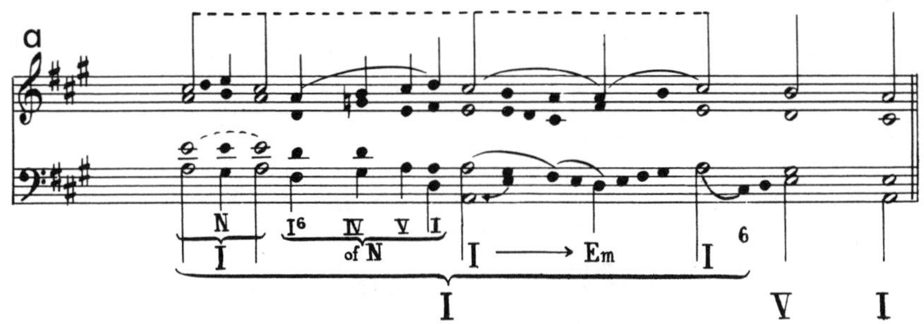

b

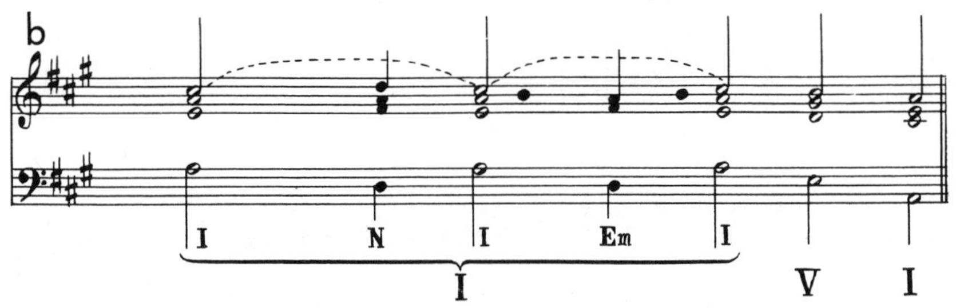

314

a

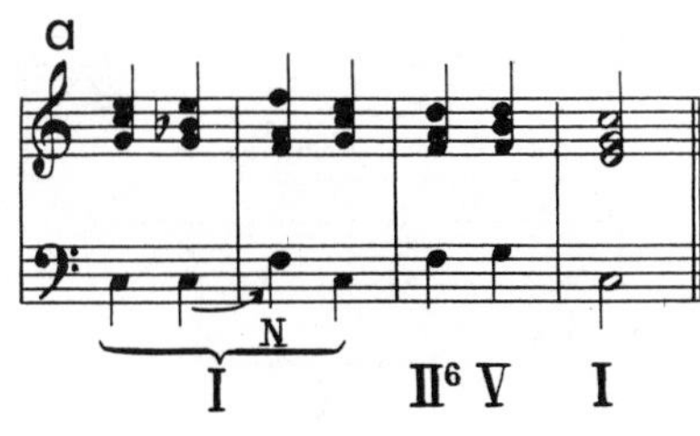

b

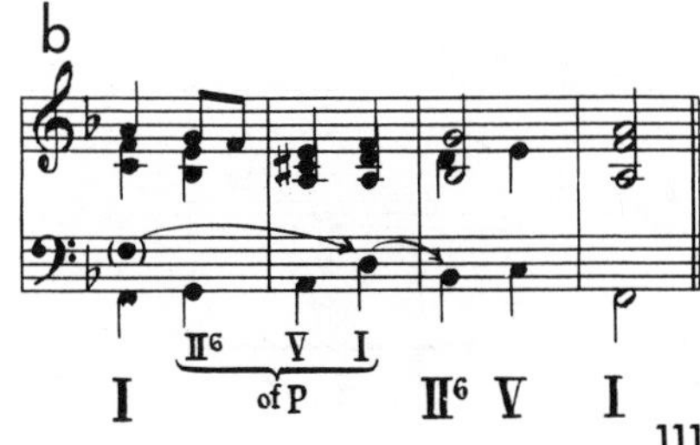

315 CHOPIN Mazurka, Op 68, No. 2 (Posth.)

Poco piu mosso
mf
pp
a
I
III
(II)
V
I

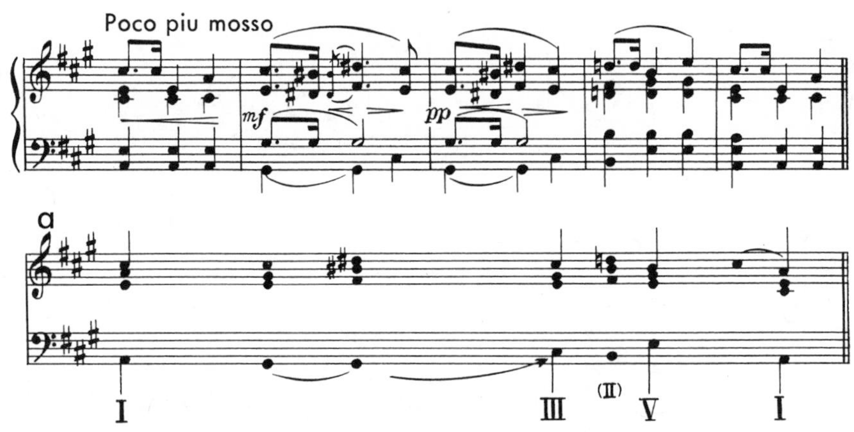

316 SCHUBERT German Dance, No. 7

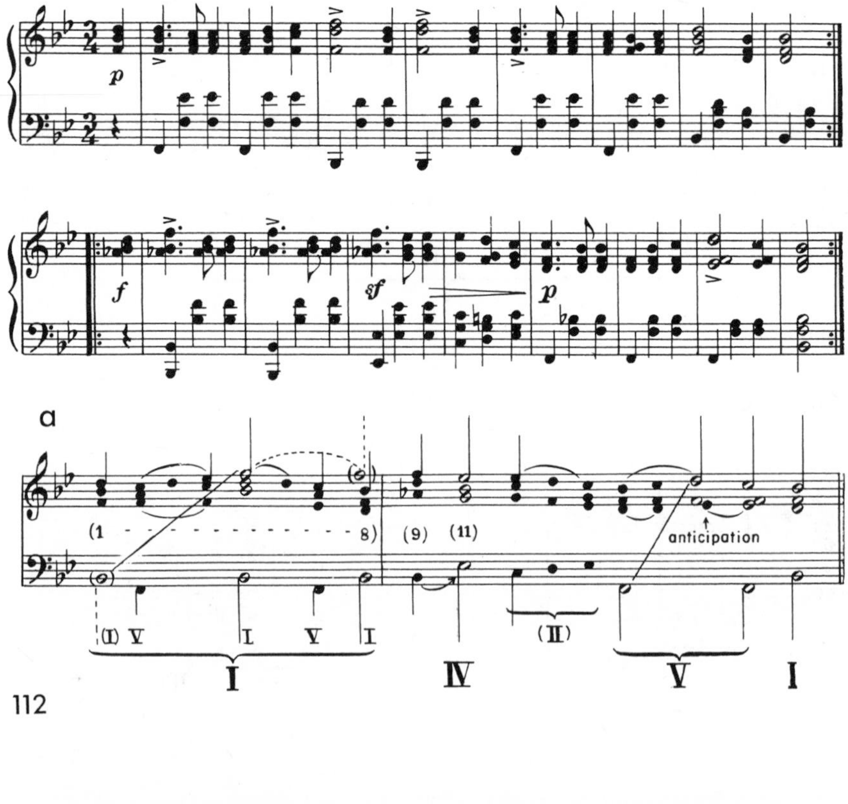
p
f
sf
p
a
(1
8)
(9)
(11)
anticipation
(I) V
I
V
I
I
IV
(II)
V
I

316 cont'd

317

318 HAYDN Piano Sonata, G minor, No. 44

319 PURCELL Overture, "Dido and Aeneas"

a

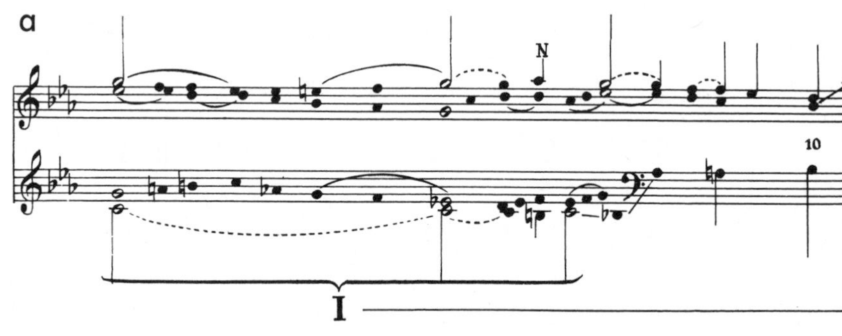

b

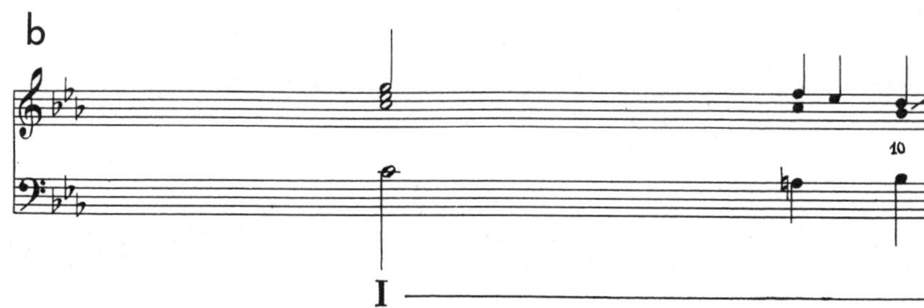

320 PEERSON The Primerose

319 cont'd

f
p
(10)
pp

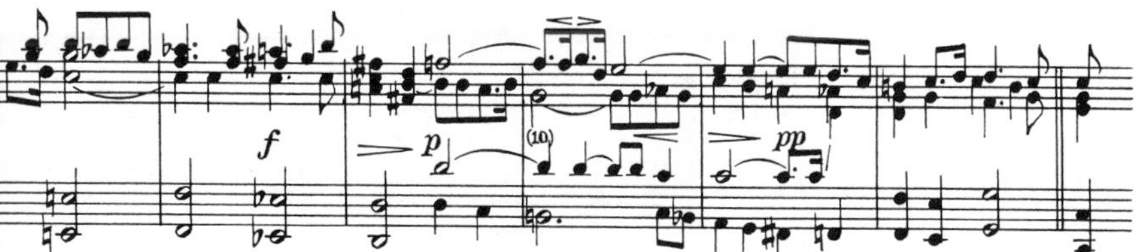

cont'd

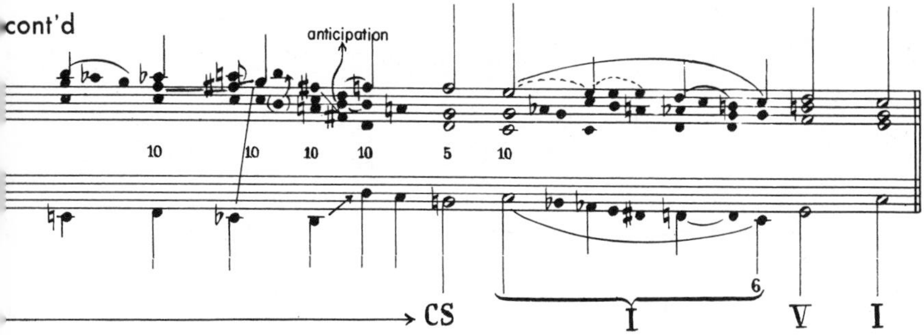

anticipation
10
10
10
10
5
10
6
CS
I
V
I

cont'd

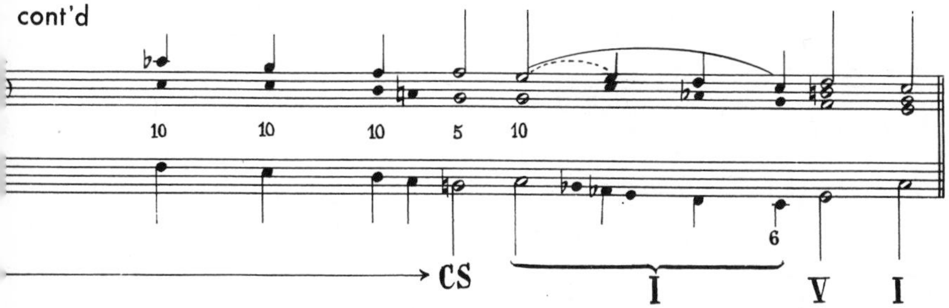

10
10
10
5
10
6
CS
I
V
I

320 cont'd

a

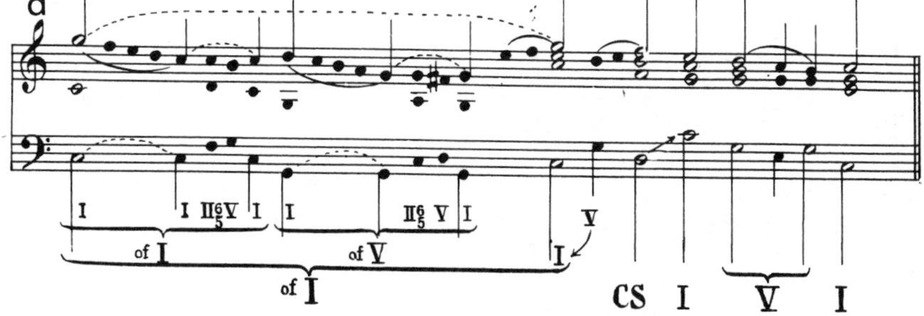

I
I II6/5 V I
I
II6/5 V I
of I
of V
V
I
of I
CS
I
V
I

321 BACH Chorale (No. 229)

322

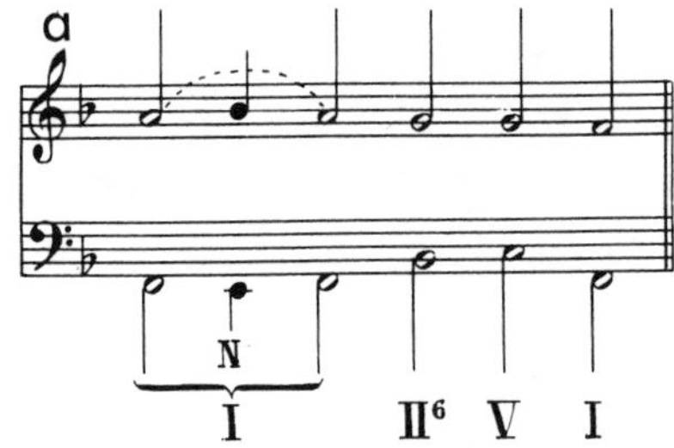

323 COUPERIN La Bandoline

324 CHOPIN Nocturne, Op 9, No. 2

324 cont'd

a

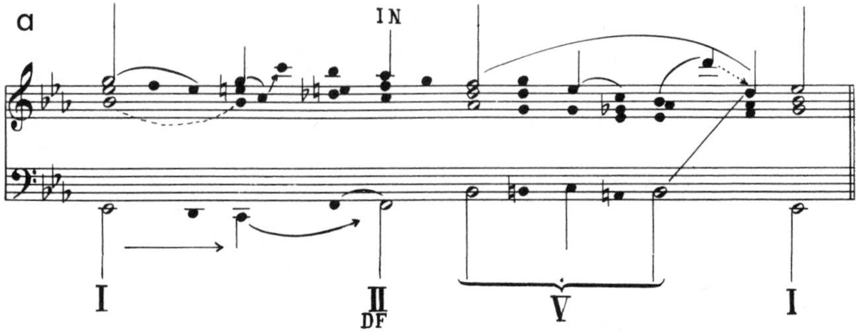

IN

I II DF V I

b

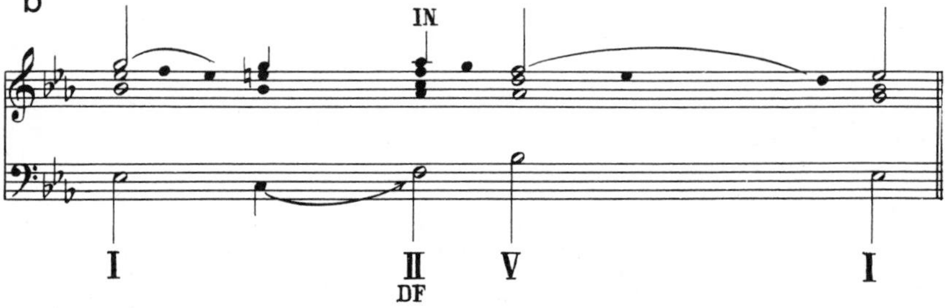

IN

I II DF V I

325 SCHUMANN Piano Concerto

325 cont'd

a

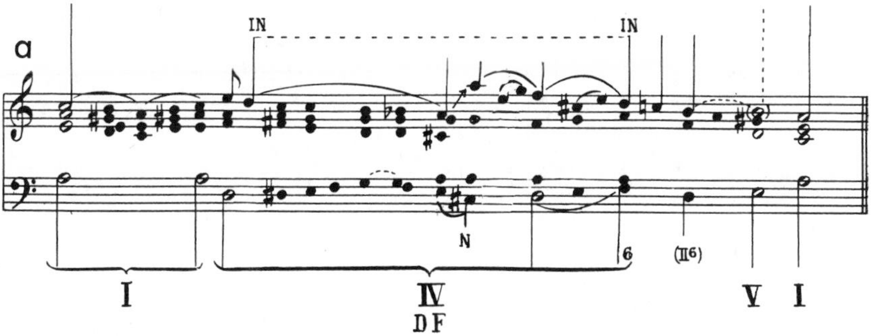
IN
IN
N
6
(II6)
I
IV
DF
V
I

b

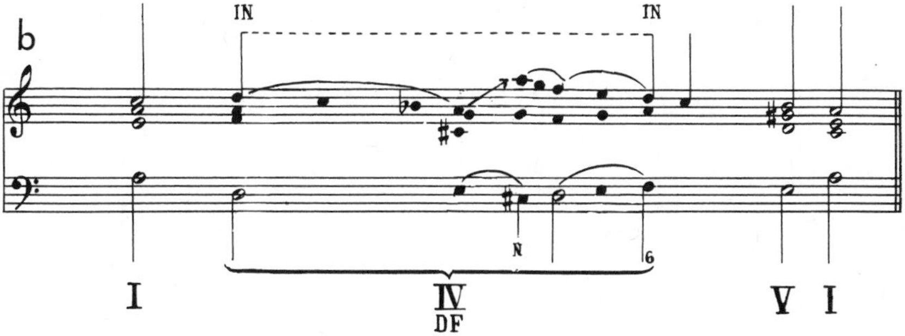
IN
IN
N
6
I
IV
DF
V
I

c

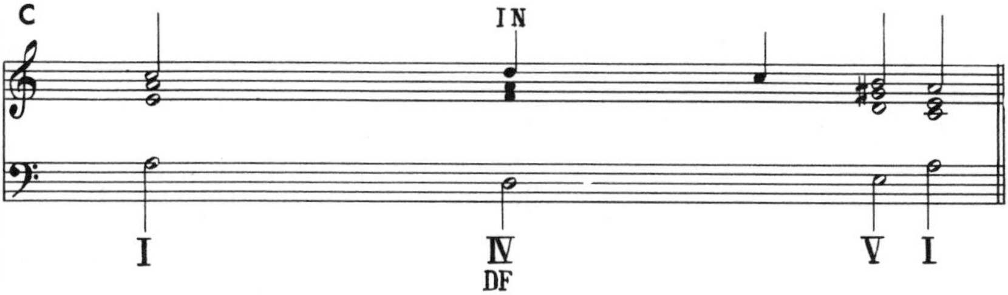
IN
I
IV
DF
V
I

326

a

I
V
II
DF
V
I

b

I
IV
DF
V
I

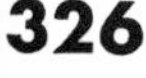

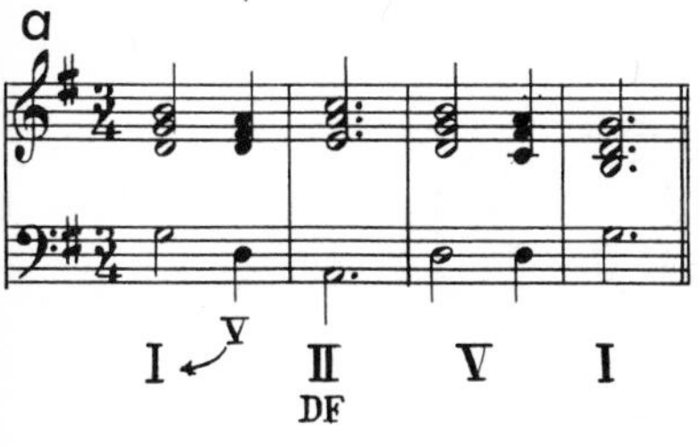

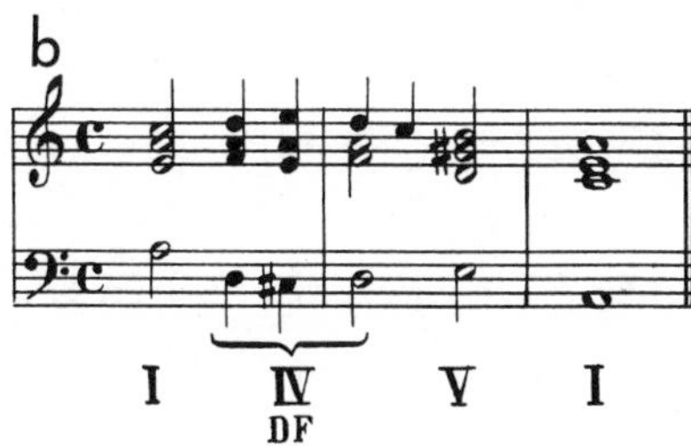

327 BACH Chorale (No. 320)

a

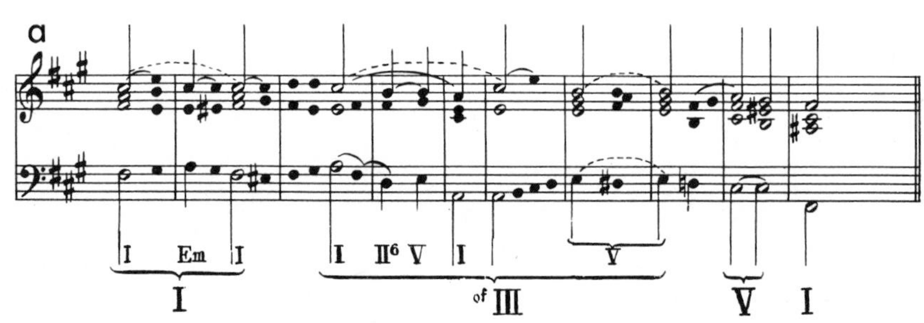

b

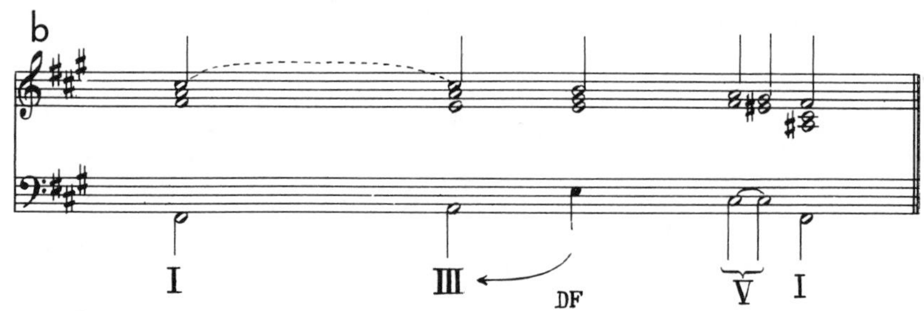

328 BACH Chorale (No. 280)

329 HANDEL Courante (Suite No. 14)

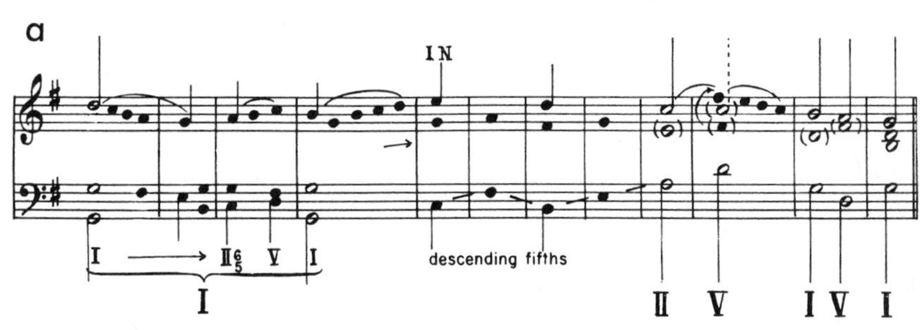

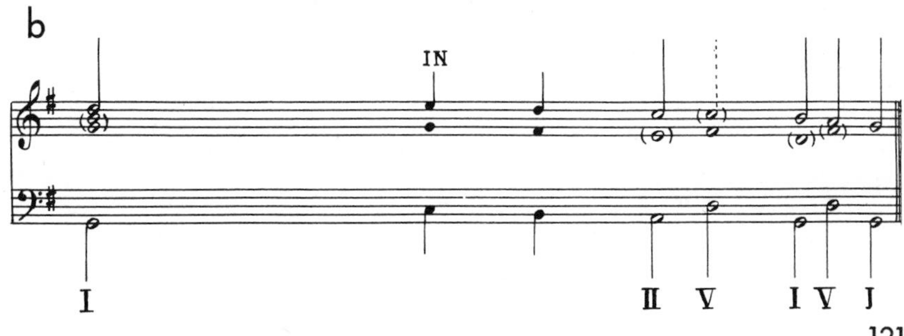

330 SCHUBERT Impromptu, Op 90, No. 2

331 VAUGHAN-WILLIAMS Symphony No. 5

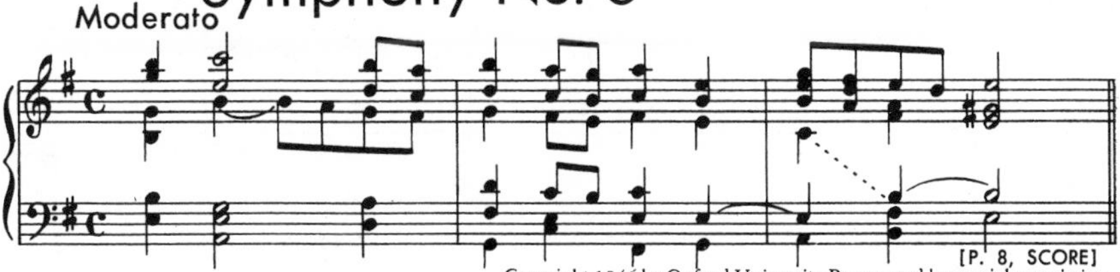

Moderato

[P. 8, SCORE]

a

IN

I ⟶ CS I6 CS V I

b

IN

I CS I6 CS V I

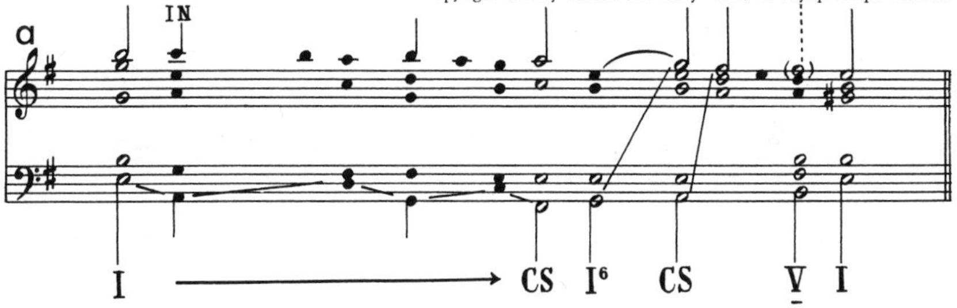

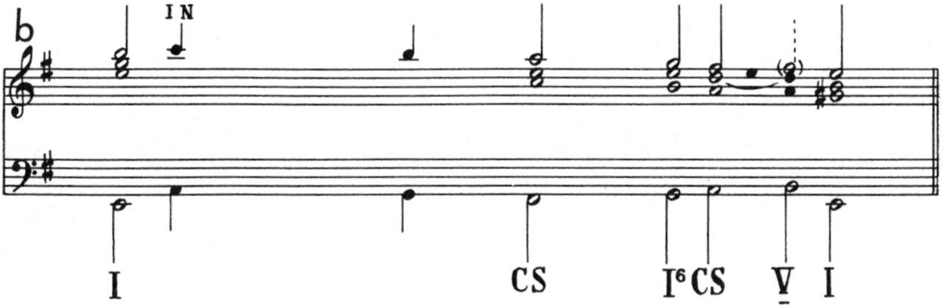

332 MOZART Rondo, K. 494

332 cont'd

b

5 6 7 6 7 6
I → V I

c

I → V I

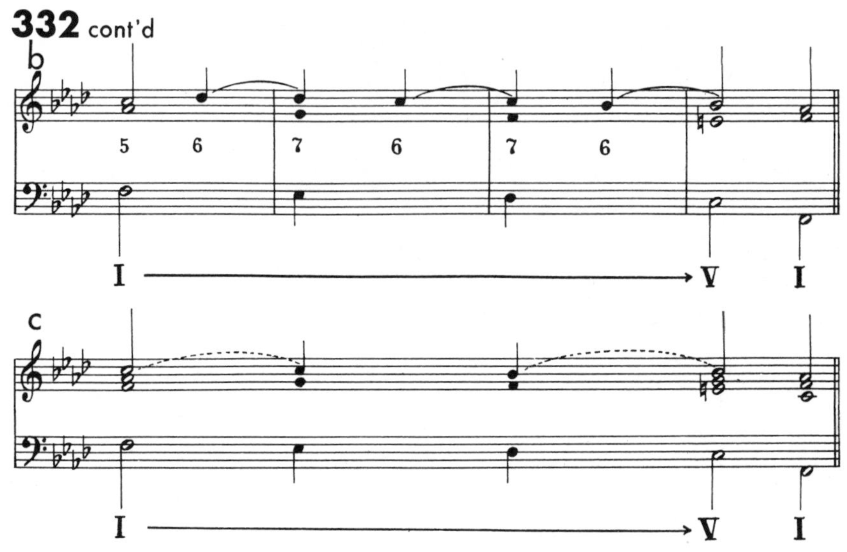

333 SCHUBERT Waltz Op 77, No. 10

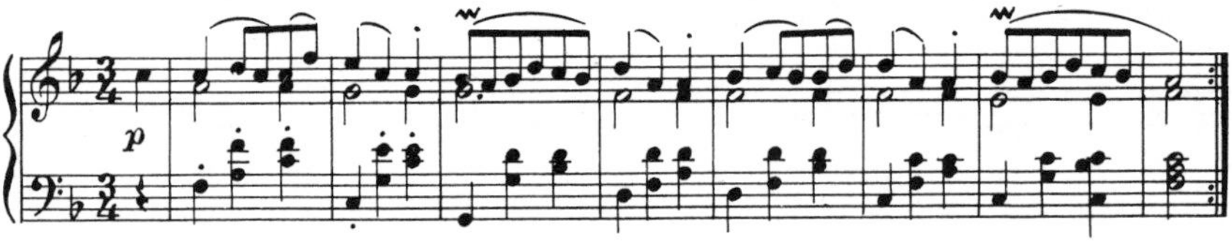

p

a

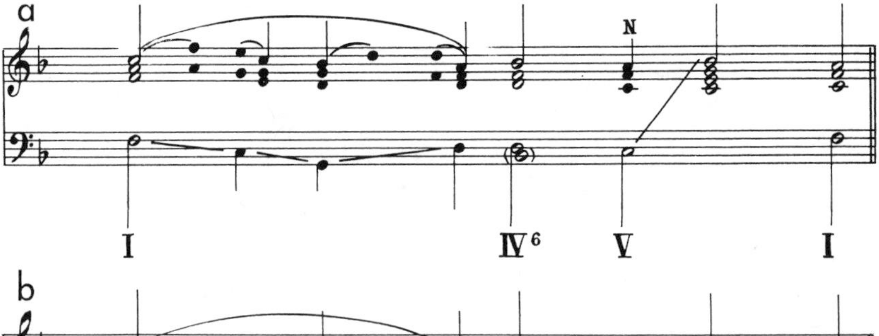

N
I IV6 V I

b

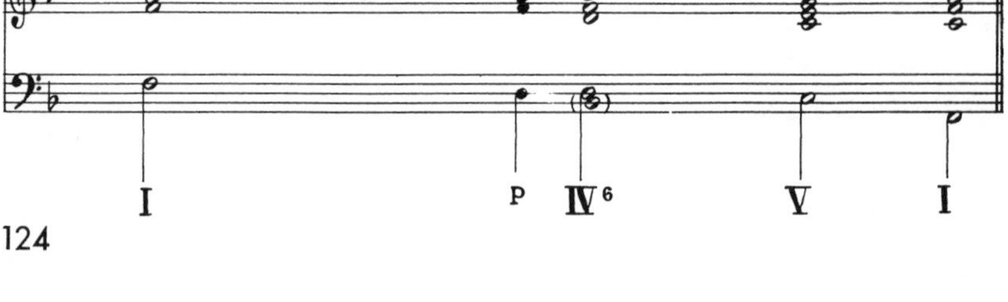

I P IV6 V I

334 SCHUBERT Täuschung

335 WEBER Overture, "Der Freischütz"

Molto vivace

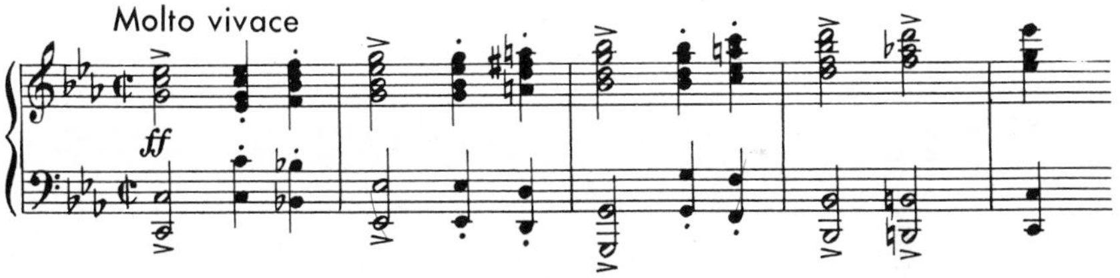

ff

a

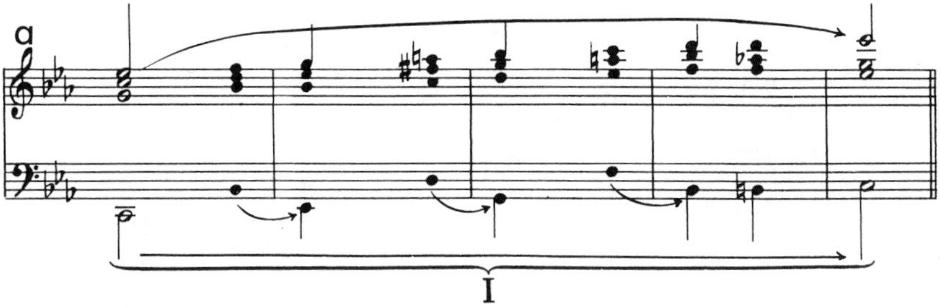

I

b

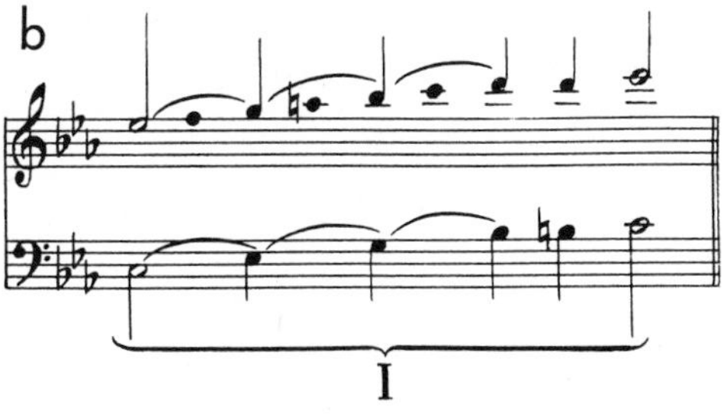

I

c

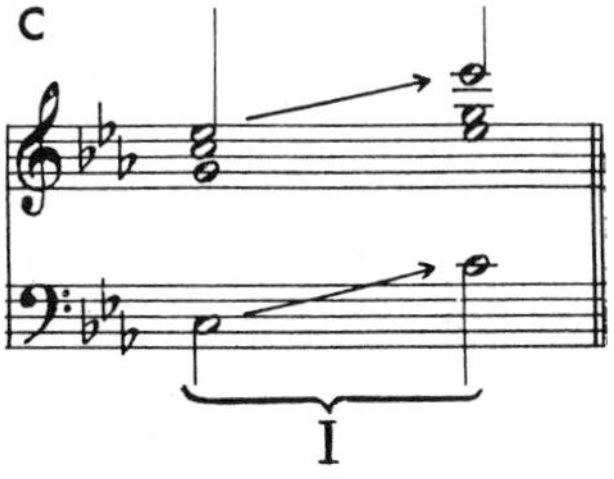

I

336 HAYDN String Quartet, Op 76, No. 4

337 SCHUBERT Piano Sonata, B♭ Major

Molto moderato

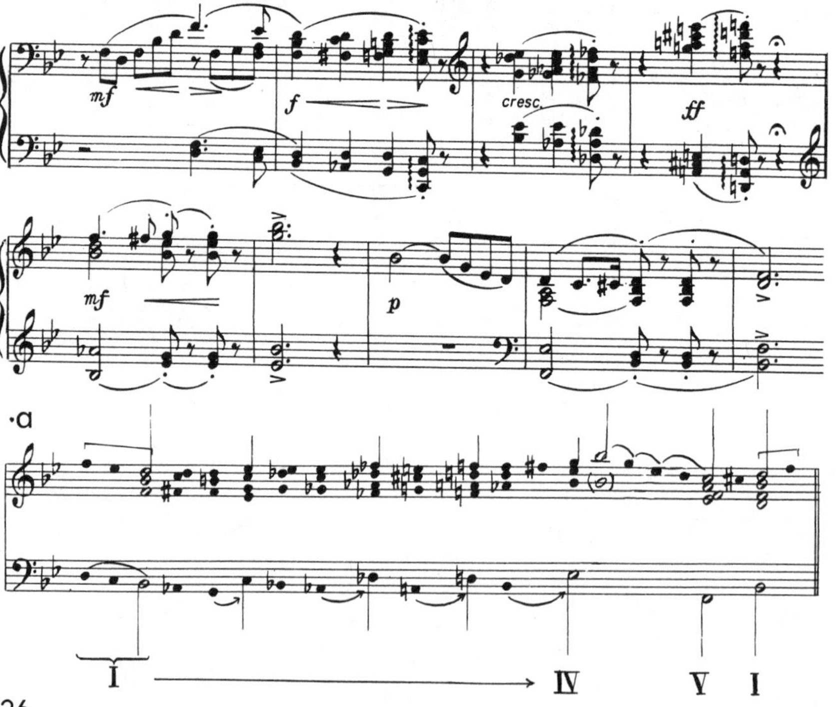

mf

f

cresc.

ff

mf

p

a

I ⟶ IV V I

338

a

c

b

I VII V I

c

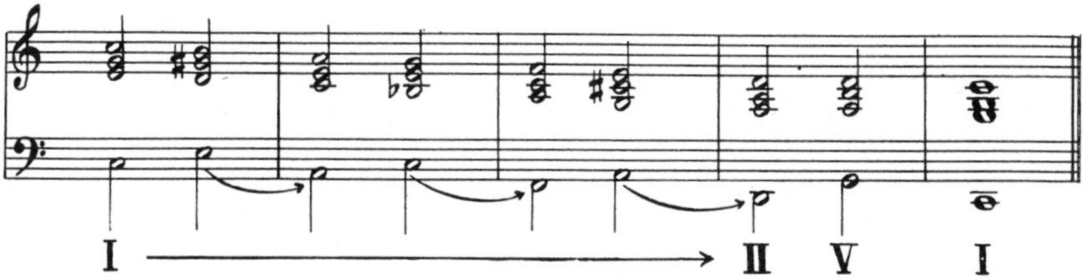

I → II V I

d

I → II V I

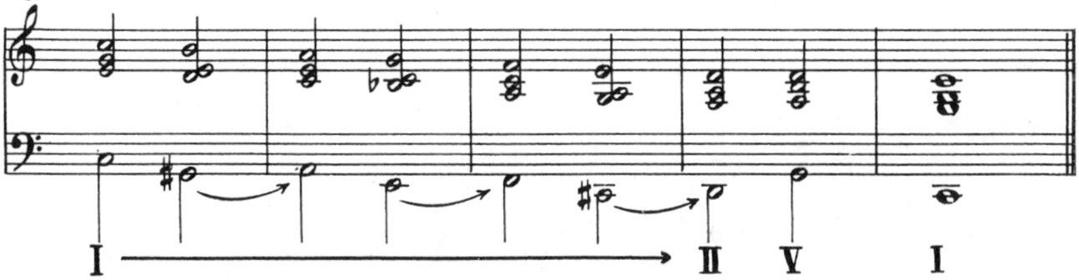

339 BACH Chorale (No. 361)

a

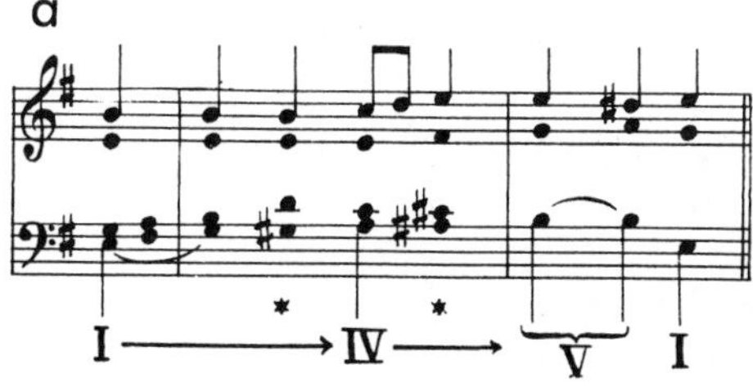

340

341

342

343

344

345

a

b

346

347 BACH Chorale (No. 166)

348 BACH Chorale (No. 167)

349 HAYDN String Quartet, Op 76, No. 1

350 CHOPIN Mazurka, Op 24, No. 3

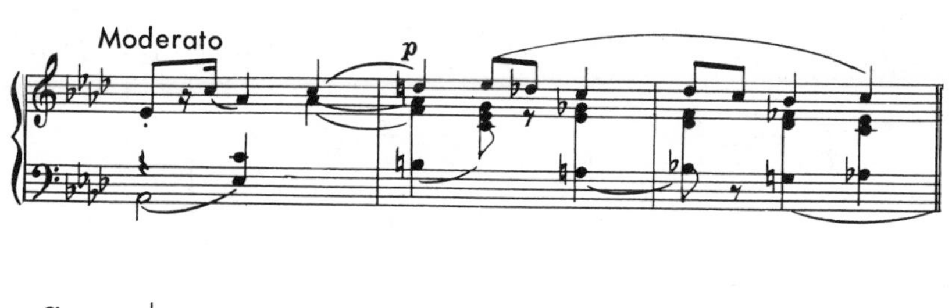

351 WOLF Schlafendes Jesuskind

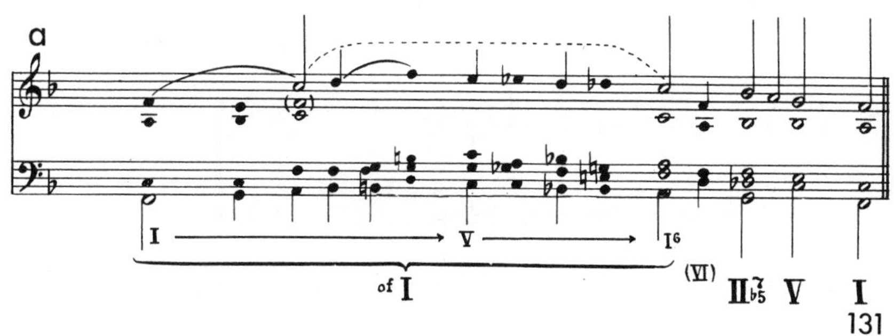

352

353

354

355

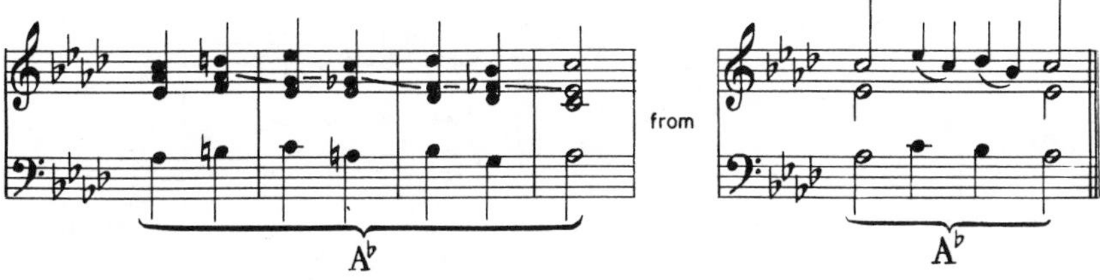

356

357 CHOPIN Mazurka, Op 30, No. 4

358 SCHUMANN Novelette, Op 21, No. 2

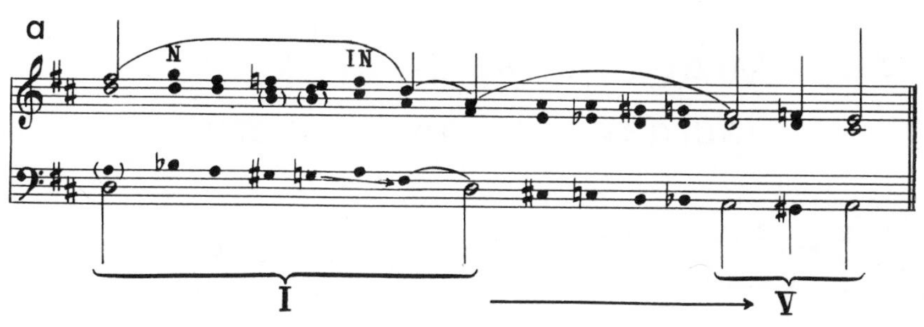

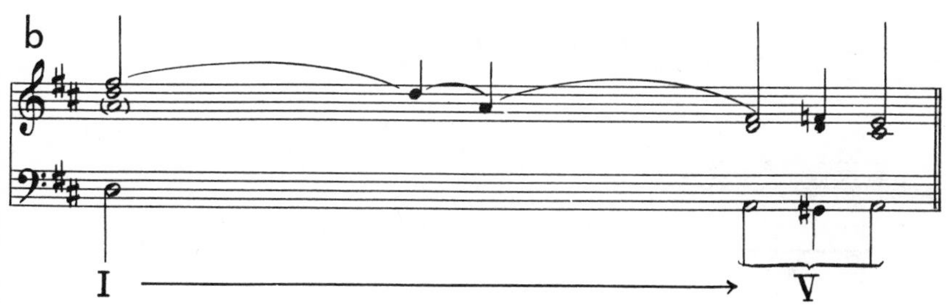

359 CHOPIN Mazurka, Op 17, No. 4

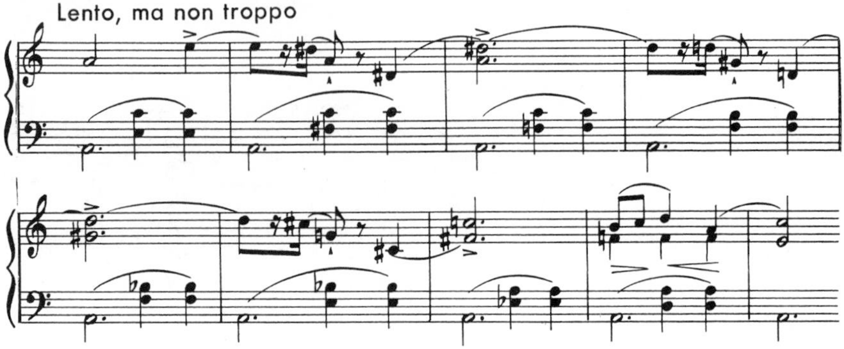

Lento, ma non troppo

a

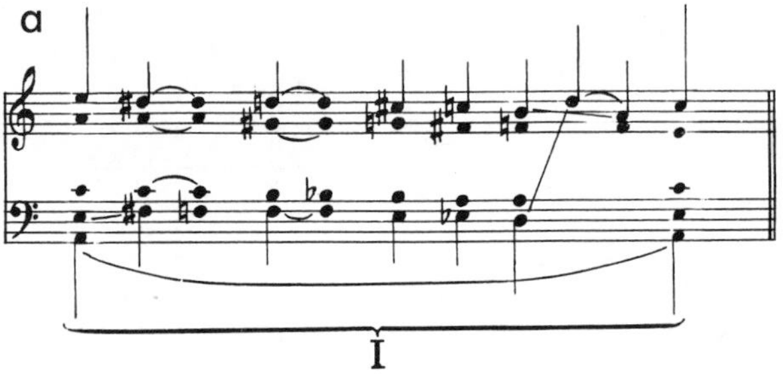

I

b

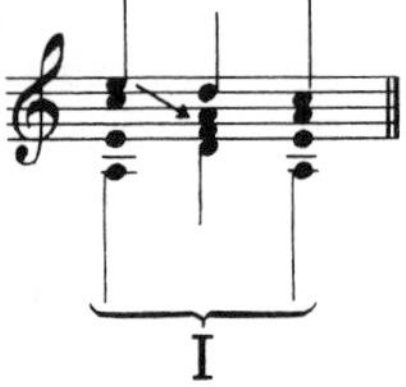

I

360 WAGNER Siegfried's Rhine Journey ("Götterdämmerung")

Rasch
f vigoroso

a

F

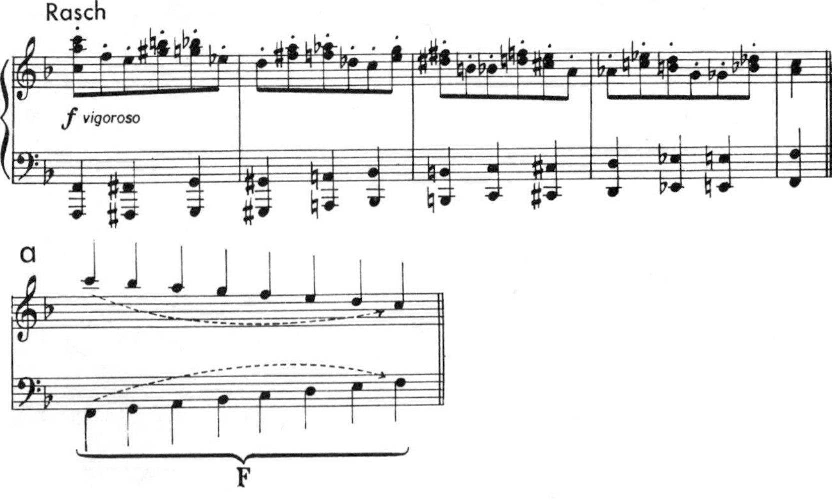

361 CHOPIN Mazurka, Op 7, No. 2

362 CHOPIN Mazurka, Op 6, No. 1

a

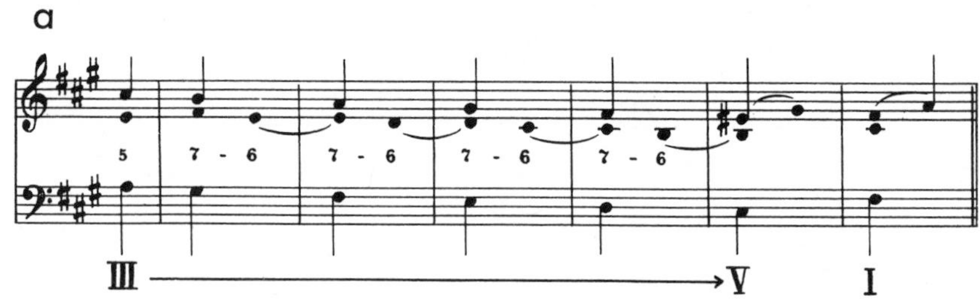

b

c

362 cont'd

d

e

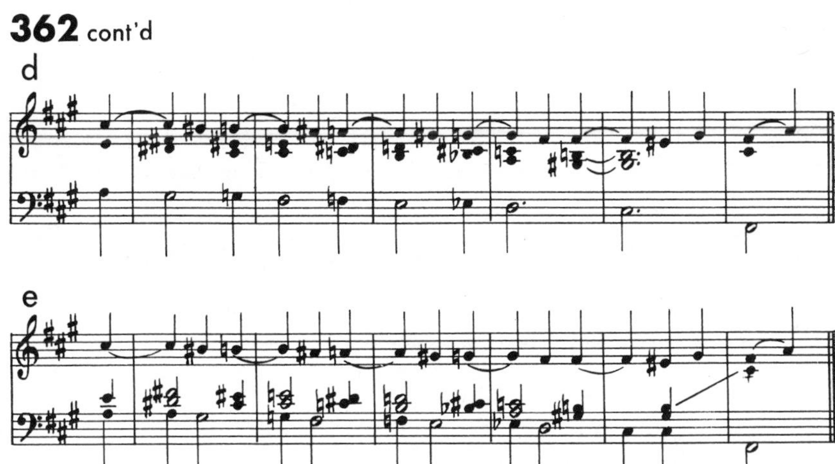

363 SCHUMANN Novelette, Op 21, No. 8

Munter, nicht zu rasch

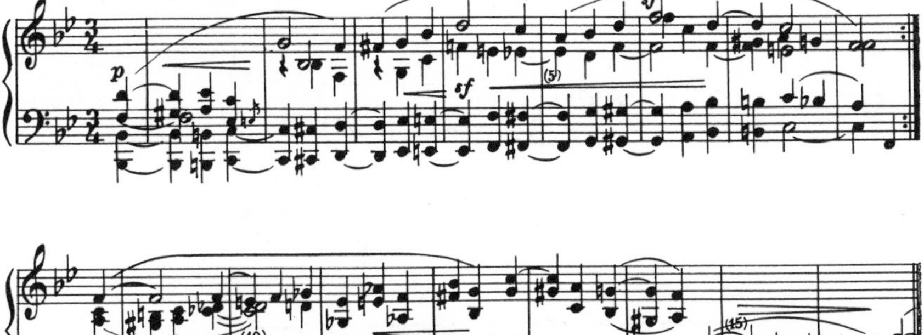

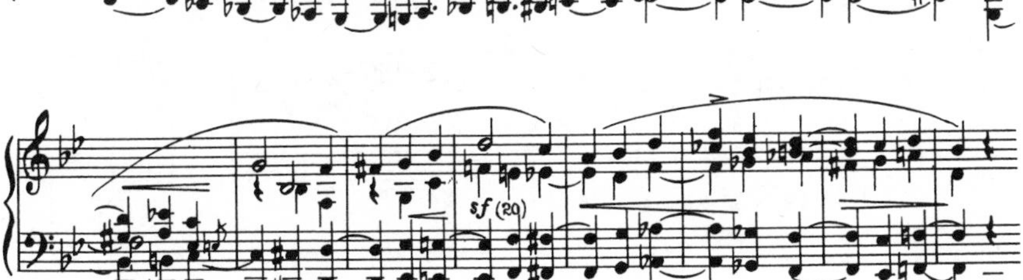

363 cont'd

363 cont'd

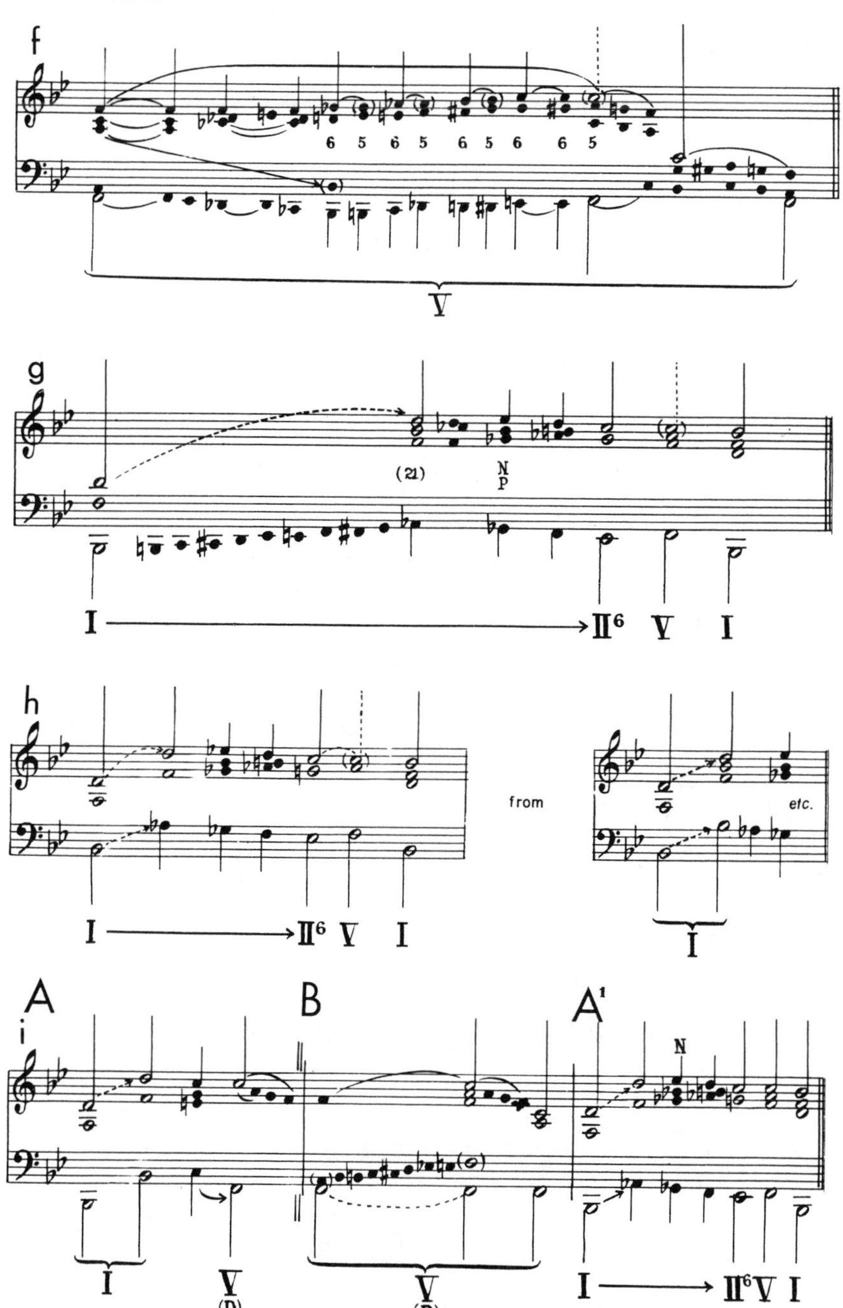

f
6 5 6 5 6 5 6 6 5
V
g
(21)
N
P
I
II6
V
I
h
I
II6
V
I
from
etc.
I
A
B
A1
i
N
I
V
(D)
V
(D)
I
II6
V
I

364

a

I V I

b

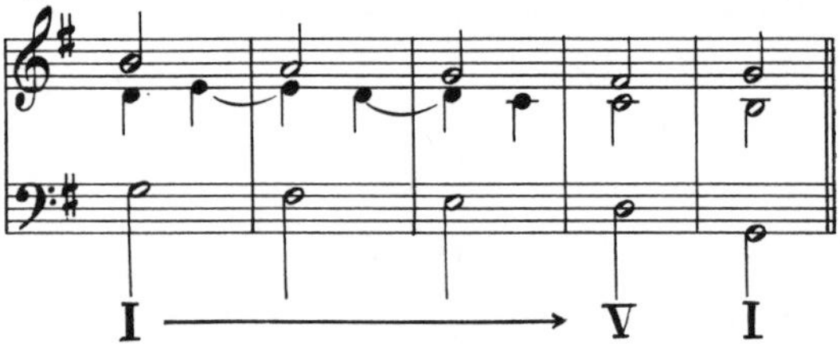

I ⟶ V I

c

I ⟶ V I

365

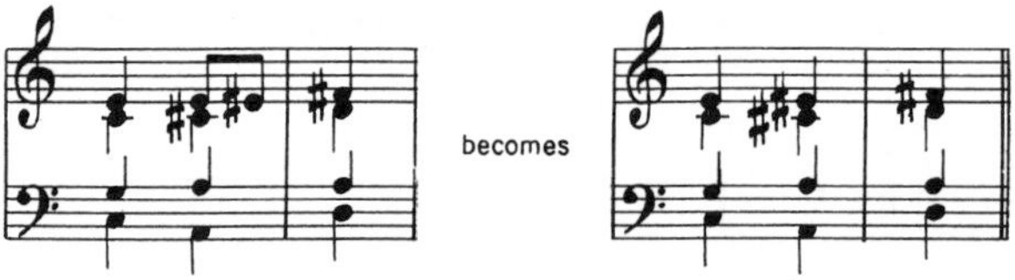

becomes

366 SCHUBERT Tränenregen

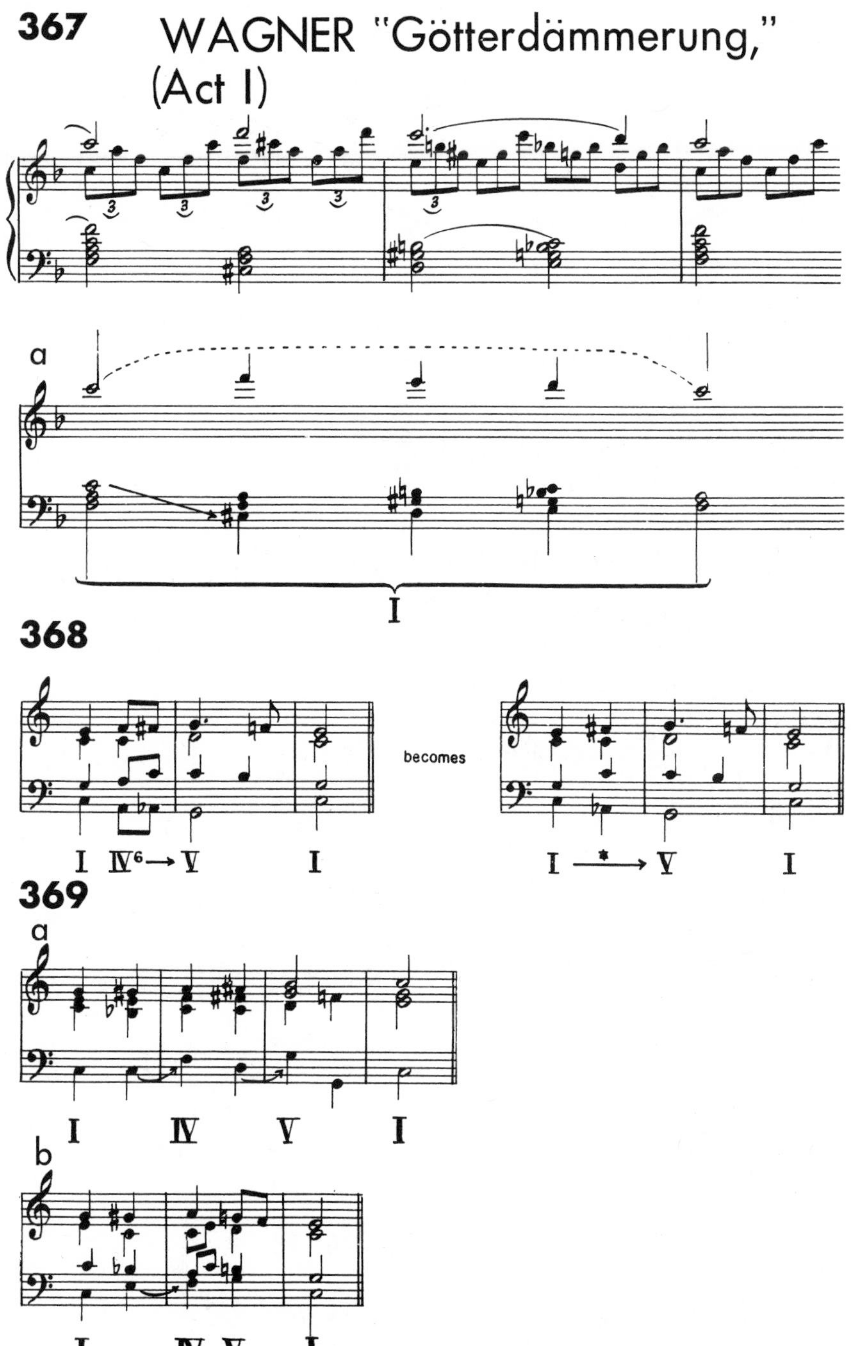
367
WAGNER "Götterdämmerung," (Act I)
3
a
I
368
I IV6 → V I
becomes
I → V I
369
a
I IV V I
b
I IV V I

370

371 WAGNER Prelude, "Tristan und Isolde"

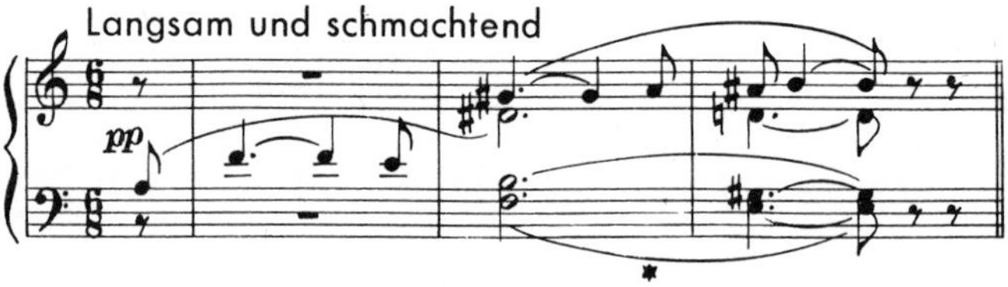

Langsam und schmachtend

pp

*

372

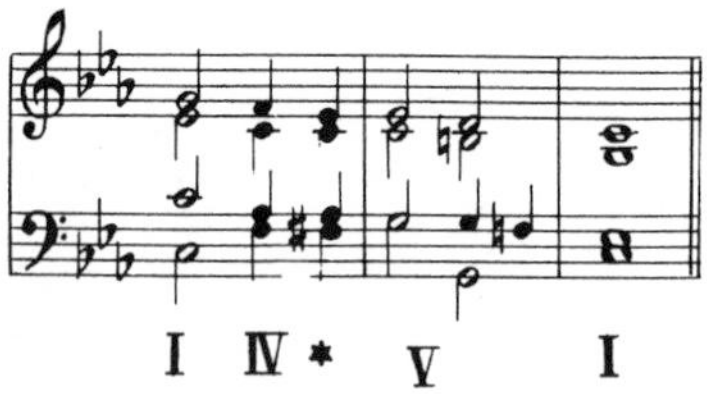

I IV * V I

373

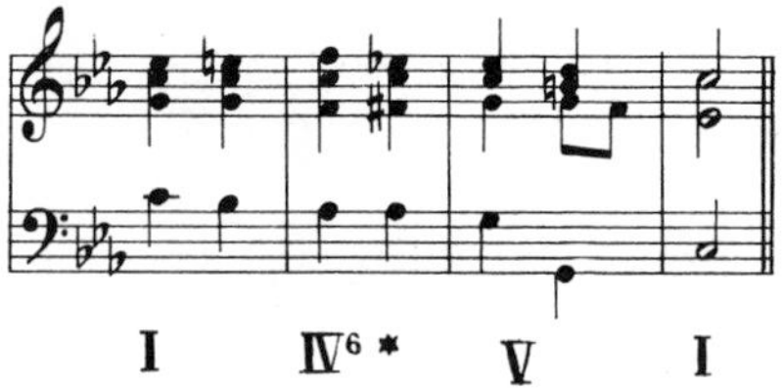

I IV⁶ * V I

374

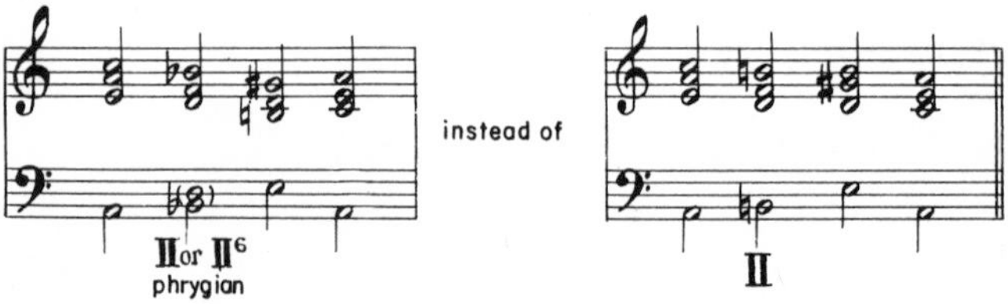

instead of

II or II⁶
phrygian

II

375 BEETHOVEN Piano Sonata, C# minor, Op 27, No. 2

Adagio sostenuto
pp
a
N
I ⟶ II6 phr. V I

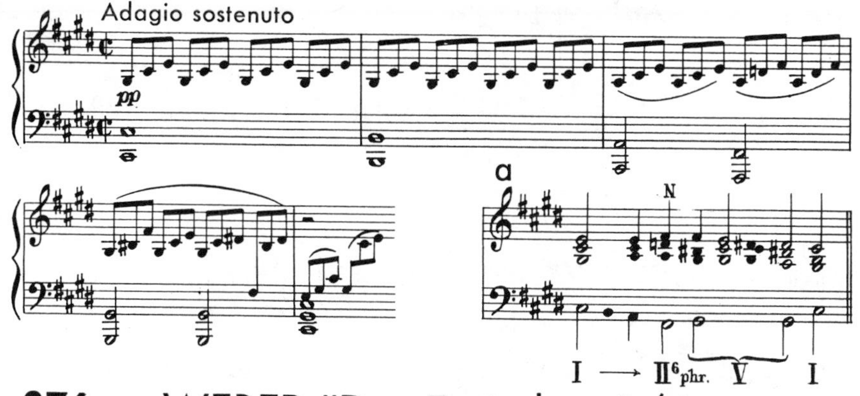

376 WEBER "Der Freischütz" (Act II, No. 6)

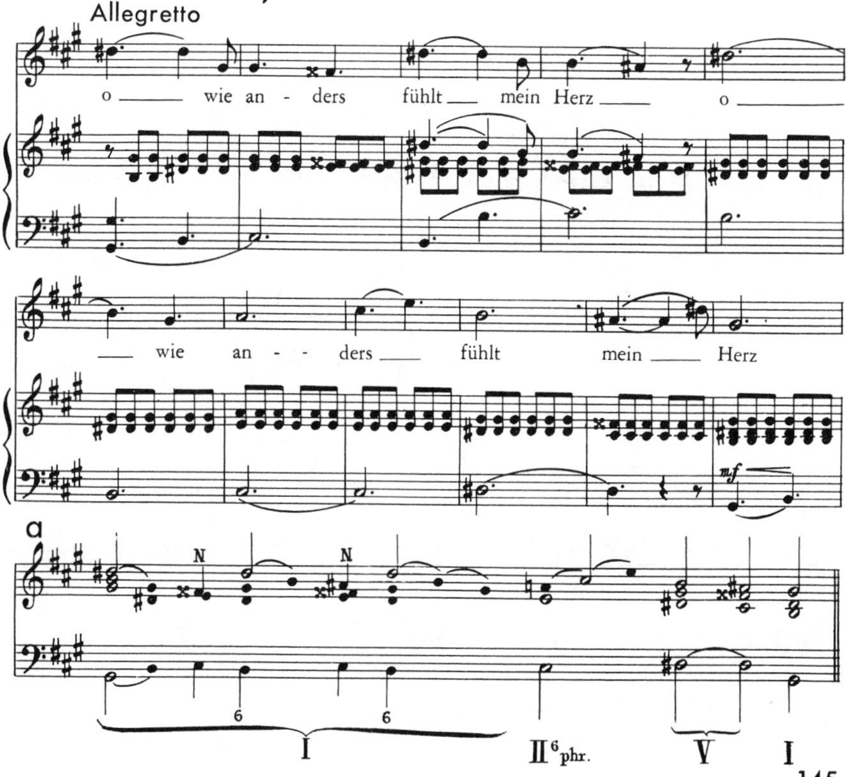
Allegretto
o — wie an - ders fühlt — mein Herz — o —
— wie an - - ders — fühlt mein — Herz
mf
a
N
N
6
6
I
II6 phr.
V
I

377 R. STRAUSS "Ariadne auf Naxos"

Mezzo movimento
p

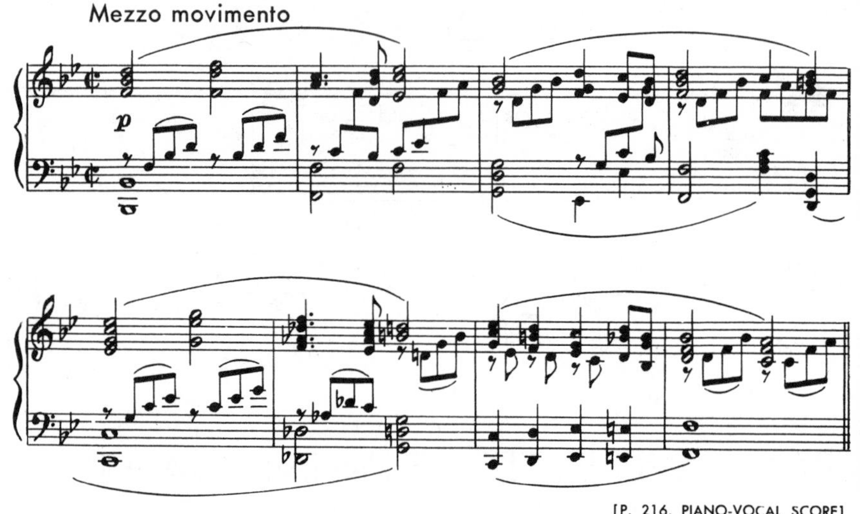

[P. 216, PIANO-VOCAL SCORE]

a

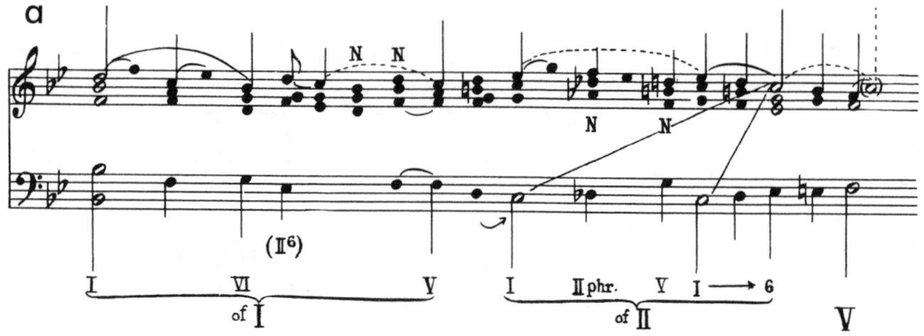

N N
N N
(II^6)
I VI V
of I
I II phr. V I → 6
of II
V

b

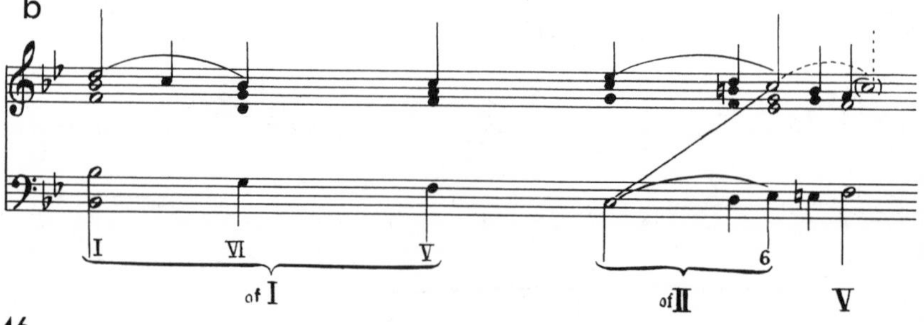

I VI V
of I
6
of II
V

378 CHOPIN Nocturne, Op 27, No. 1

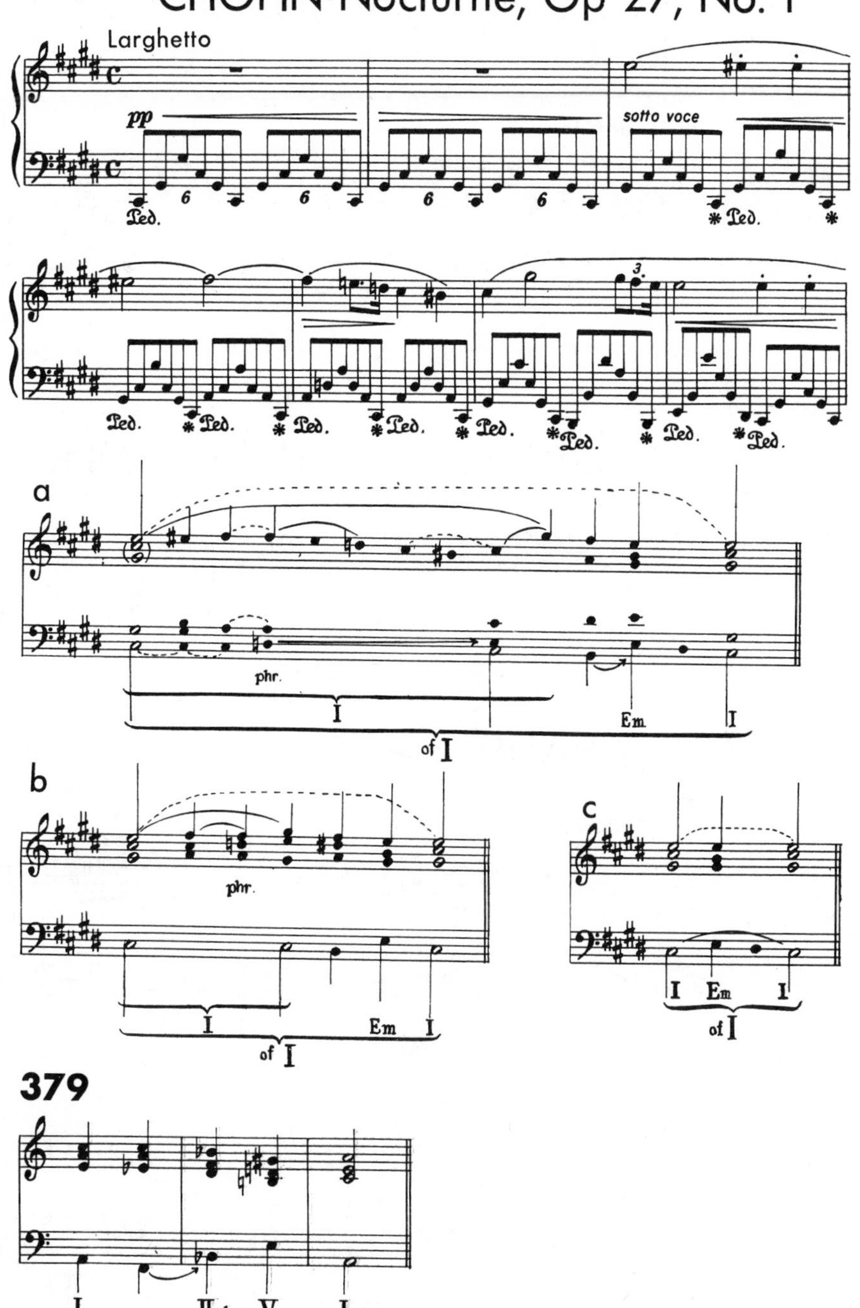

380 PROKOFIEFF Gavotte, Op 77, No. 4

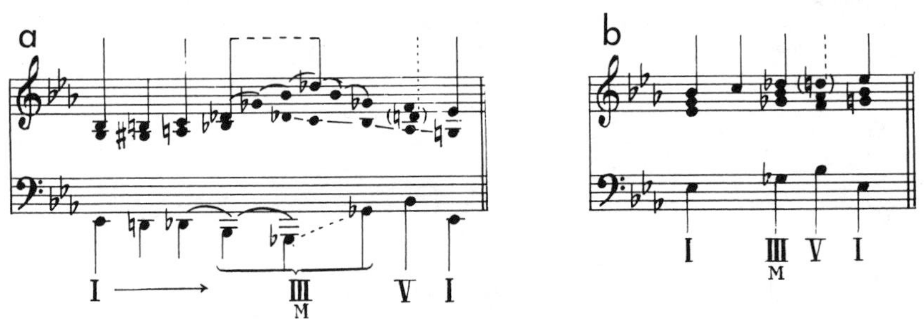

381 R. STRAUSS Don Juan

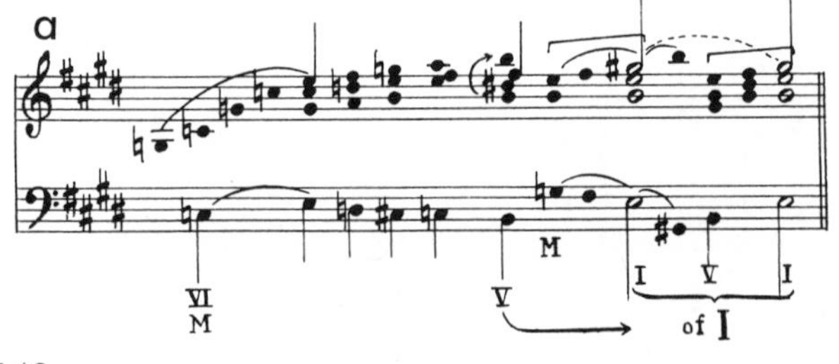

382 WOLF In dem Schatten meiner Locken

382 cont'd

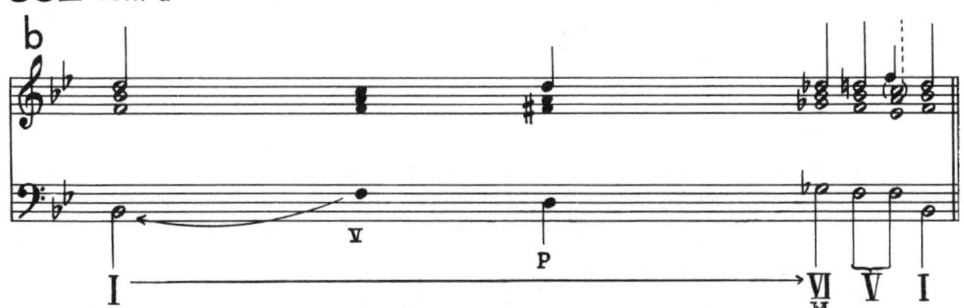

383 BEETHOVEN Piano Sonata, C minor, Op 13

Adagio cantabile

383 cont'd

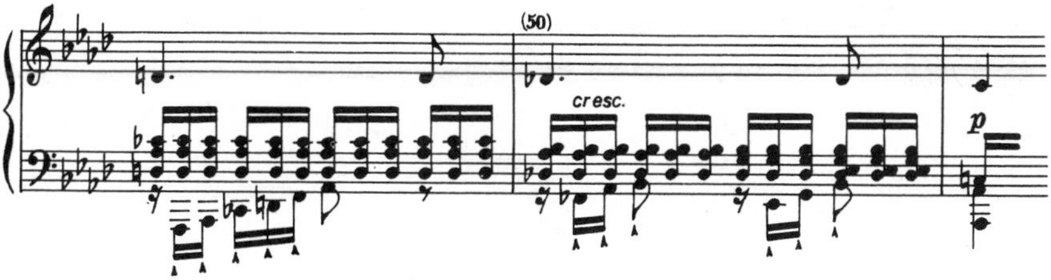
(50)
cresc.
p

a

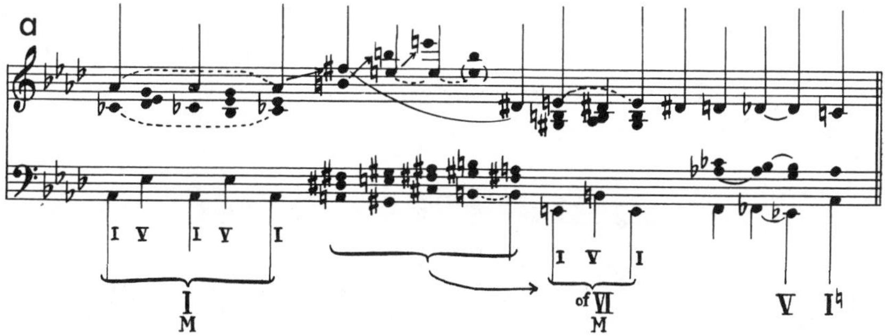
I V I V I
I
M
I V I
of VI
M
V I♮

b

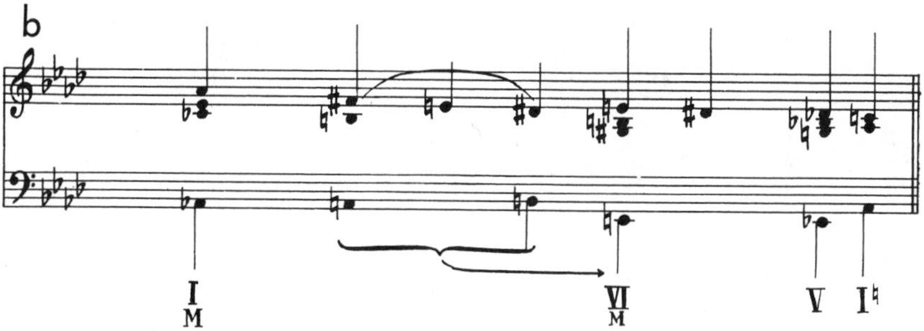
I
M
VI
M
V I♮

384 SCHUBERT Piano Sonata, C minor

Adagio

ppp
pp
un poco cresc.
p

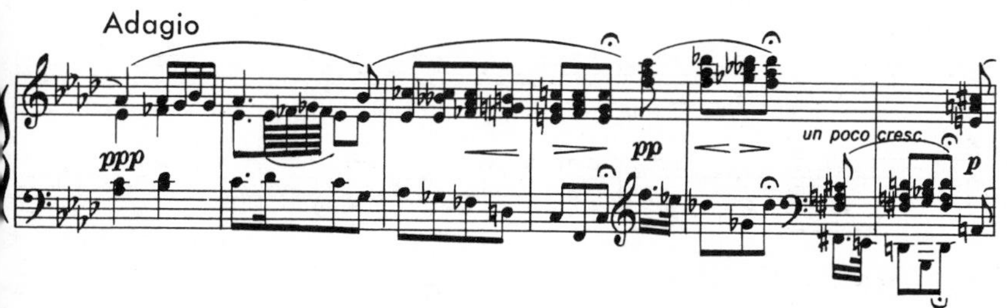

384 cont'd

f
p

a

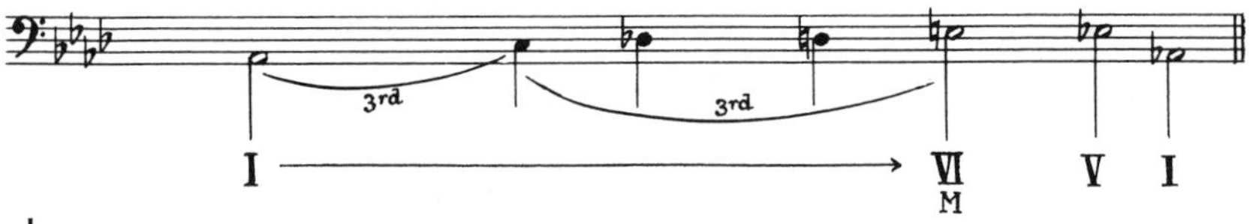

3rd 3rd

I → VI V I
M

b

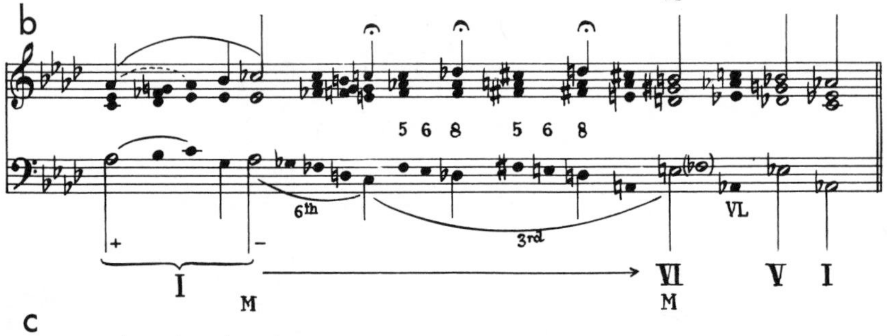

5 6 8 5 6 8

6th 3rd VL

+ −

I → VI V I
M M

c

I♭ VI V I♮

385 SCHUBERT Pause

Ziemlich geschwind

385 cont'd

(50)
Lüft - chen ü - ber die Sai - ten dir, und streift ei - ne Bie - ne mit
3

3
(55)
ih - ren Flü-geln dich, da wird mir so ban - ge, und es durchschauert mich.
pp
(60)
War-um liess ich das Band auch hän-gen so lang? Oft

fliegt's um die Sai - ten mit seuf - zen dem Klang. Ist es der Nach-klang

385 cont'd
(65)
(69)
— mei-ner Lie - bes - pein? Soll es das Vor - spiel- neu - er Lie - der sein?
a
N
N
(46)
(52)
(55)
5
(63)
6
5
(67)
(69)
M
double mixture
M
I
II
(DF)
V
I
b
N
N
5
5
M
M
I
II
V
I
386 MAHLER Das Lied von der Erde, No. 6
Langsam
54
Ich — su - che Ru - he, Ru - he für - mein - ein - - - - - sam Herz!
espress.
pp
p
pp

386 cont'd

387 CHOPIN Mazurka, Op 68, No. 4 (Posth.)

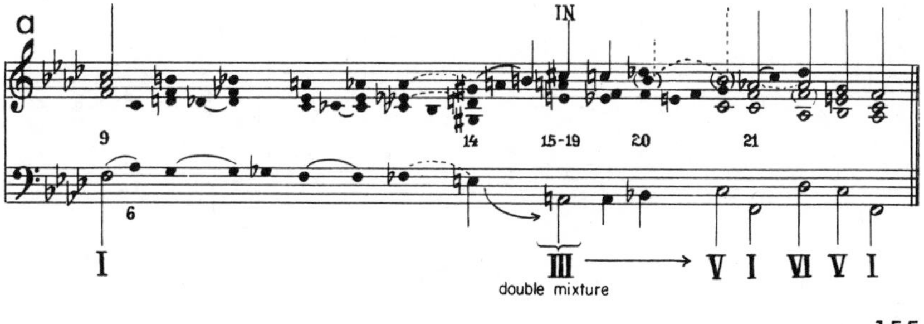

Andantino

9

sempre legatissimo

Ped. *

cresc.

15

Ped. * Ped. * Ped. * Ped. *

20

tr

Ped. * Ped. * Ped. *

a

IN

9 14 15-19 20 21

6

I III → V I VI V I

double mixture

387 cont'd

388 MOZART Piano Sonata, F Major, K. 280

Adagio

tr

p

f

p

f

p

f

p

f

a

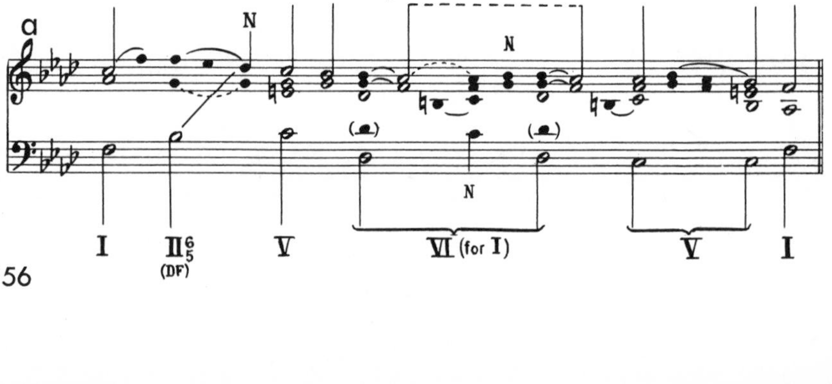

N

N

N

I II^6_5 (DF) V VI (for I) V I

389 SCHUBERT Trio, B♭ Major, Op 99

390 HAYDN Piano Sonata, F Major, No. 29

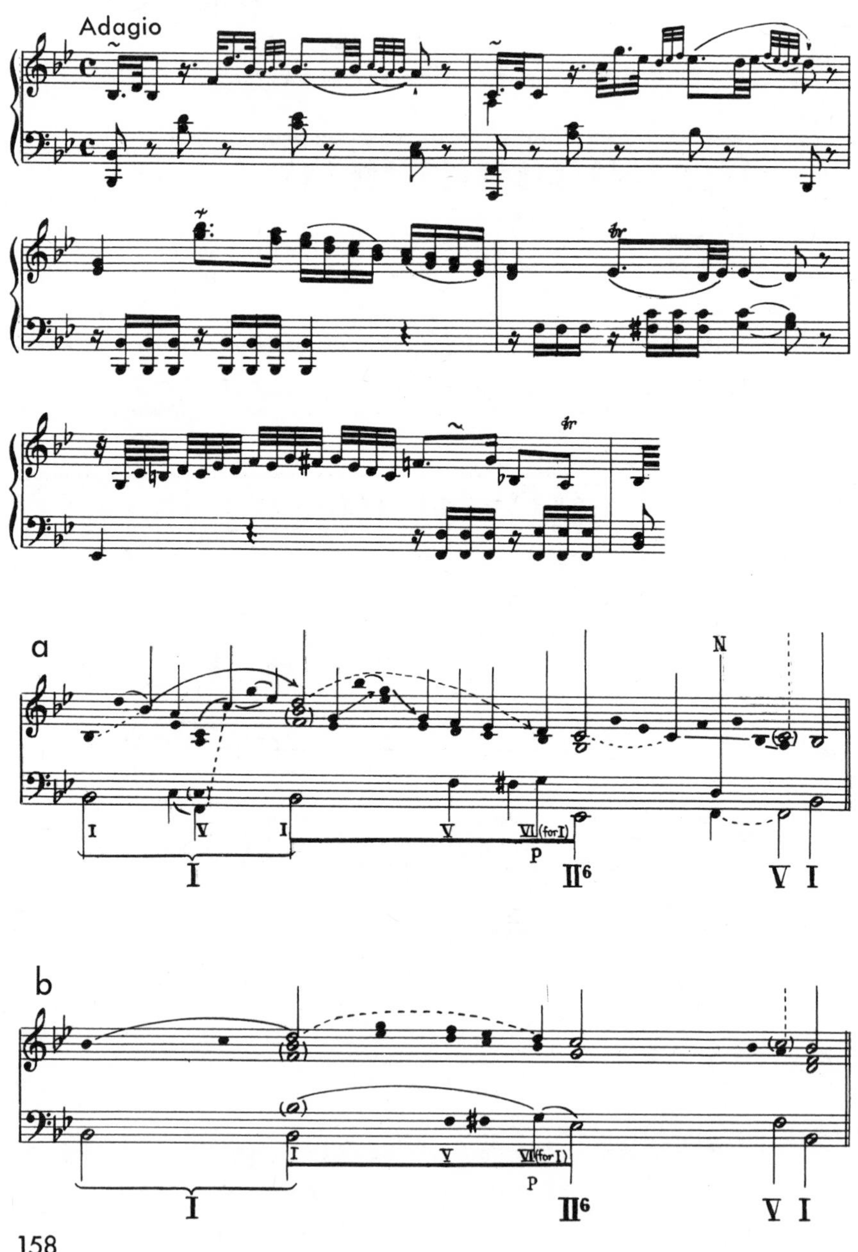

391 SCHUMANN Forest Scenes, No. 6

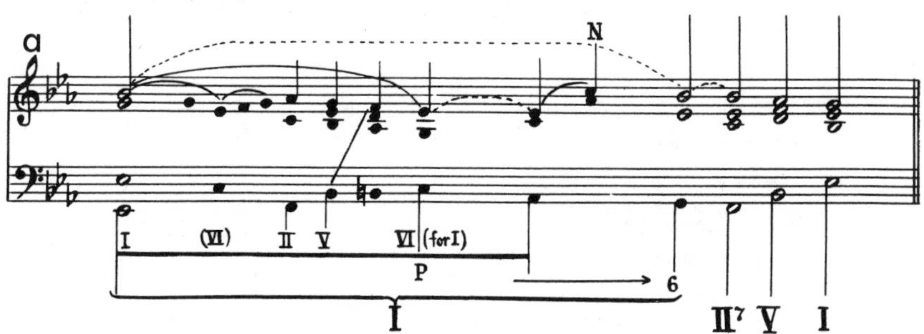

392 BACH Chorale (No. 5)

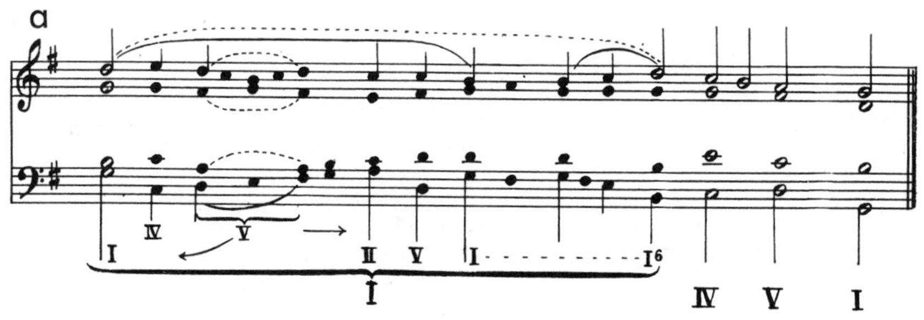

393 CHOPIN Waltz, Op 64, No. 2

394 SCHUBERT Piano Sonata, B♭ Major

pp
(30)
cresc.
(35)
f
(40)
cresc.
decresc.
cresc.
decresc.
(44)

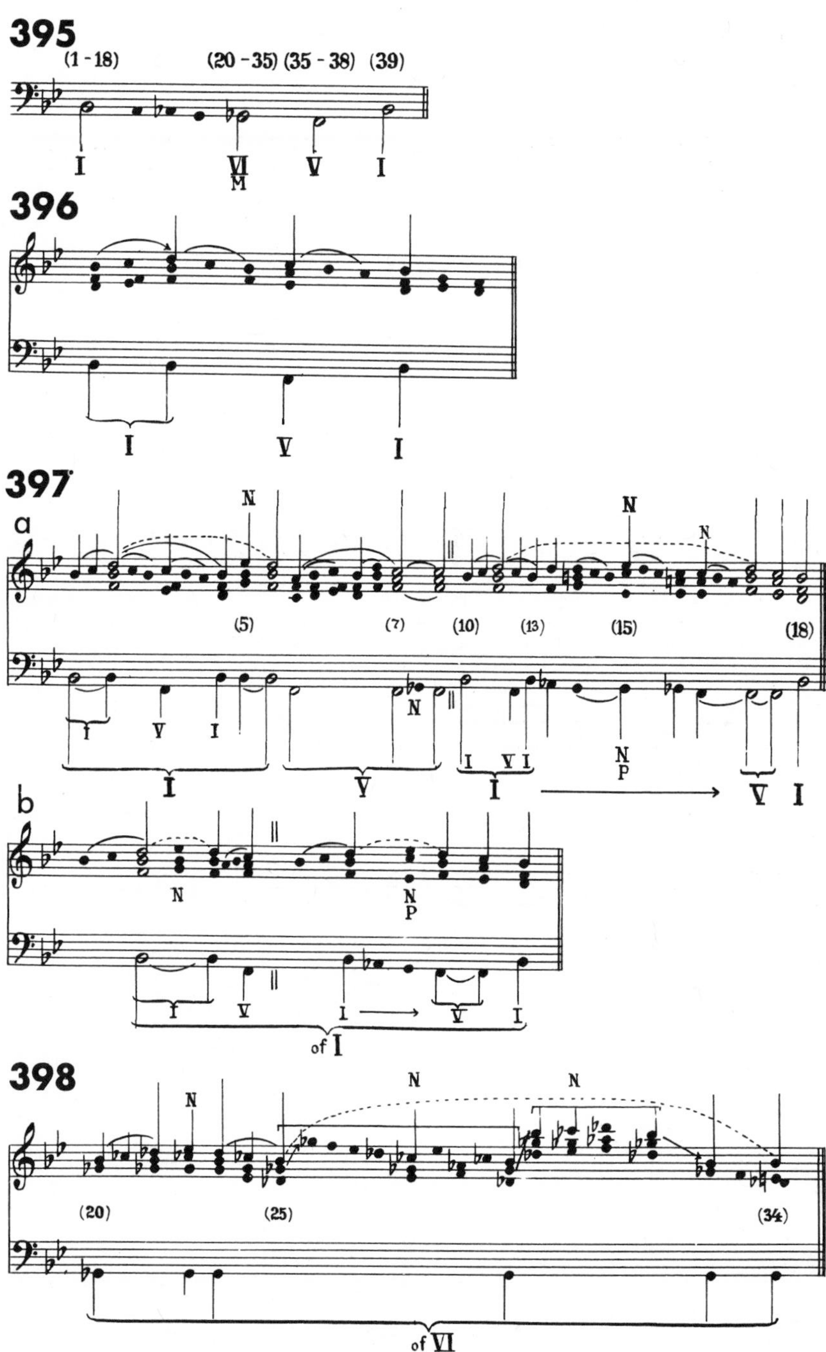
395
(1 - 18)
(20 - 35) (35 - 38) (39)
I VI/M V I
396
I V I
397
a
N N N
(5) (7) (10) (13) (15) (18)
N
I V I
N/P
I V I I V I
I V I
b
N N/P
I V I V I
of I
398
N N N
(20) (25) (34)
of VI/M

399

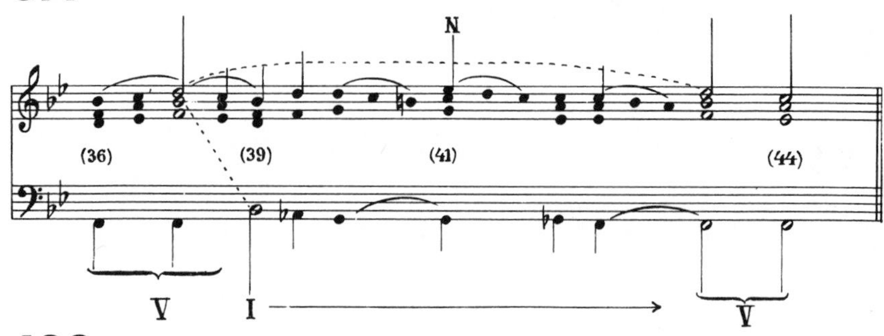

400

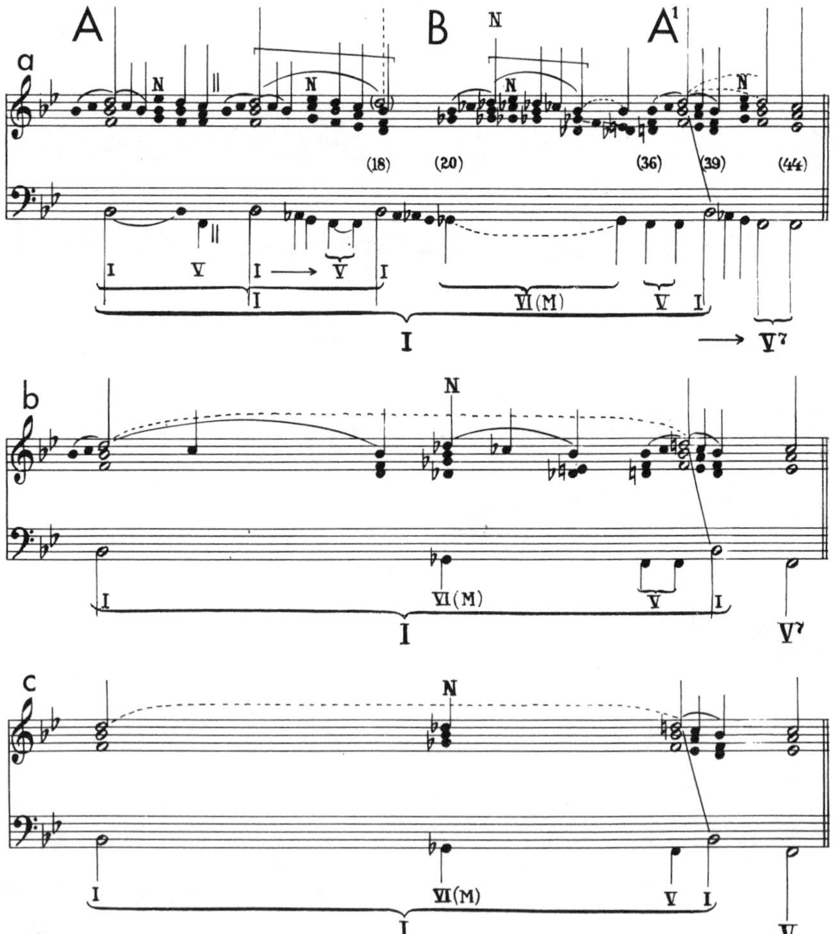

a

A B A[1]

N N N N N

(18) (20) (36) (39) (44)

I V I V I

I

VI (M) V I

I

V[7]

b

N

I VI (M) V I

I

V[7]

c

N

I VI (M) V I

I

V

401 HAYDN String Quartet, Op 20, No. 5

402 LASSO Motet: Recordare Jesu pie

402 cont'd

[From *OL*, Vol. 15]

403 GASTOLDI Balletto: Speme amorosa

[From SHM, No. 20]

a

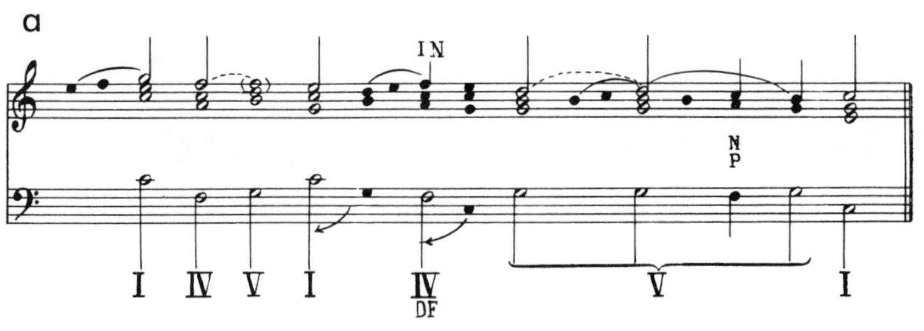

b

404 WAGNER "Tristan und Isolde" (Act II)

405 FRANCK Prelude, Aria and Finale

Allegro moderato e maestoso

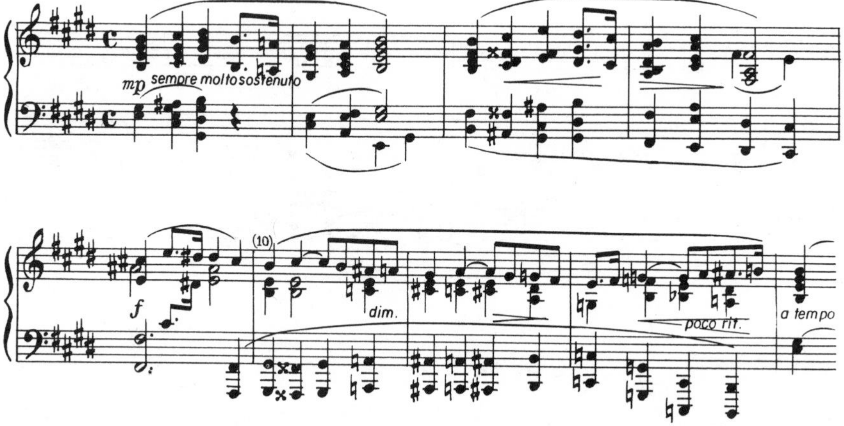

mp sempre molto sostenuto
f
(10)
dim.
poco rit.
a tempo

a

5 8 5 5
Em
Em
I
V
I

b

5 5 5 5
Em Em
I

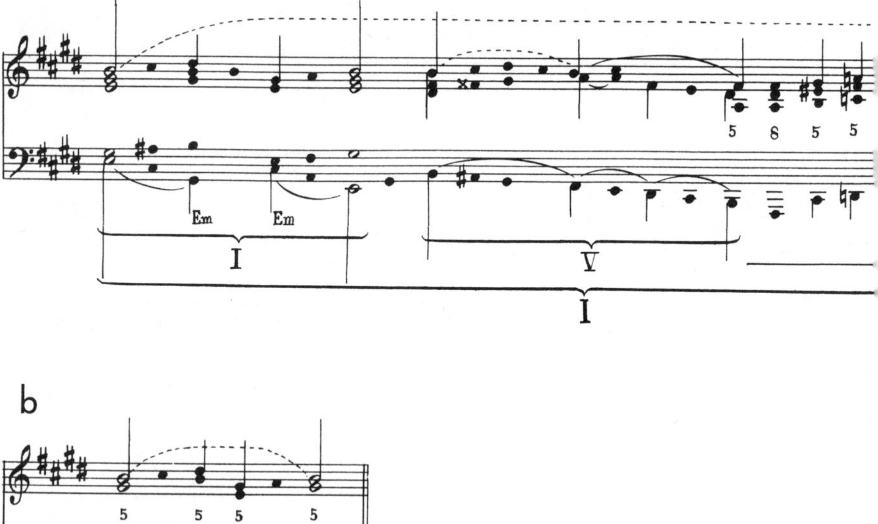

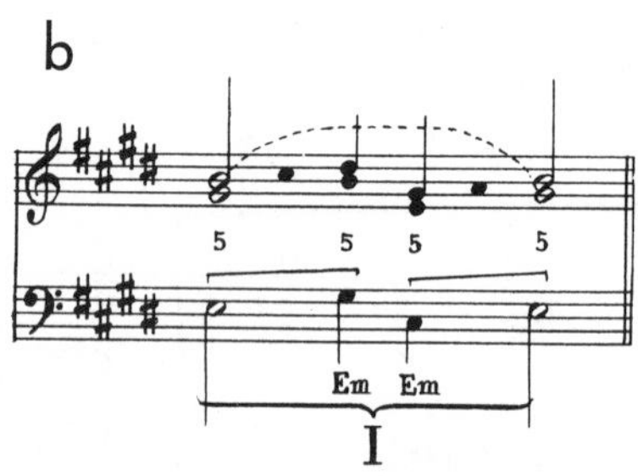

405 cont'd

(5)
mf
poco cresc.

cont'd

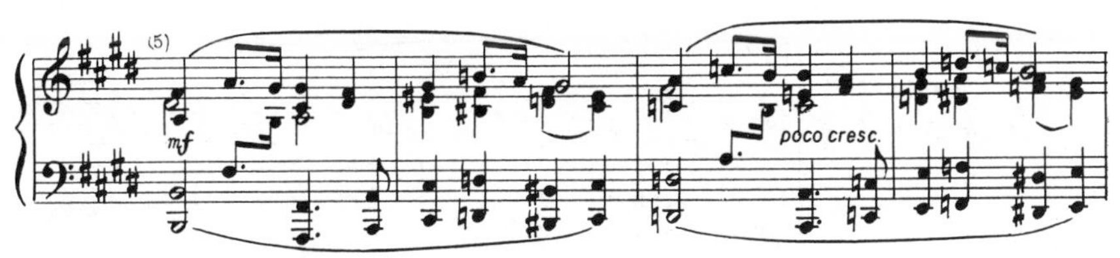

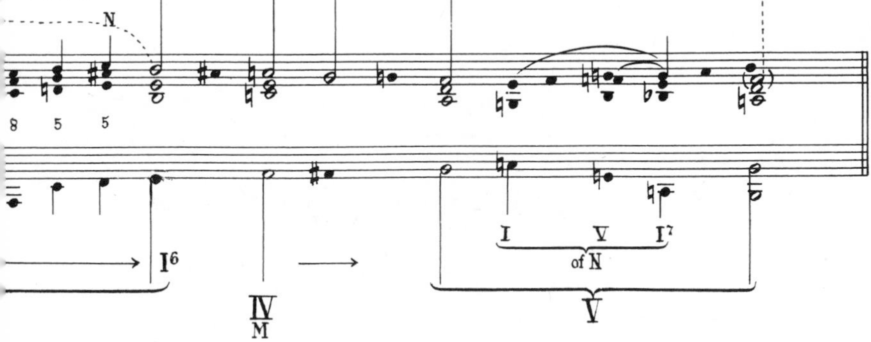
N
8
5
5
I6
IV
M
I
V
I7
of N
V

C

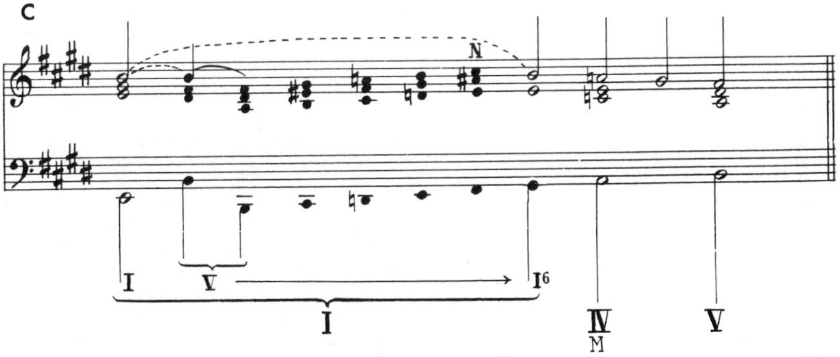
N
I
V
I6
I
IV
M
V

406 R. STRAUSS Quintet ("Ariadne auf Naxos")

a

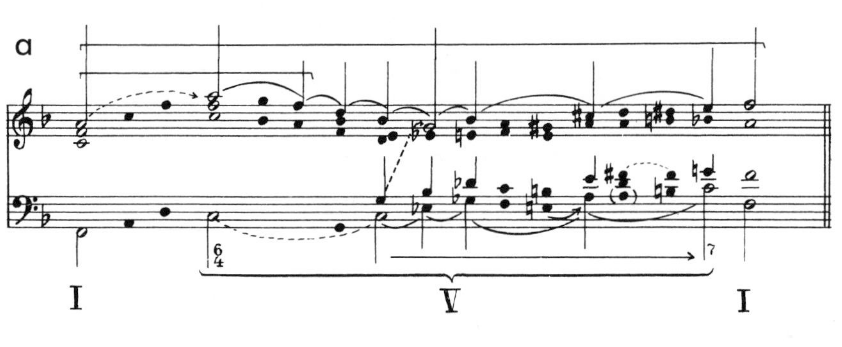

b

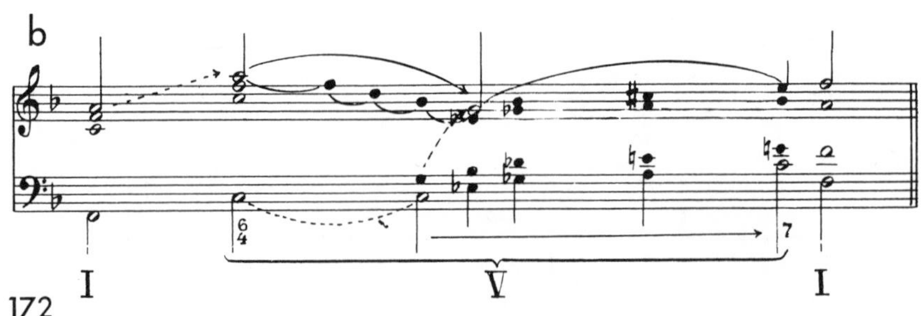

407 R. STRAUSS Quintet ("Ariadne auf Naxos")

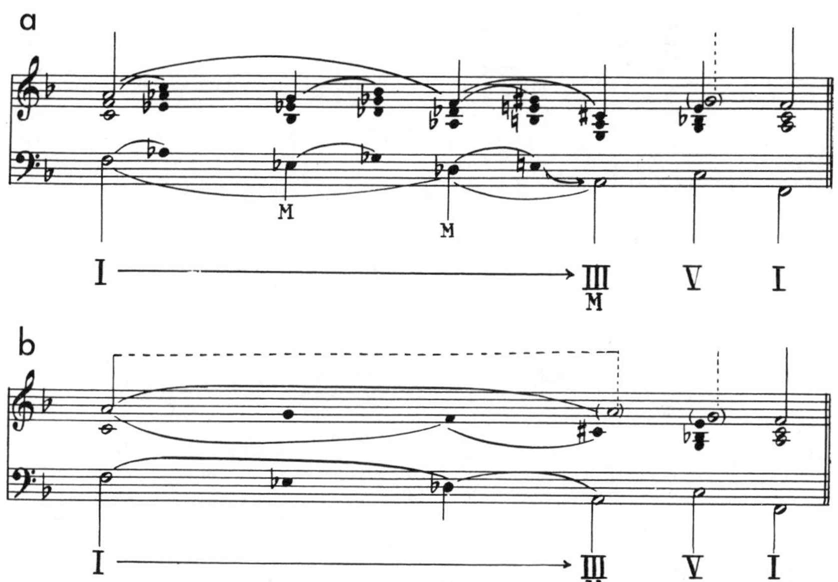

408 BIZET Seguidilla ("Carmen," Act I)

408 cont'd

409 CHOPIN Polonaise-Fantasy

a

408 cont'd

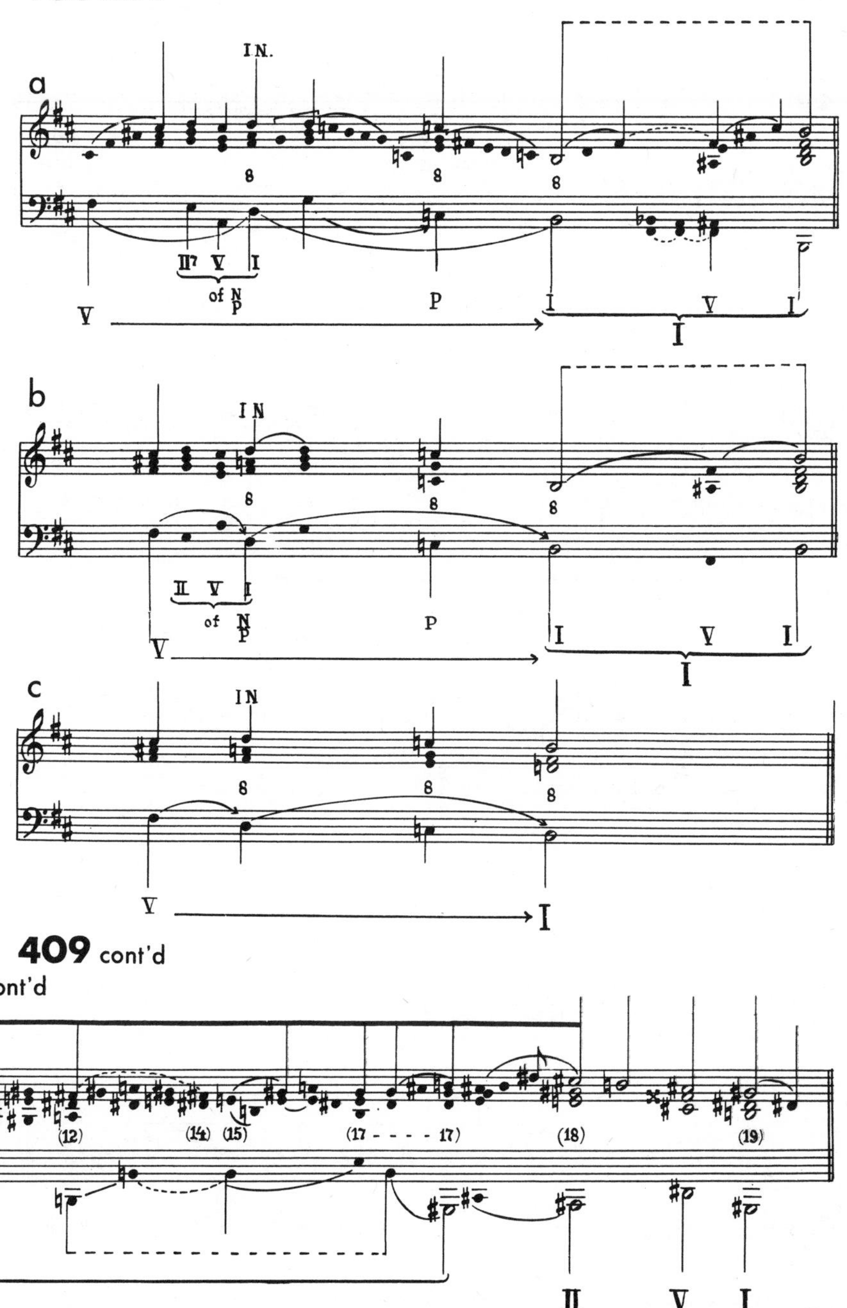

409 cont'd

cont'd

409 cont'd

b
(1)
(5)
(10) (12) (17 - - - - - - 17) (18) (19)
I
II7 V I
c
(1 - - - - - - - - - - - - - - - - - 17) (18) (19)
I
II7 V I
d
(1 - 17) (18) (19)
(21) (22) (24) (26) (27)
I II V I
I
II6 phr.
IV V I
e
(26) (27)
3
f
I
II6/5 V I

410 HINDEMITH Piano Sonata No. 2.

a

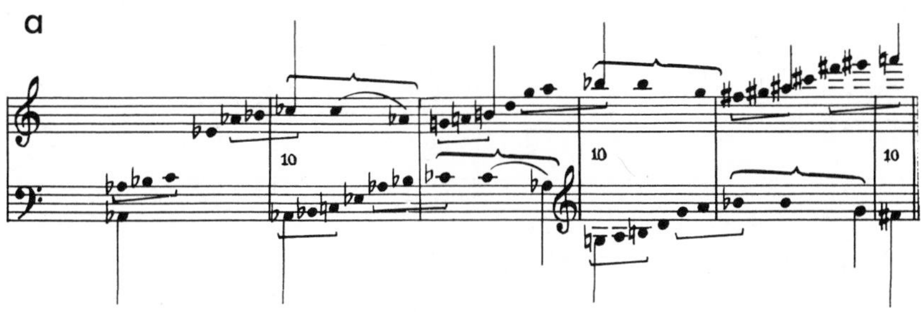

b

c

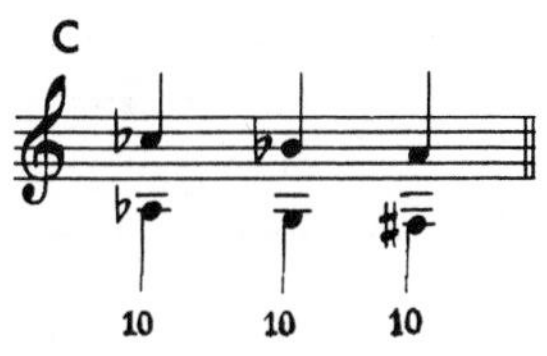

411 MARTINŮ Sonata for Cello and Piano No. 2.

412 COPLAND 3 Excerpts from "Our Town," No. 1

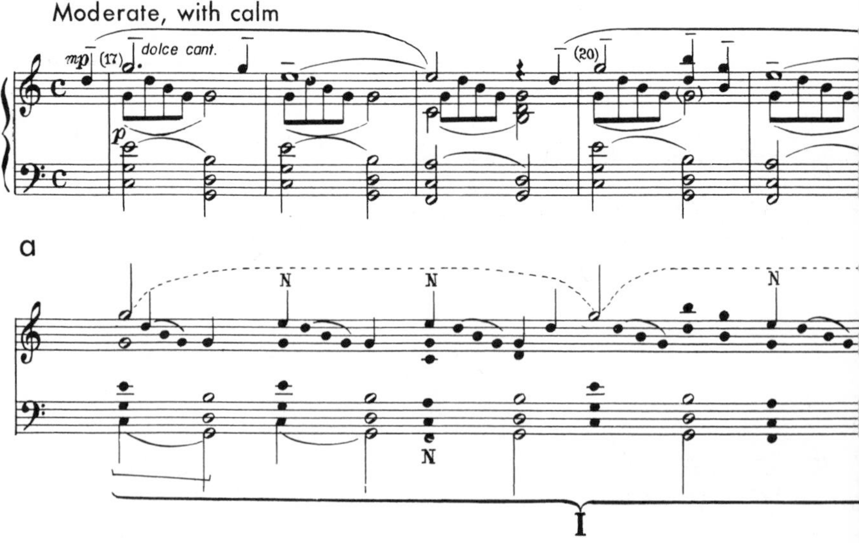

411 cont'd

412 cont'd

413 WAGENAAR Ciacona

414 MARTINŮ Sonata for Violin and Piano No. 2

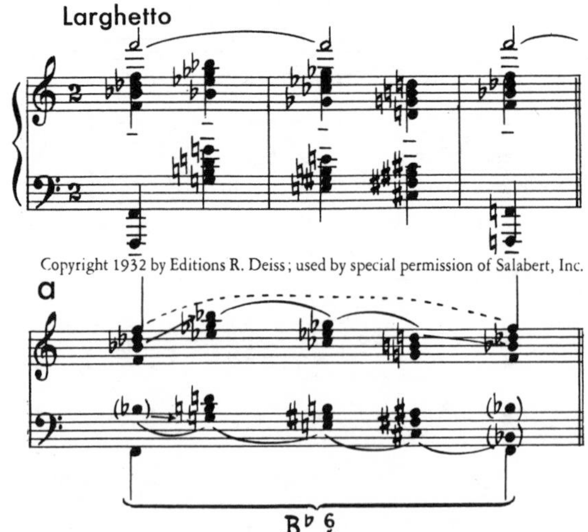

415 RAVEL Jeux d'eau

415 cont'd

a

416 COPLAND Piano Sonata

415 cont'd

cont'd

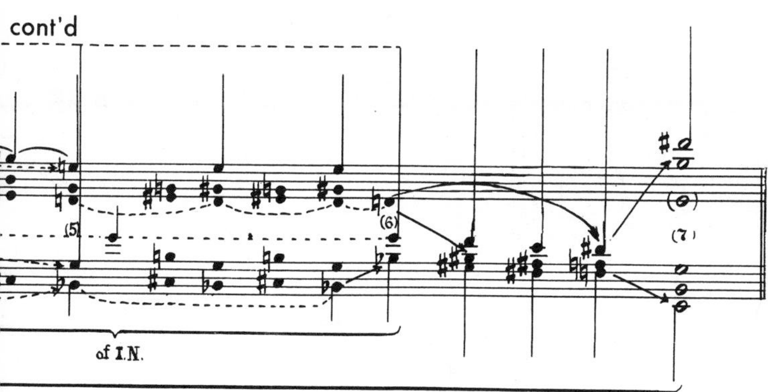

c

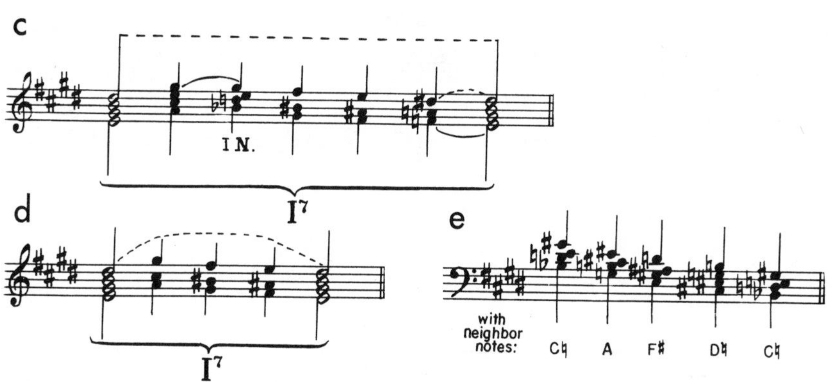

416 cont'd

(205)
eloquently
meno f
p

(210)
mp
pp
p

(215)
mp
p

(220)
espr
mp
pp
p

(225)

(230)
(235)
cresc.
f
dim.

8
(240)
r.h.
l.h.
mf
più f
mp
f
ff
mf

416 cont'd

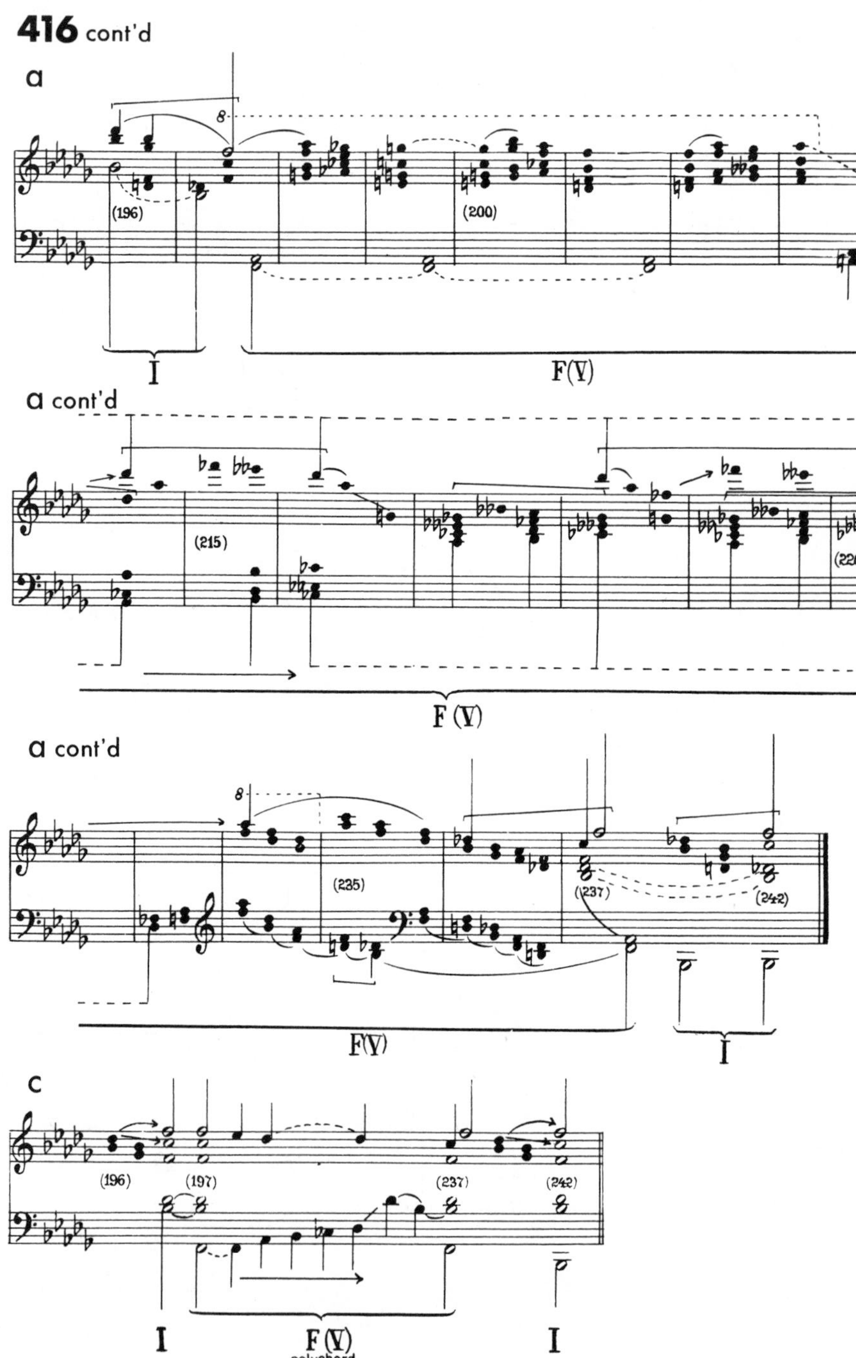
a
8
(196)
(200)
I
F(V)
a cont'd
(215)
(220)
F (V)
a cont'd
8
(235)
(237)
(242)
F(V)
I
c
(196)
(197)
(237)
(242)
I
F(V)
polychord
I

416 cont'd

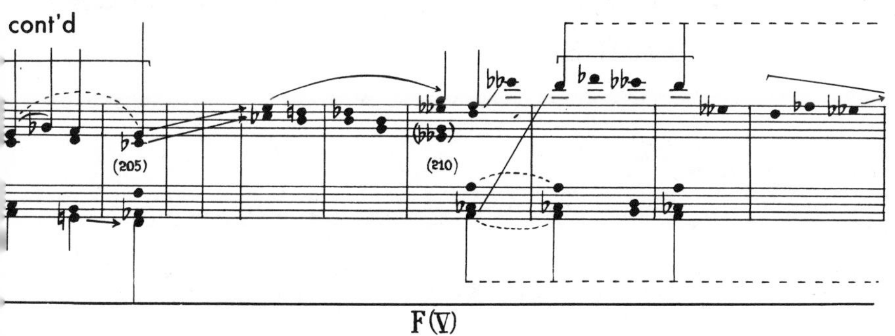
cont'd
(205)
(210)
F(V)

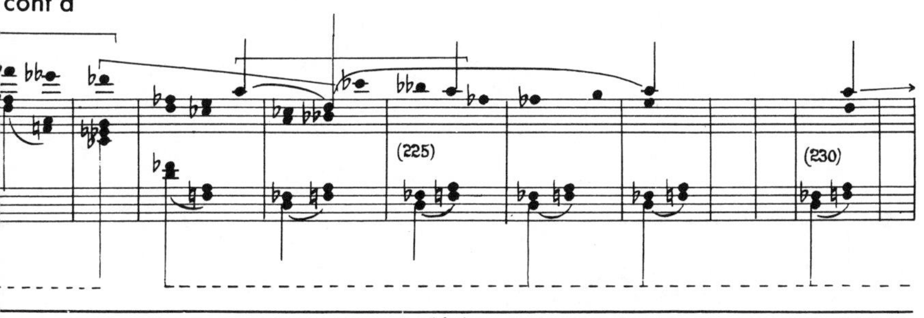
cont'd
(225)
(230)
F(V)

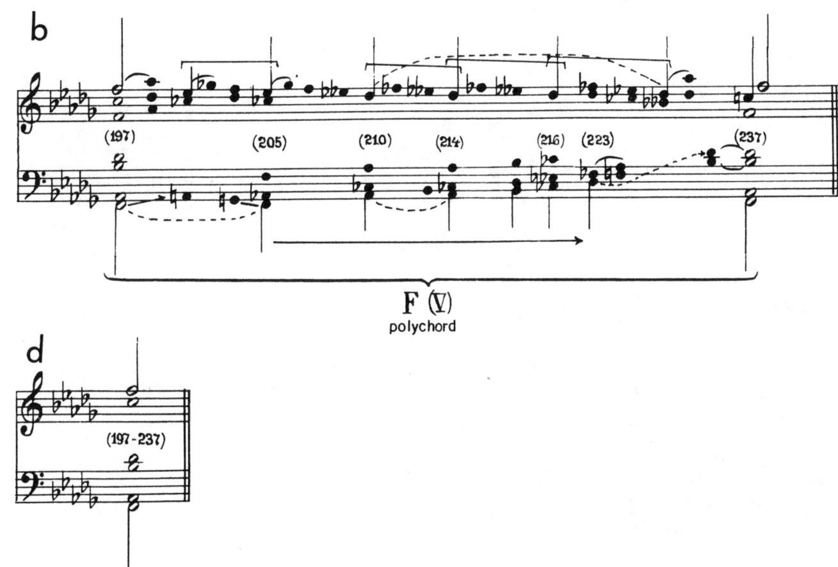
b
(197)
(205)
(210)
(214)
(216)
(223)
(237)
F (V)
polychord
d
(197-237)

417 STRAVINSKY Symphony in Three Movements

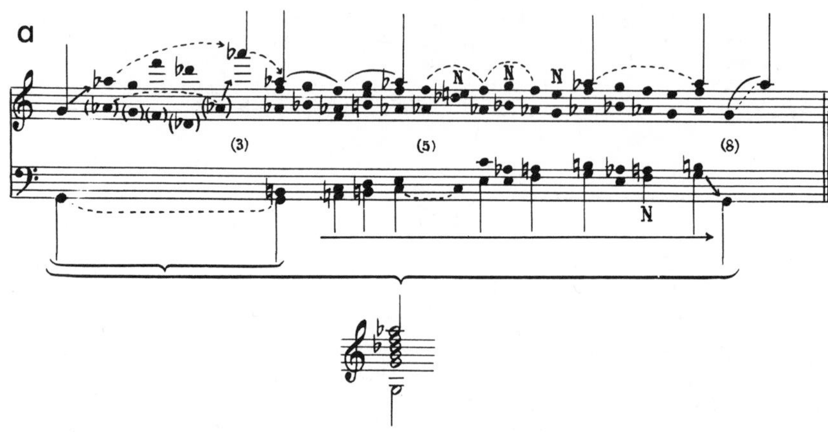

418 BARTOK Bagatelle Op 6, No. 4

419 R. STRAUSS "Elektra"

420 BEETHOVEN Piano Concerto No. 4, G Major

a

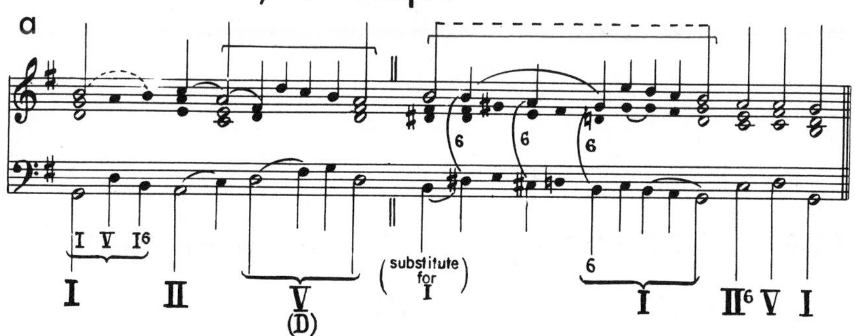

421

a

b

422

a

b

423

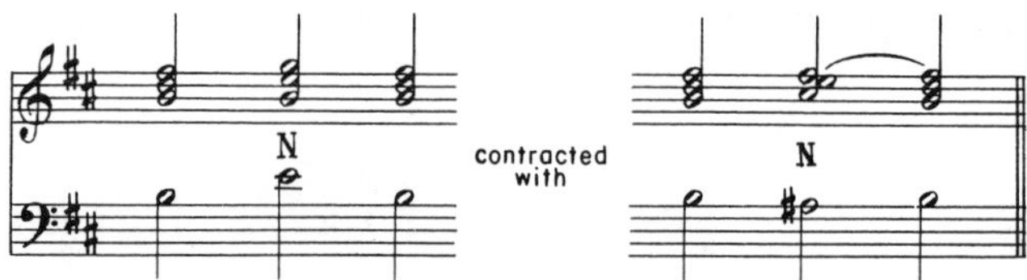

424 BACH Cantata: Du wahrer Gott und Davids Sohn

425 SCHUMANN Romance, Op 28, No. 1

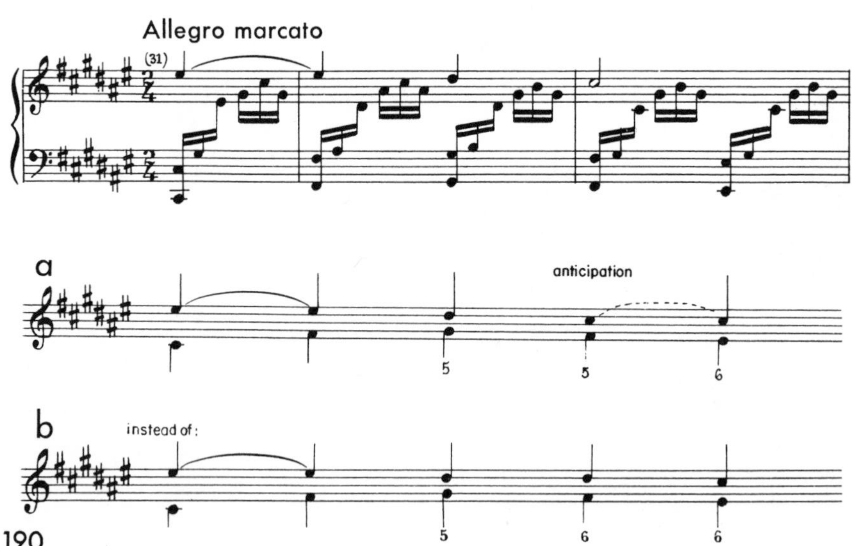

426 COUPERIN La Favorite

427 BYRD Sacerdotes Domini

428 MOUSSORGSKY Ballet of the Unhatched Chickens (Pictures from an Exhibition)

429 VERDI Oro supplex (Requiem)

430 BEETHOVEN Piano Sonata, C Major, Op 53. Introduzione

431 CHOPIN Polonaise, Op 26

431 cont'd

b

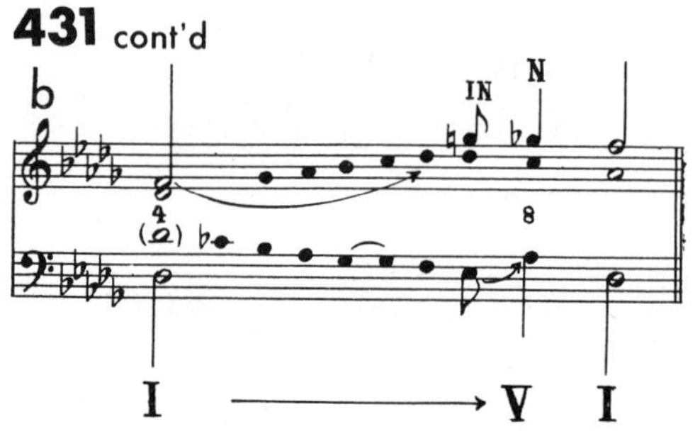

432 CHOPIN Mazurka, Op 59, No. 2

a

b

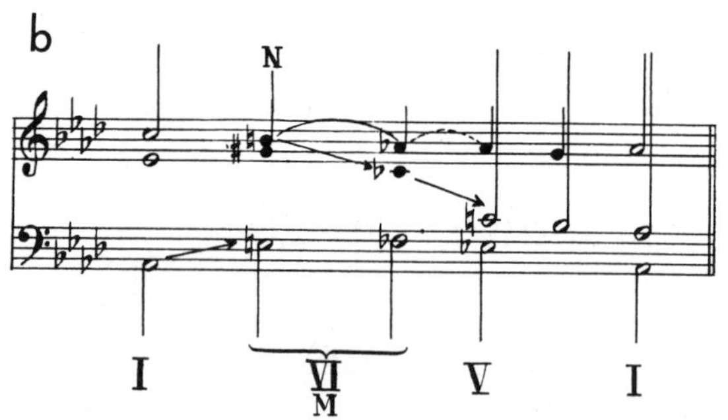

431 cont'd

432 cont'd

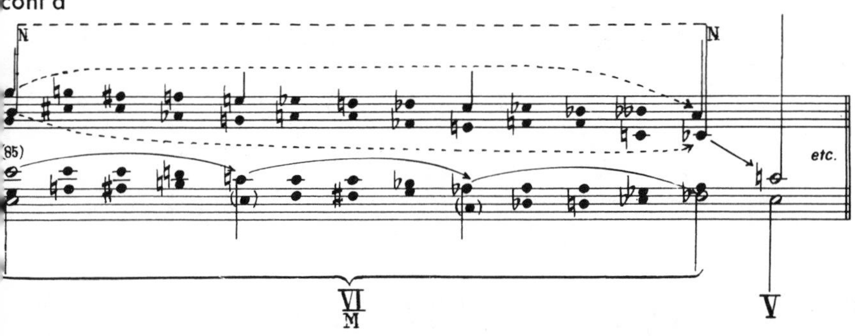

433 CHOPIN Polonaise, Op 40

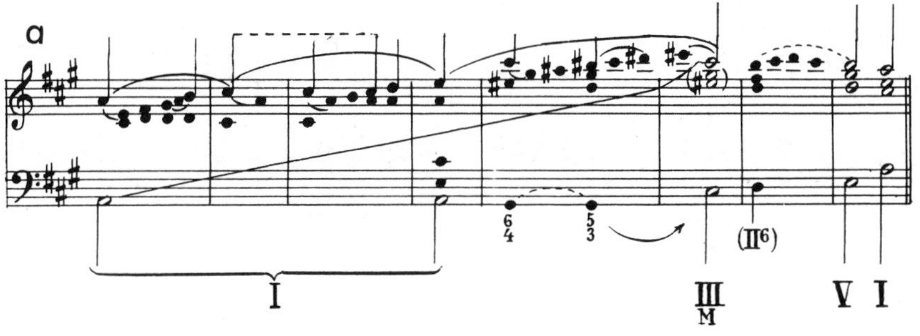

434

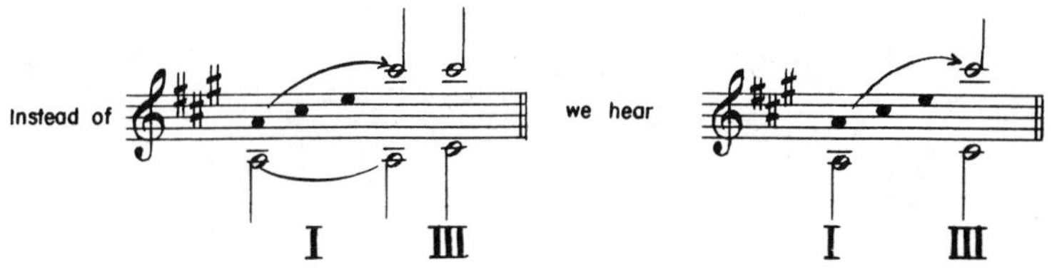

435 FARNABY A Toye

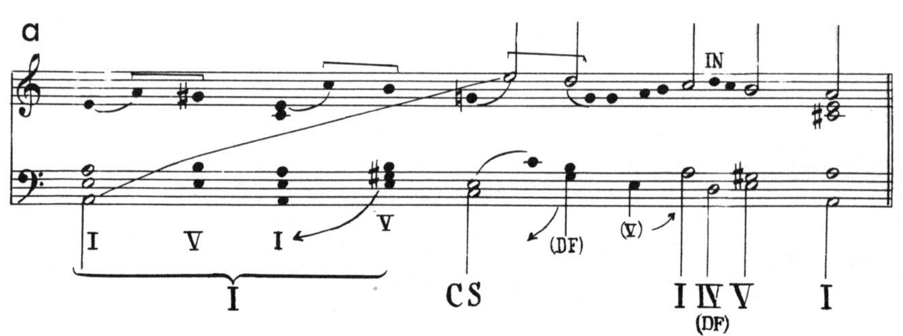

436 MENDELSSOHN Overture, "A Midsummer Night's Dream"

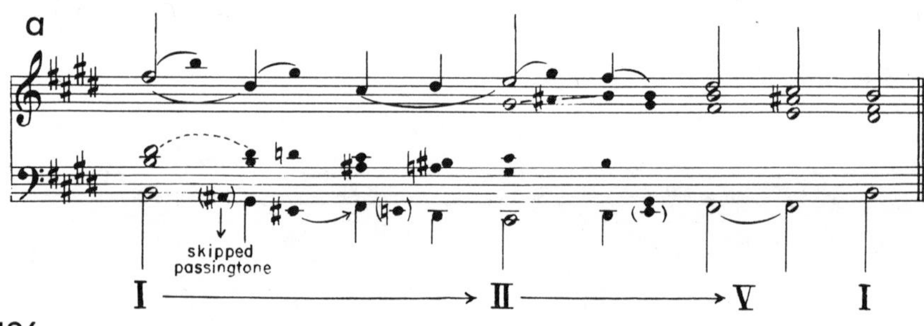

437 SCHUBERT Piano Sonata, C minor

a

b

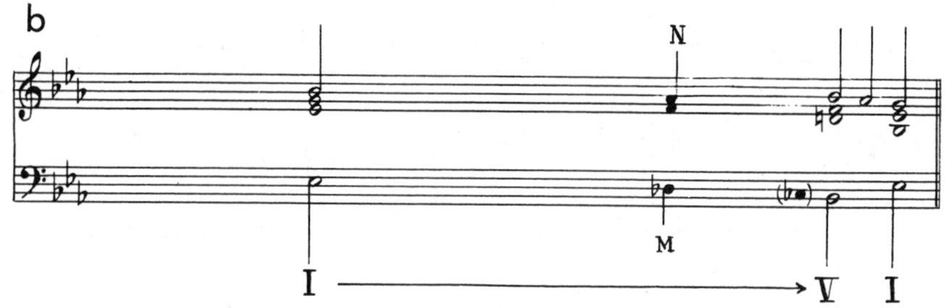

438 SCHUBERT Fantasia-Sonata

a

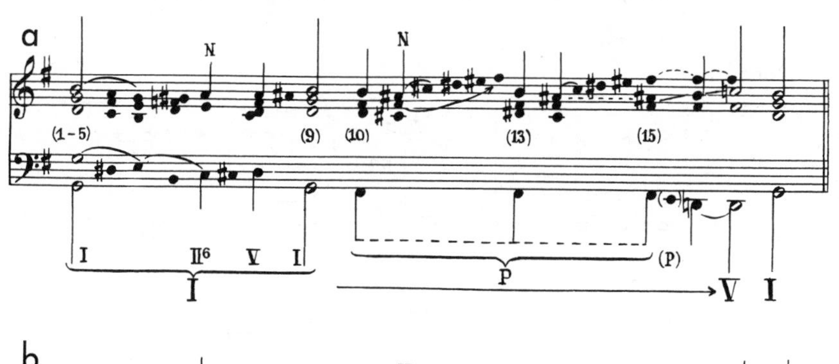

b

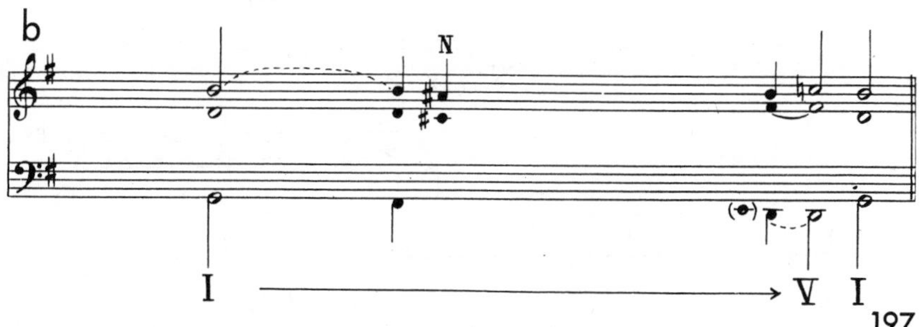

439 SCHUMANN Piano Quintet

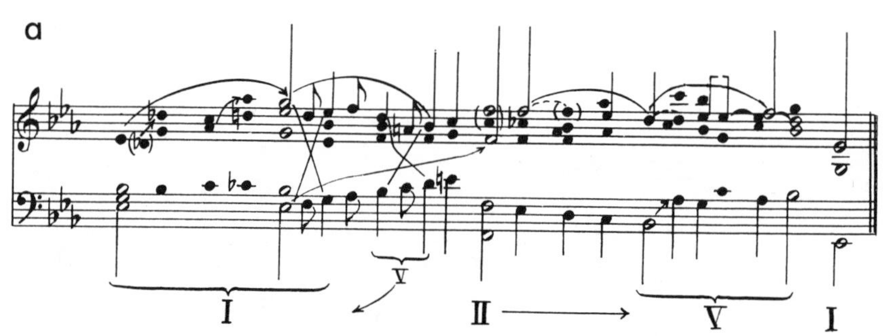

441 BARTÓK From 10 Easy Pieces for Piano

439 cont'd

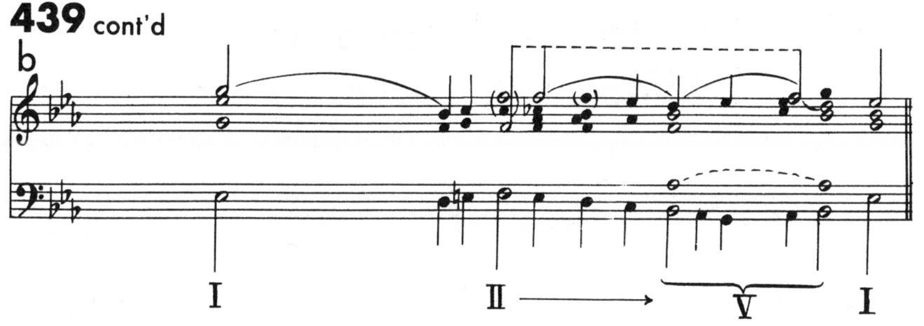

440 BEETHOVEN Piano Sonata, G Major, Op 31, No. 1

441 cont'd

442 BEETHOVEN Piano Sonata, F minor, Op 2, No. 1

a

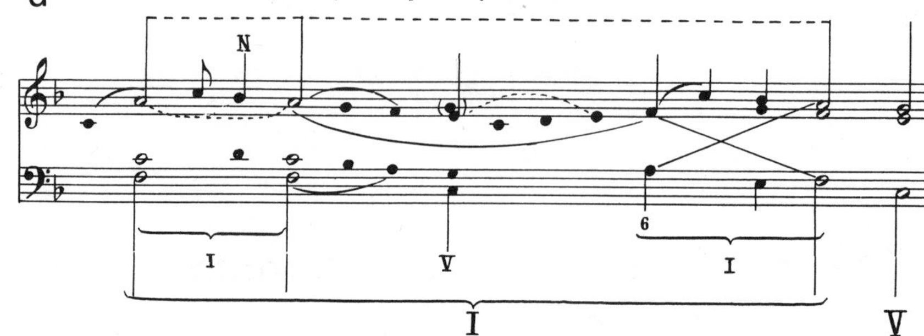

443 BEETHOVEN Piano Sonata, C minor, Op 10, No. 1.

a

444 MOZART Piano Sonata, C Major, K. 279

a

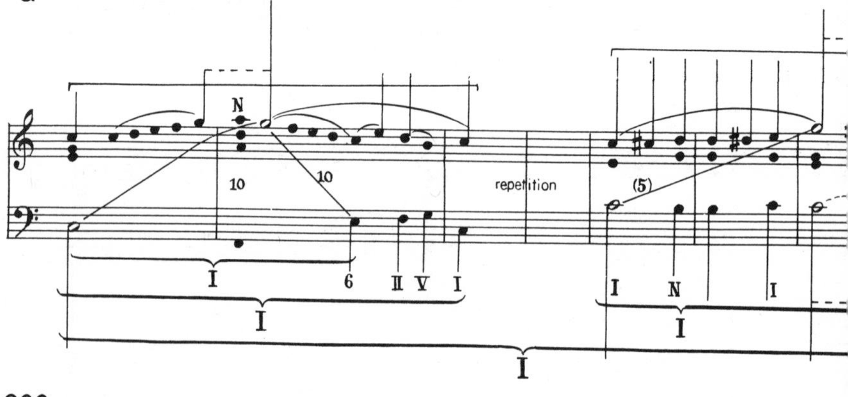

442 cont'd

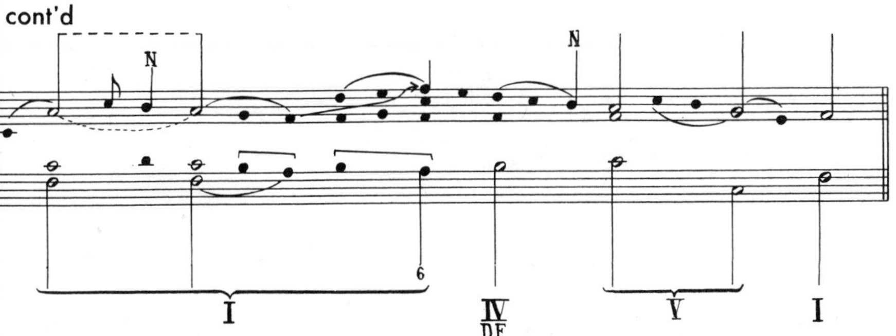

443 cont'd

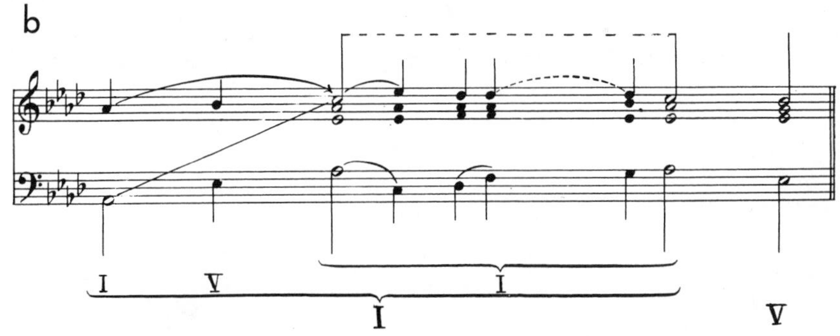

444 cont'd

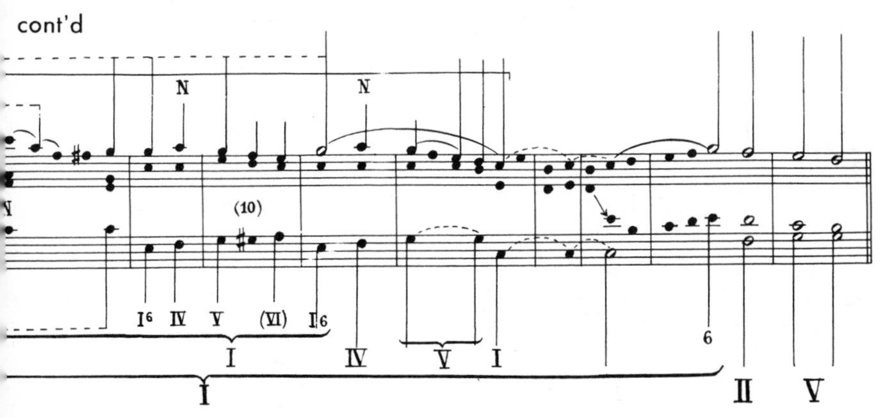

445 MAHLER Kindertotenlieder, No. 1

a

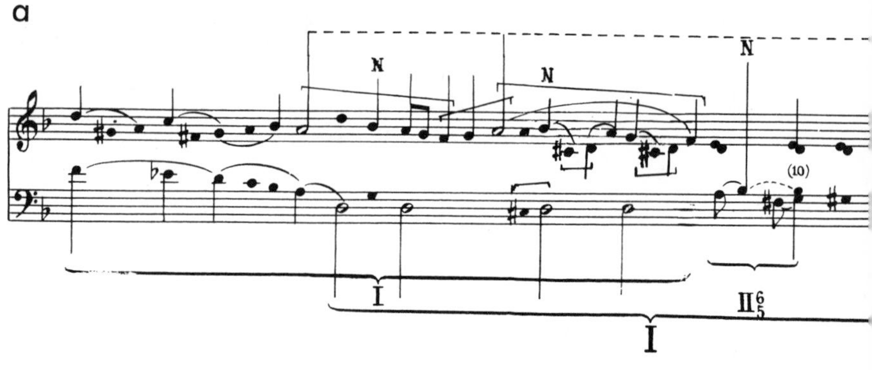

446

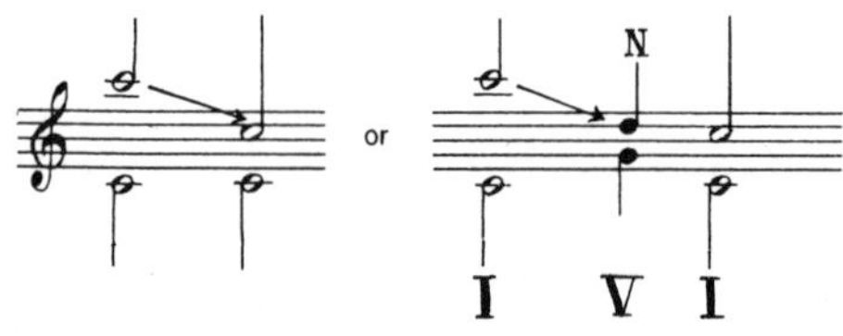

445 cont'd

cont'd

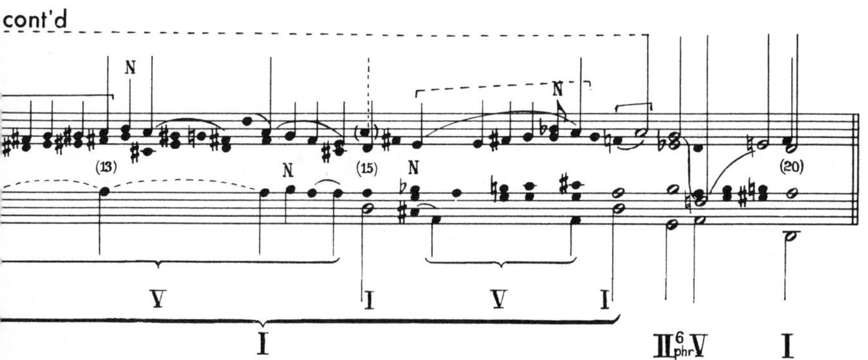

447 ALLEMANDE

447 cont'd

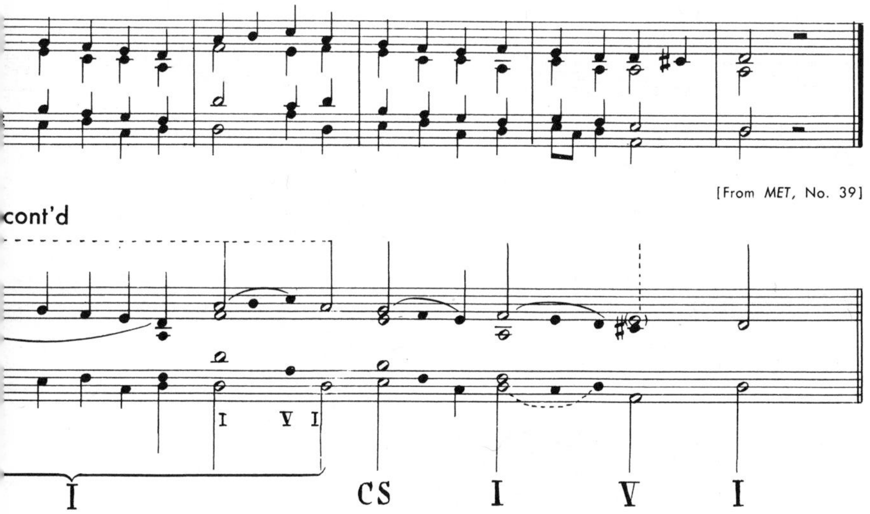

[From *MET*, No. 39]

448 SCHUBERT Die Krähe

449 RAMEAU Choeur des Spartiates ("Castor et Pollux," Act I)

450 BEETHOVEN Piano Sonata, E minor, Op 90

449 cont'd

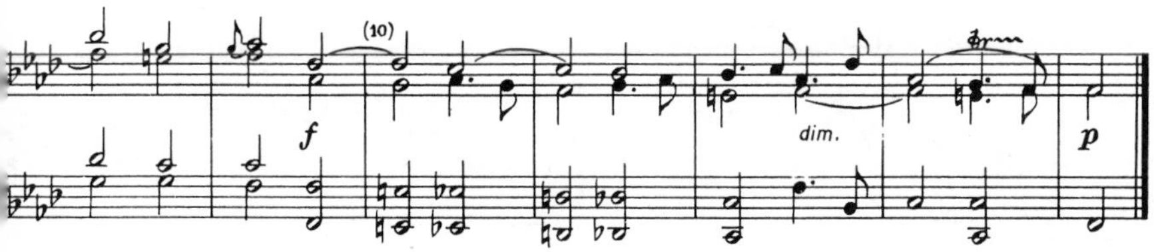

(10)
f
dim.
p

cont'd

I N
V
I
IV
DF
V
I

b

I N
I
V
I
IV
DF
V
I

450 cont'd

c

6
I
II6 5
V
I

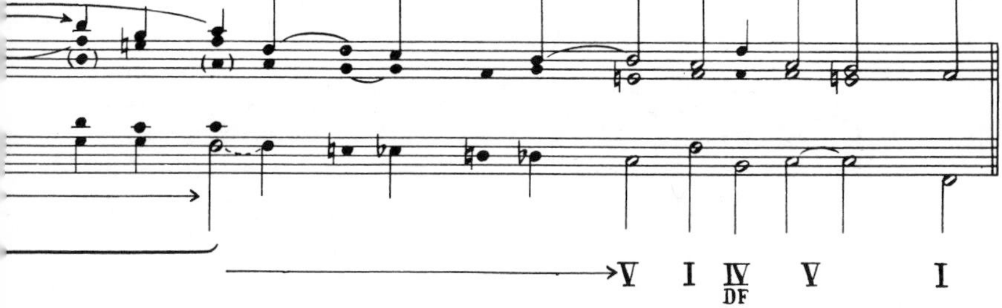

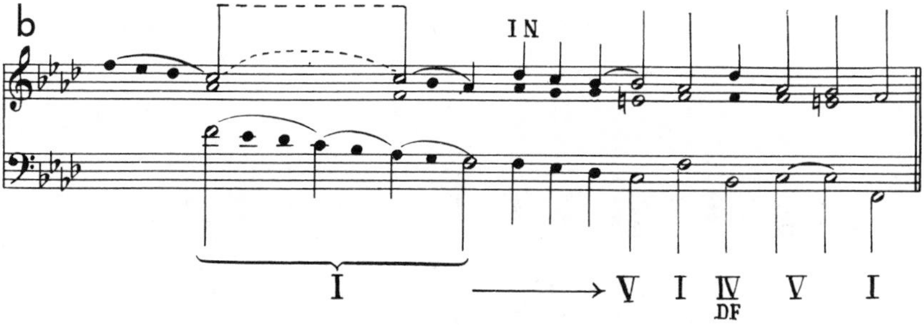

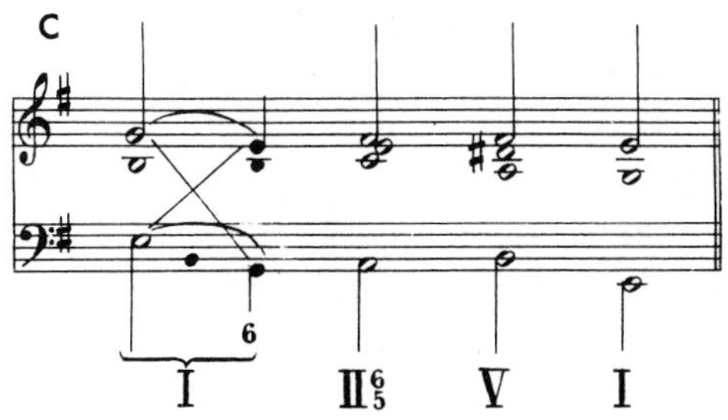

451 PROKOFIEFF Piano Sonata No. 8, Op 84

451 cont'd

452 BARTÓK String Quartet No. 5

Adagio molto

452 cont'd

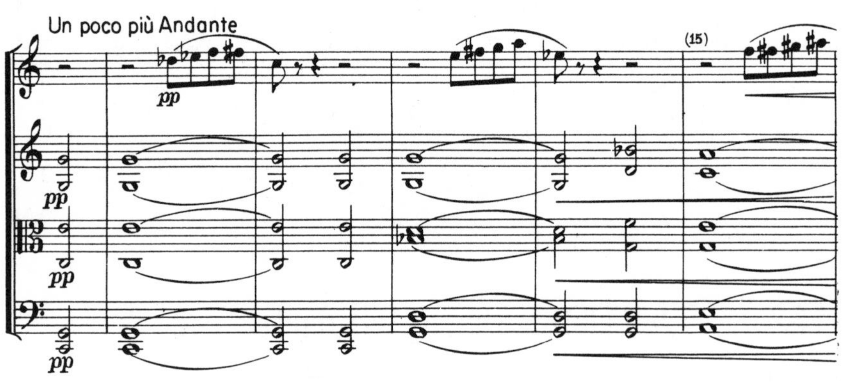

a

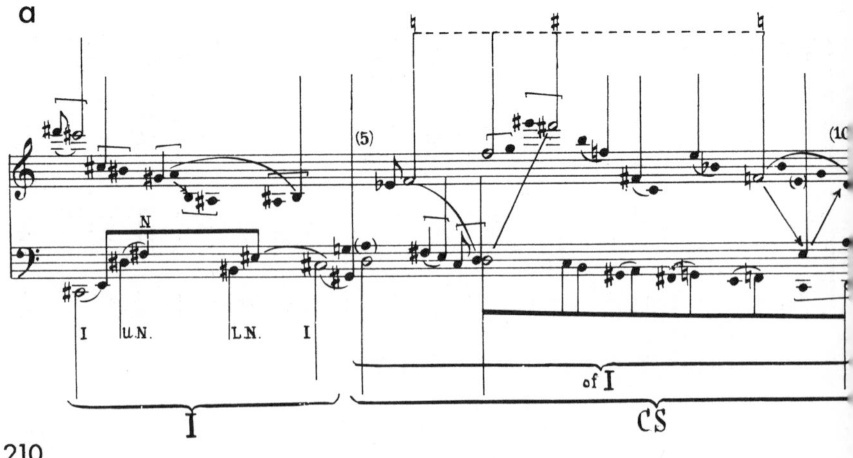

452 cont'd

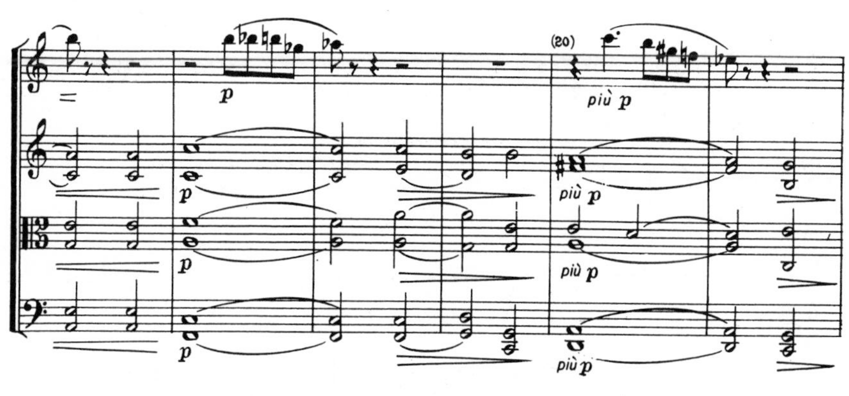

cont'd

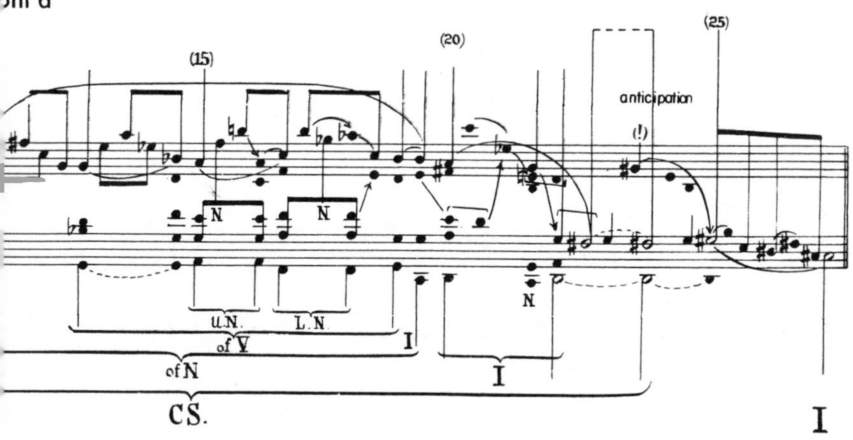

452 cont'd

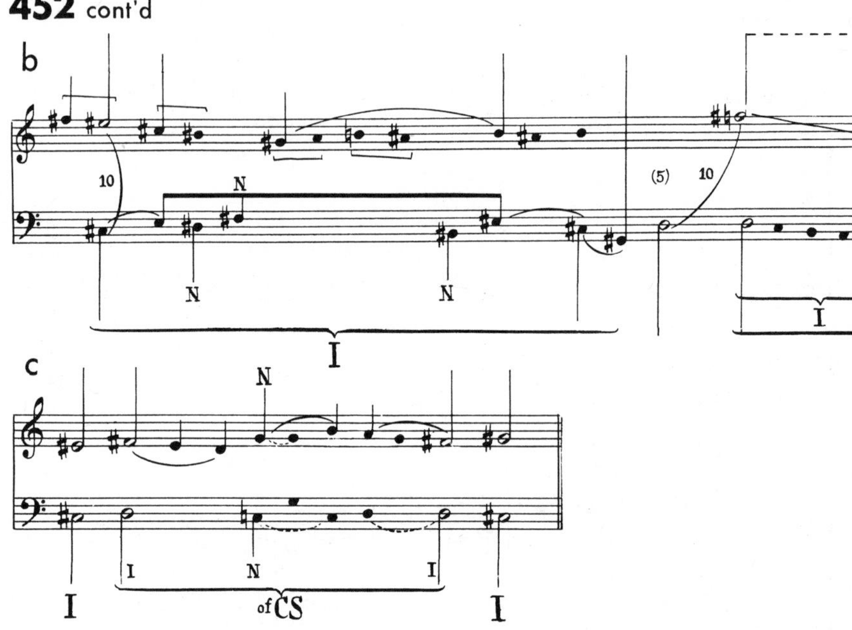

453 HINDEMITH Piano Sonata No. 1

With quiet motion, in quarters

452 cont'd

b cont'd

d

453 cont'd

453 cont'd

a

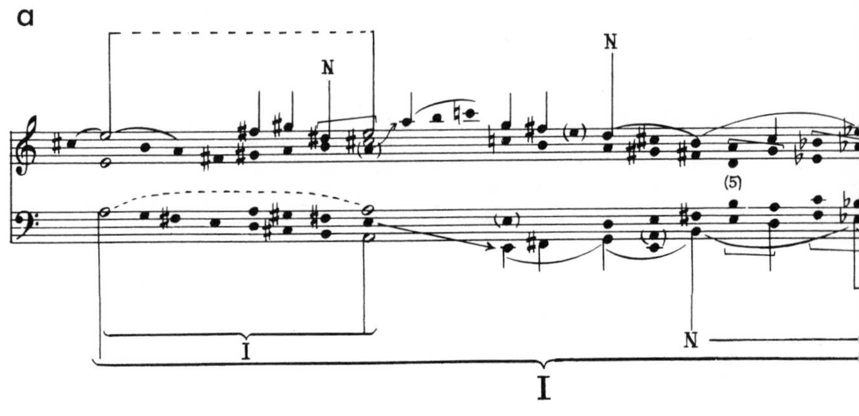

a cont'd

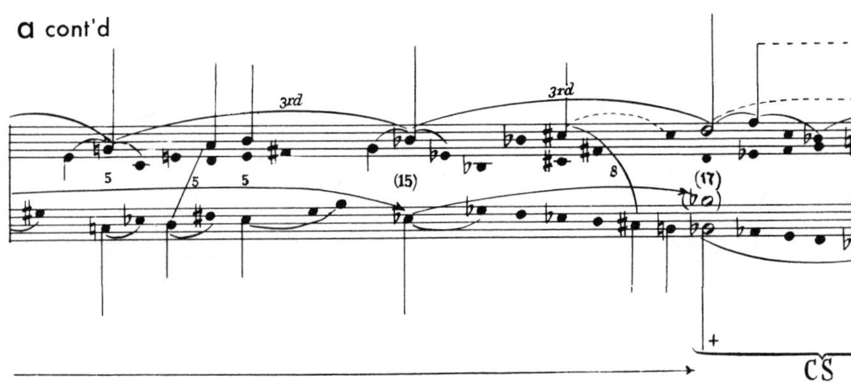

b

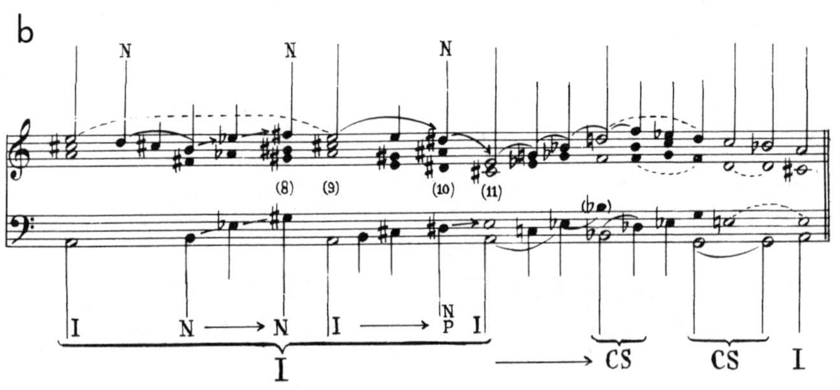

453 cont'd

cont'd

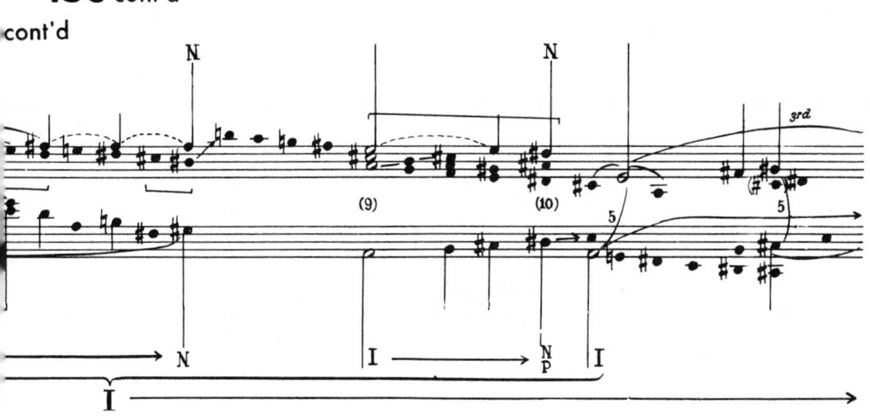

cont'd

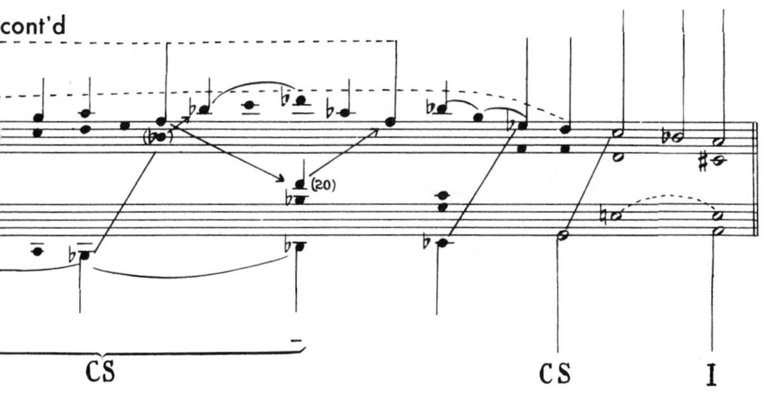

C

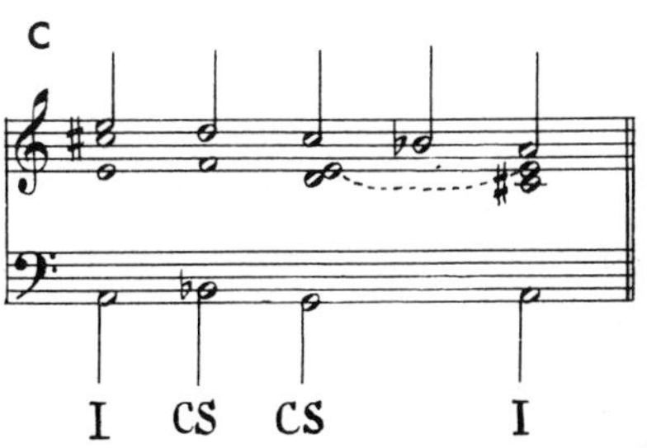

a

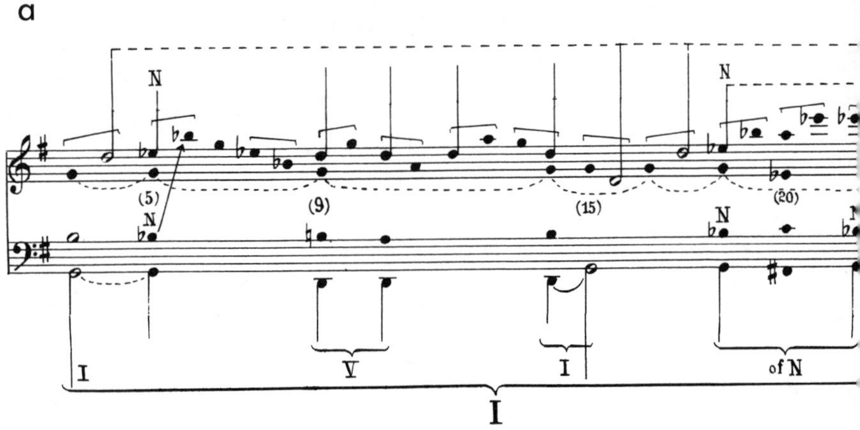
N
(5)
N
(9)
(15)
N
(20)
N
I
V
I
of N
I

a cont'd

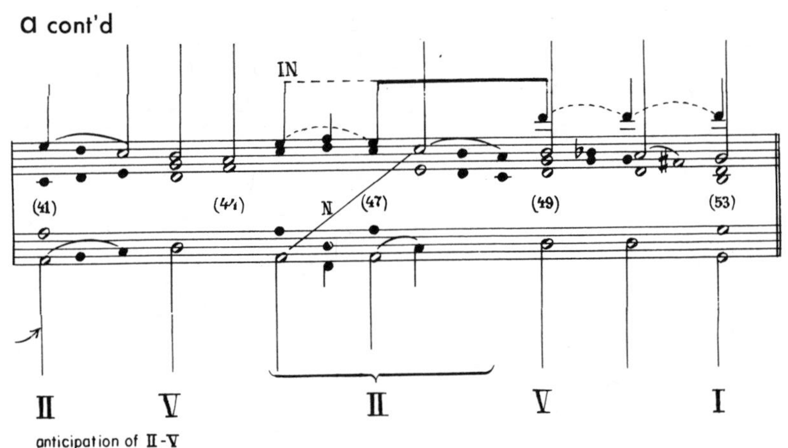
IN
(41)
(44)
N
(47)
(49)
(53)
II
V
II
V
I
anticipation of II - V

454 cont'd

cont'd

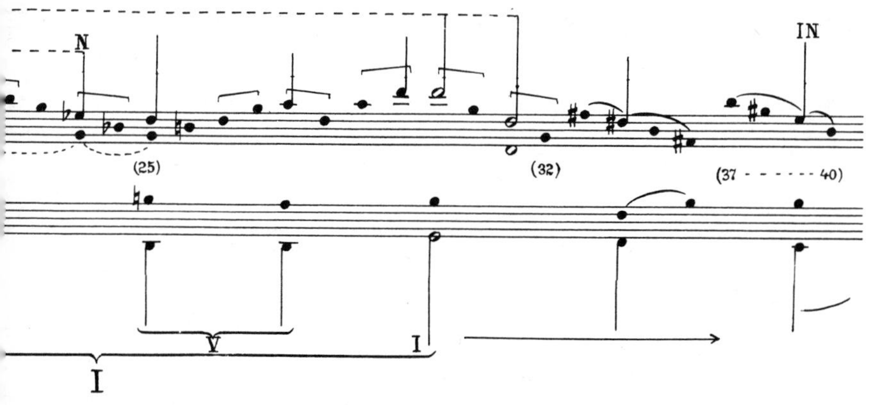

b

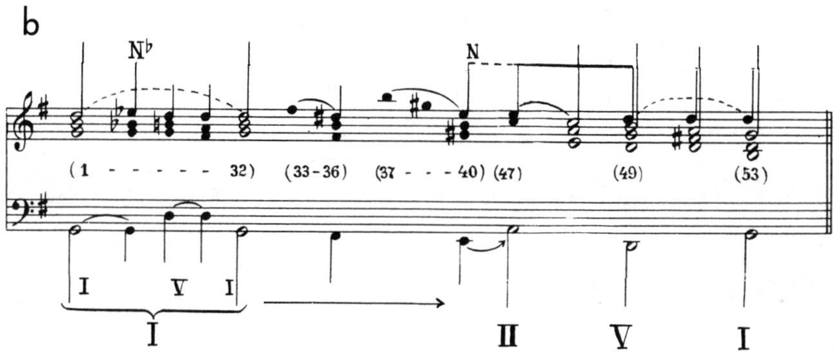

455 DEBUSSY Prélude à l'après-midi d'un faune

455 cont'd

cont'd
(13)
(14)
(19)
V
I
N
N
I
cont'd
N
N
N
(27)
(28)
(29)
N
(30)
I
I
V
cont'd
N
N
N
N
(13)
(19)
(21)
(23)
(25)
(26)
(27
(30)
I
N - - N
I
V
I
I
V

456 CHOPIN Nocturne, Op 48, No. 2

a

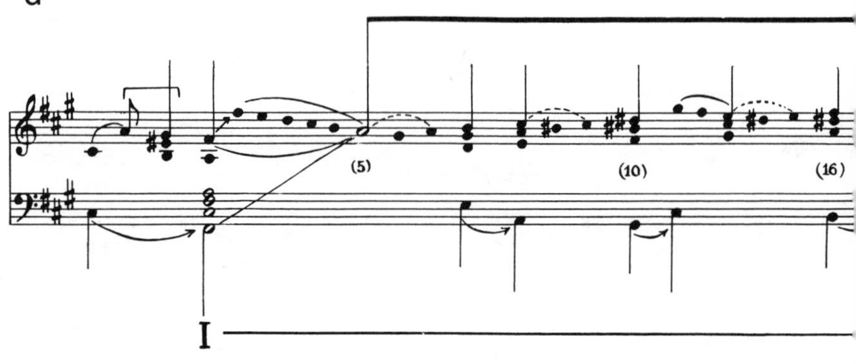

b

457 PROKOFIEFF Piano Sonata No. 3

a

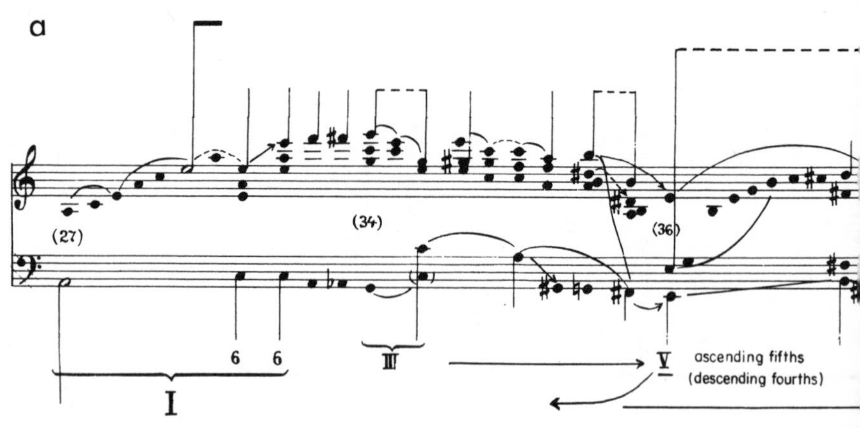

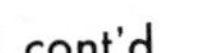

456 cont'd

a cont'd

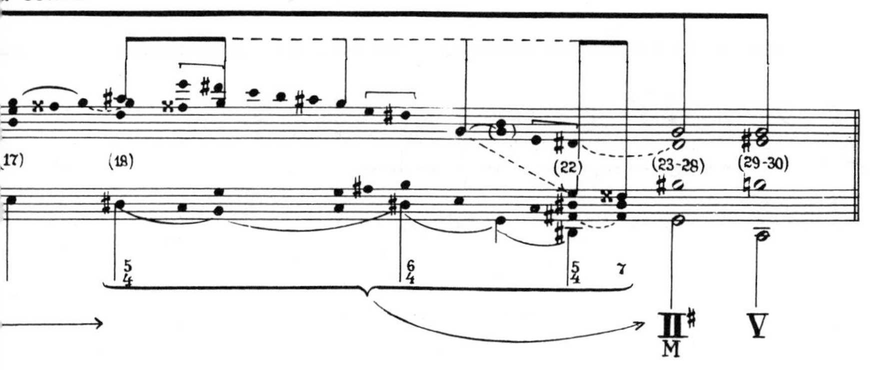

457 cont'd

cont'd

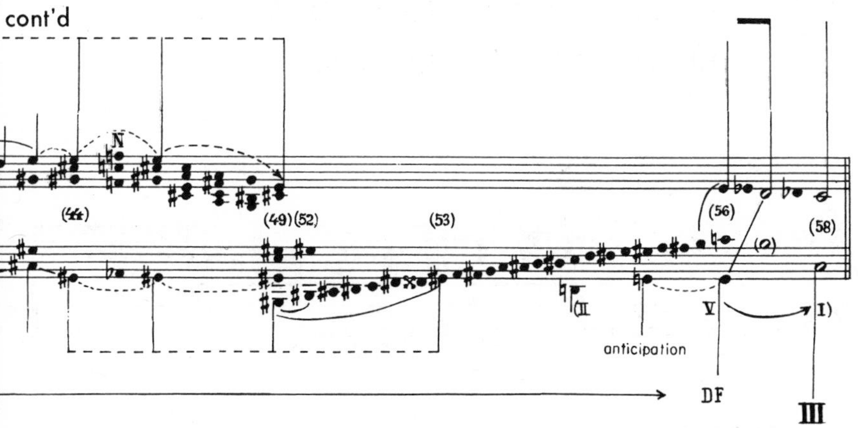

457 cont'd

b

d

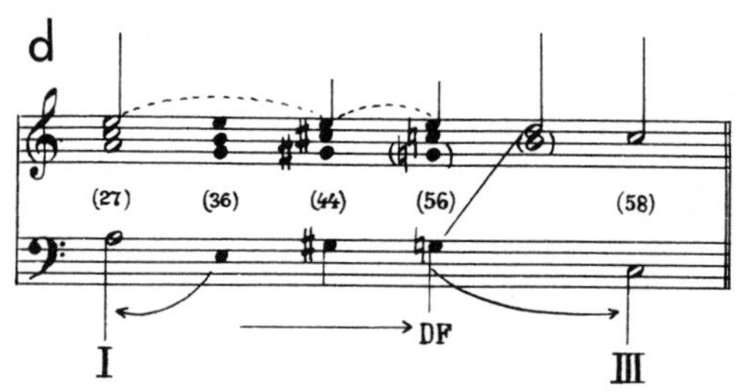

458 BEETHOVEN Piano Sonata, D Major, Op 10, No. 3

a

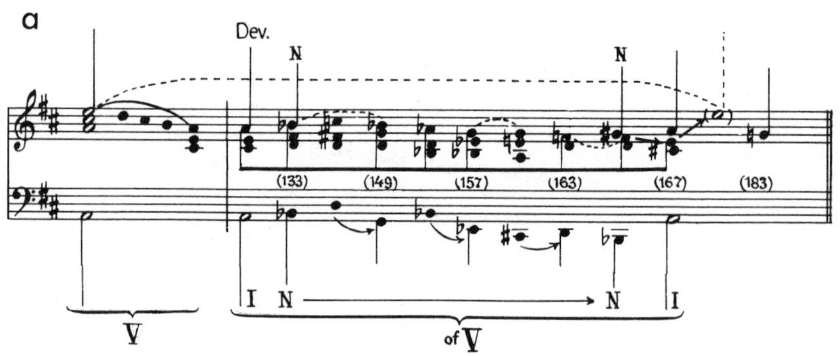

457 cont'd

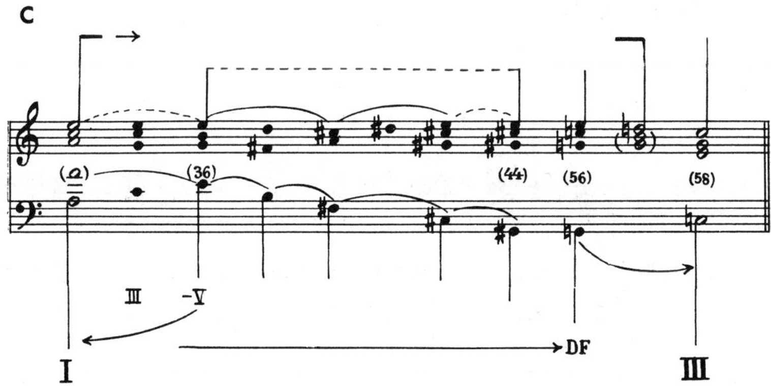

458 cont'd

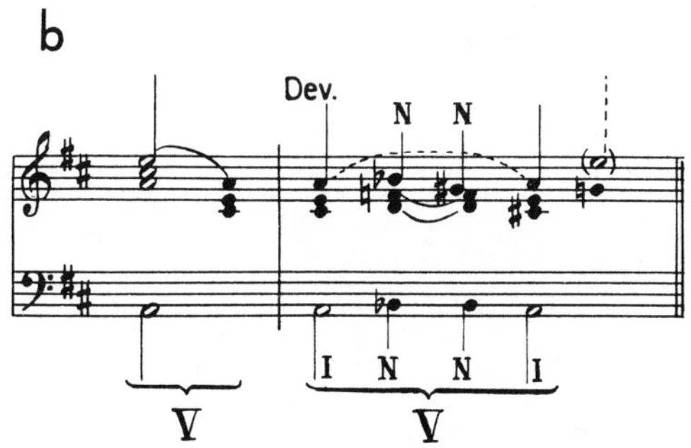

459 HAYDN Symphony D Major, No. 104

a

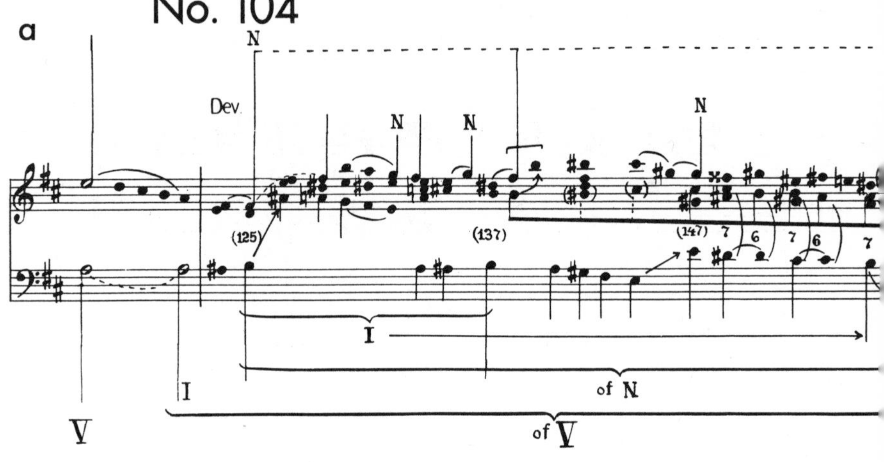

b

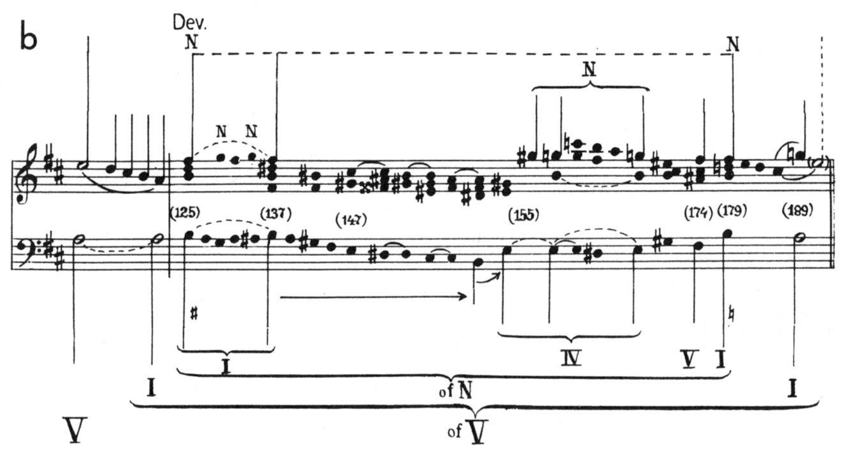

d

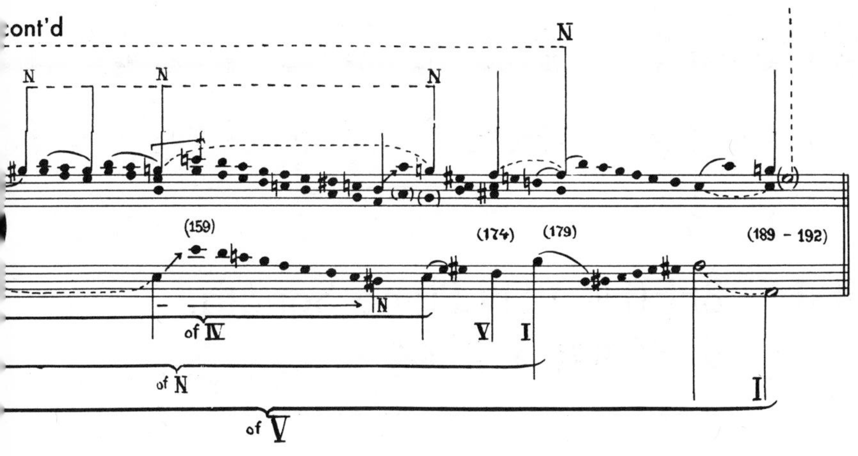
cont'd
N
N
N
N
(159)
(174)
(179)
(189 - 192)
N
of IV
V
I
of N
I
of V

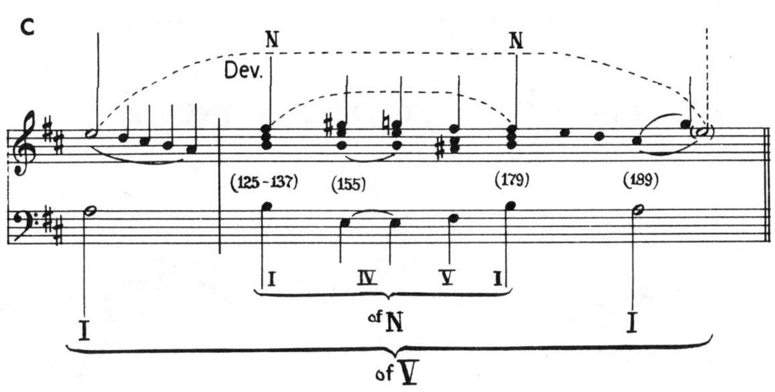
C
N
N
Dev.
(125-137)
(155)
(179)
(189)
I
IV
V
I
of N
I
I
of V

460

461 BEETHOVEN Piano Sonata, B♭ Major, Op 22

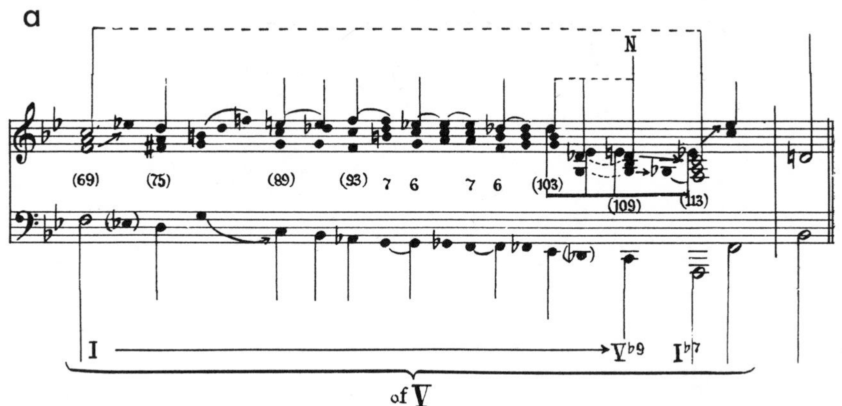

462 BEETHOVEN Symphony No. 7

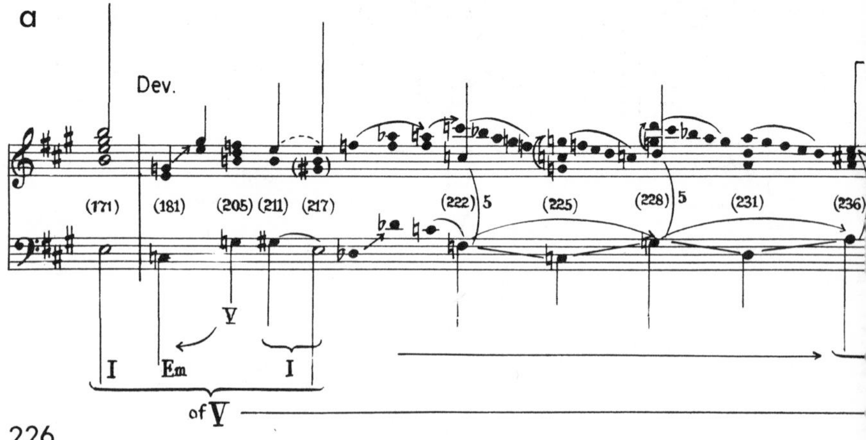

460 cont'd

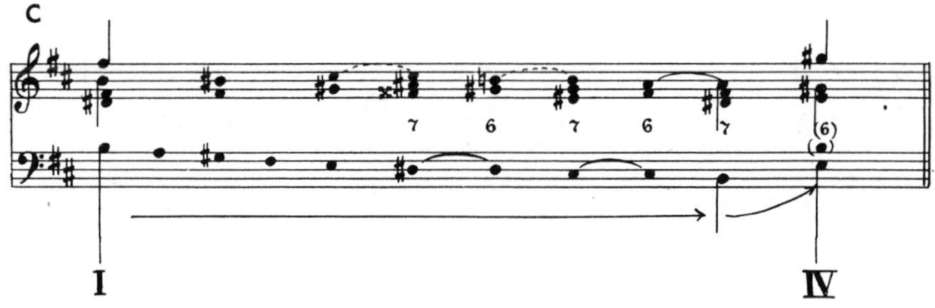

c

7 6 7 6 7 (6)
I
IV

461 cont'd

b

N
I
V♭9
I♭7
of V

c

N
I
V♭9
I♭7
of V

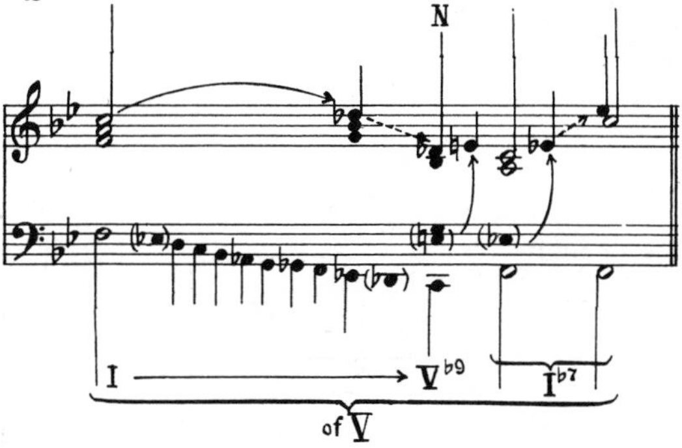

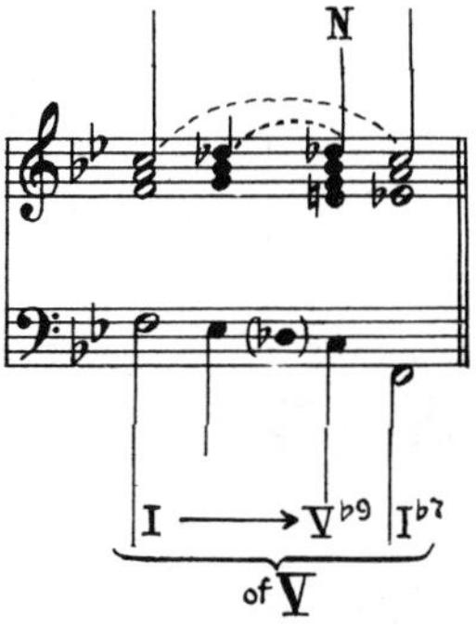

462 cont'd

cont'd

Rec.
N
N
(250)
(254)
(258)
(264)
(272)
(278)
I

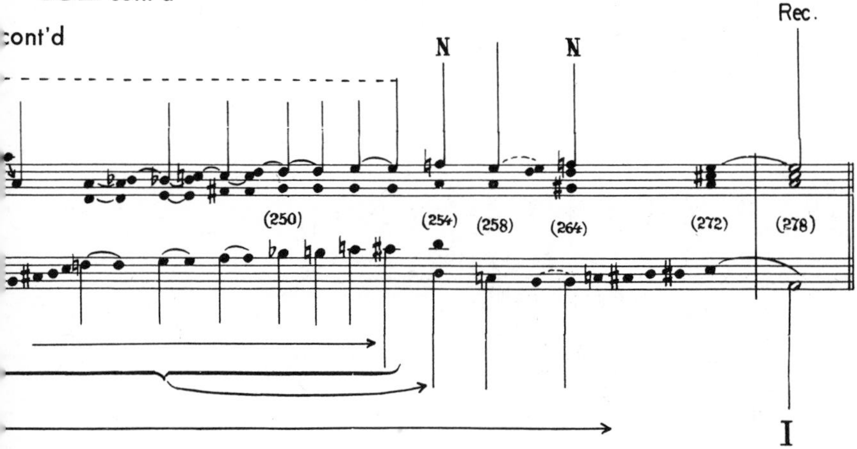

462 cont'd

b

N
N
(171)
(181)
(217)
5
5
5
(254)
(264)
I
Em
I
V
I

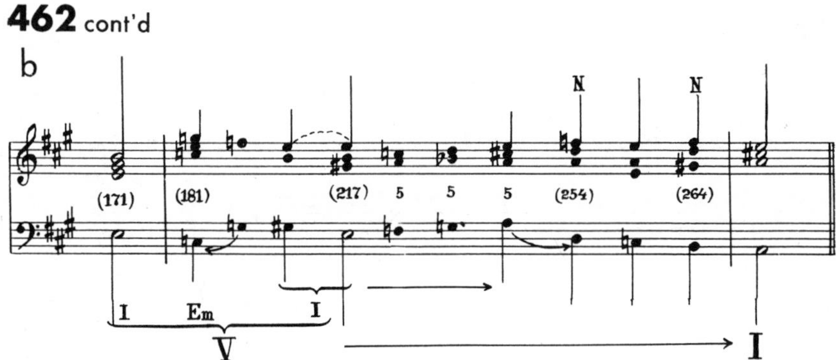

463 BEETHOVEN Piano Sonata, C minor, Op 10, No. 1

a

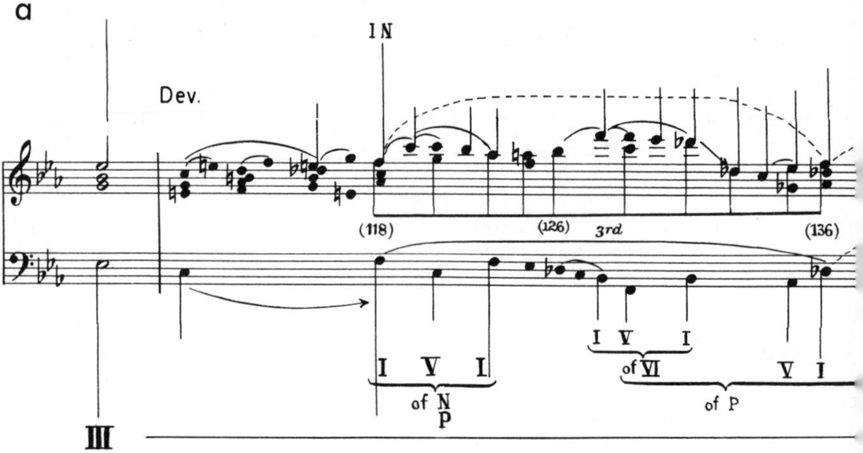

I N
Dev.
(118)
(126)
3rd
(136)
I V I
of VI
V I
I V I
of N P
of P
III

b

I N
3
3
4
4
4
VI V I
of P
N P
P
P
P
III
V

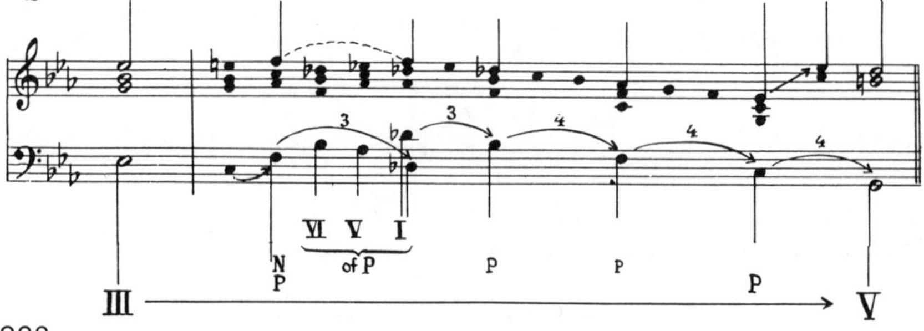

462 cont'd

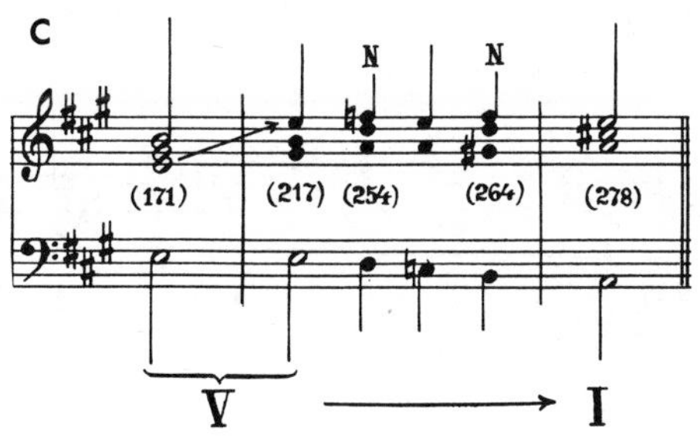

463 cont'd

cont'd

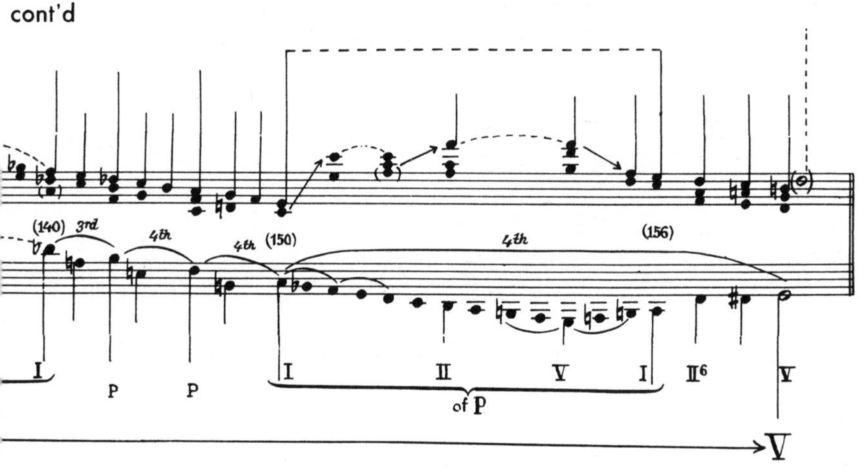

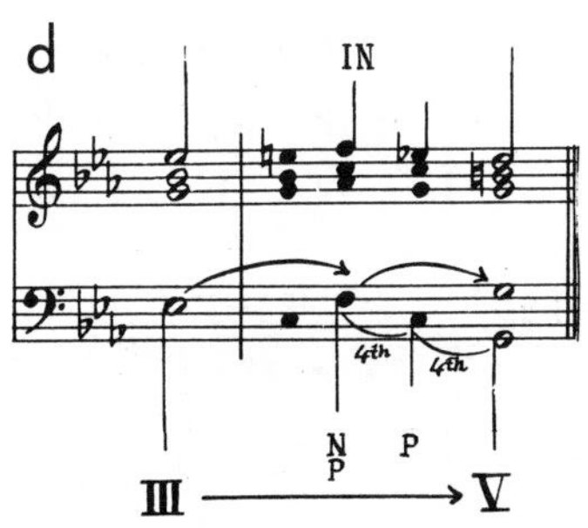

464 BEETHOVEN Piano Sonata, F minor, Op 57

a

b

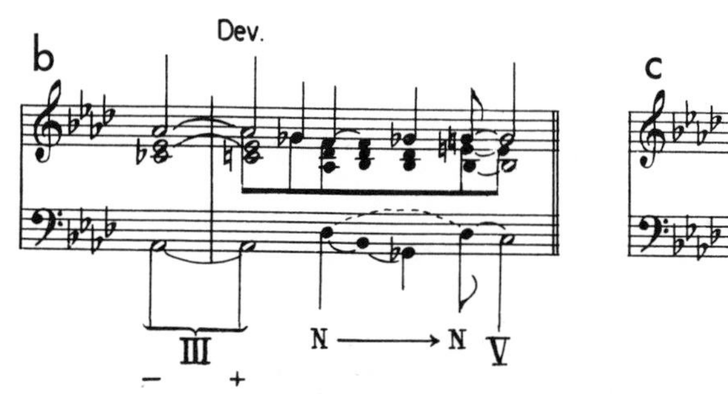

c

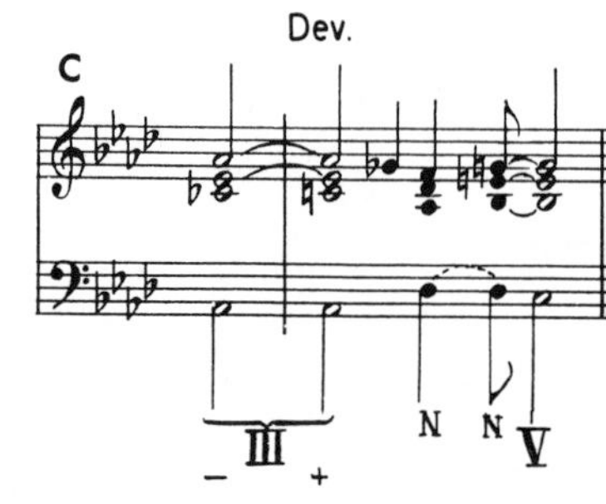

465

a

b

466

a

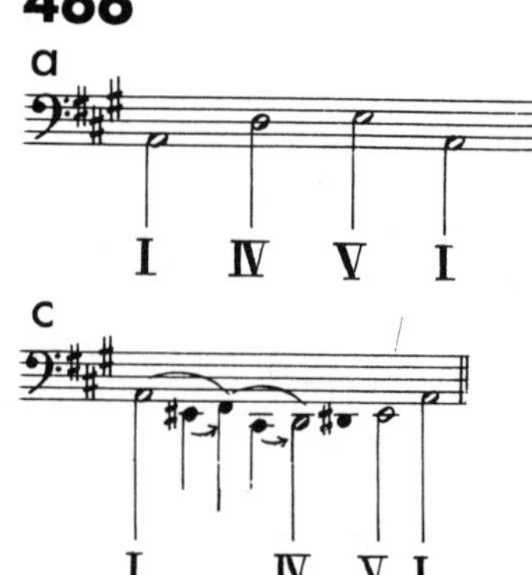

b

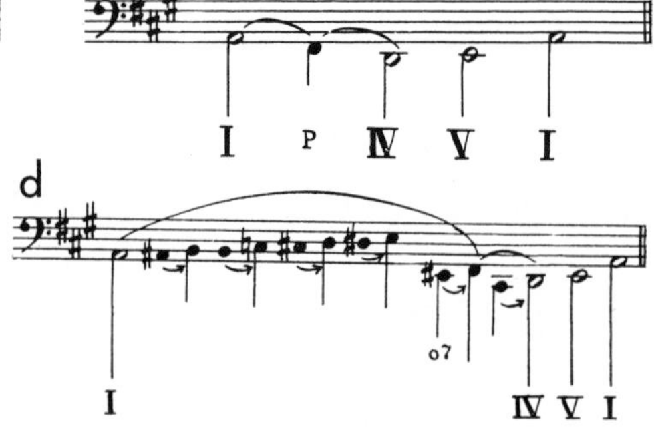

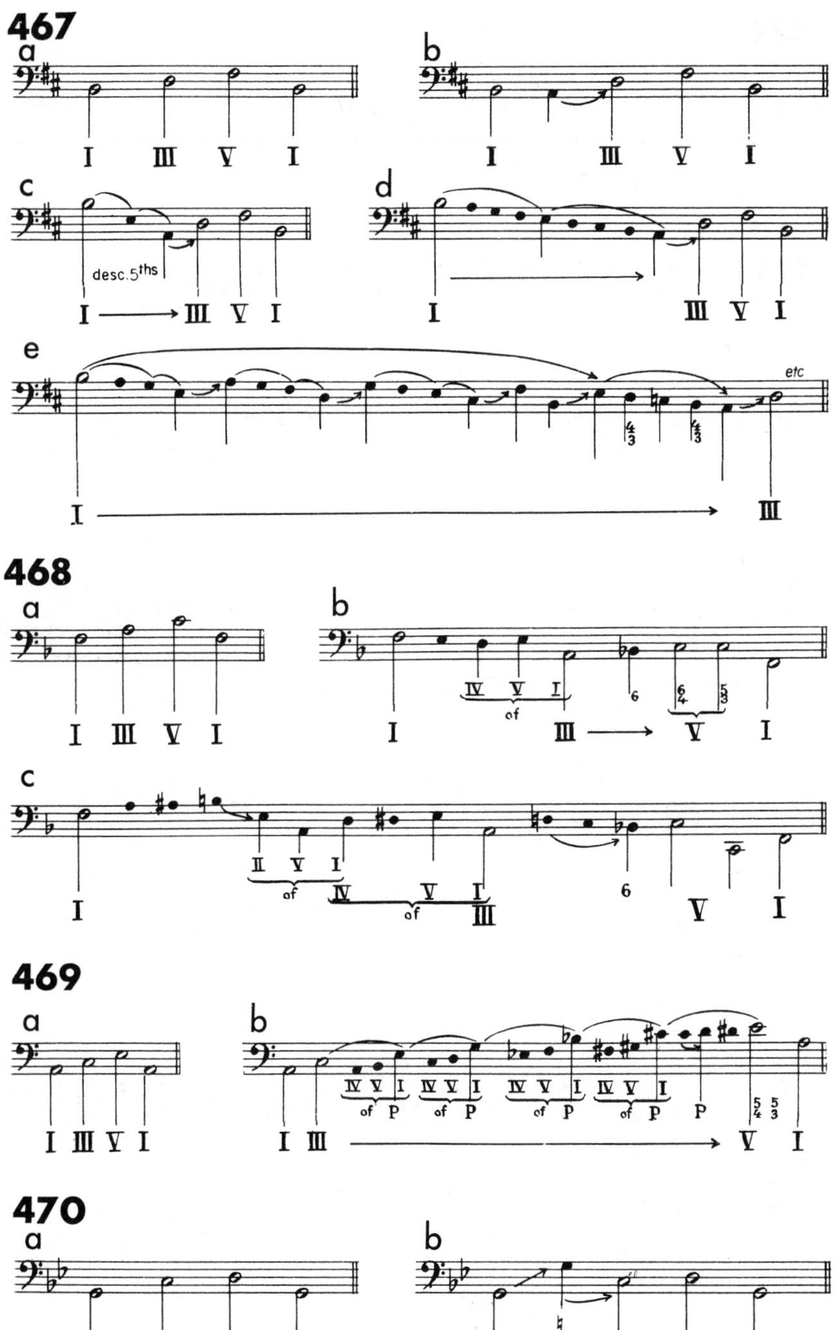
467
a
I III V I
b
I III V I
c
desc. 5ths
I → III V I
d
I → III V I
e
etc
4 3
4 3
I → III
468
a
I III V I
b
IV V I
of
6
6 4
5 3
I III → V I
c
II V I
of
IV V I
of
6
I III V I
469
a
I III V I
b
IV V I
of P
IV V I
of P
IV V I
of P
IV V I
of P
P
5 4
5 3
I III → V I
470
a
I IV V I
b
♮
I IV V I

470 cont'd

c

o7
I
IV
V
I

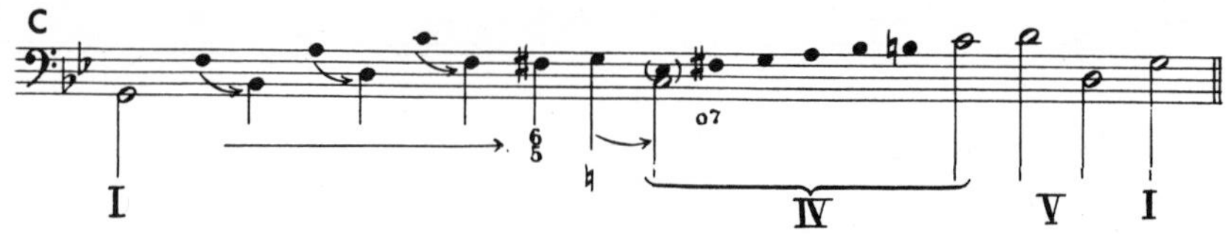

471 WAGNER "Parsifal," (Act I)

a

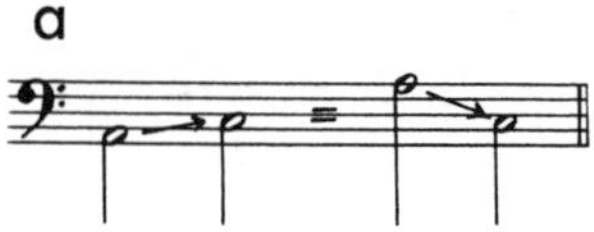

b

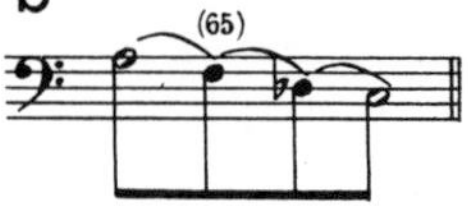

(65)

c

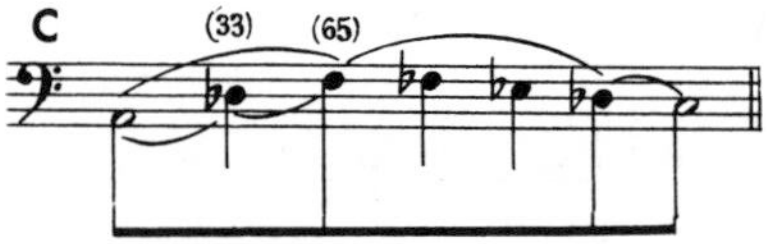

(33)
(65)

d

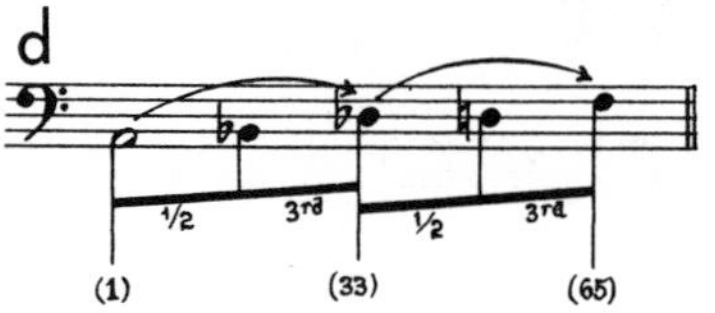

½
3rd
½
3rd
(1)
(33)
(65)

e

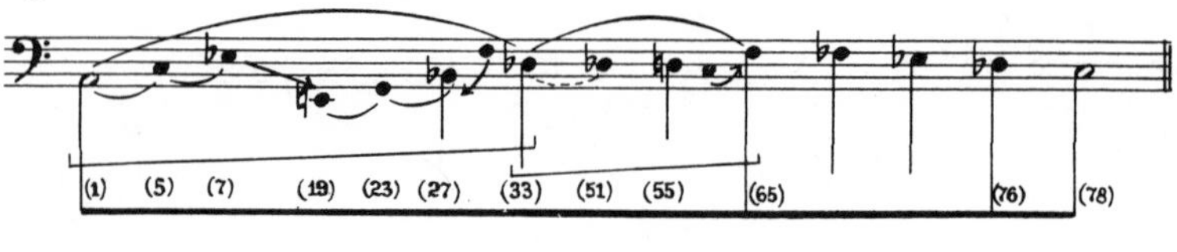

(1)
(5)
(7)
(19)
(23)
(27)
(33)
(51)
(55)
(65)
(76)
(78)

g cont'd

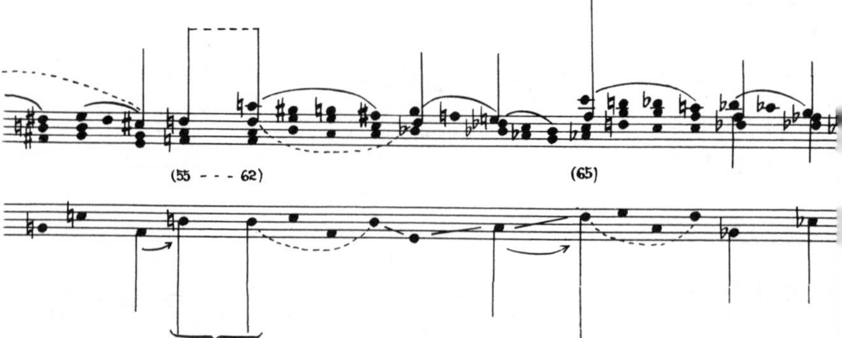

(55 - - - 62)
(65)

471 cont'd

f
(1) (5) (7) (19) (23) (27) (33 - - - 51) (55) (65) (68) (70) (76) (78)
D♭
F
D♭
A
C
g
(5) (7) (12) 4th 4th 4th (19) (23) (27) (33 - - - - 51)
+
−
g cont'd
(70) (76) (78)
+
−

472 STRAVINSKY Symphony in Three Movements

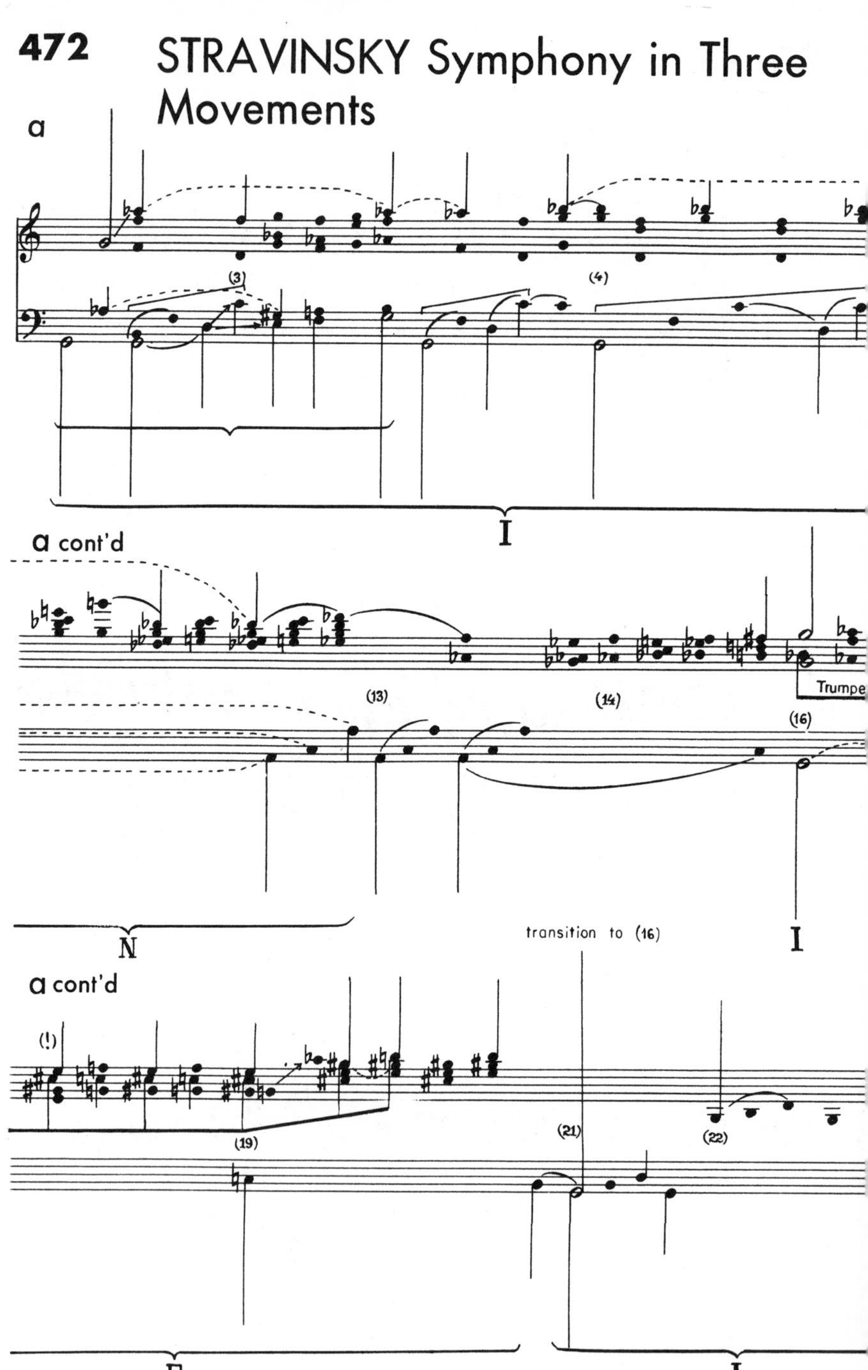

472 cont'd

472 cont'd

b

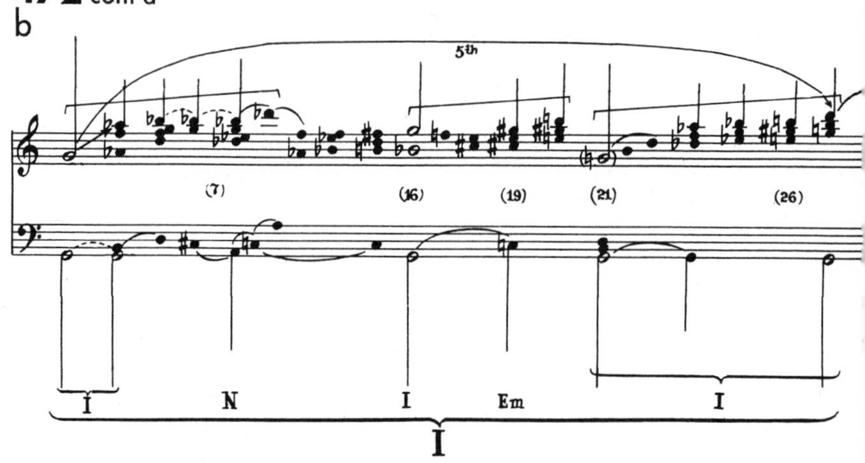
5th
(7)
(16)
(19)
(21)
(26)
I
N
I
Em
I
I

c

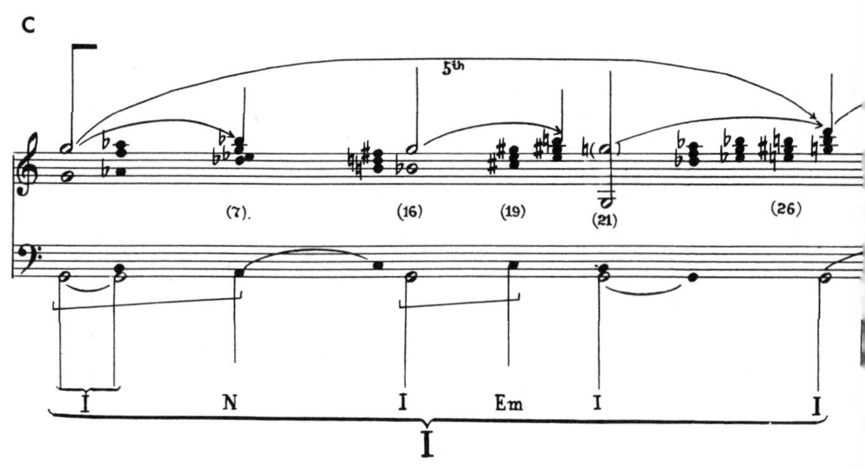
5th
(7).
(16)
(19)
(21)
(26)
I
N
I
Em
I
I
I

d

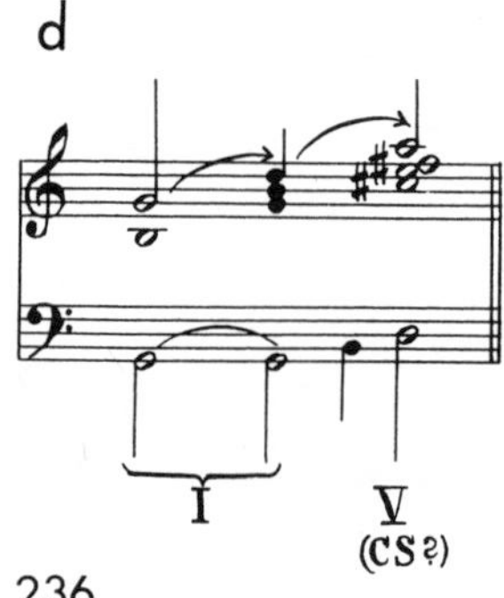
I
V
(CS?)

472 cont'd

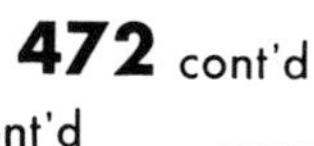

cont'd

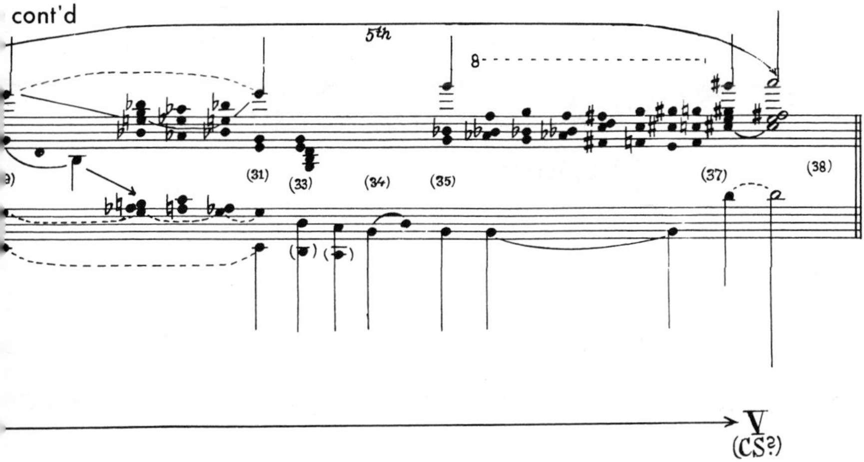
5th
8
(31)
(33)
(34)
(35)
(37)
(38)
V
(CS?)

cont'd

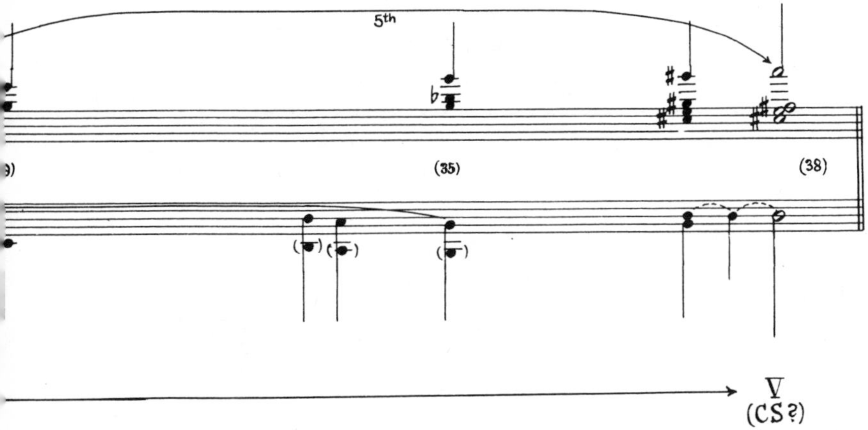
5th
(35)
(38)
V
(CS?)

473 DOWLAND Ayre: What if I never speed

[From *HAM*, Vol. I, No. 163]

a

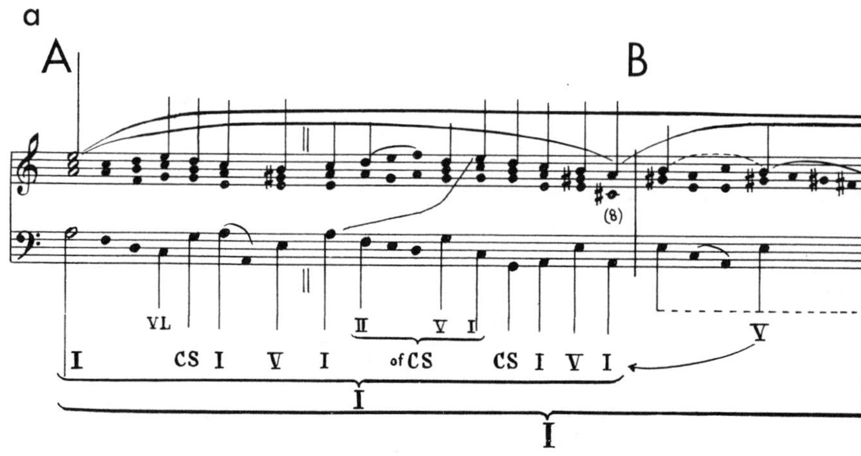

b

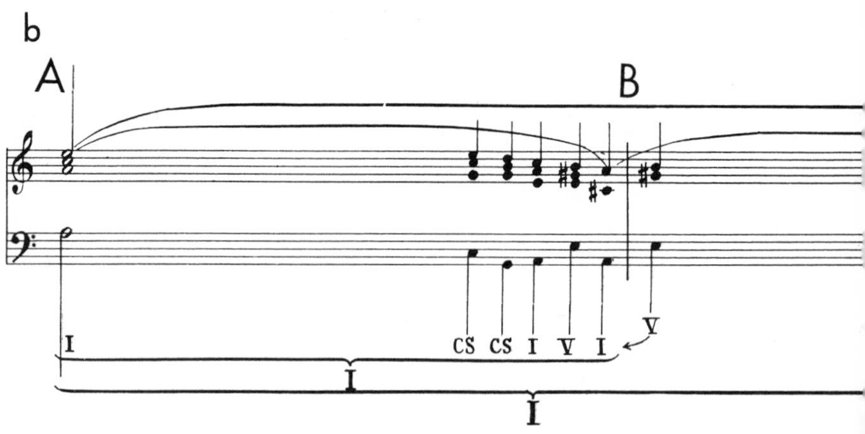

473 cont'd

cont'd

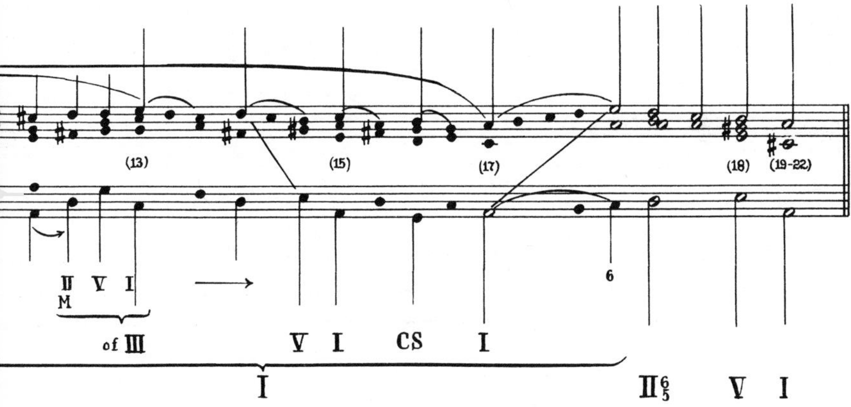

cont'd

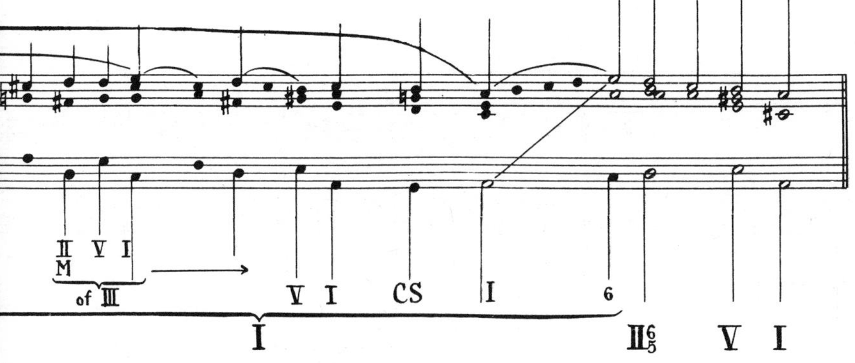

474 BACH Fugue No. 5 (Well-Tempered Clavier, Bk I)

a

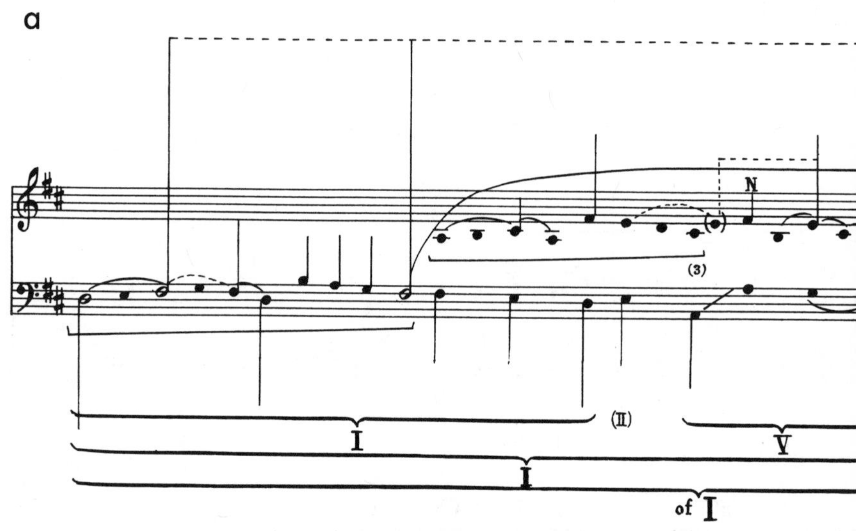

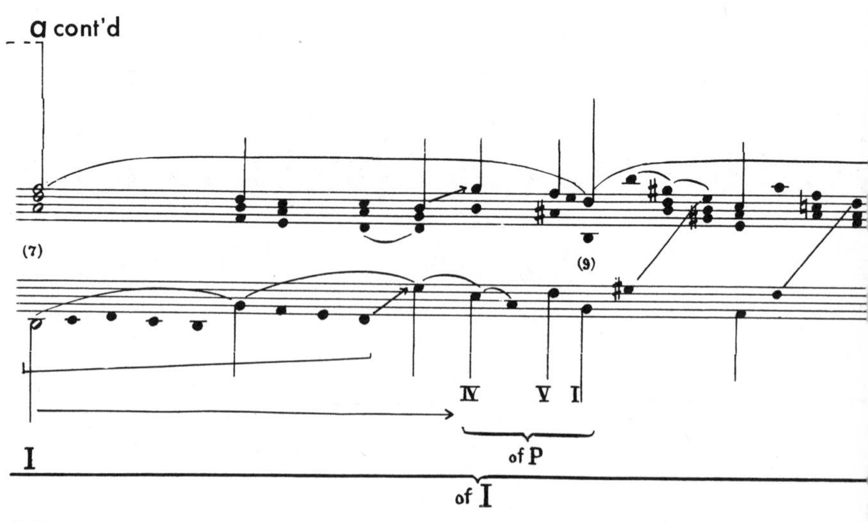

474 cont'd

cont'd

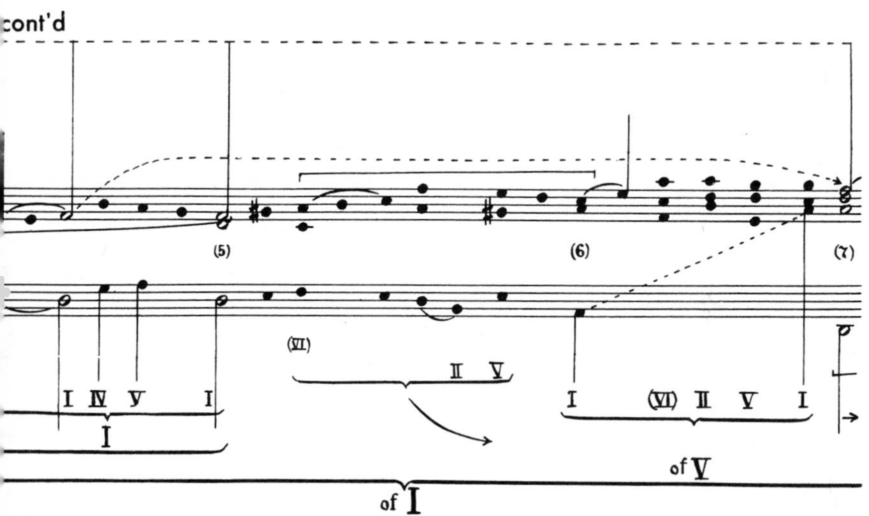

cont'd

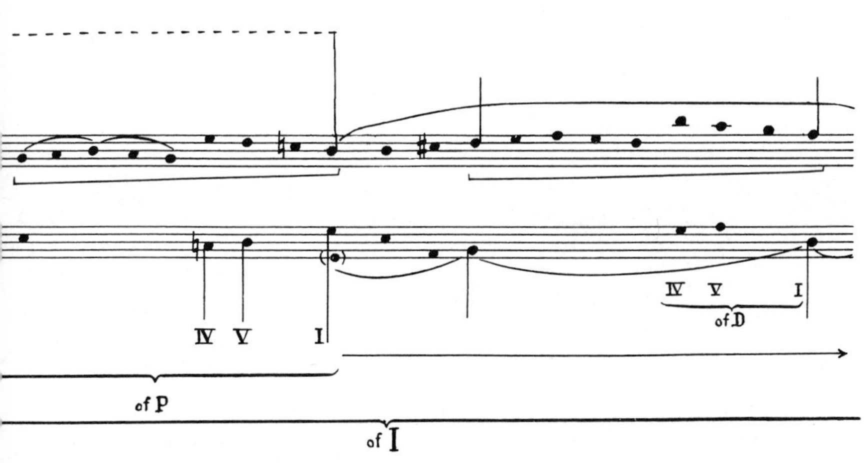

474 cont'd

a cont'd

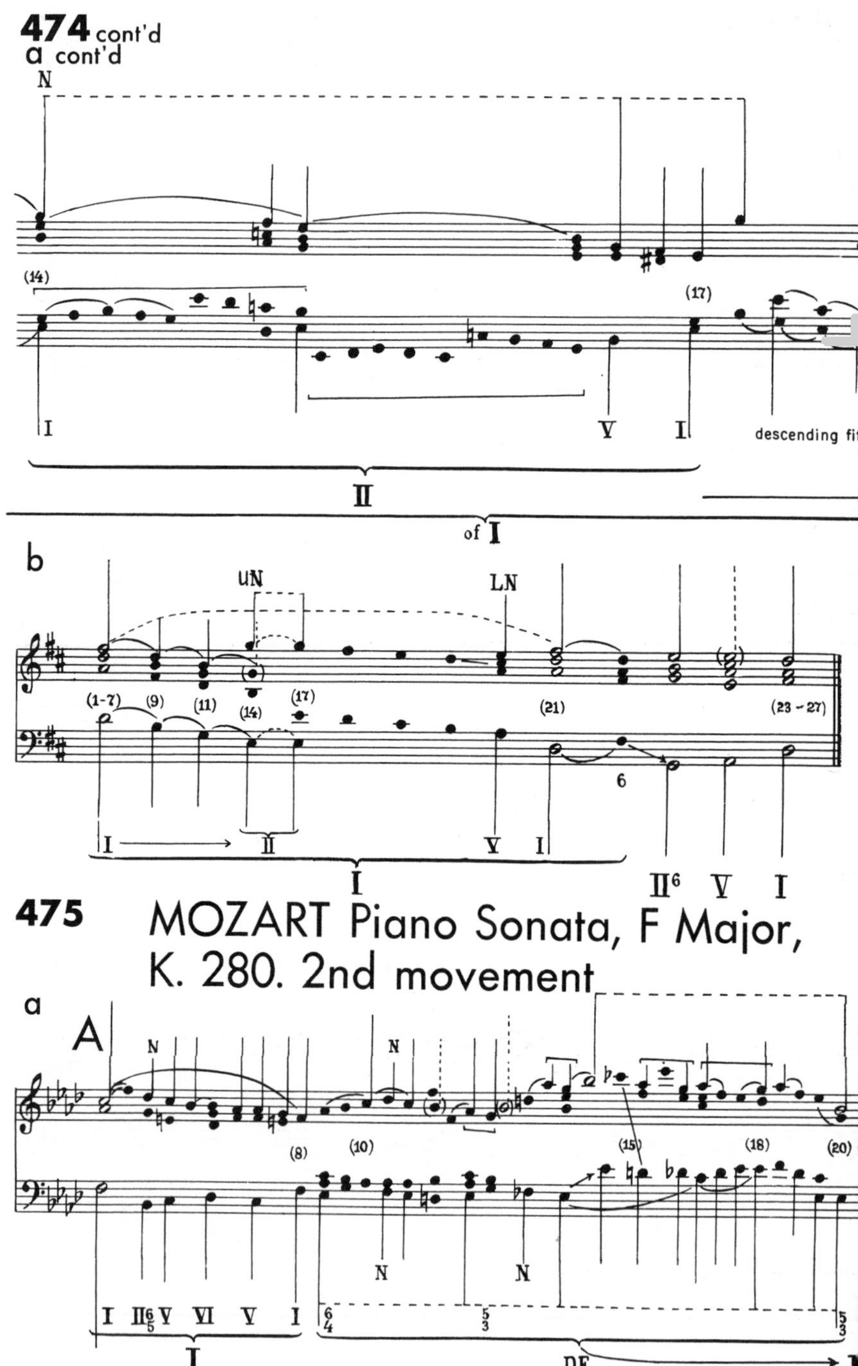

475 MOZART Piano Sonata, F Major, K. 280. 2nd movement

474 cont'd

a cont'd

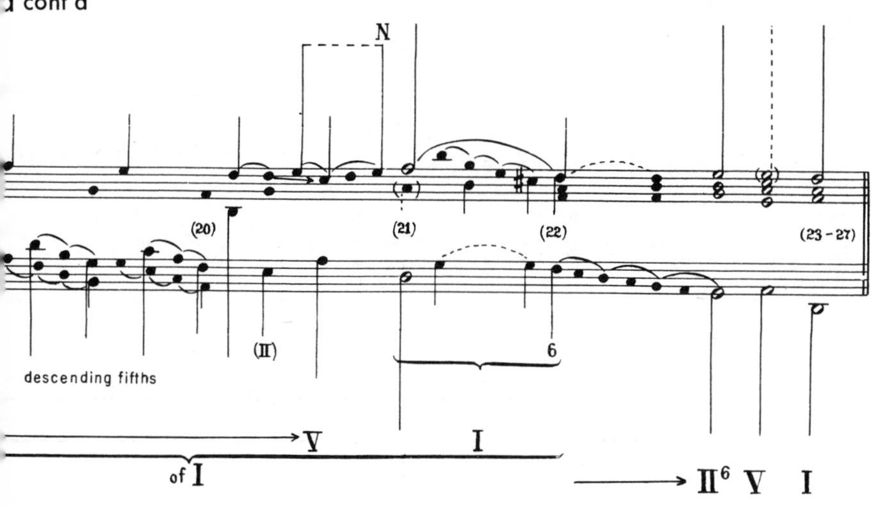

475 cont'd

cont'd

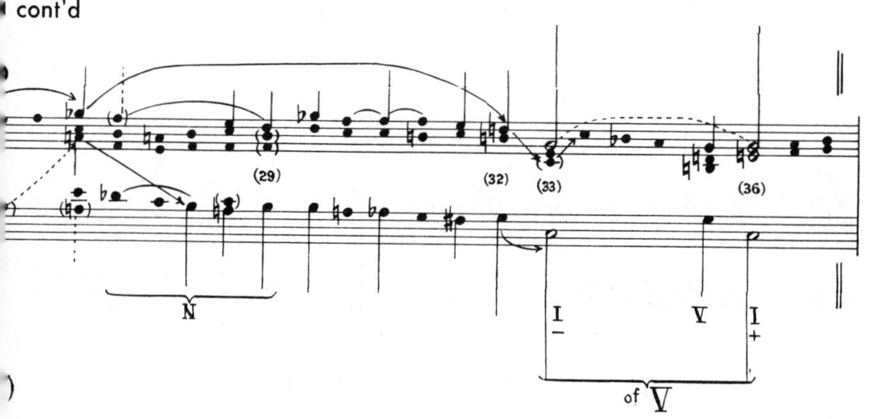

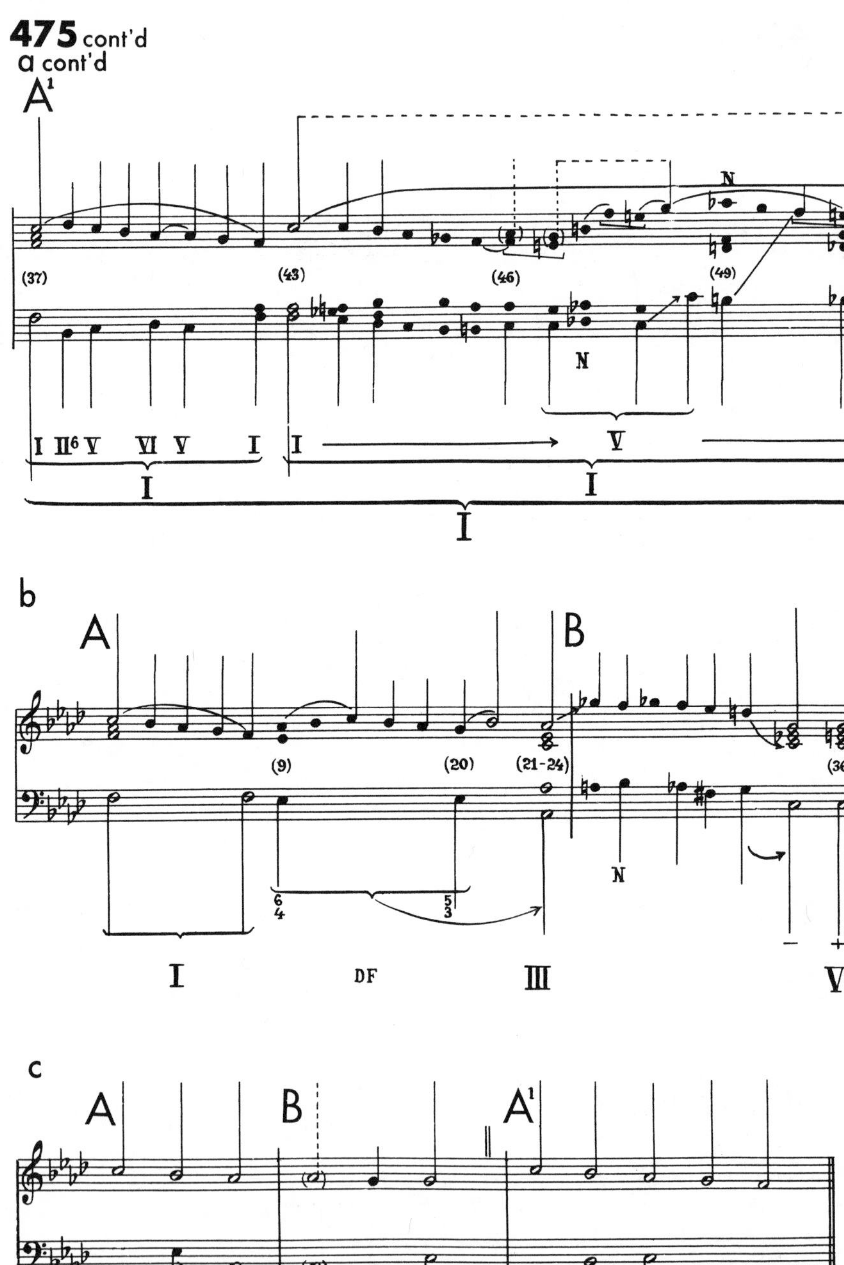
475 cont'd
a cont'd
A1
N
(37)
(43)
(46)
(49)
N
I II6 V VI V I
I
V
I
I
I
b
A
B
(9)
(20)
(21-24)
(36)
6 4
5 3
N
– +
I
DF
III
V
c
A
B
A1
I DF III (III) V I II6/5 V I

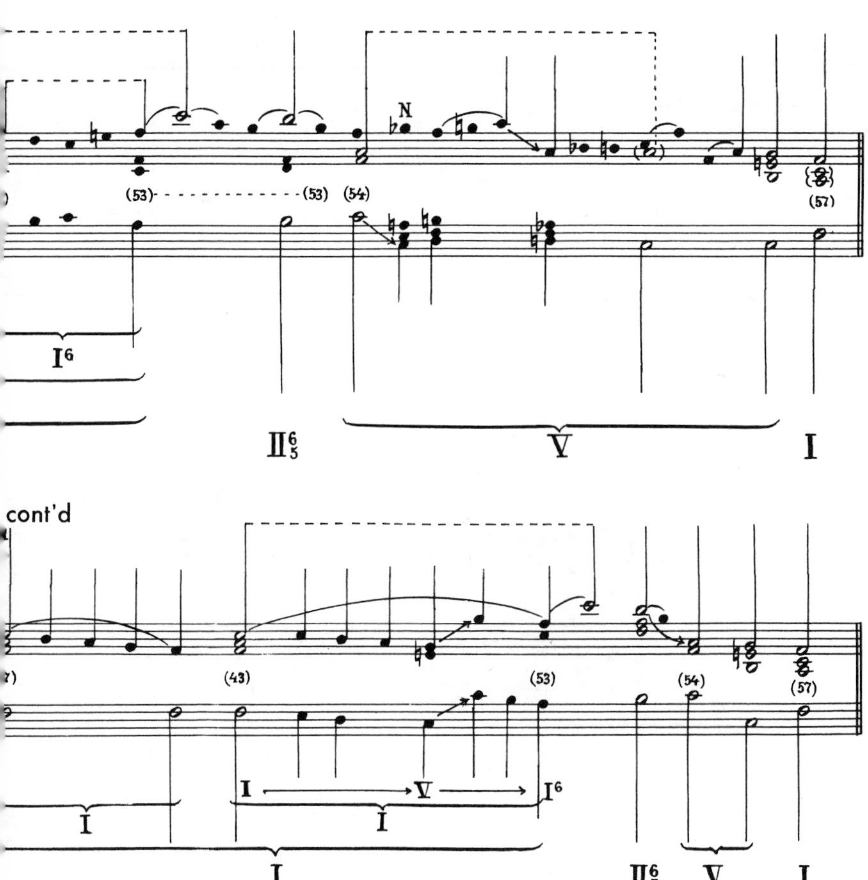
cont'd
N
(53)
(53)
(54)
(57)
I6
II6 5
V
I
cont'd
(43)
(53)
(54)
(57)
I
V
I6
I
I
I
II6 5
V
I

a
A
N
N
UN
LN
(6)
twice
III V I
of
I V I
II
V
I6 V I
I
I
I
a cont'd
N
N
(29)
(32)
8
8 (36)
8
I V I V I
I II V
I
P
P
II
a cont'd
B
IN
N
(51)
52 - - 63 like 6 - - 17
(64)
(68)
P I V I
V
(D)
I
IV
V
I

476 cont'd

cont'd
N
(15)
(17)
(18)
(20)
(25)
6
I
II
V
P
cont'd
(40)
(44)
(48)
III
M
b
A
B
N
Stanza 1
2
3
Piano
4
IV
(D)

477 BRAHMS Intermezzo, Op. 119, No. 1

a

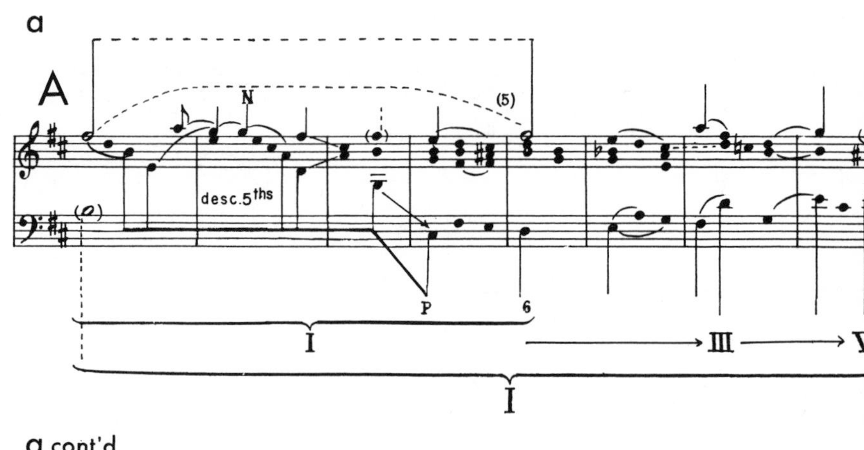

a cont'd

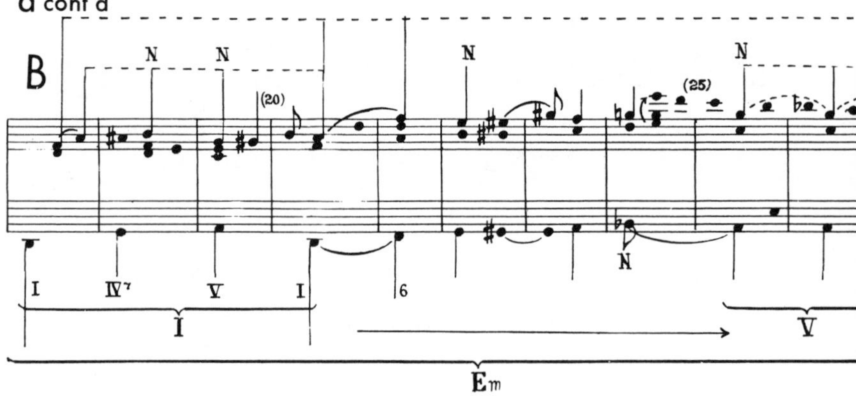

a cont'd

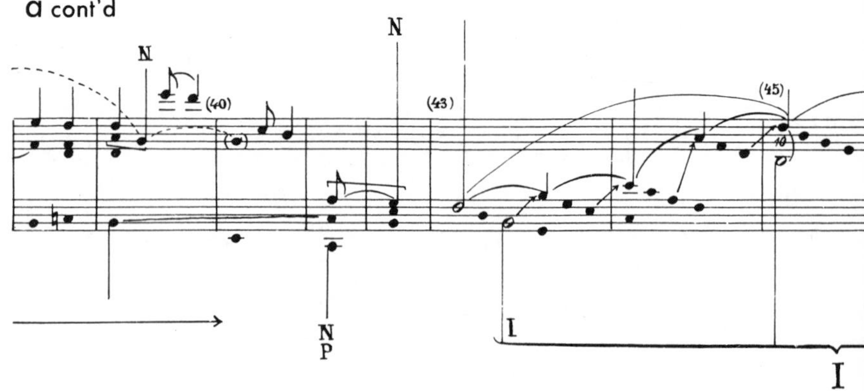

a cont'd
(10)
N
10
9
10
9
10
10
(15)
I
VI
V
I
I
of V
I
a cont'd
N
(30)
N
(35)
6
N
(V)
V
I
IV
V
Em
a cont'd
A1
(50)
(55)
10
(meas.47–54 like meas.1–8)
anticipation
III
V
I
I
I

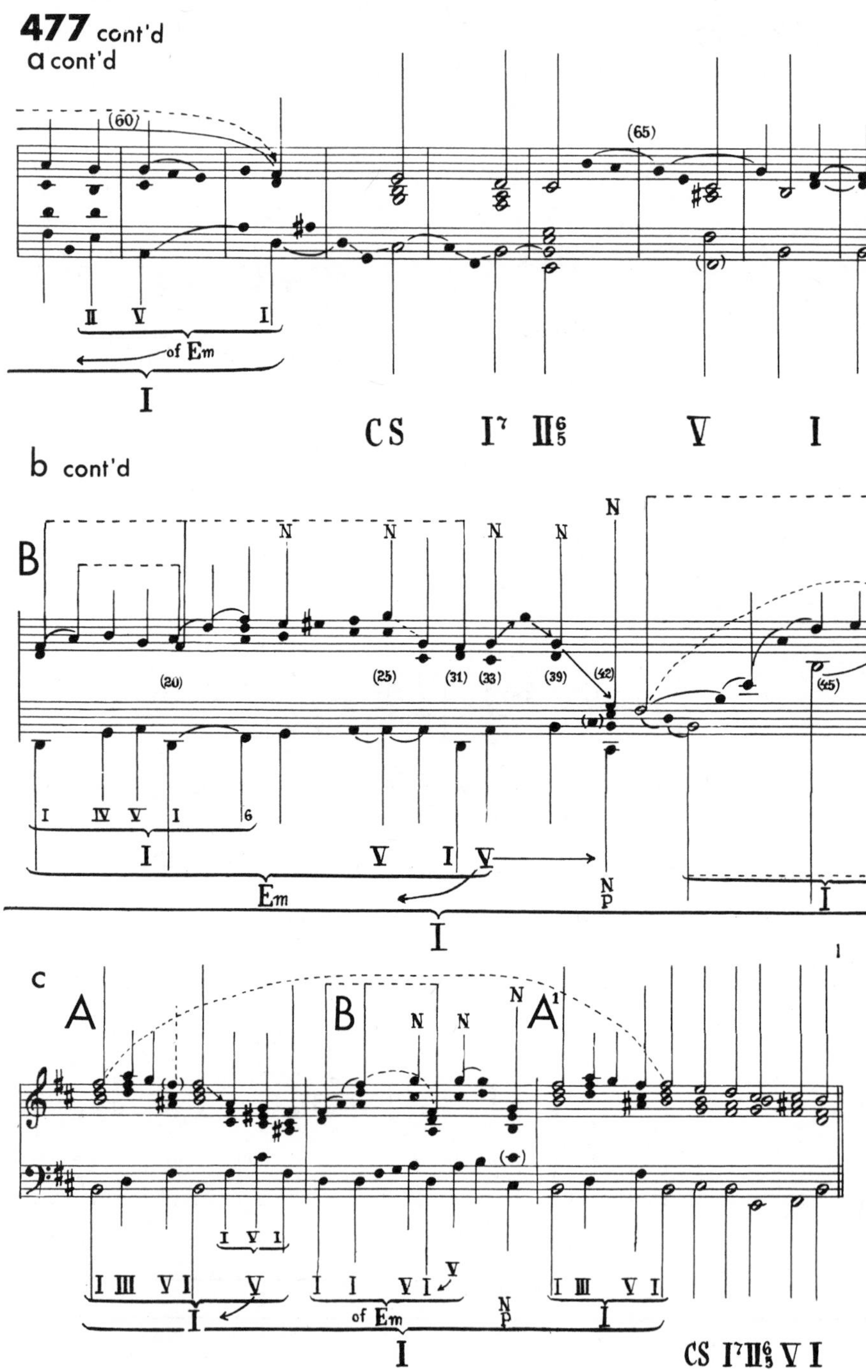
477 cont'd
a cont'd
(60)
(65)
II V I
of Em
I
CS I7 II6/5 V I
b cont'd
B
N N N N N
(20) (25) (31) (33) (39) (42) (45)
I IV V I 6
I
V I V
N P
Em
I
I
c
A B A1
N N N
I V I
I III V I V
I I V I V
I III V I
I of Em I
N P
I
CS I7 II6/5 V I

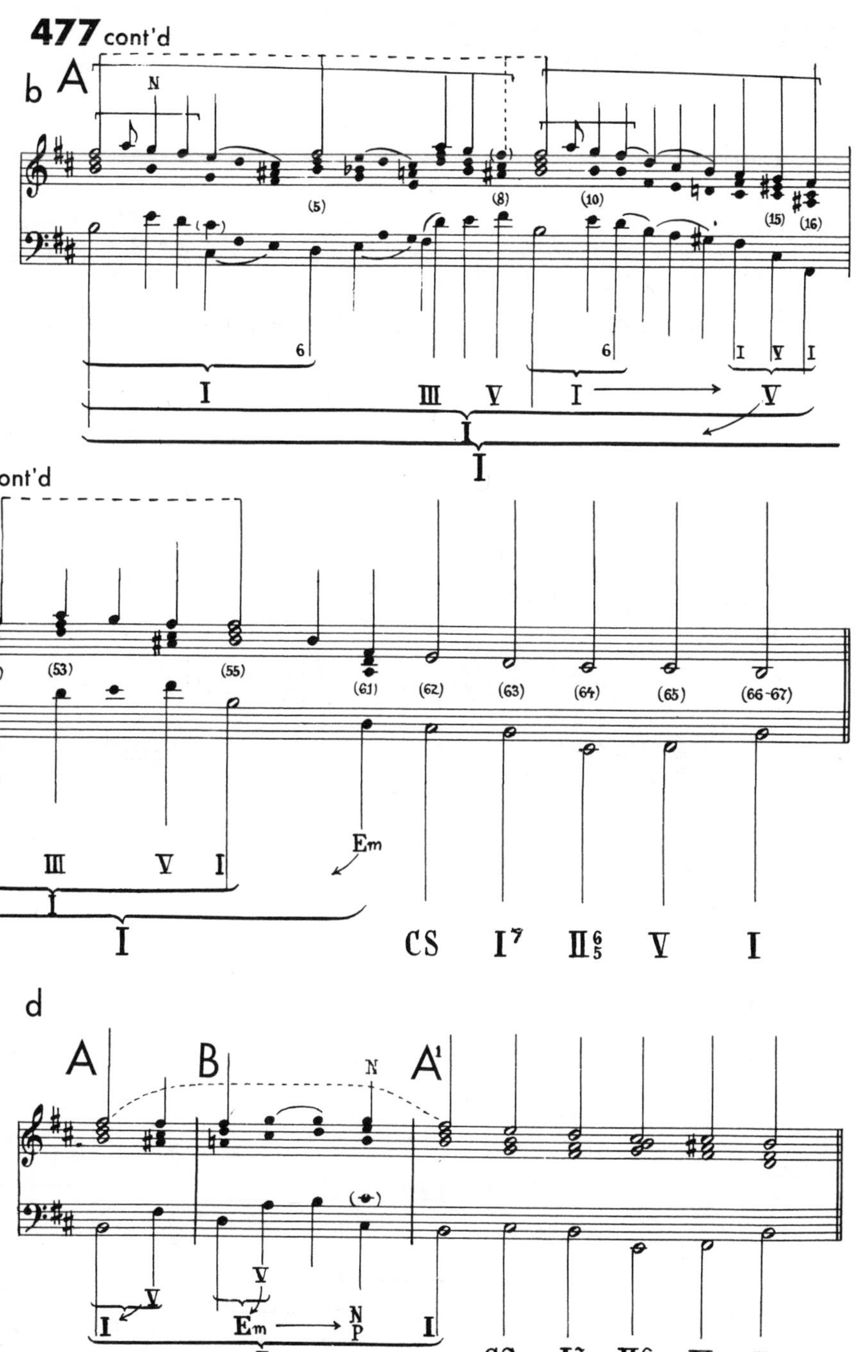
477 cont'd
b A
N
(5)
(8)
(10)
(15)
(16)
6
6
I V I
I
III
V
I
V
I
I
cont'd
(53)
(55)
(61)
(62)
(63)
(64)
(65)
(66-67)
I III V I
Em
I
I
CS
I7
II6 5
V
I
d
A
B
N
A1
V
V
I
Em
N P
I
I
CS
I7
II6 5
V
I

478 DEBUSSY Bruyères

a

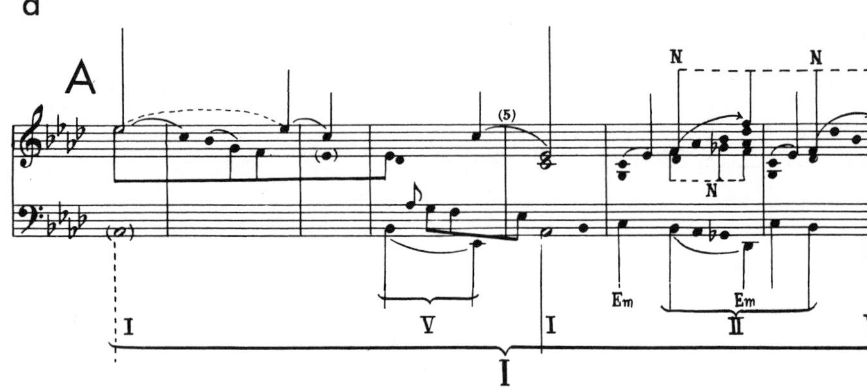

a cont'd

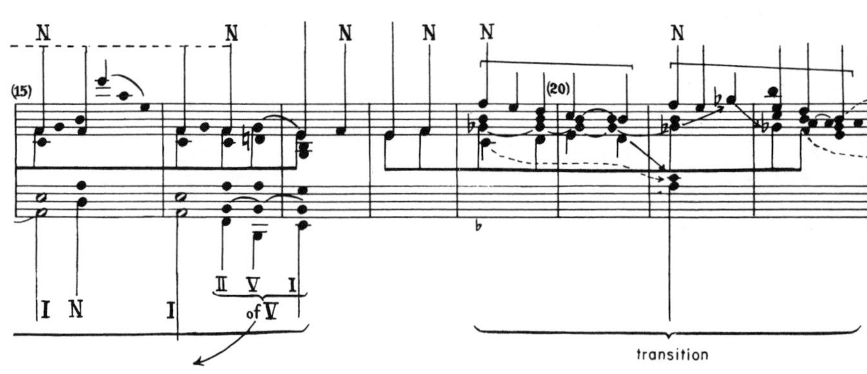

a cont'd

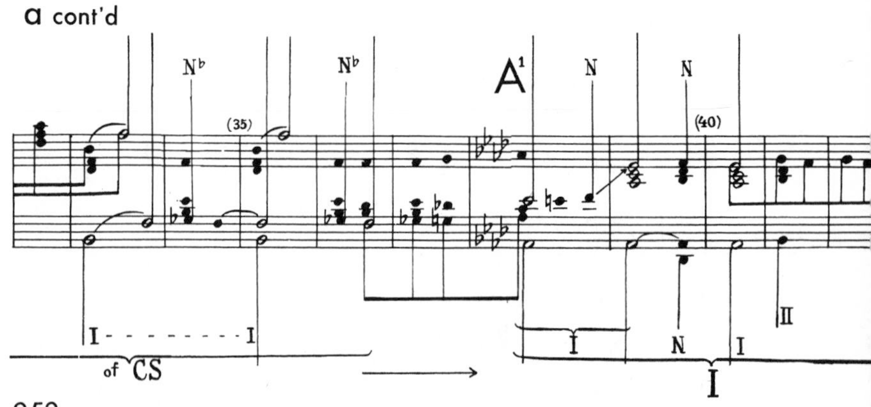

478 cont'd

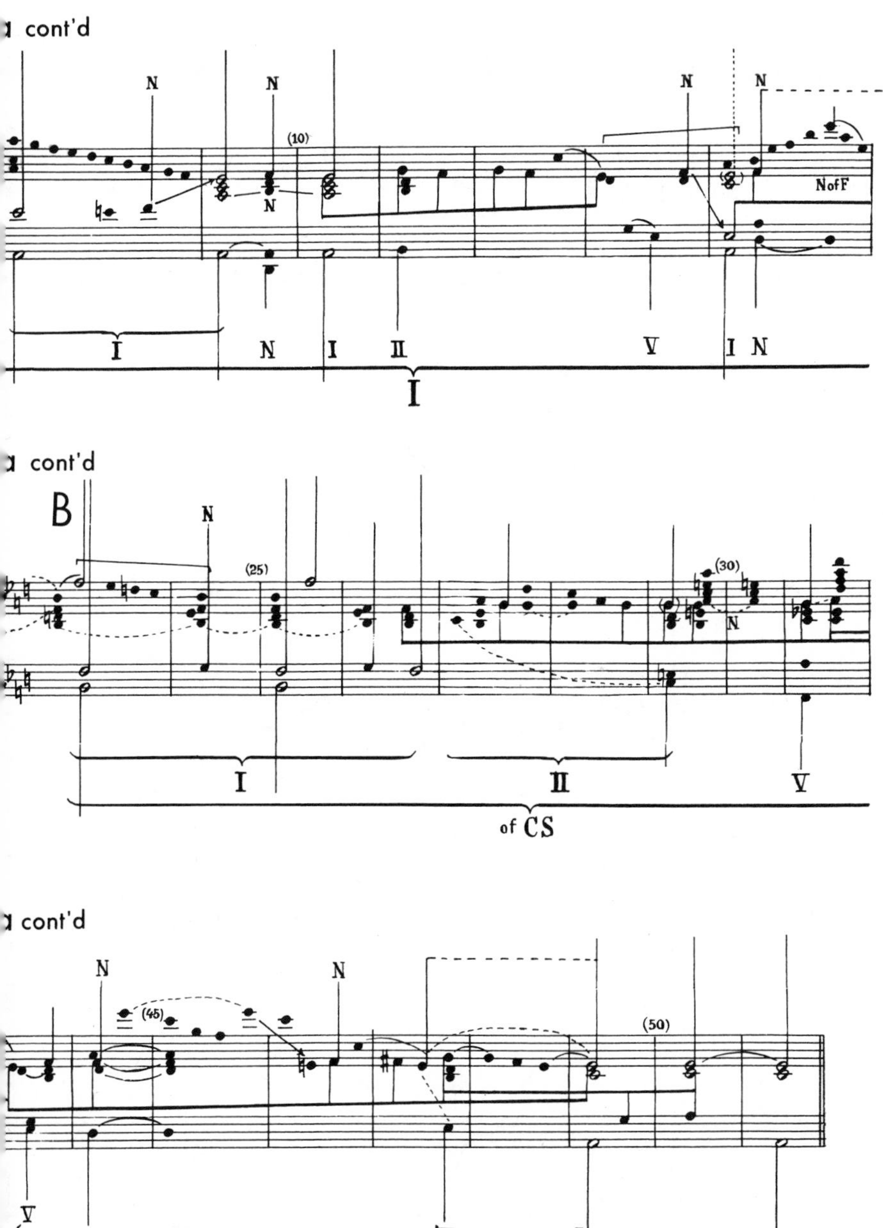
cont'd
N
N
N
(10)
N
N
NofF
I
N
I
II
V
I N
I
cont'd
B
N
(25)
(30)
N
I
II
V
of CS
cont'd
N
(45)
N
(50)
V
IV
V
I
I

478 cont'd

b

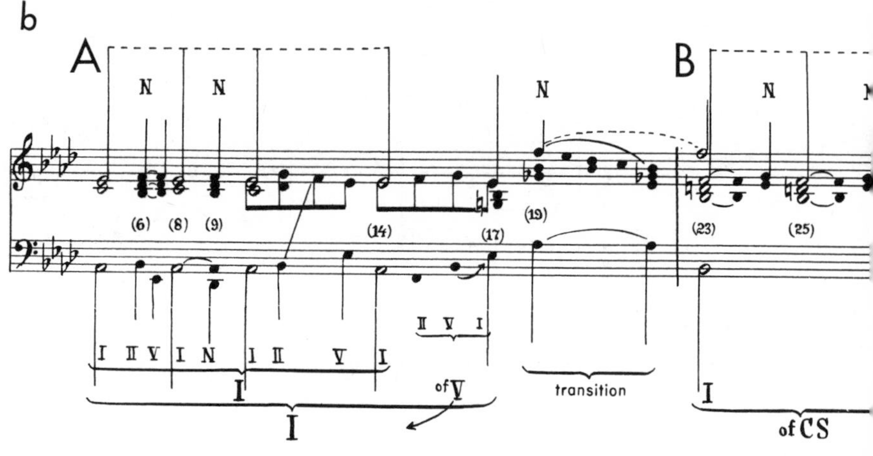

c

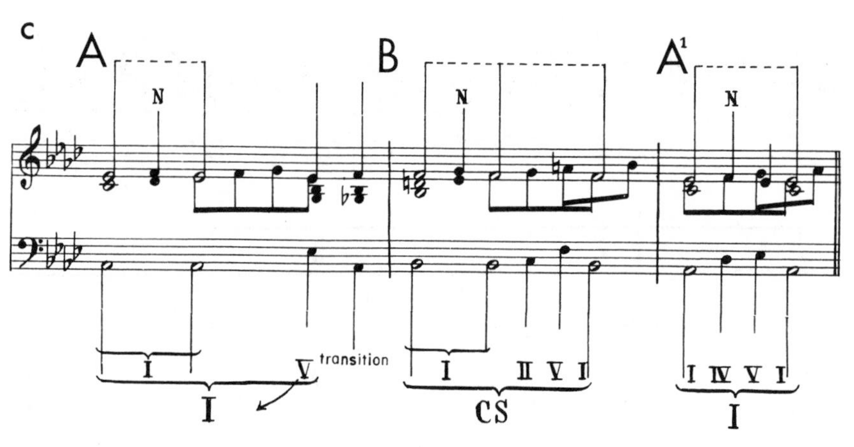

d

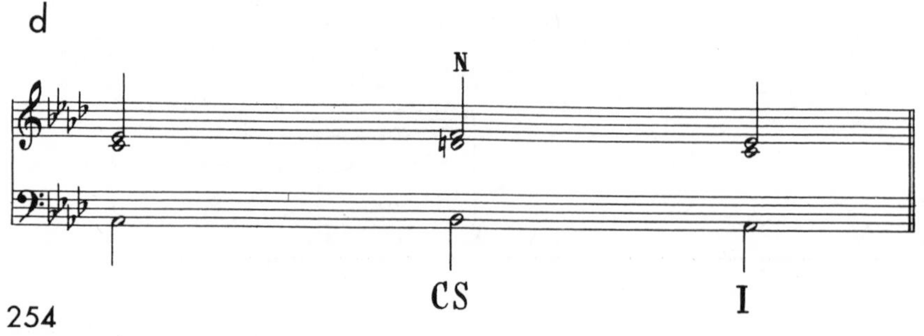

478 cont'd

b cont'd
A¹
N
N
N
(26)
(33)
(35)
(38)
(40)
(44)
N
I III♮ V I I
of CS
I I IV V I
I
e
Melodic prolongations:
A
N
B
N
N♭
N
A¹
N
N

479 GESUALDO Madrigal: Io pur respiro

[From *HAM*, Vol. I, No. 161]

ont'd
N
(14) (15)
(16)
(19)
(23) (25)
(27)
(31)
I
V
I
5th
5th
I
CS
cont'd
(52)
(55)
(60)
(61)
(66)
3rd
3rd
3rd
V
I
I
cont'd
C
(52) (60) (61)
(66)
I
I
I CS I

480 BARTÓK Piano Concerto No. 3. 1st movement

a

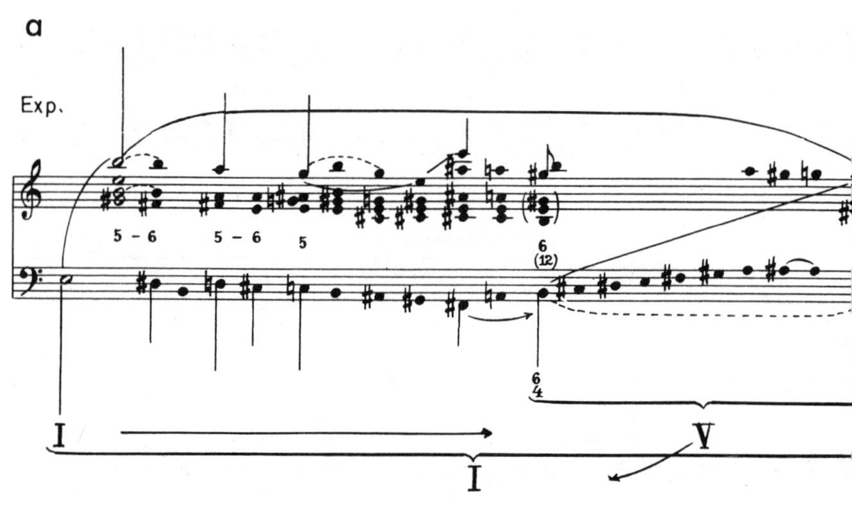

a cont'd

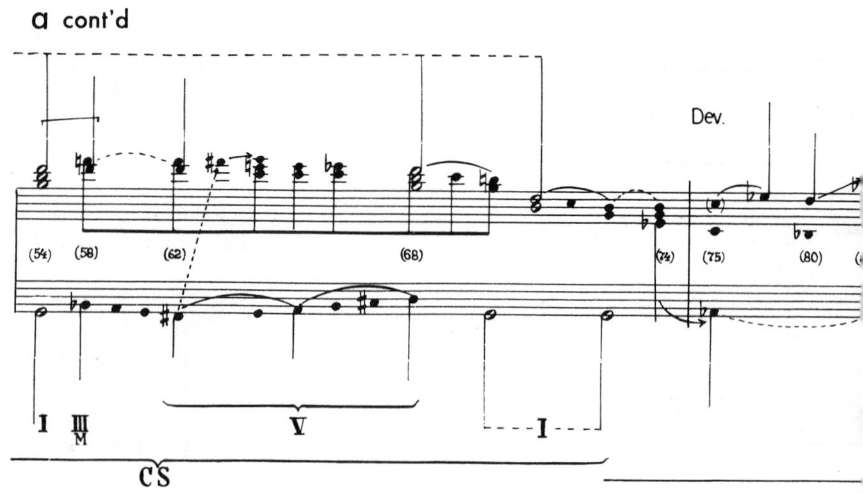

480 cont'd

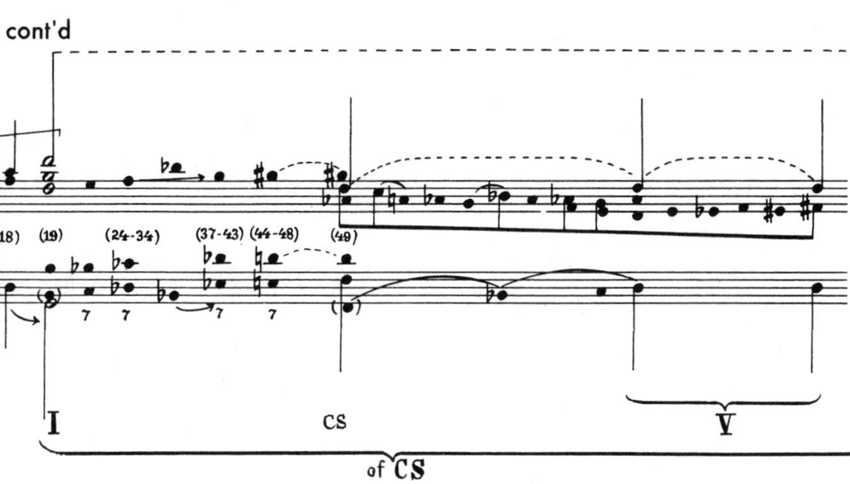
cont'd
(18)
(19)
(24-34)
(37-43)
(44-48)
(49)
7 7 7 7
I
CS
V
of CS

cont'd

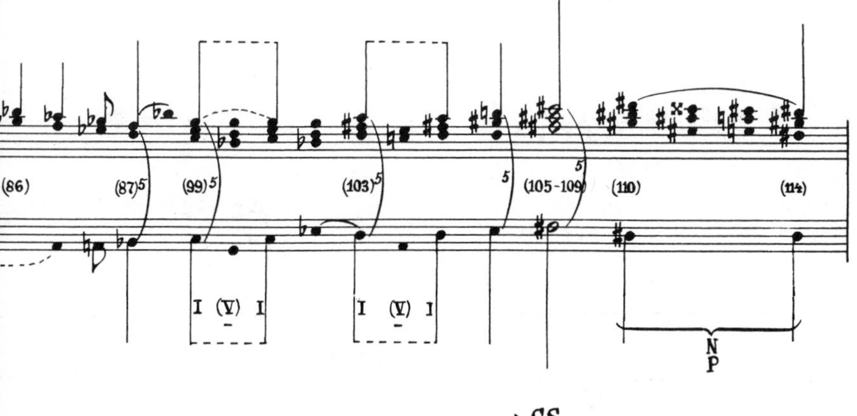
(86)
(87)
(99)
(103)
(105-109)
(110)
(114)
I (V) I
I (V) I
N
P
CS

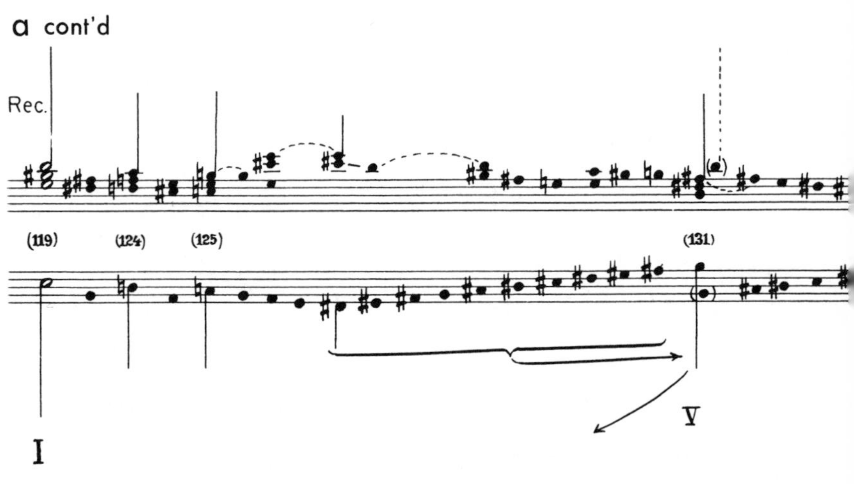
a cont'd
Rec.
(119)
(124)
(125)
(131)
V
I

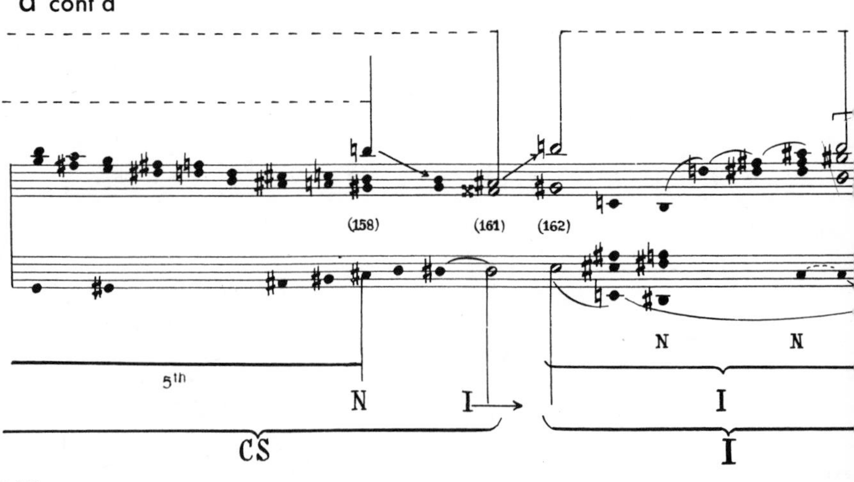
a cont'd
(158)
(161)
(162)
N
N
5th
N
I
I
CS
I

cont'd

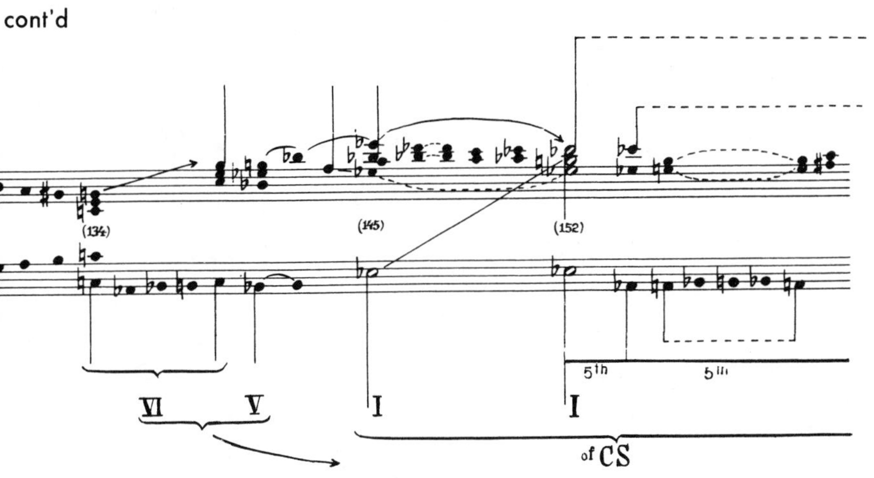
(134)
(145)
(152)
5th
5th
VI
V
I
I
of CS

cont'd

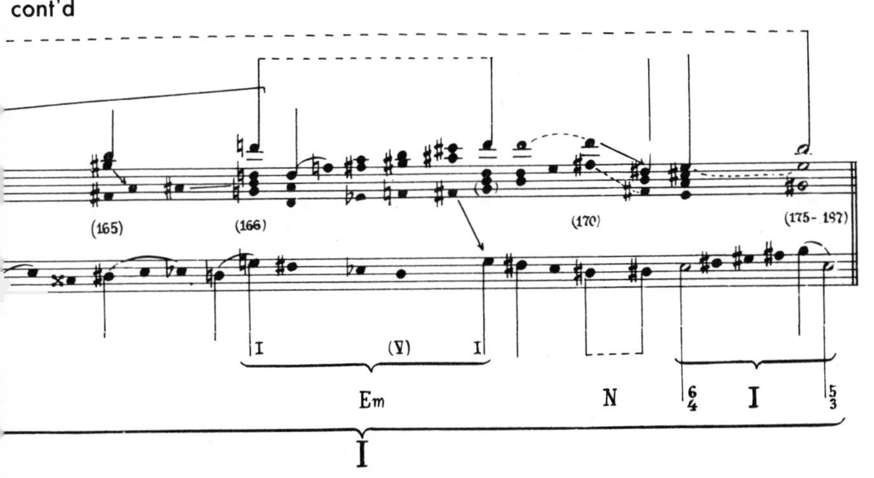
(165)
(166)
(170)
(175- 187)
I
(V)
I
Em
N
6
4
I
5
3
I

480 cont'd

b

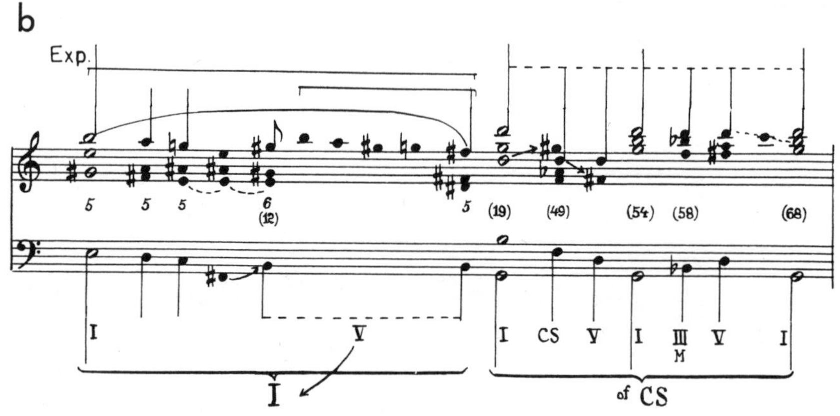

b cont'd

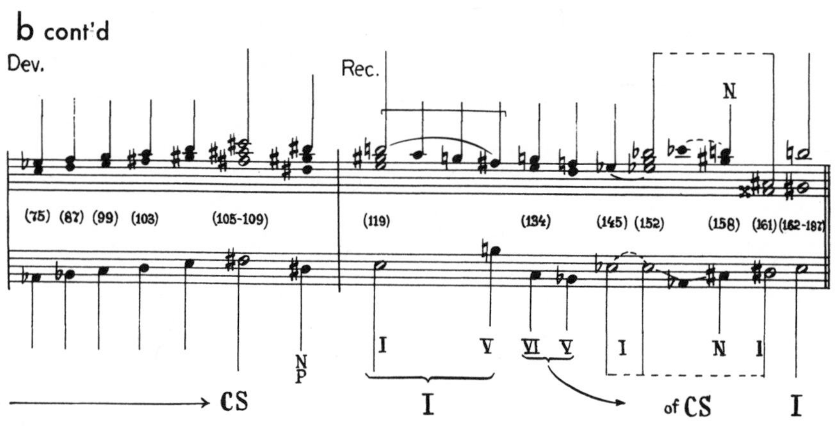

c

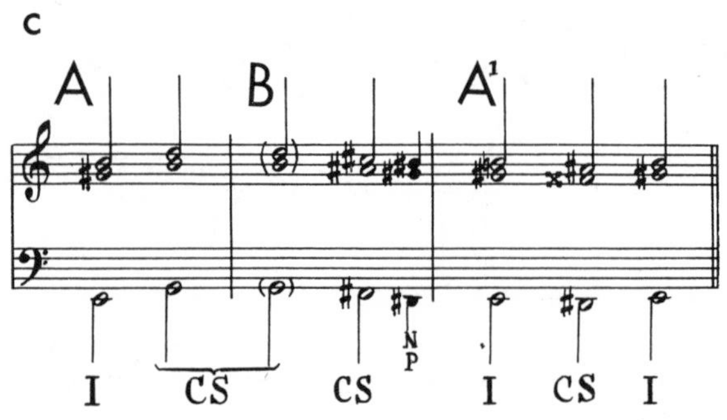

481

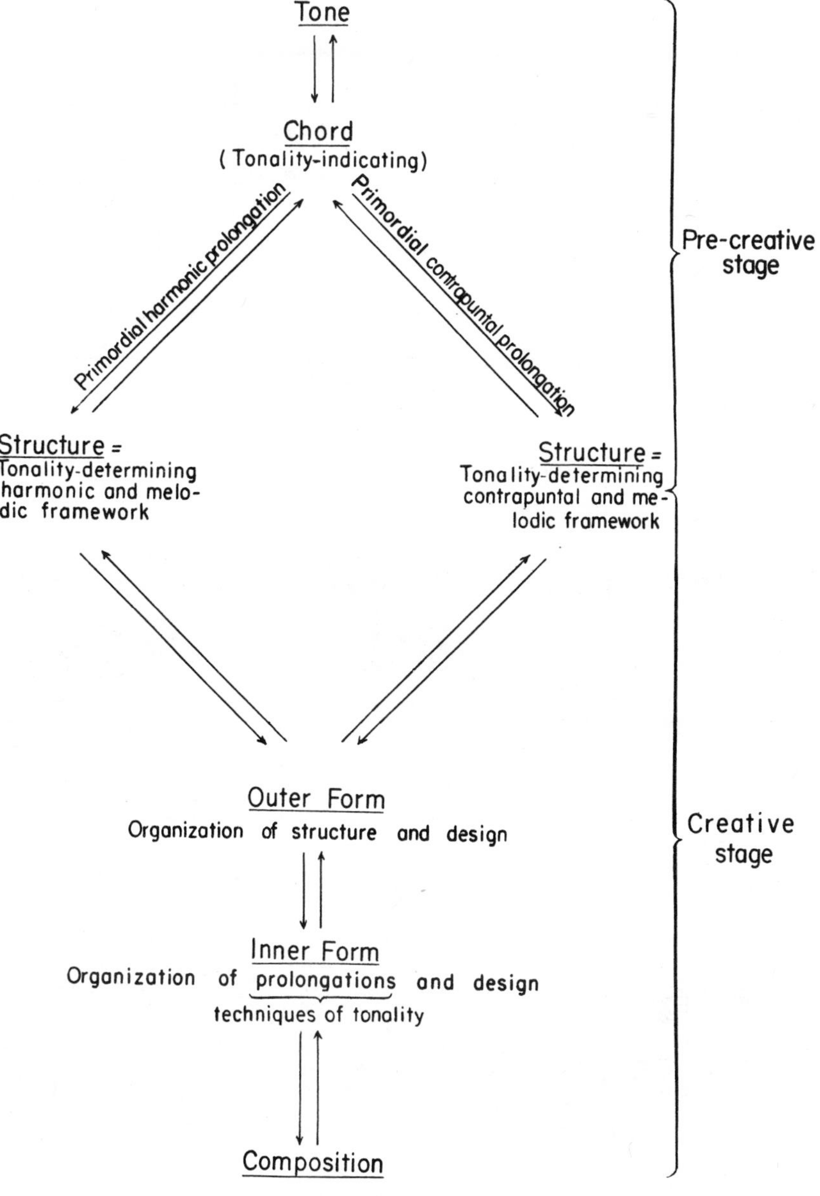

Tone
Chord
(Tonality-indicating)
Primordial harmonic prolongation
Primordial contrapuntal prolongation
Structure = Tonality-determining harmonic and melodic framework
Structure = Tonality-determining contrapuntal and melodic framework
Pre-creative stage
Outer Form
Organization of structure and design
Inner Form
Organization of prolongations and design
techniques of tonality
Creative stage
Composition

482 MARENZIO Madrigal: Io piango

[From *SHM*, No. 18]

a

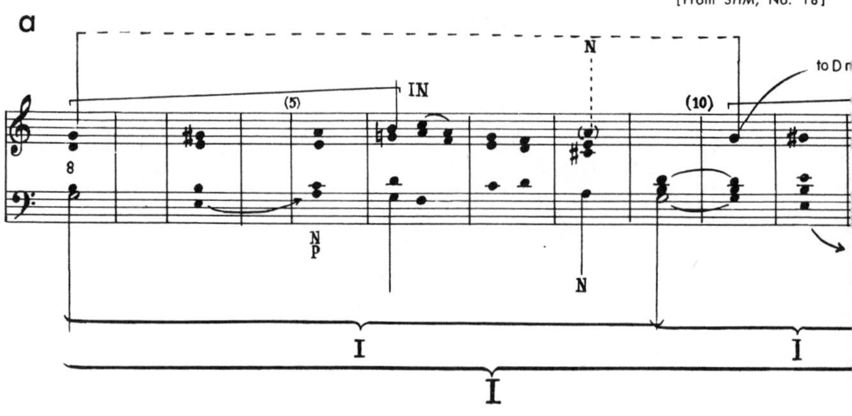

a cont'd

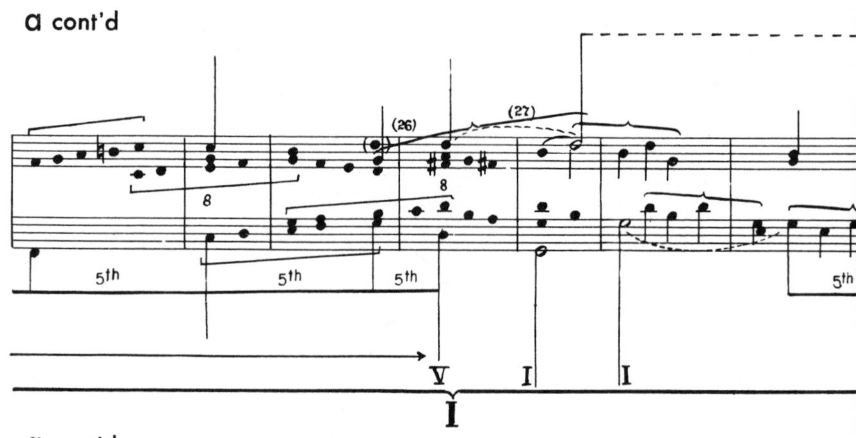

a cont'd

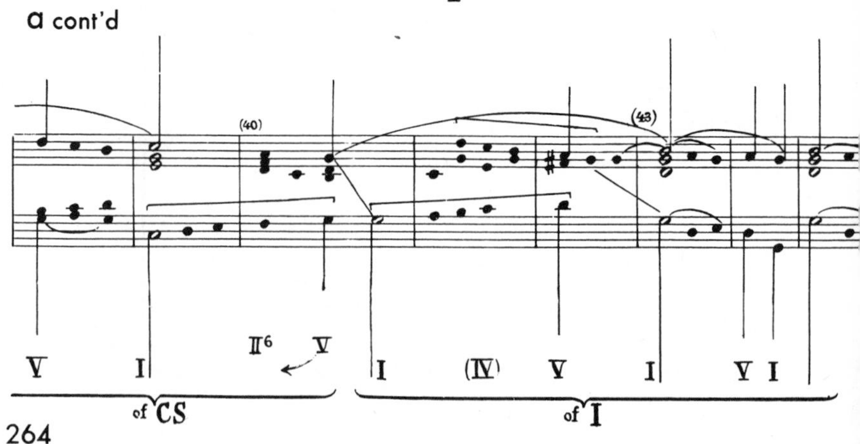

482 cont'd

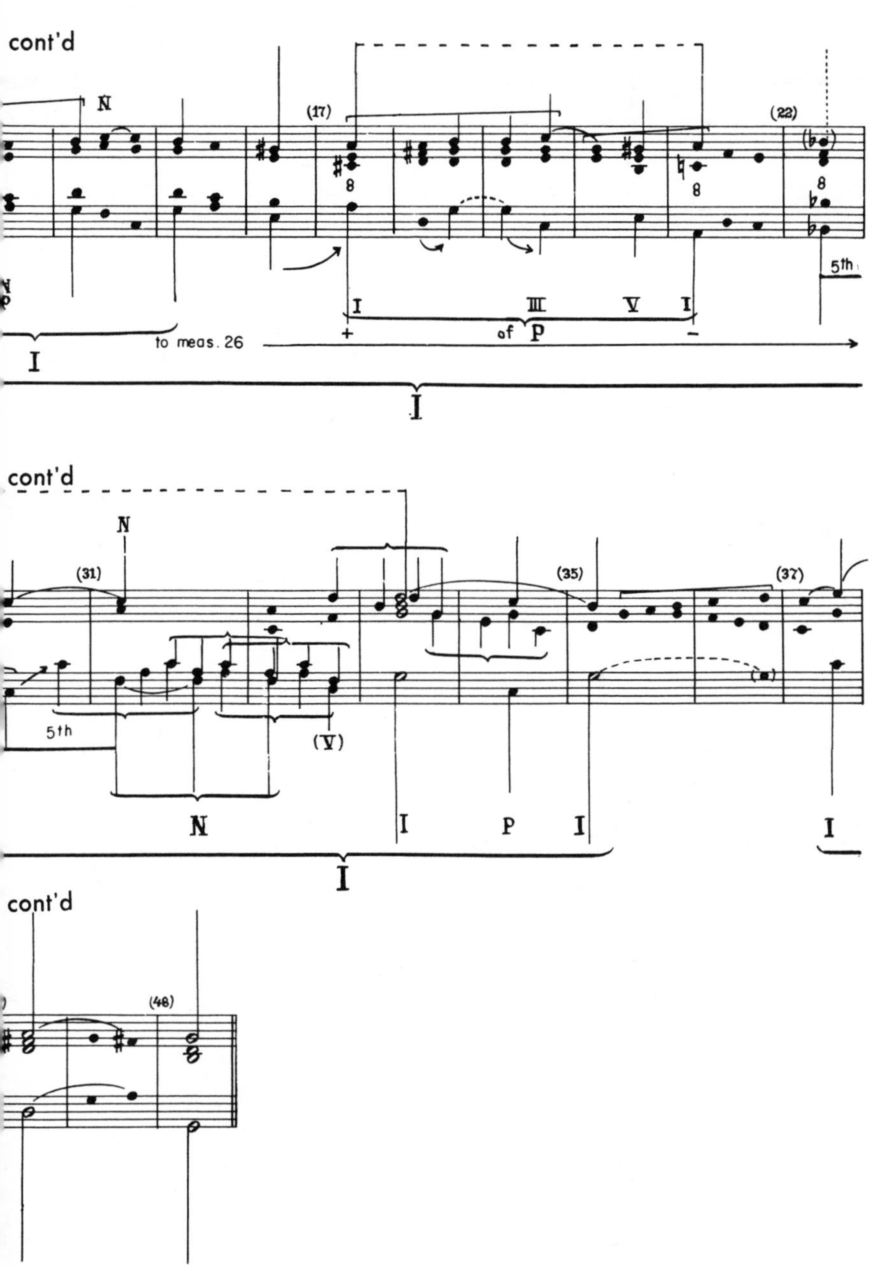
cont'd
N
(17)
(22)
8
8
8
5th
I
III
V
I
+
of P
−
I
to meas. 26
I
cont'd
N
(31)
(35)
(37)
5th
(V)
N
I
P
I
I
I
cont'd
(48)
V
I

482 cont'd

483 MOZART Aria ("The Magic Flute")

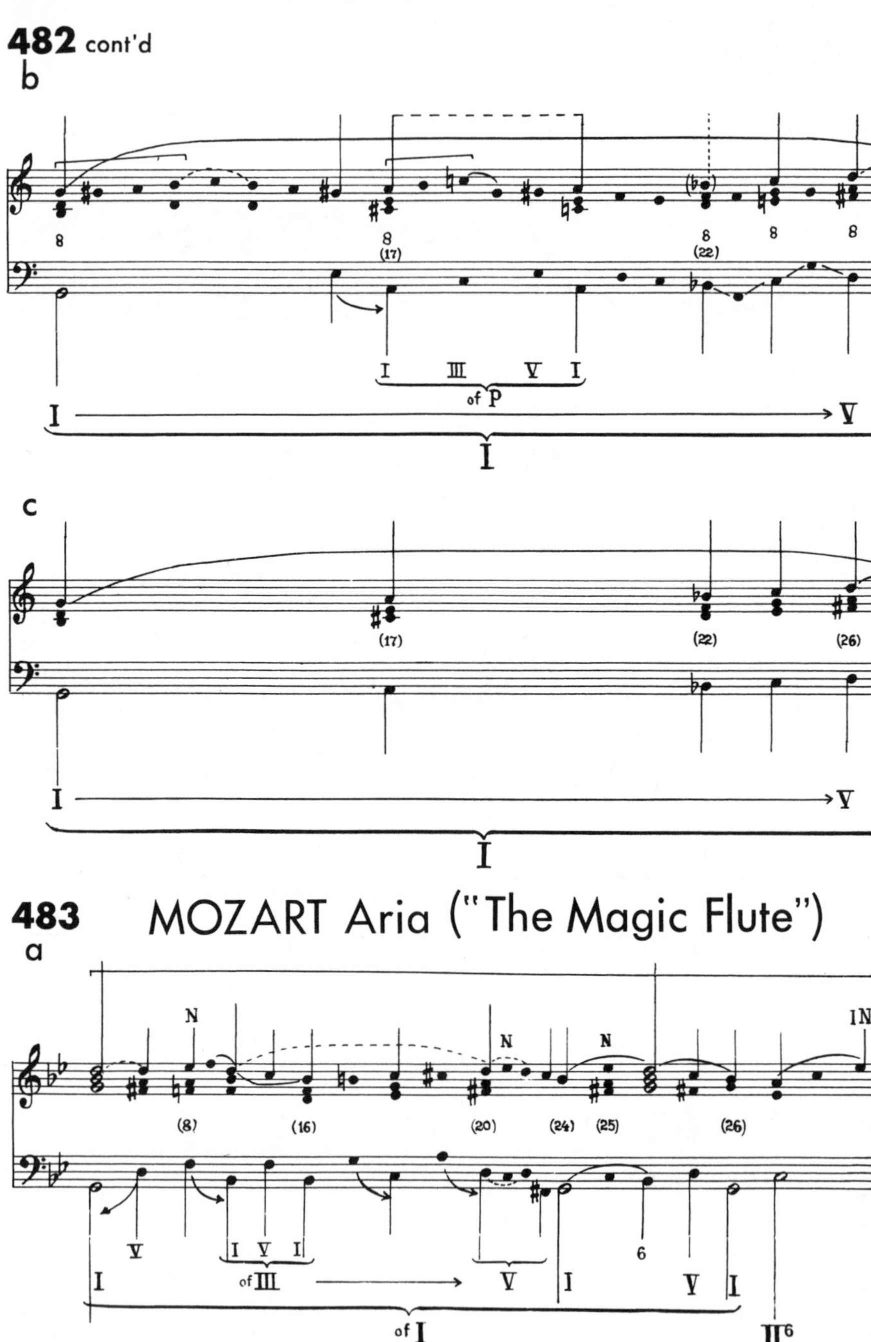

482 cont'd

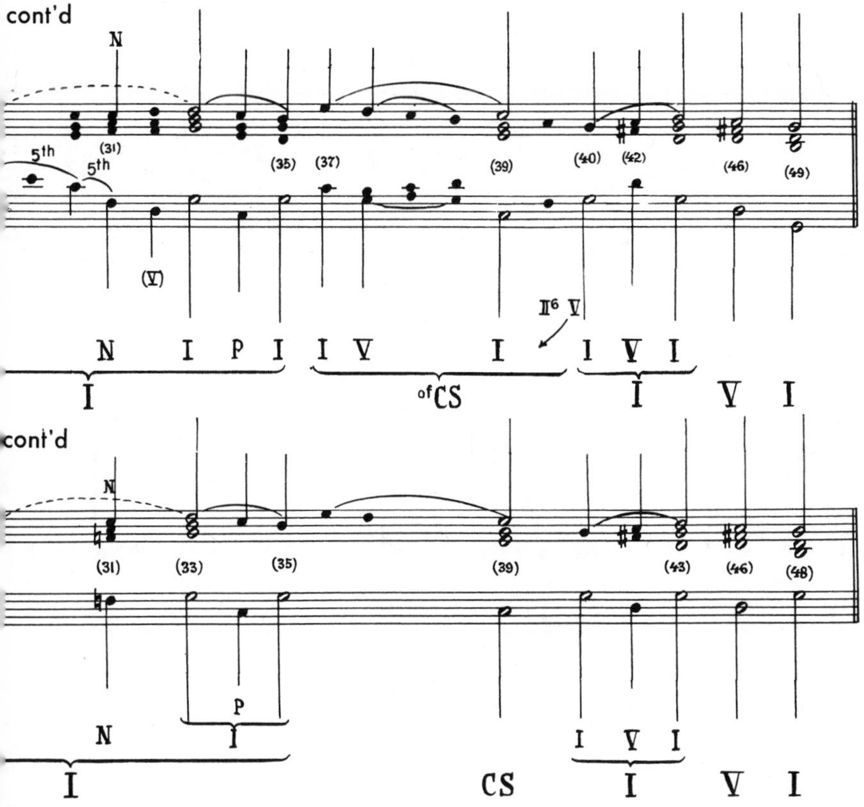

cont'd

N I P I I V I I V I
I ofCS I V I

cont'd

N P I
I V I
I CS I V I

483 cont'd

cont'd

V I V I
V N (VI) I II6phr. V N V I

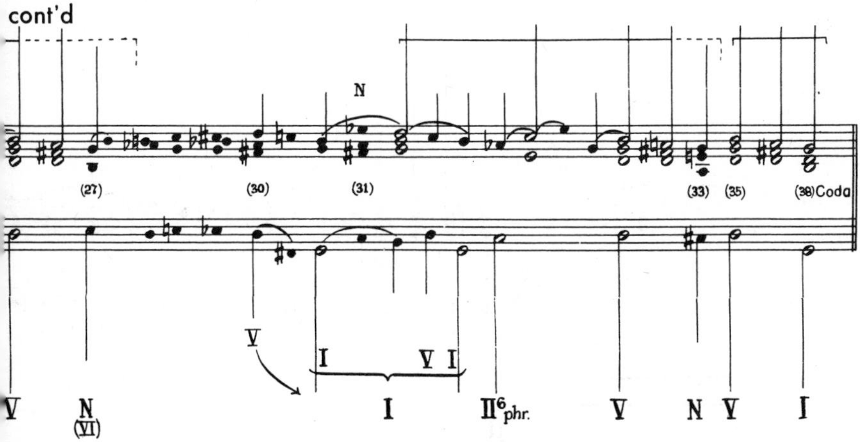

484 FRESCOBALDI Corrente

[From *AMI*, Vol. III, P. 207]

a

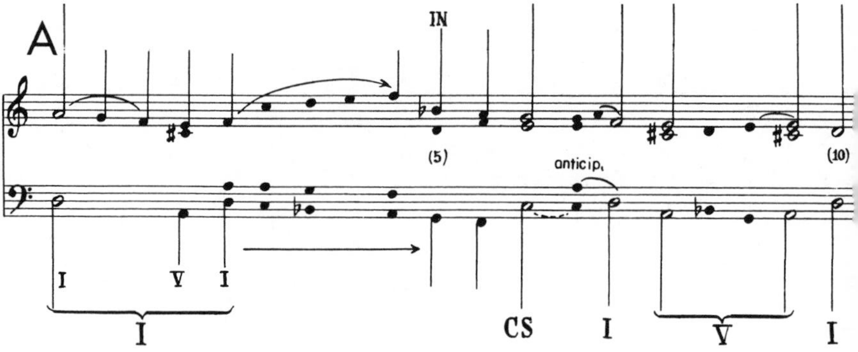

A
IN
(5)
anticip.
(10)
I V I
I
CS
I
V
I

b

A
IN
B
IN
I
CS
I
V
I
I
CS
I ⟶ II6
V
I

485 cont'd

a cont'd

B
N
(12)
(17)
(19)
(21)
6
I
II
V
I
I
I

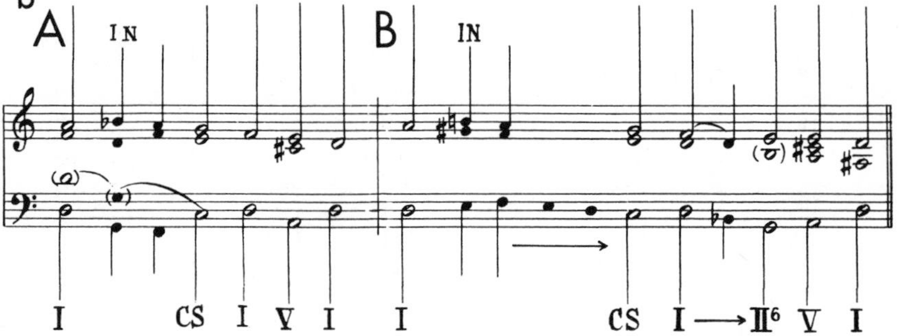

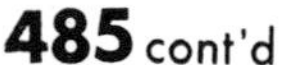

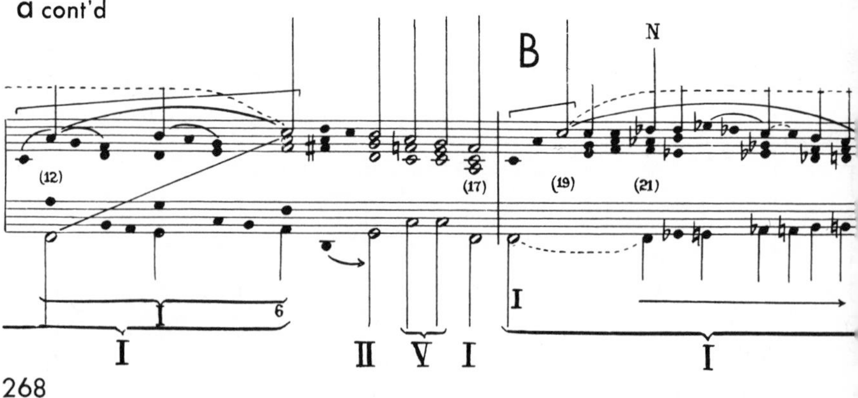

484 cont'd

cont'd

IN
(16)
(22)
(26)
CS → I → II6 V I

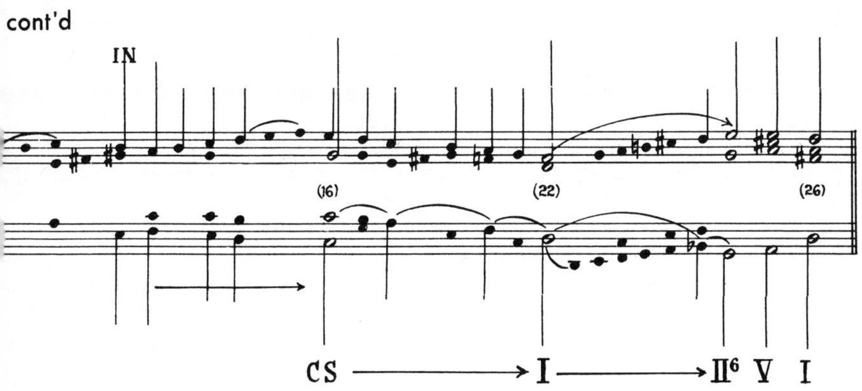

485 BRAHMS Feldeinsamkeit

a

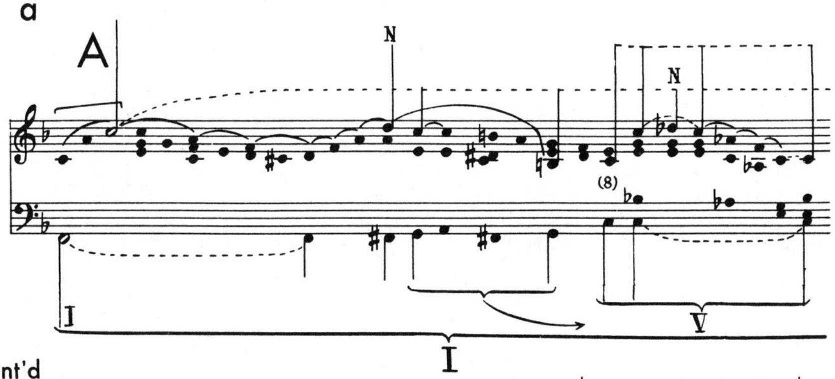

A
N
N
(8)
I
V
I

cont'd

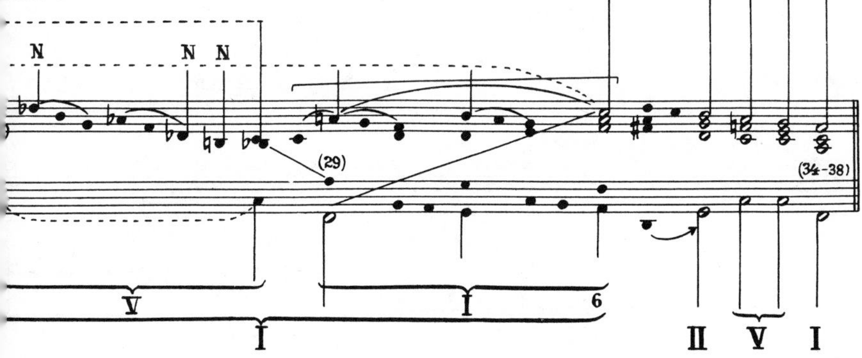

N
N N
(29)
(34-38)
V
I
6
I
II V I

486 FRESCOBALDI La Frescobalda

[From *EPM*, P. 33]

a

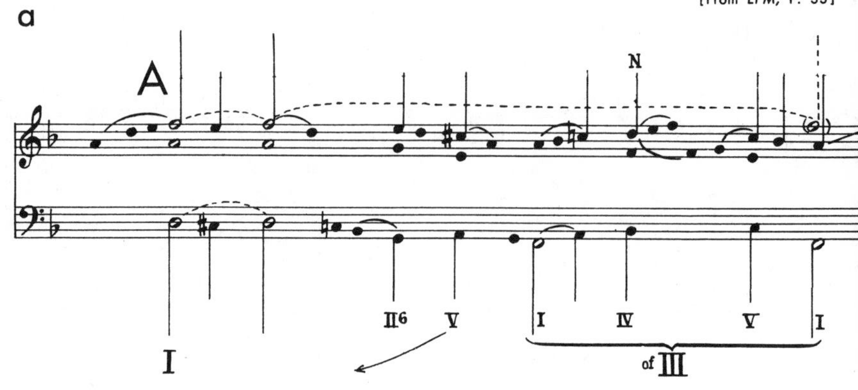

b

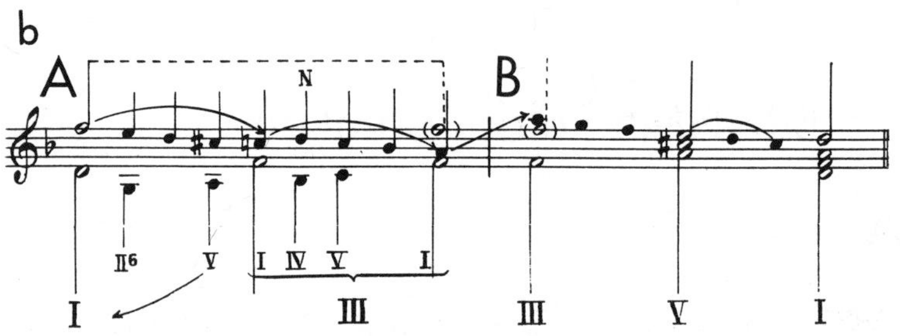

487 D. SCARLATTI Sonata, G Major, L. 490

a

486 cont'd

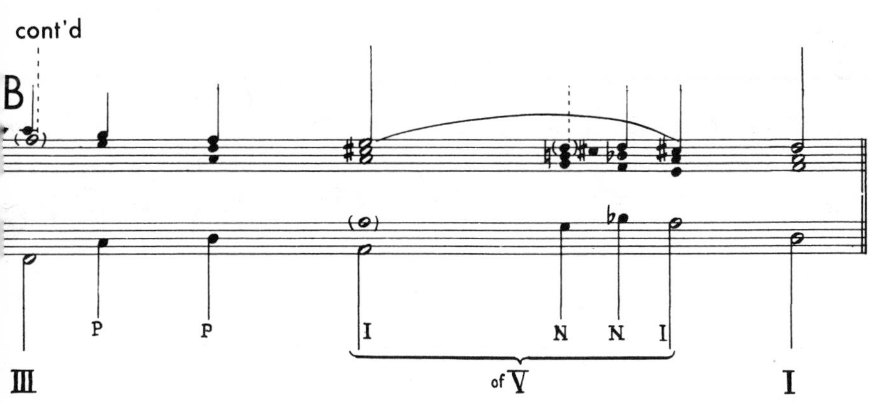

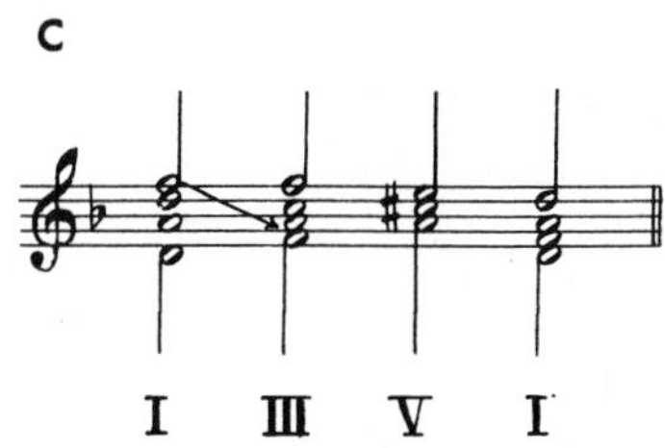

487 cont'd

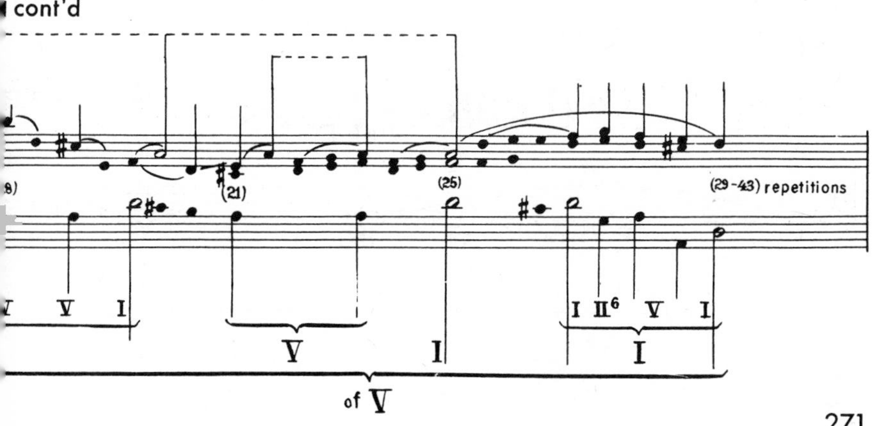

487 cont'd

488 WOLF In der Frühe

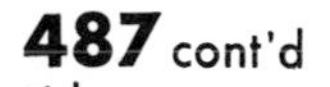

487 cont'd

cont'd

N
(56)
V

b

A
B
I II6 V I
I II6 V I
I
of V
V
of I

488 cont'd

cont'd

(11)
(14)
(16)
(18)
(22)
CS
I

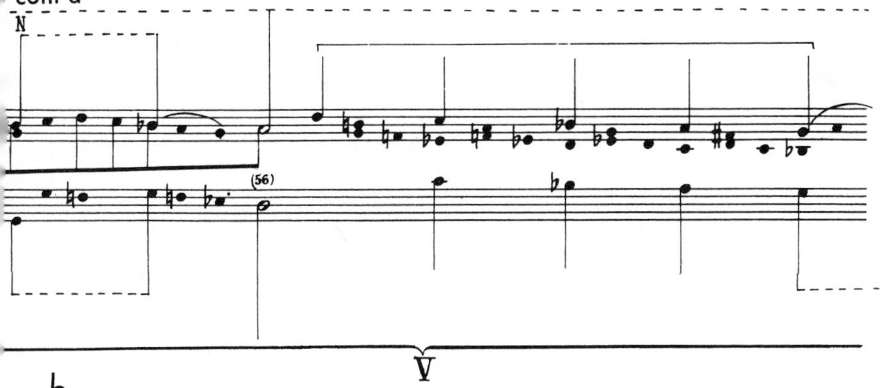

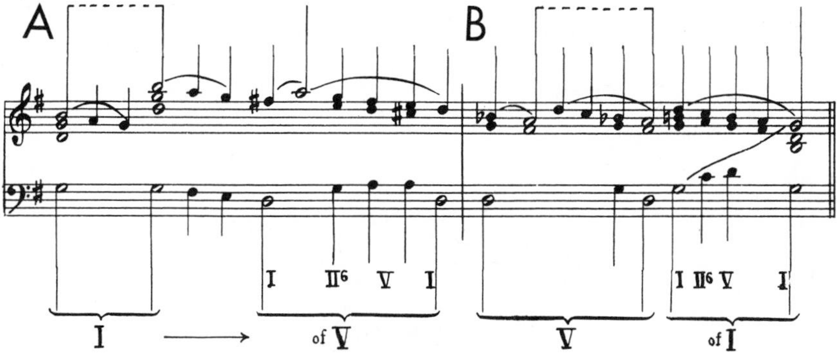

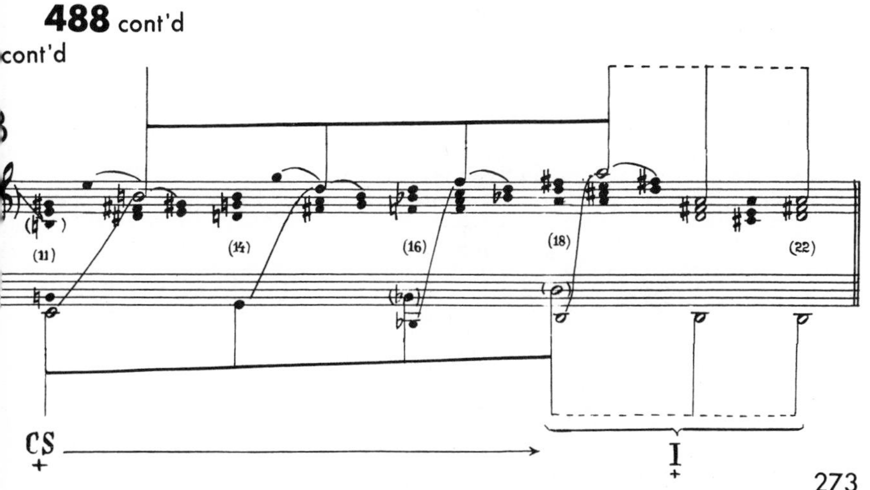

488 cont'd

b

A
B
(1)
4th
4th
(8)
(11)
(18 - 22)
I
CS
CS
I

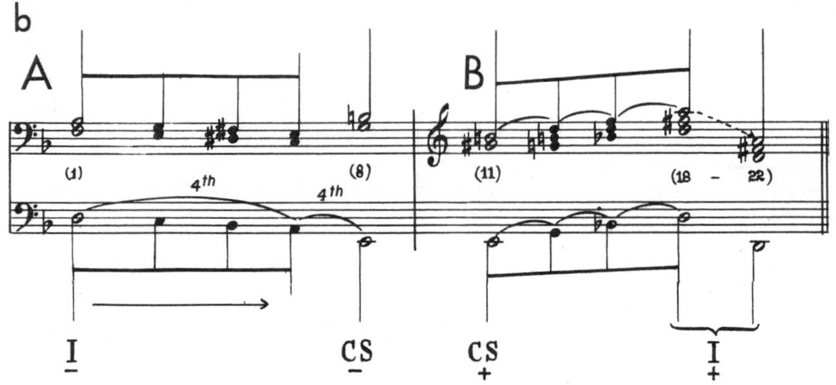

489 HINDEMITH Interludium (Ludus Tonalis)

a

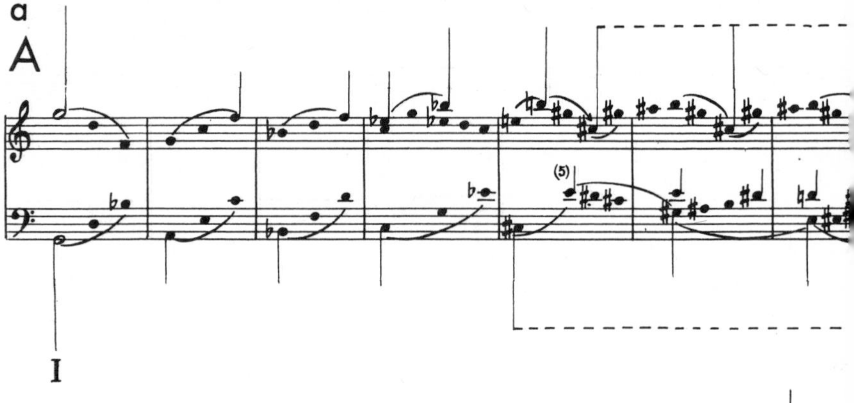

A
(5)
I

a cont'd

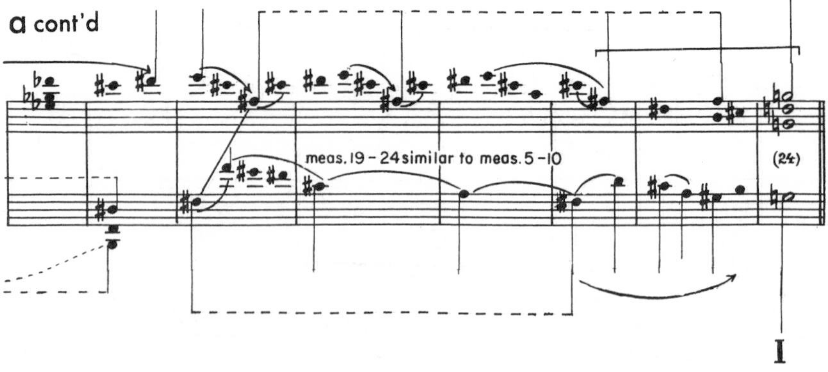

meas. 19 - 24 similar to meas. 5 - 10
(24)
I

488 cont'd

c

A
B
I
CS
CS
I
−
−
+
+

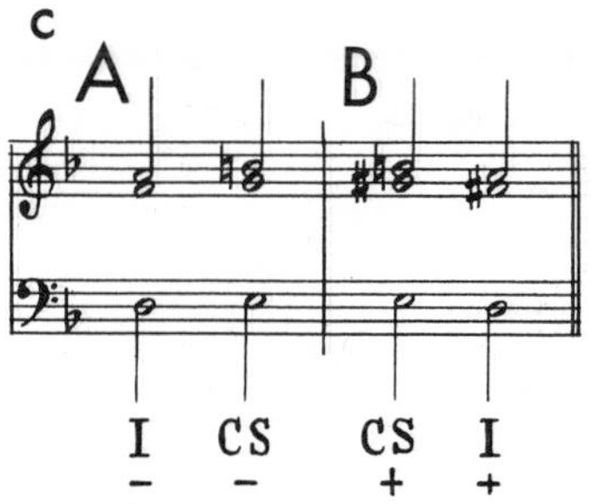

489 cont'd

cont'd

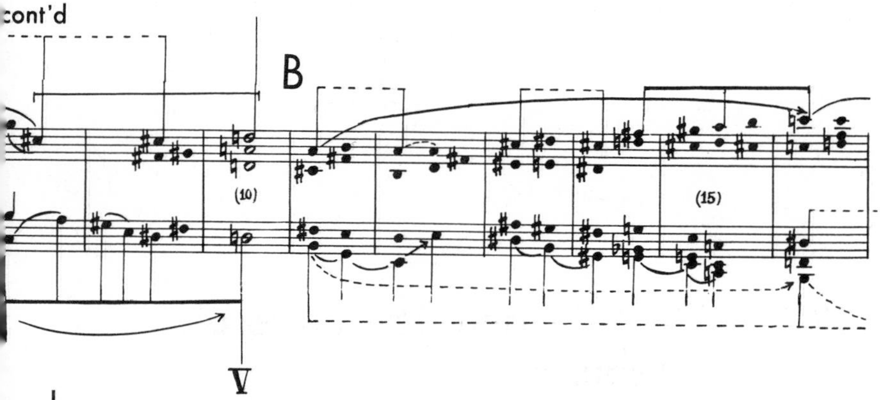

B
(10)
(15)
V

b

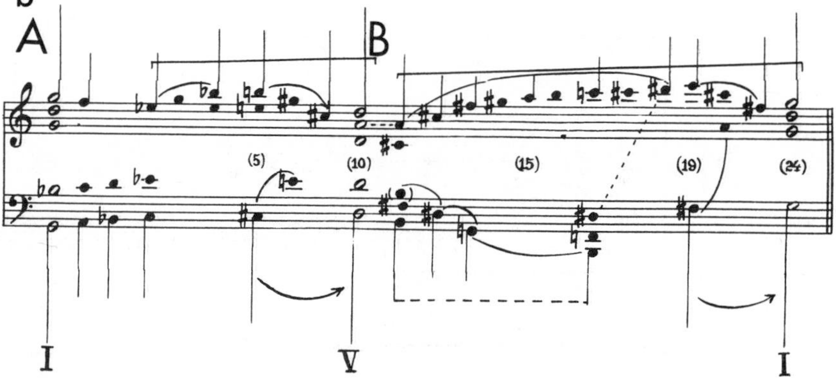

A
B
(5)
(10)
(15)
(19)
(24)
I
V
I

489 cont'd

c

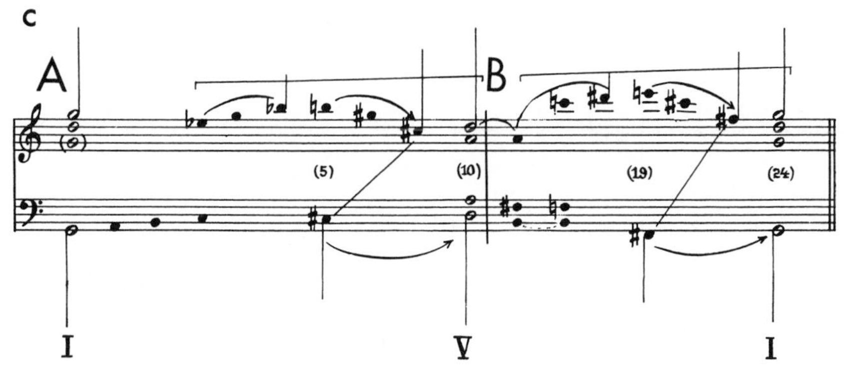

e

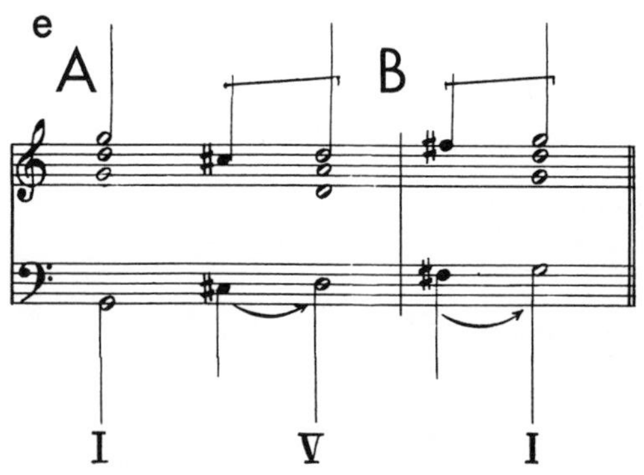

490 BYRD Pavane: The Earle of Salisbury

a

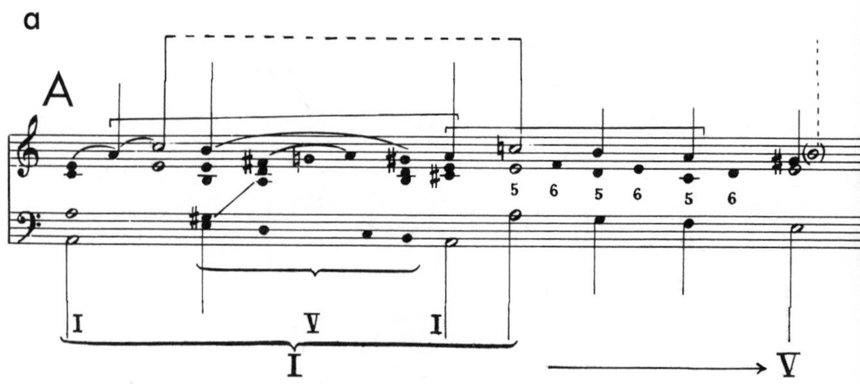

489 cont'd

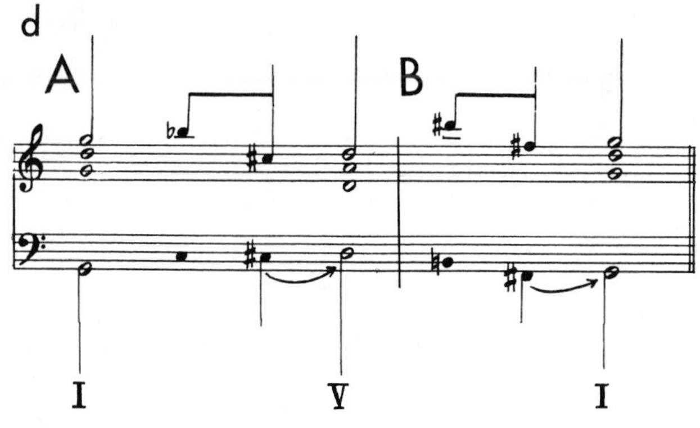

490 cont'd

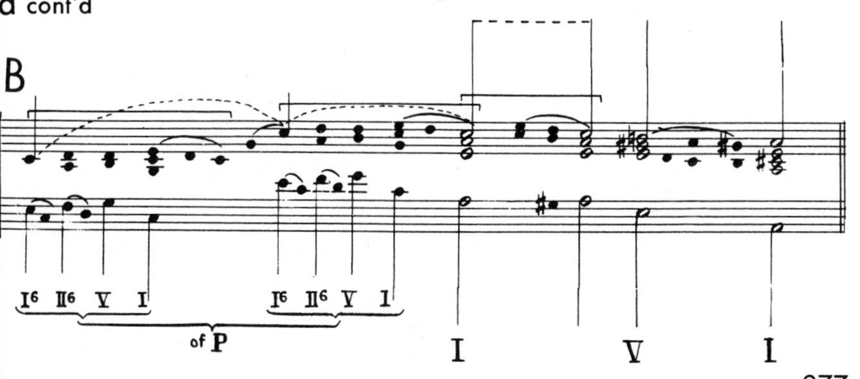

490 cont'd

b

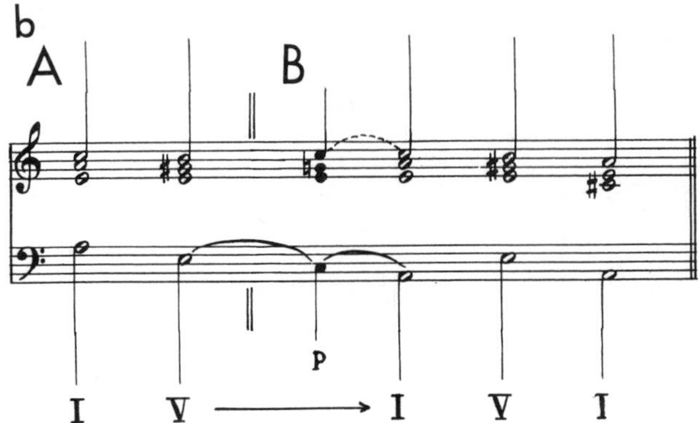

491 BEETHOVEN String Quartet, Op 18, No. 5. 3rd movement

a

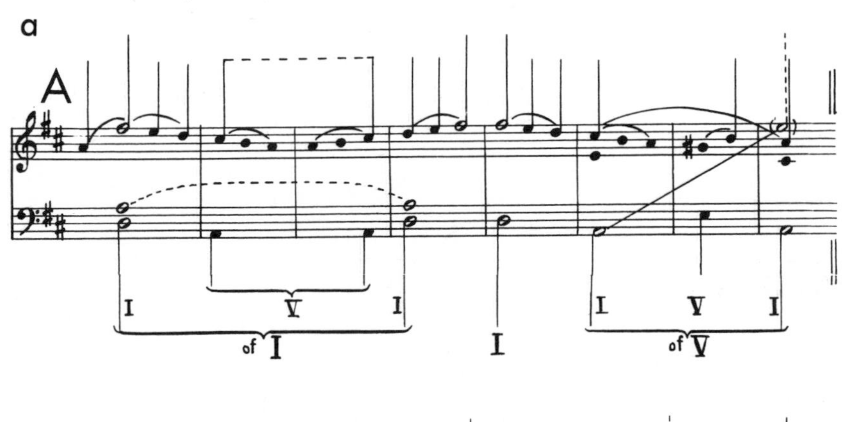

a cont'd

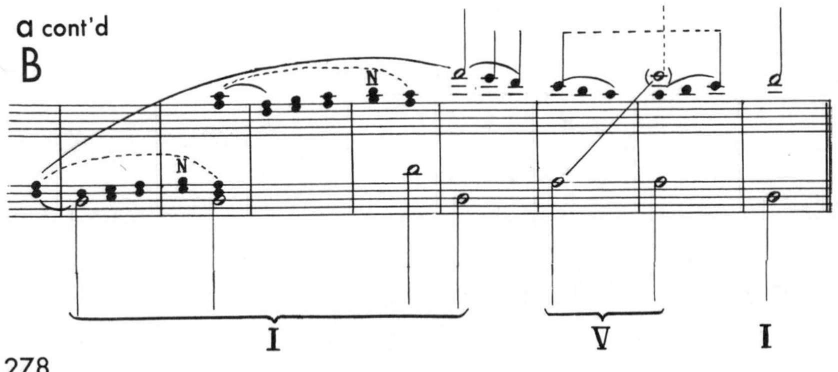

491 cont'd

b

A
B
I V I
of V
I
I
V
I

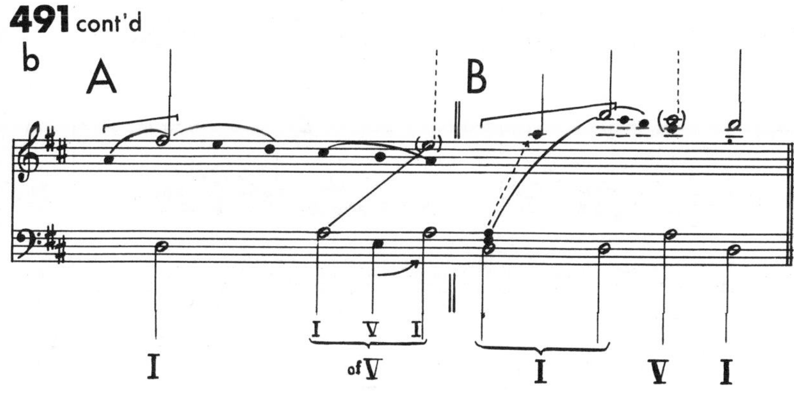

492 CHOPIN Prelude, Op 28, No. 1

a

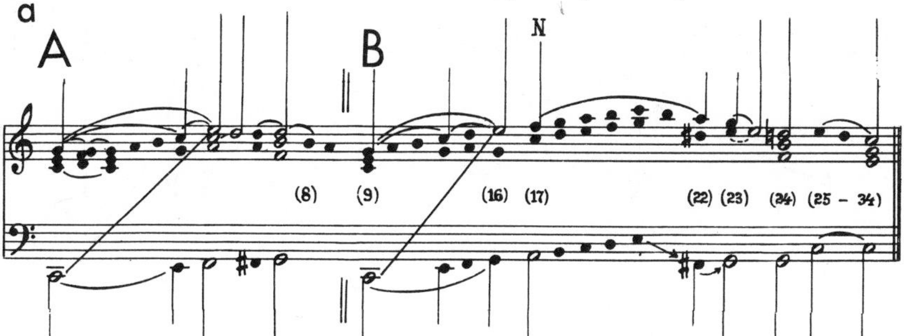

A
B
N
(8) (9) (16) (17) (22) (23) (24) (25 – 34)
I
II 6/5
V
I
IV6 DF
V
I

b

A
B
N
I
II 6/5
V
I
IV6 DF
V
I

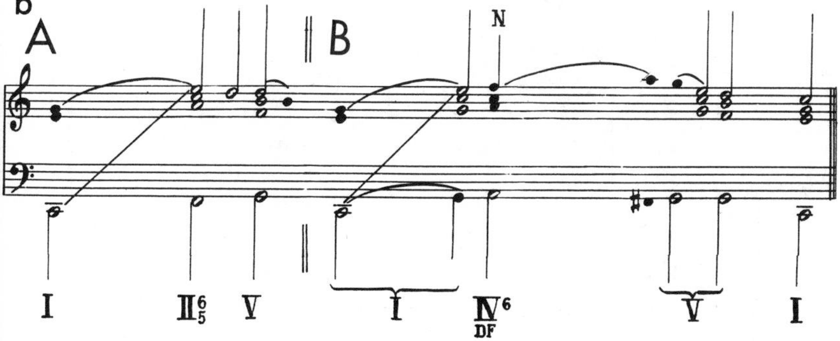

493 BACH Little Prelude, G minor

a

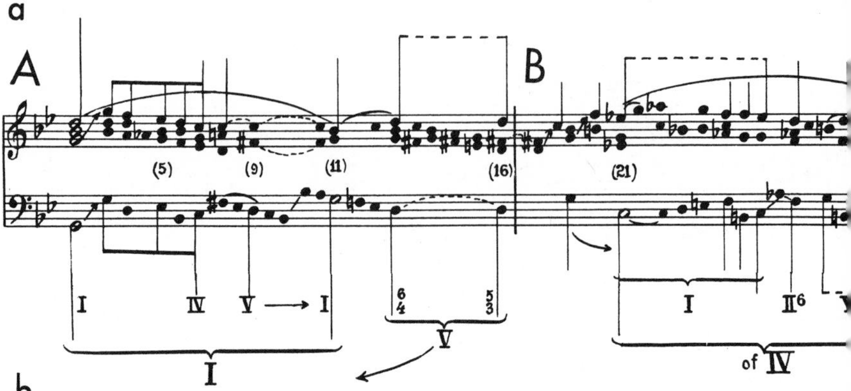

A
B
(5)
(9)
(11)
(16)
(21)
I
IV
V → I
6 4
5 3
V
I
I
II6
of IV

b

A
B
8
5 6 5
V
I
IV
V
I II6 V I

494 BRAHMS Waltz, Op 39, No. 8

a

N
A
B
(1)
(12)
(13 – 15)
(27)
V
I
III
M
(DF)
V
I

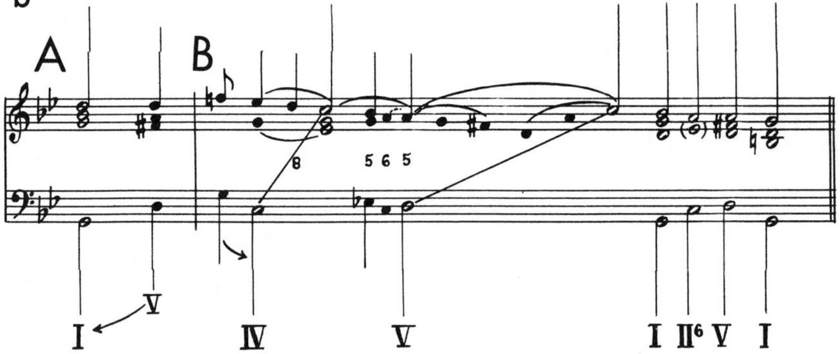

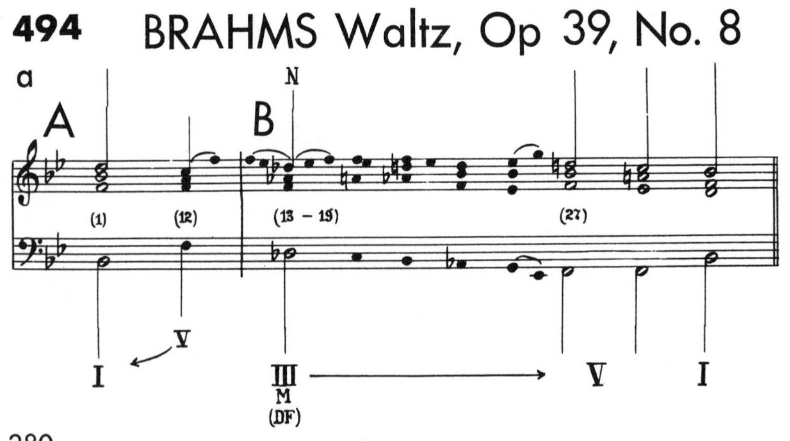

493 cont'd

ont'd

5
6
5
(35)
(39)
(42)
V
I II6 V I

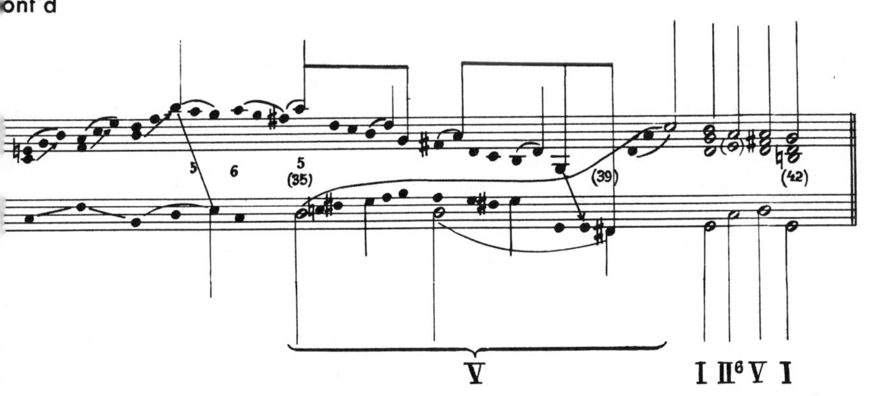

495 BACH Minuet 2 (Partita No. 1)

a

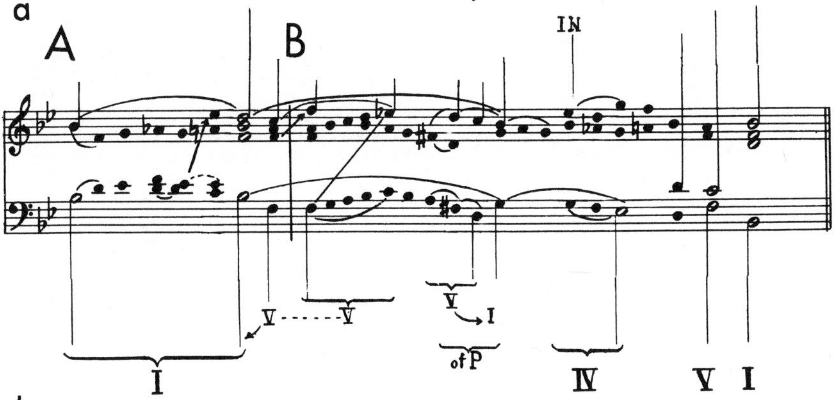

A
B
IN
V
V
V
I
of P
I
IV
V I

b

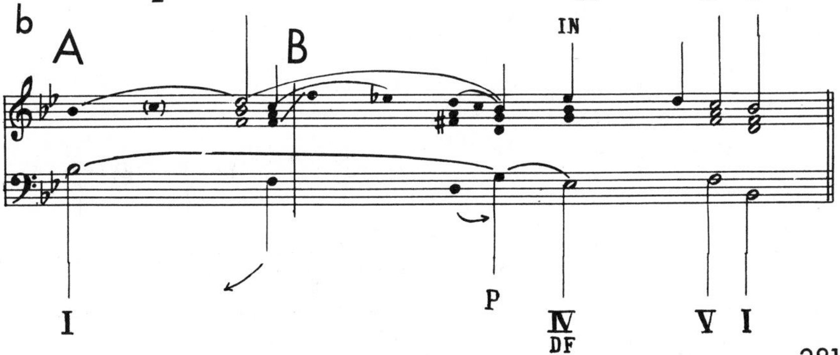

A
B
IN
P
I
IV
DF
V I

496

a

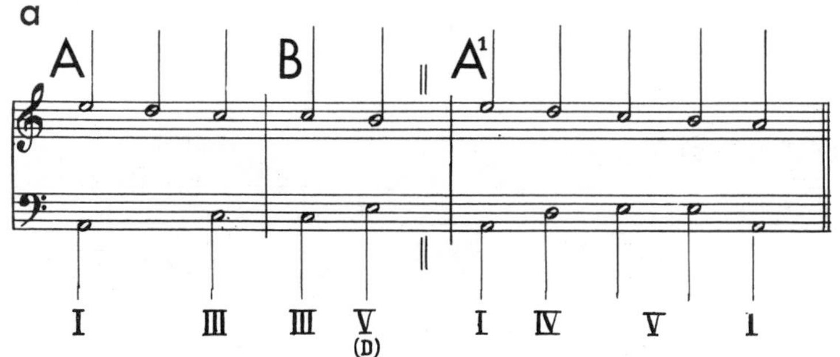

497 SCHUBERT Symphony, B minor. 1st movement

a

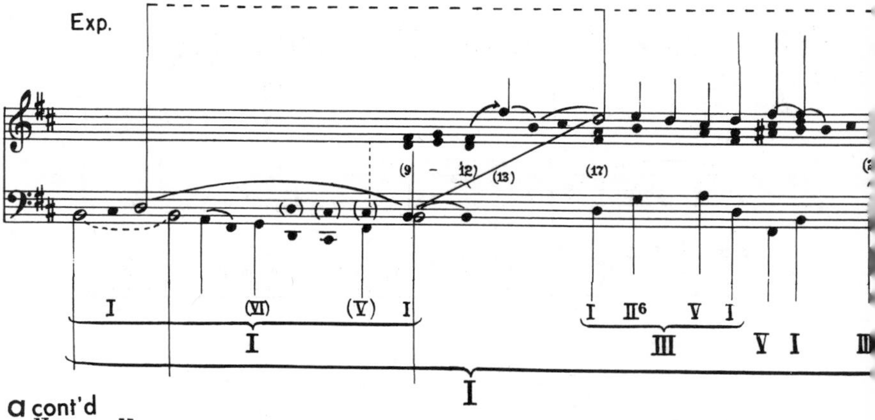

Exp.

(9 - 12) (13) (17)

I (VI) (V) I

I

I II6 V I

III

V I III

I

a cont'd

N N

(63) (74) 5 6 5 6 5

II

I N P I → IV V

!

V

VI

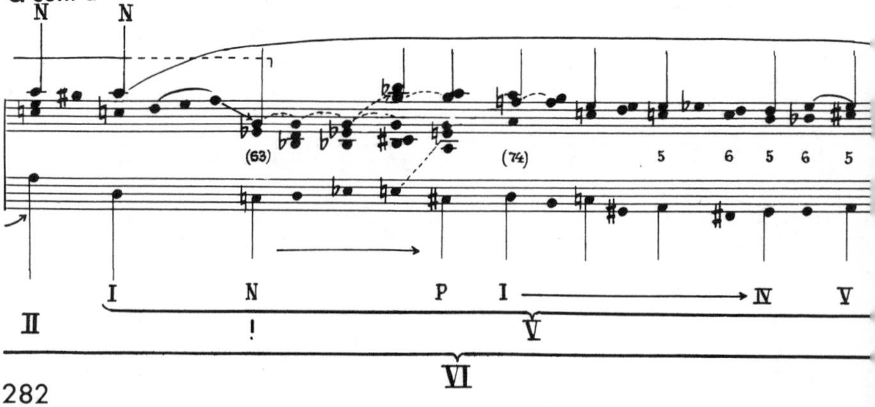

496 cont'd

b

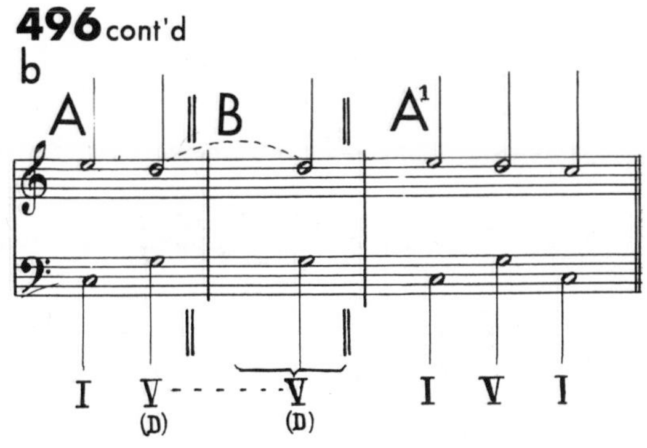

497 cont'd

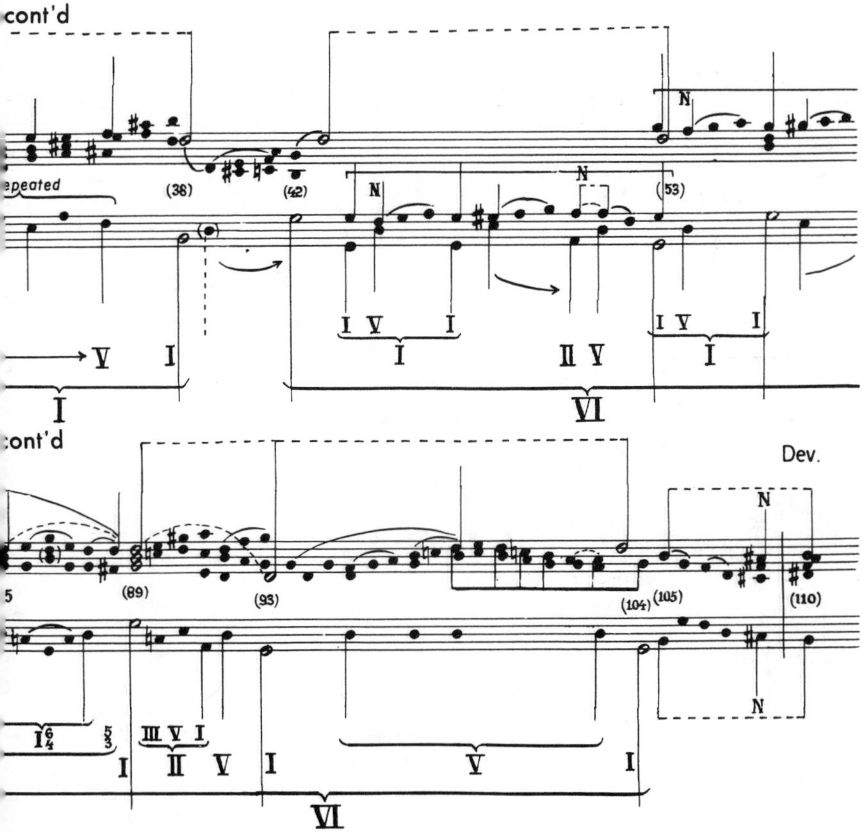

cont'd

repeated

(38) (42) (53)

N N N

I V I

I

V I

I

II V

I V I

I

VI

cont'd

Dev.

5 (89) (93) (104) (105) (110)

N

N

I^6_4 $^5_3$

III V I

I II V I V I

VI

497 cont'd
a cont'd
Dev.
IN
(110)
(114)
(124)
I
of Em
a cont'd
N
IN
(180)
(184)
N
(195)
(209
6
6
6
4
6
anticip.
N
P
I6
of Em
V
a cont'd
N N
(250 (252)
(256-271) (272)
(279)
V
I
II V
(I)
I N
III
!
of V
I

497 cont'd

cont'd
N
(134)
(146)
5
(158)
5
(166)
5
(170)
V
I
of I
of Em
cont'd
ec.
8)
(226)
(231)
(235)
(240)
repeated
V
II6 V I
of P
P
P
V
IV
V I
of P
P
I
to C#
I
ont'd
(292)
(303)
N
N
(306)
(307)
(310)
Coda
I
IV
V
I 6 4
5 3
of V
III V I
I
I
II
V
+
−
I

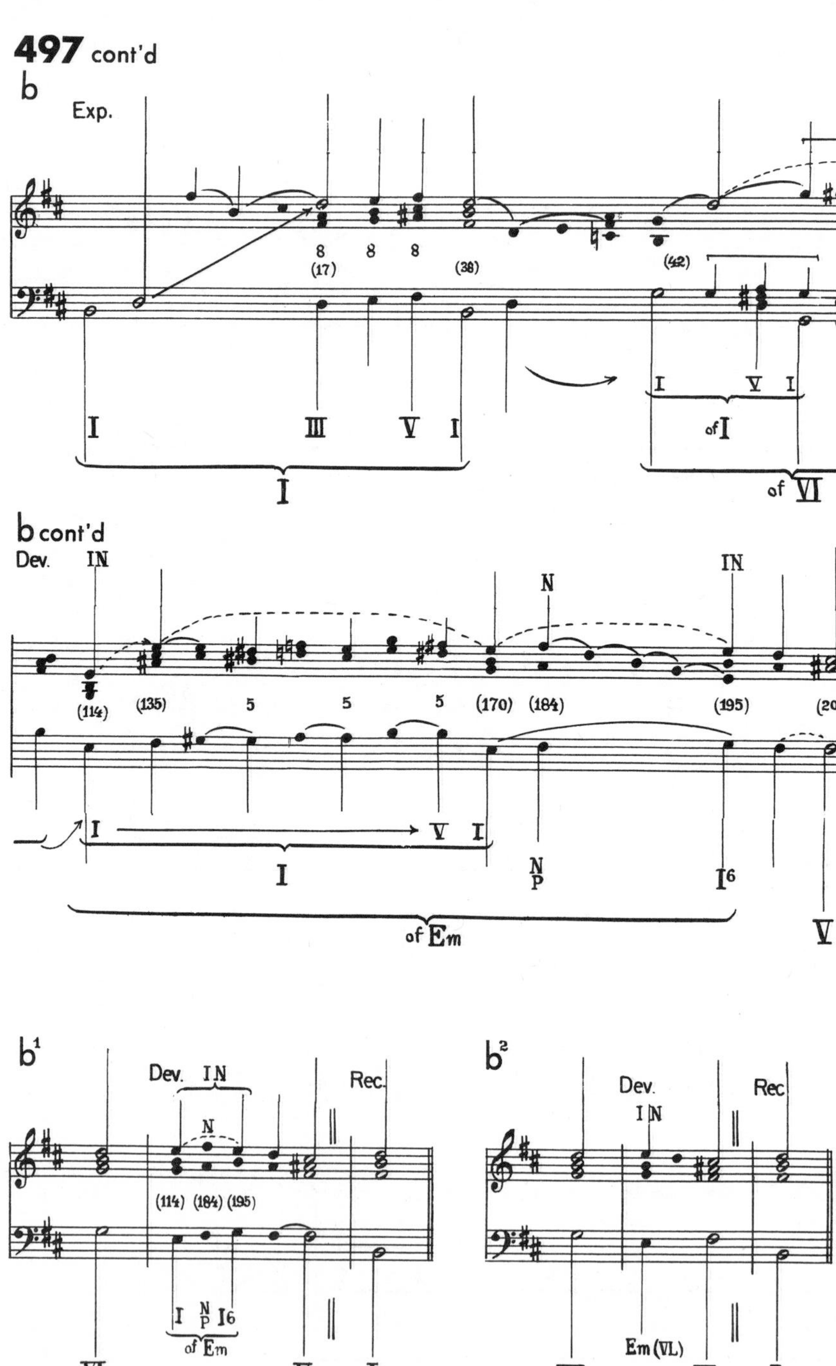
497 cont'd
b
Exp.
8 8 8
(17)
(38)
(42)
I III V I
I
I V I
of I
of VI
b cont'd
Dev.
IN
N
IN
(114) (135) 5 5 5 (170) (184) (195) (209)
I V I
I
N
P
I6
of Em
V
b1
Dev. IN
N
Rec.
(114) (184) (195)
I N P I6
of Em
VI V I
b2
Dev.
IN
Rec.
Em (VL)
VI V I

497 cont'd

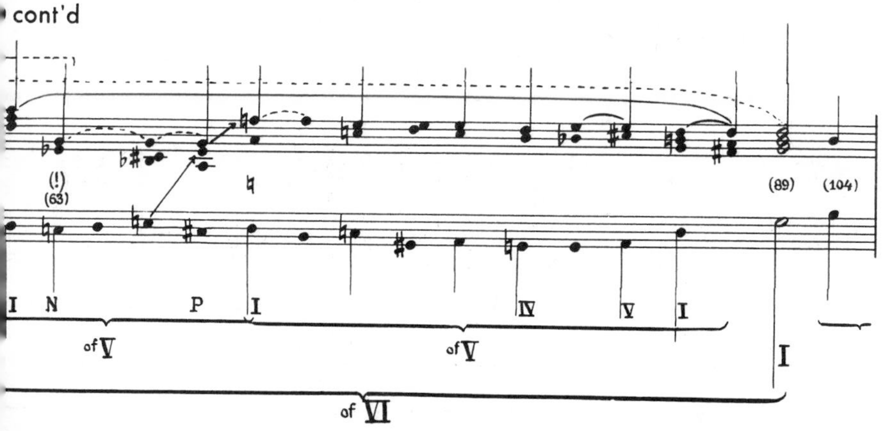
cont'd
(!)
(63)
(89)
(104)
I N P I IV V I
of V
of V
I
of VI

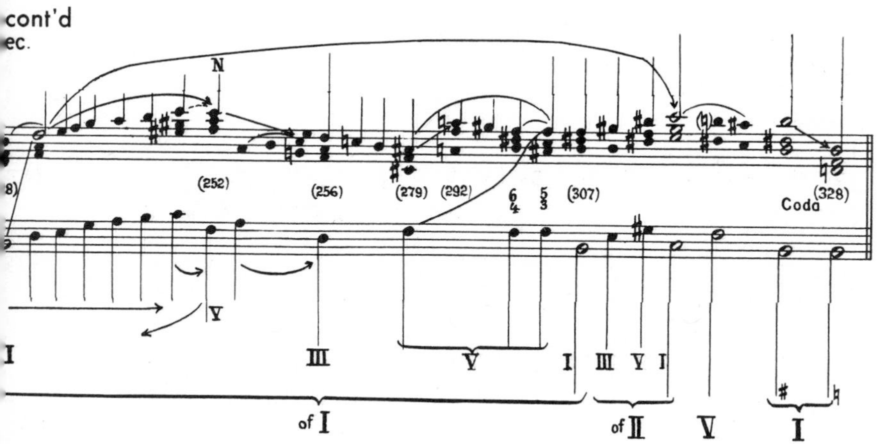
cont'd
ec.
N
(252)
(256)
(279)
(292)
6 4
5 3
(307)
Coda
(328)
V
I
III
V
I III V I
of I
of II
V
I

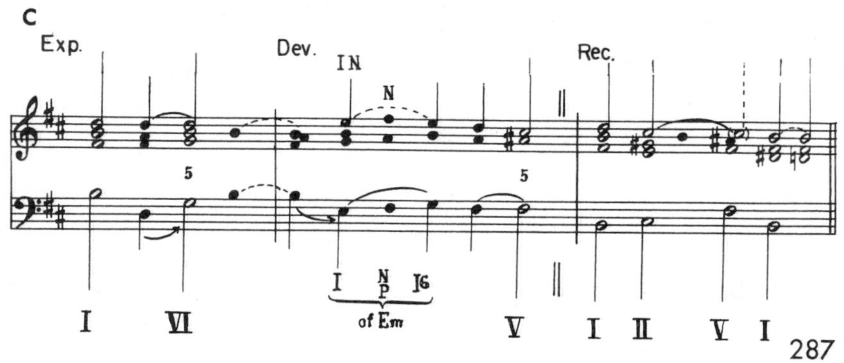
C
Exp.
Dev.
Rec.
I N
N
5
5
I N P I6
of Em
I VI V I II V I

498 RAVEL Sonatina. 1st movement

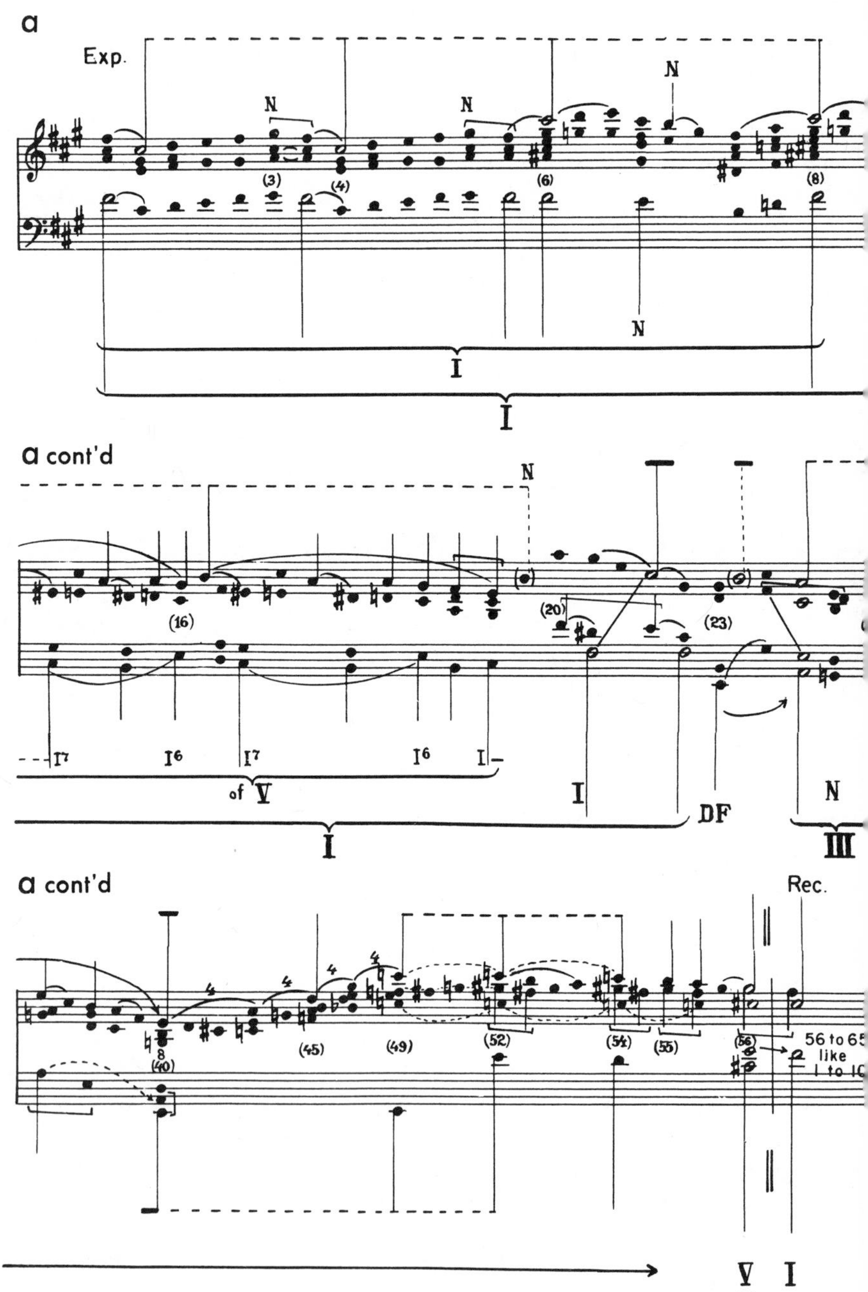

498 cont'd

cont'd
N
N
N
N
(10)
(11)
(13)
I7+
of P
of V
I
cont'd
Dev.
to E meas. 40
26)
(28)
(31)
(34)
8
to E meas 40
cont'd
(66)
(68)
(74)
(75)
(78)
(78) Coda
I7-
I7
I6
I
CS
CS
V
I

498 cont'd

b

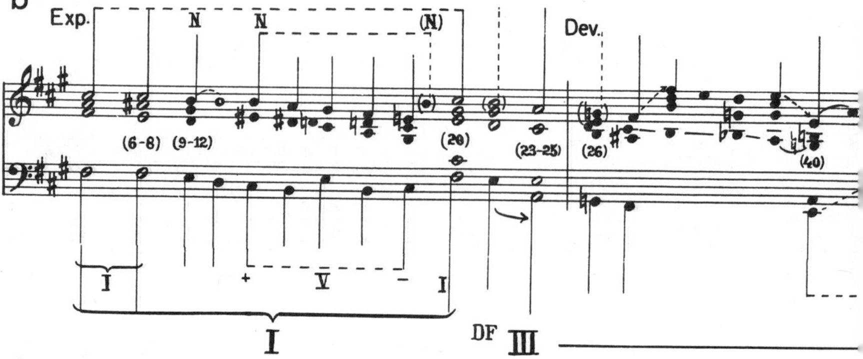

Exp.
N
N
(N)
Dev.
(6-8) (9-12)
(20)
(23-25)
(26)
(40)
I
+ V − I
I
DF III

c

A
N
B
A1
8
(8) 8 8 7 6 6 5 5
I V I
I
III
V
I CS CS V I

500 CHOPIN Nocturne, Op 9, No. 2

a

A
B
IN
5 6 5 (6)
N N
I
II
V
I
I
of I
of V

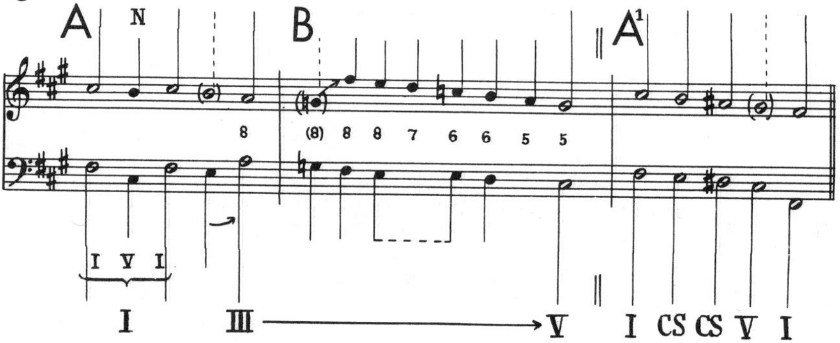

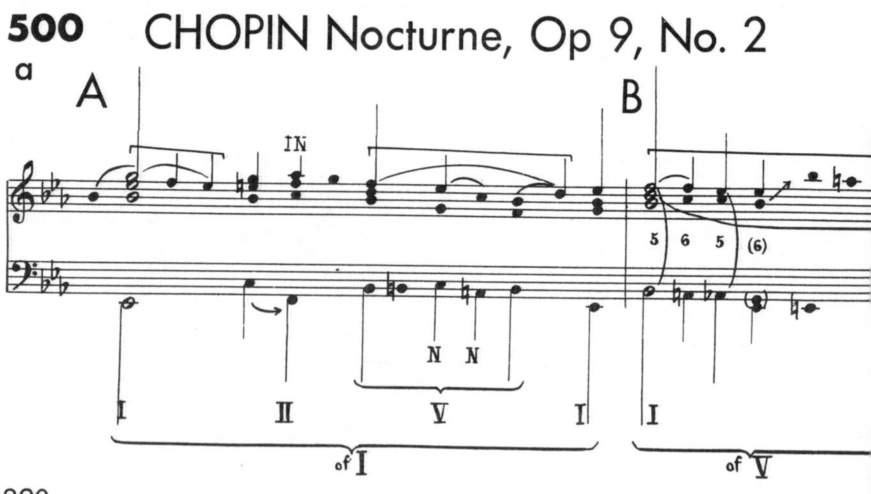

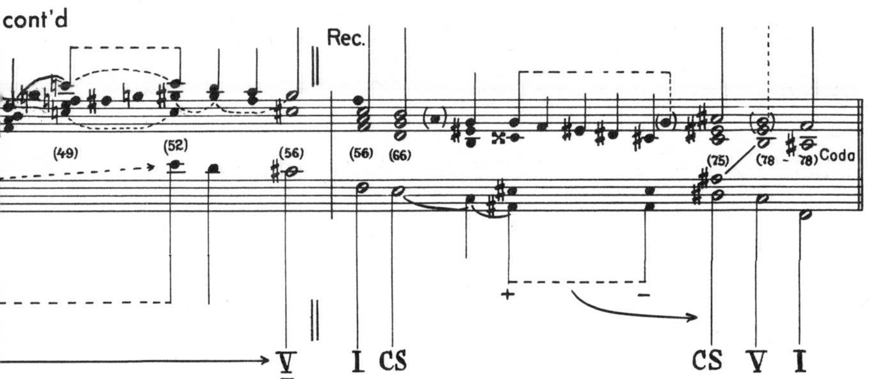

499 CHOPIN Mazurka, Op 17, No. 2

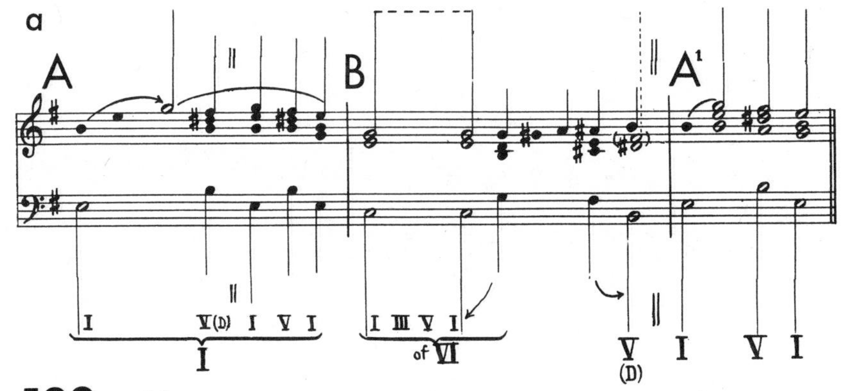

500 cont'd

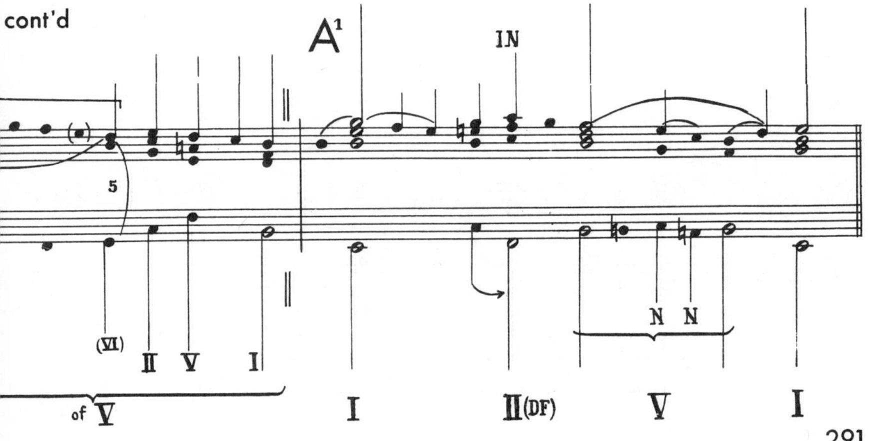

500 cont'd

b

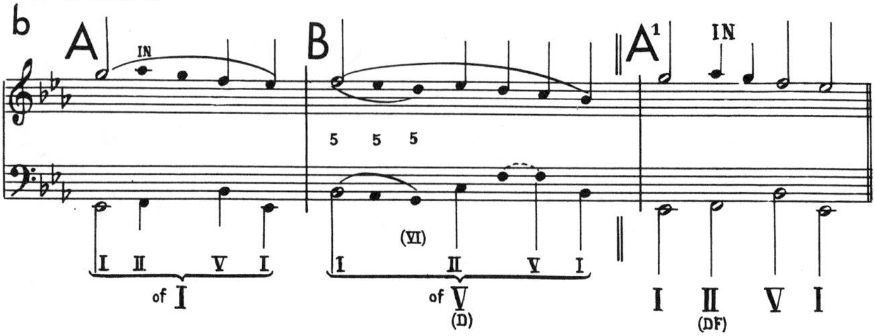

A IN

B

A[1] IN

5 5 5

(VI)

I II V I

of I

I II V I

of V (D)

I II V I

(DF)

501 cont'd

a cont'd

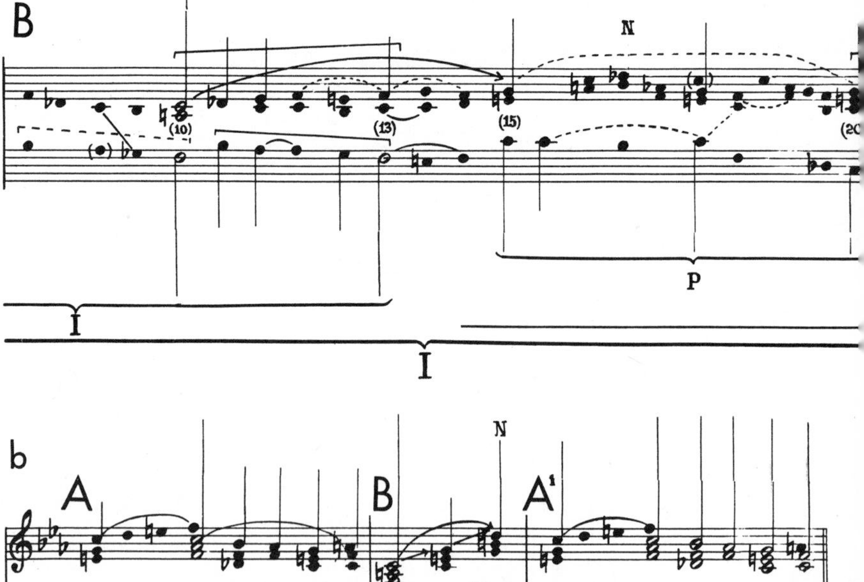

B

(10) (13) (15) (20

N

P

I

I

b

A B A[1]

N

5th 5th

V I IV V I

P

I

II(M) V I

I

IV V I

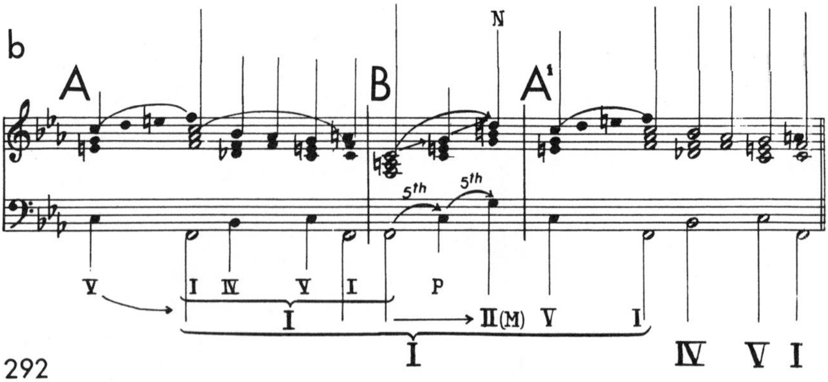

501 MONTEVERDI Madrigal: Lasciatemi morire

a

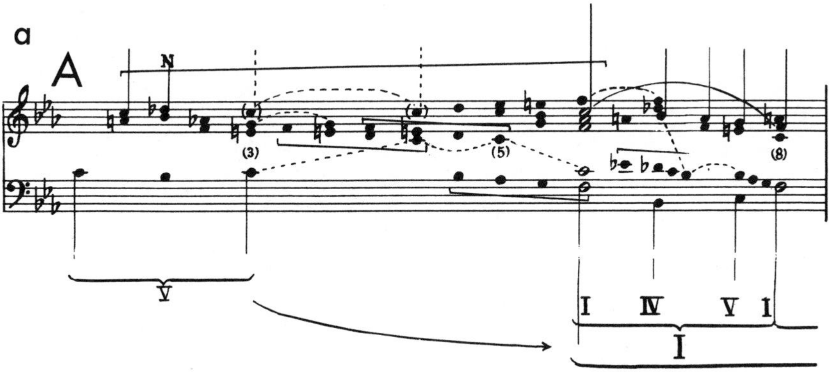

A
N
(3)
(5)
(8)
V
I
IV
V
I
I

cont'd

N
A¹
N
(24)
(26)
(27)
(34)
P
II(M)
V
I
I
IV
V
I

c

N
I
II(M)
V
I
I
IV
V
I

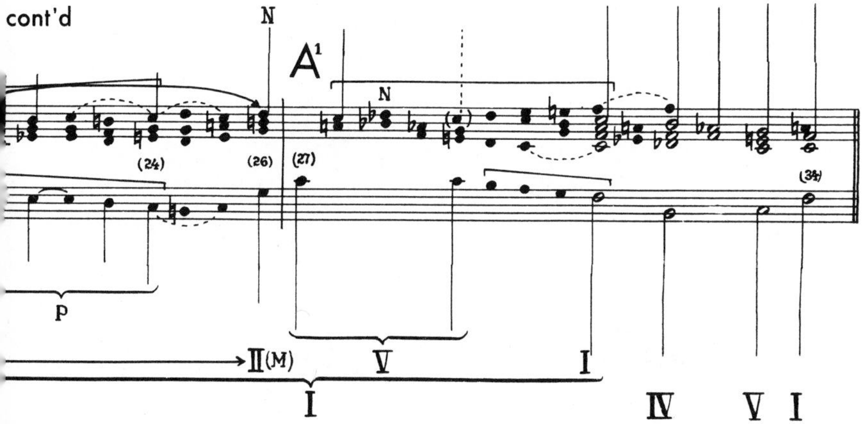

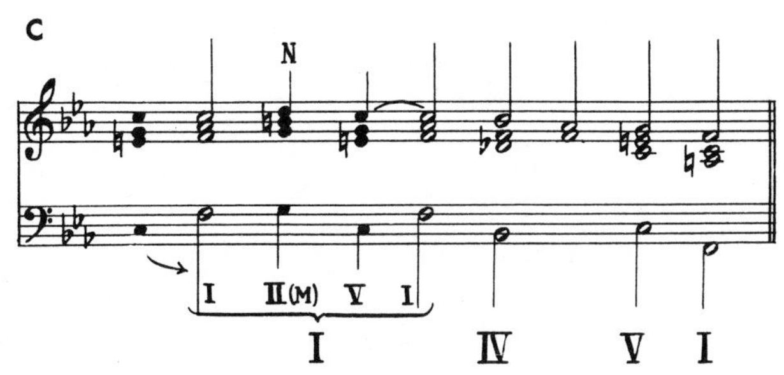

SCHUBERT Moment Musical No. 2

a

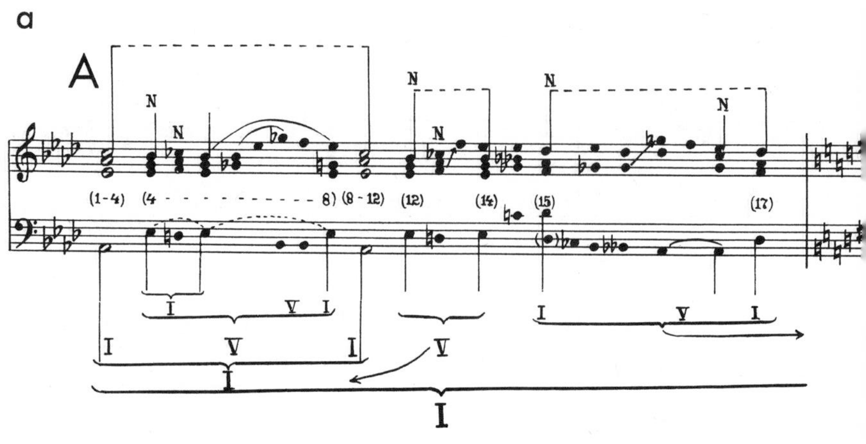

a cont'd

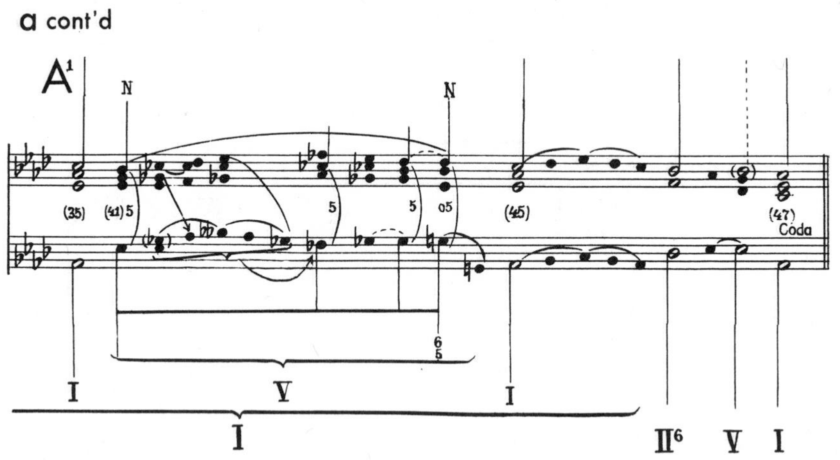

502 cont'd

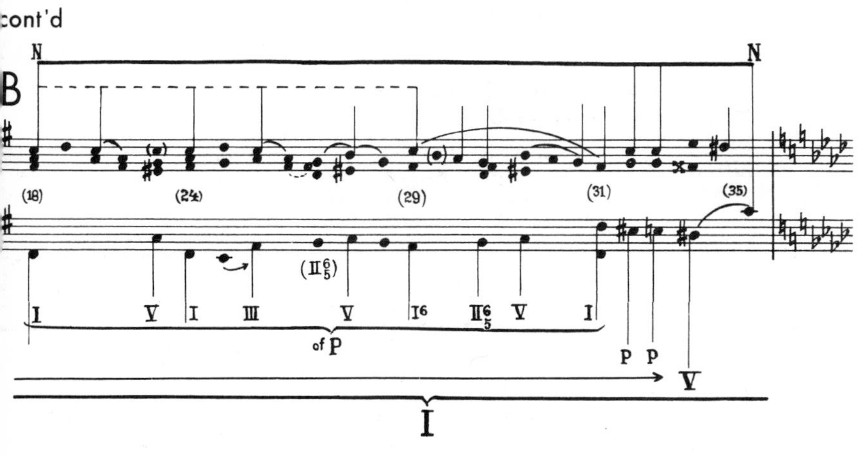
cont'd
N
N
B
(18)
(24)
(29)
(31)
(35)
(II 6 5)
I
V
I
III
V
I6
II 6 5
V
I
of P
P
P
V
I

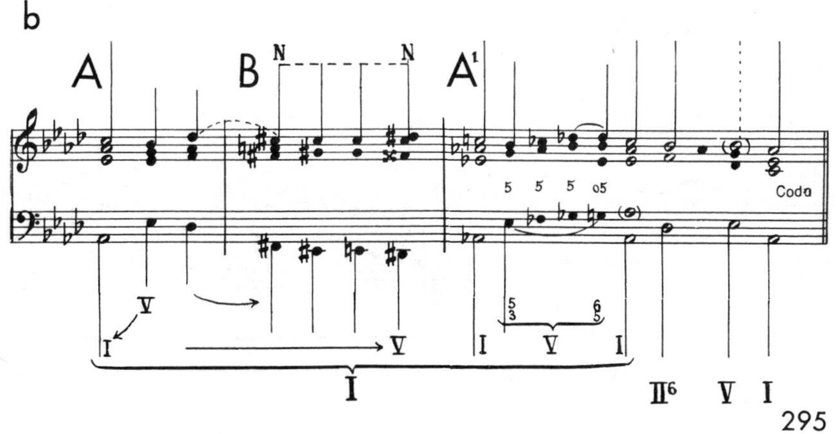
b
A
B
N
N
A1
5
5
5
05
Coda
V
I
V
5 3
6 5
I
V
I
I
II6
V
I

503 BRAHMS Symphony No. 3. 1st movement

a

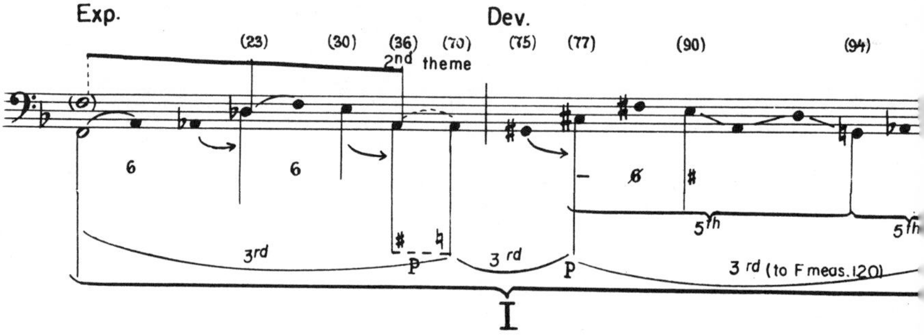

Exp. (23) (30) (36) (70) Dev. (75) (77) (90) (94)

2nd theme

3rd — P — 3 rd — P — 3 rd (to F meas. 120)

5th 5th

I

a cont'd

(119) Rec. (120-136) (140-142) (143) (149 - - 181) (183 - - 187) (195-199) (209-224)

2nd theme

VI V I

VI M V $\frac{6}{4}$ $\frac{5}{3}$ $\frac{7}{5}$ I

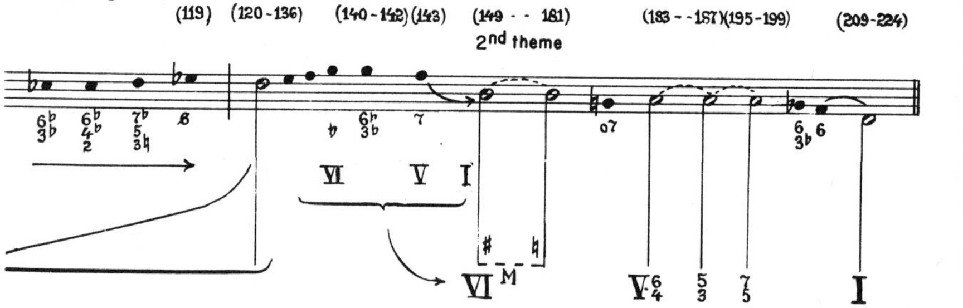

504 BARTÓK Bourrée (Mikrokosmos, Bk IV)

a

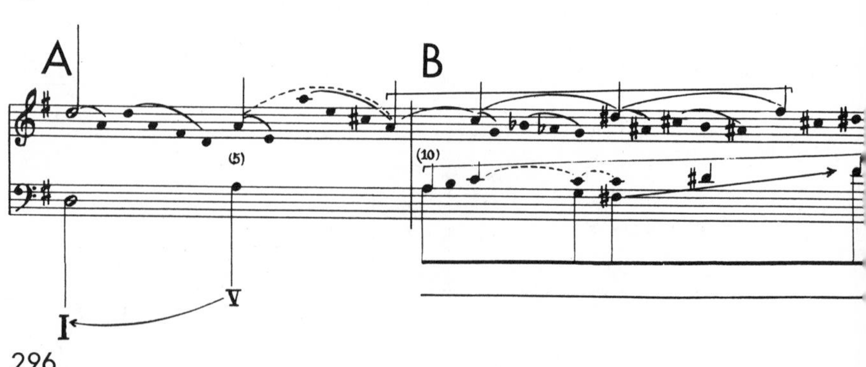

503 cont'd

a cont'd

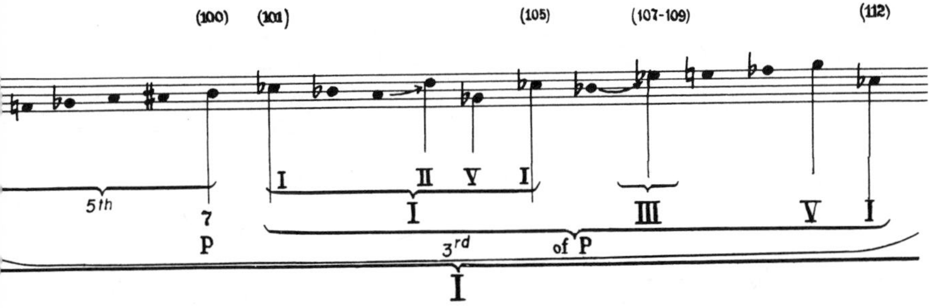

b

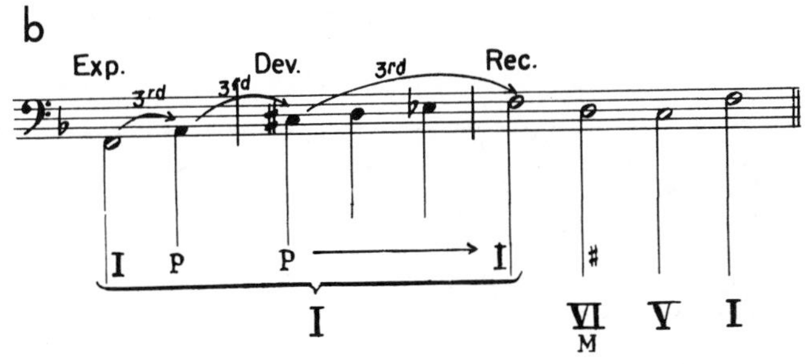

504 cont'd

a cont'd

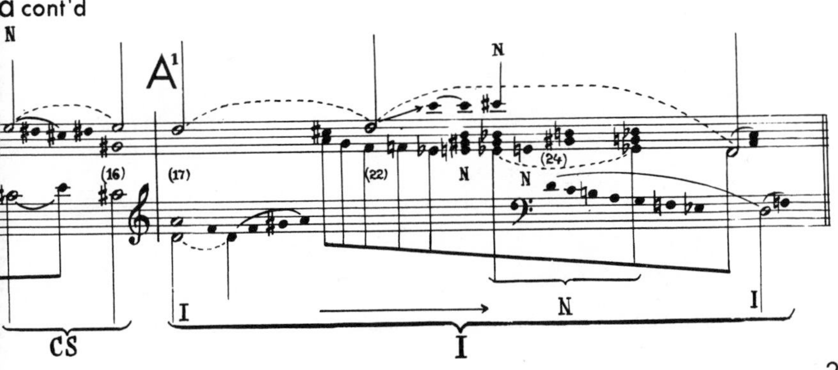

504 cont'd

b

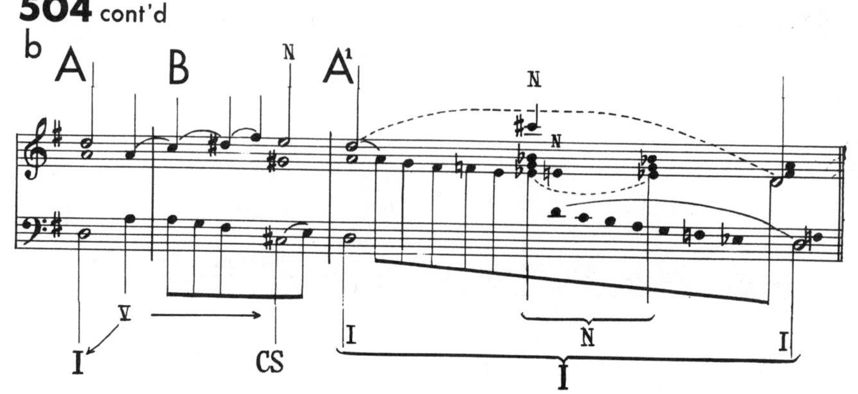

505 HINDEMITH Piano Sonata No. 2 1st movement

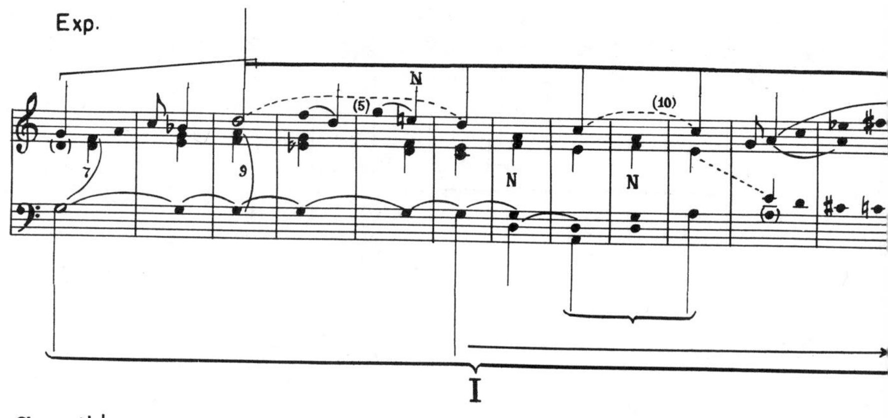

a cont'd

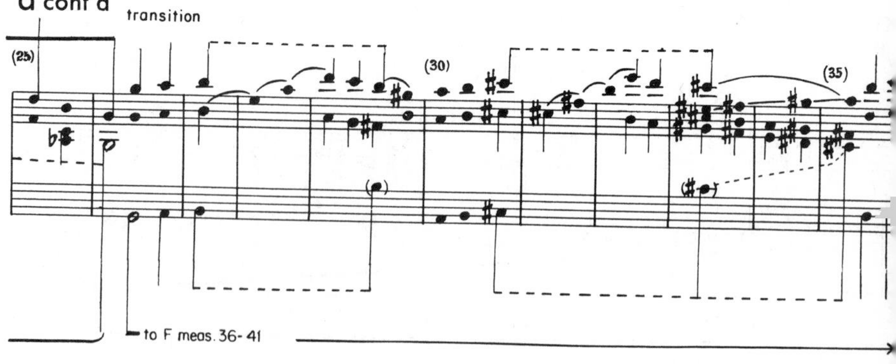

504 cont'd

C

N
N
#and♮
V
N
I
CS
I

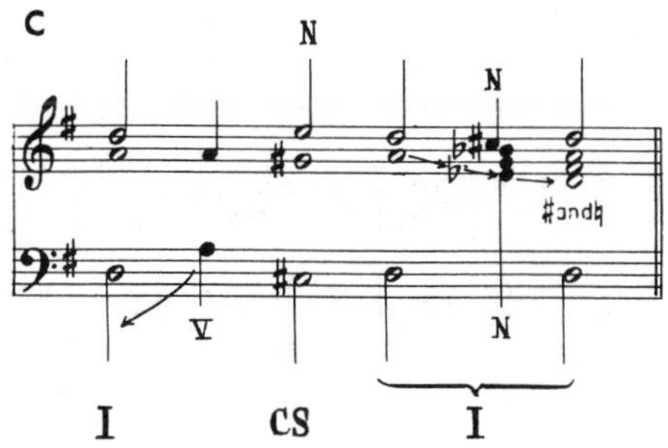

505 cont'd

cont'd

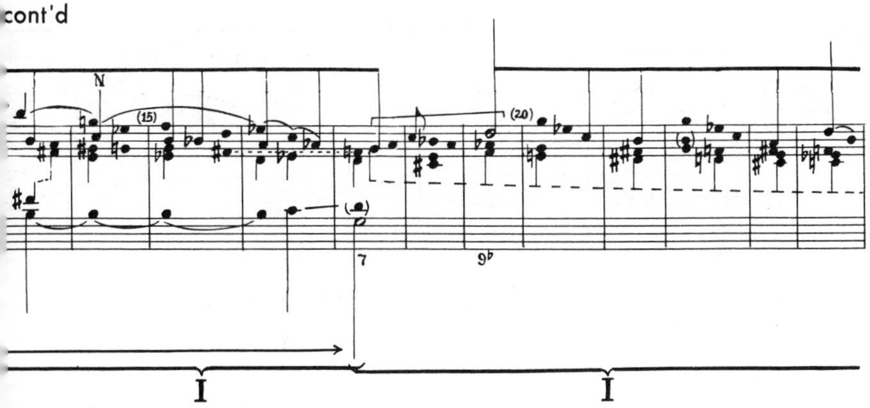

N
(15)
(20)
7
9♭
I
I

cont'd

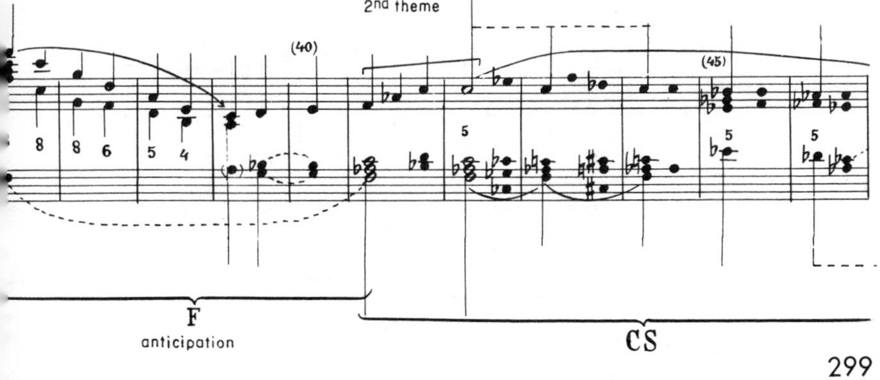

2nd theme
(40)
(45)
8
8
6
5
4
5
5
5
F
anticipation
CS

505 cont'd

a cont'd

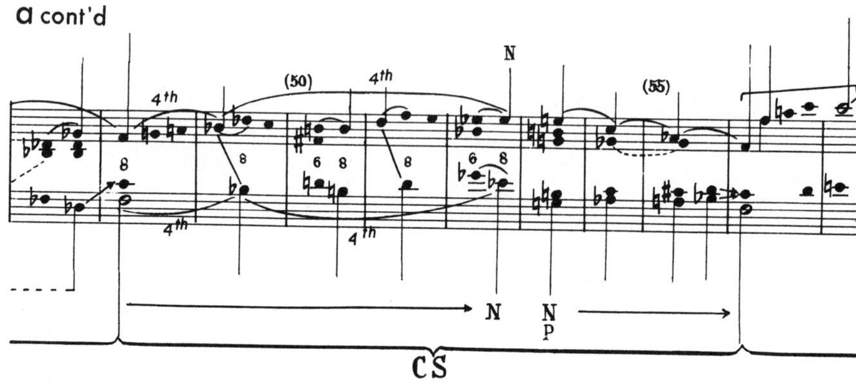

a cont'd

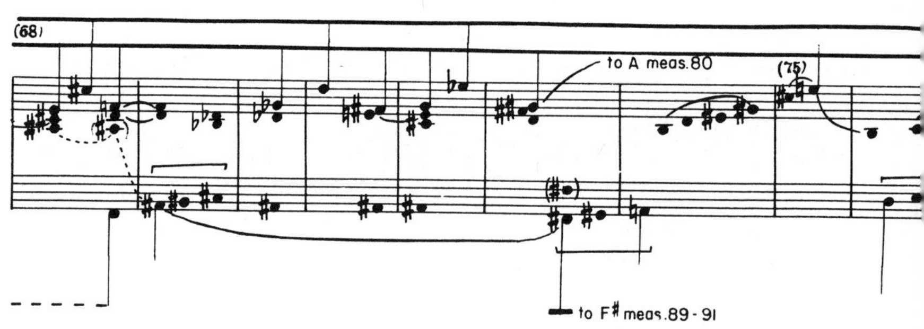

a cont'd

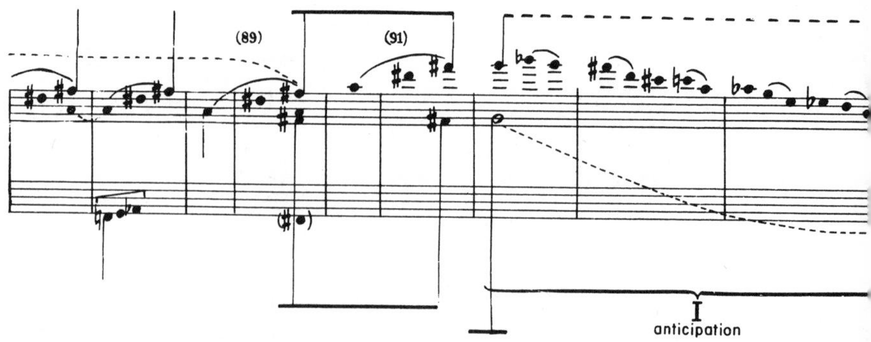

505 cont'd

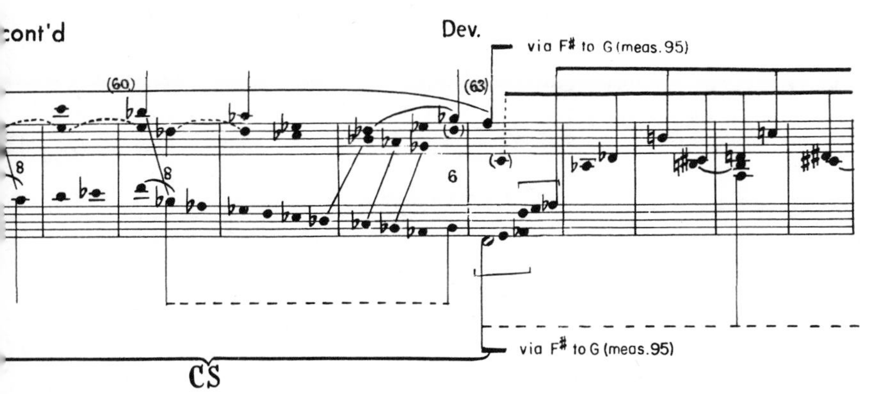
cont'd
Dev.
via F# to G (meas. 95)
(60)
(63)
8
8
6
via F# to G (meas. 95)
CS

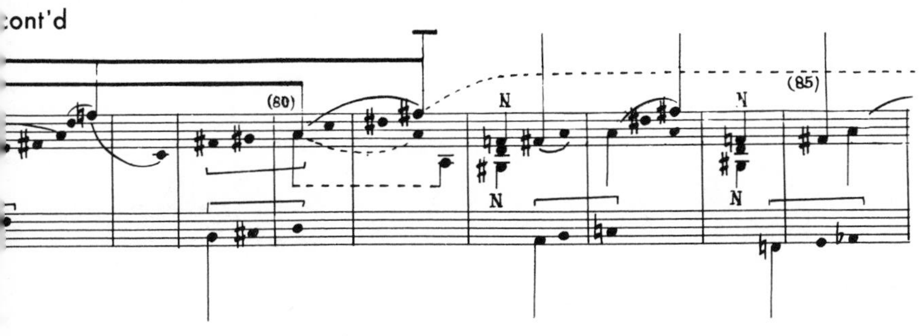
cont'd
(80)
N
N
N
N
(85)

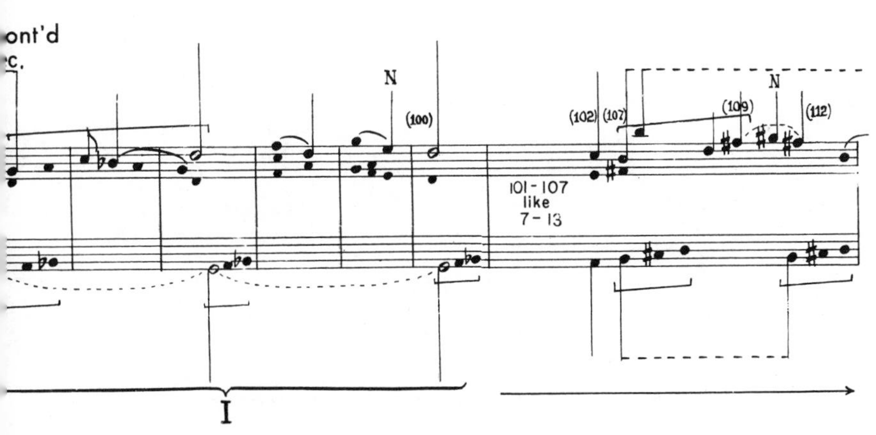
ont'd
c.
N
(100)
(102)
(107)
(109)
N
(112)
101 - 107
like
7 - 13
I

505 cont'd

a cont'd

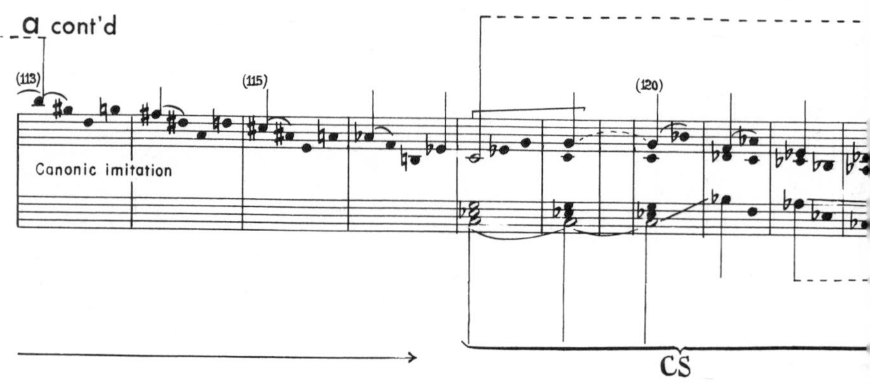

a cont'd

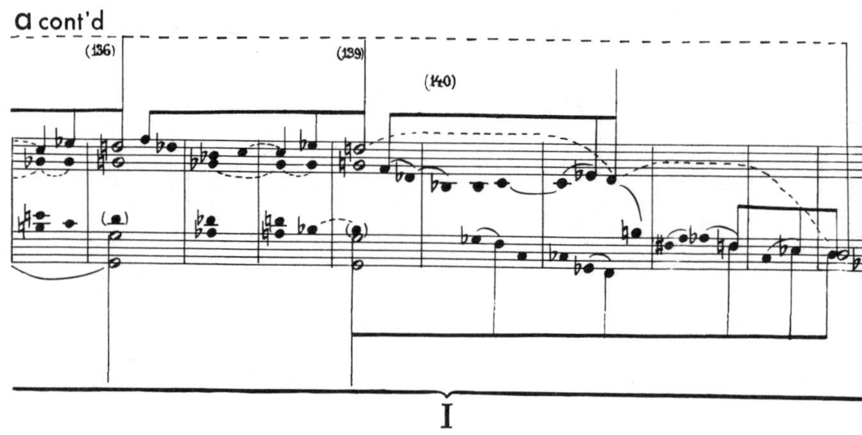

b

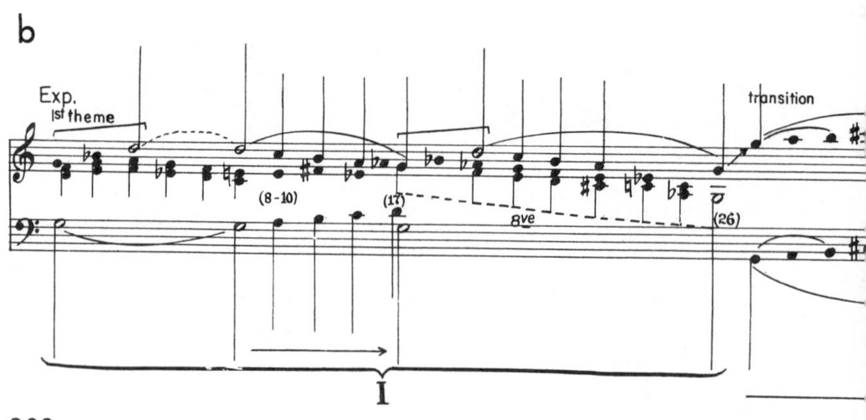

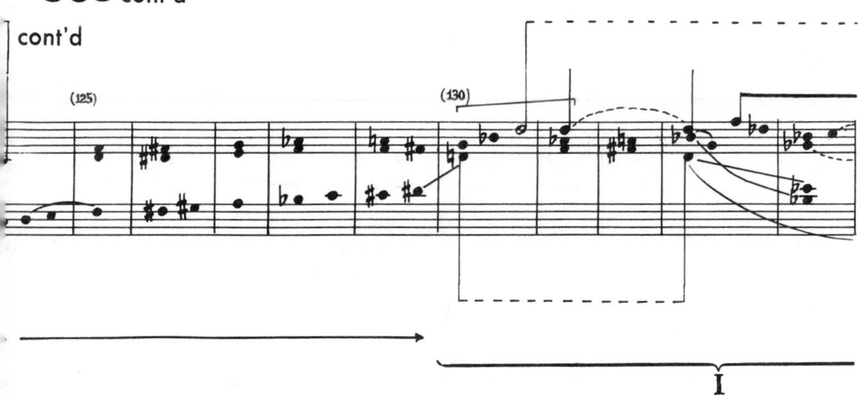

cont'd
(125)
(130)
I

cont'd
(150)
(155)
I

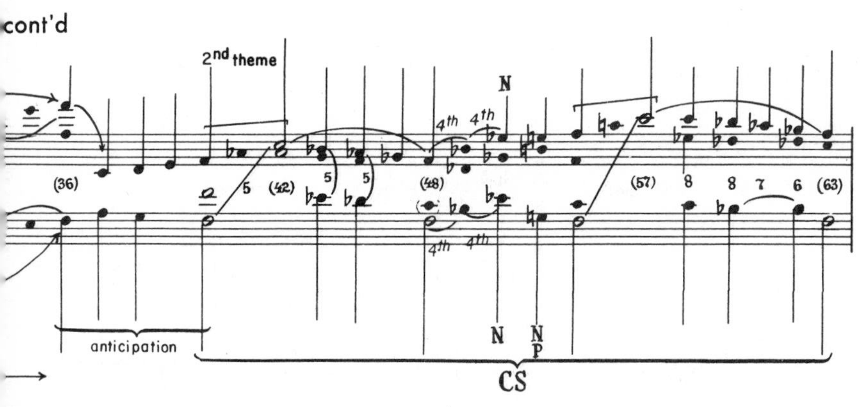

cont'd
2nd theme
N
(36)
5
(42)
5
5
(48)
4th
4th
(57)
8
8
7
6
(63)
anticipation
N
N
P
CS

505 cont'd

b cont'd

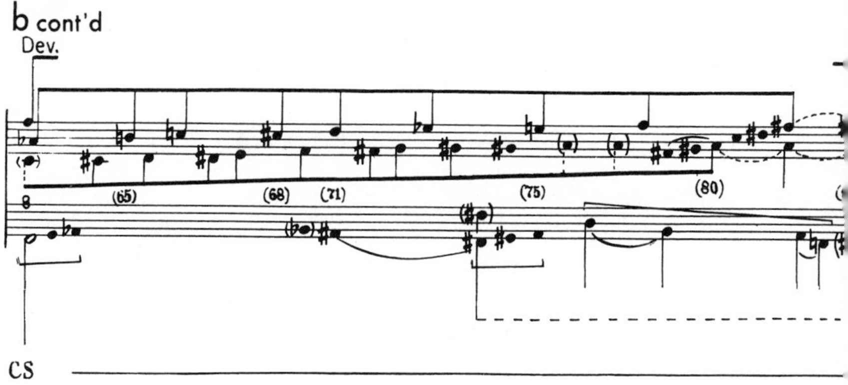

c

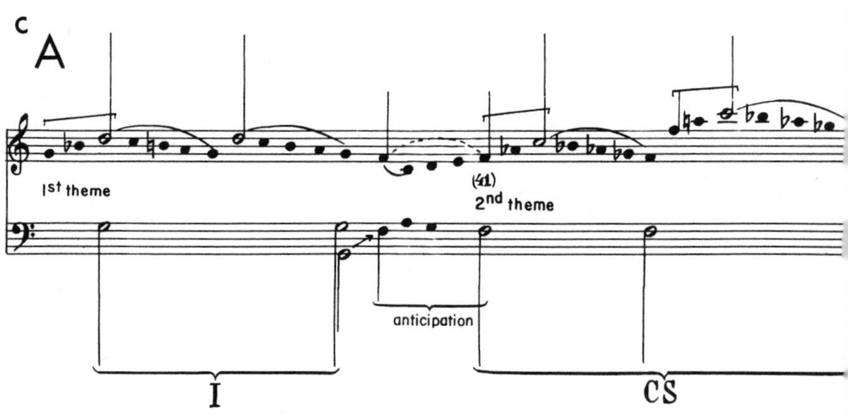

d

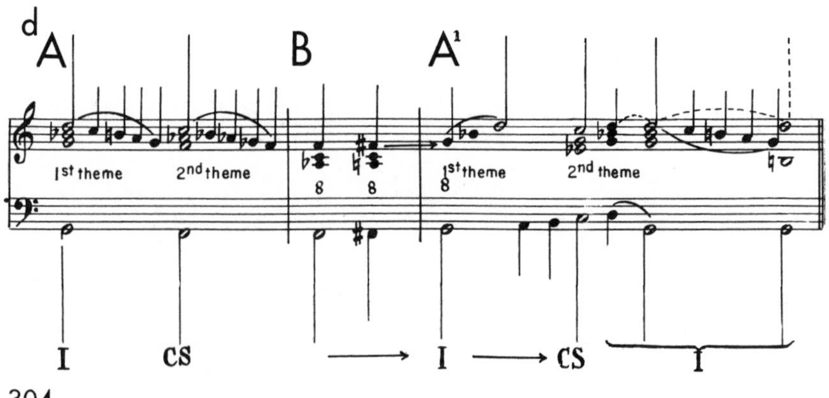

505 cont'd

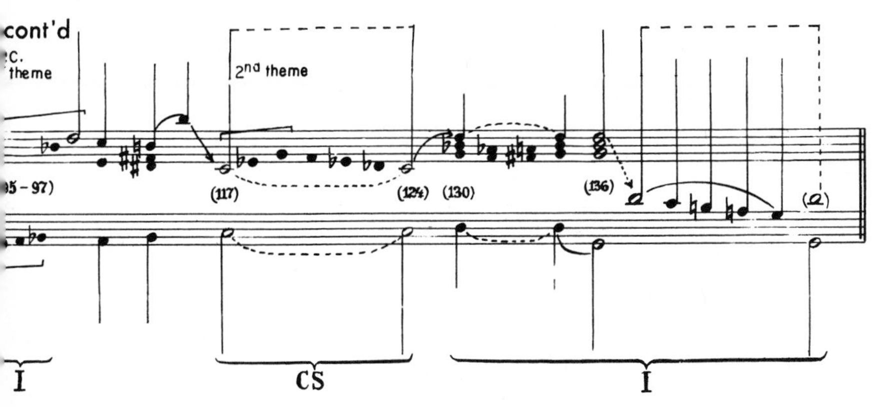
cont'd
2nd theme
(95 – 97)
(117)
(124)
(130)
(136)
I
CS
I

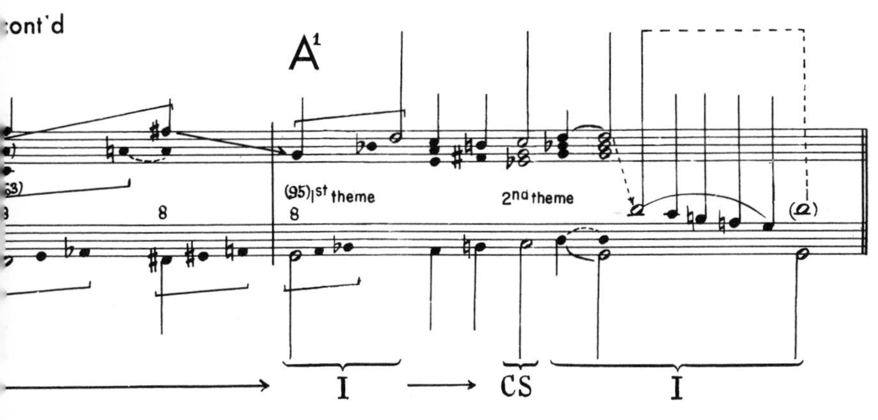
cont'd
A1
(95) 1st theme
2nd theme
8
I
CS
I

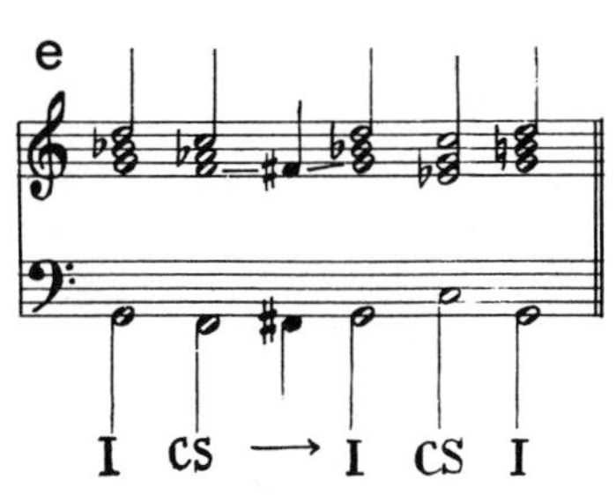
e
I
CS
I
CS
I

f
(75)
(76)
(79)
(82)
(85)

a

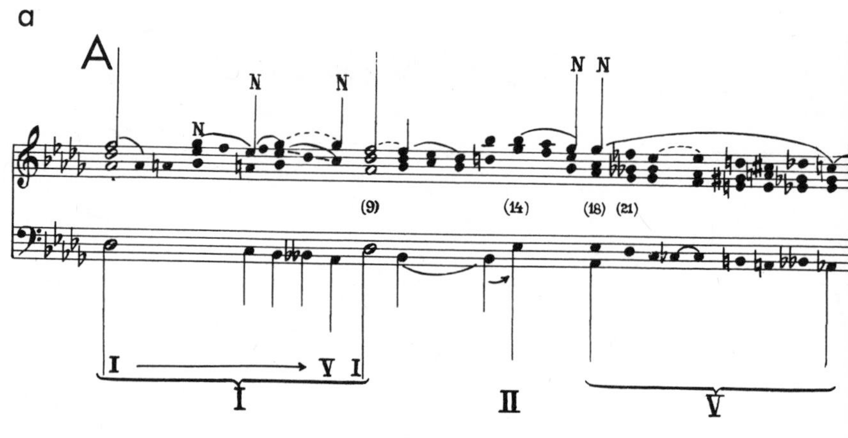

a cont'd

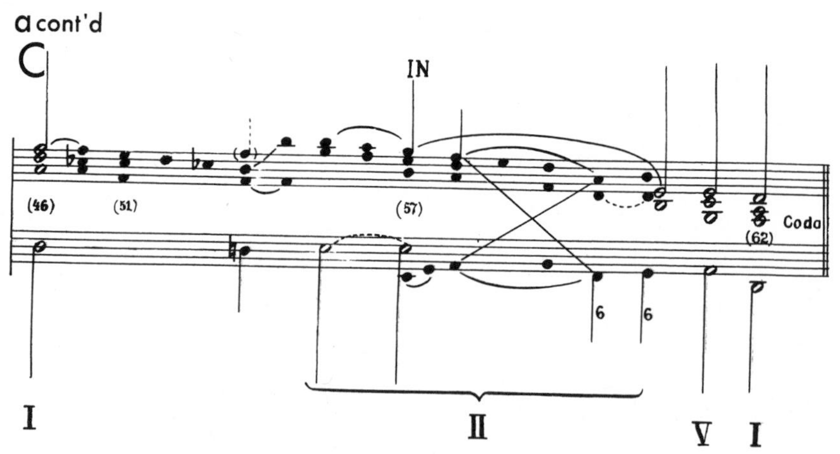

cont'd

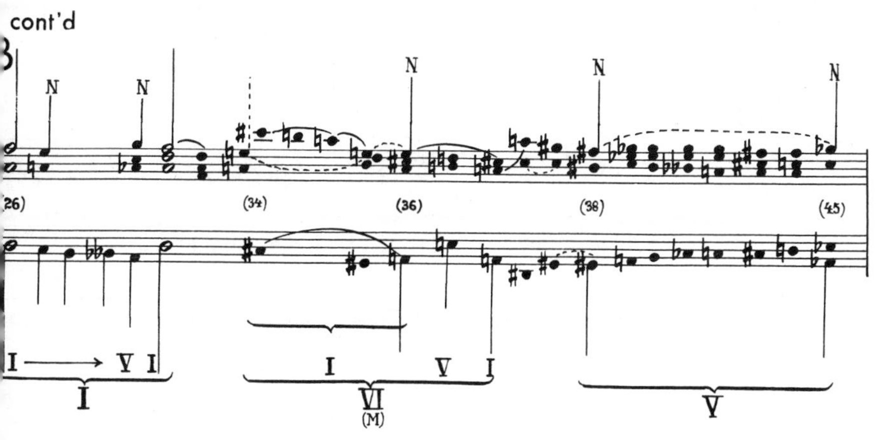
N
N
N
N
N
(26)
(34)
(36)
(38)
(45)
I ⟶ V I
I
I
V
I
VI
(M)
V

b

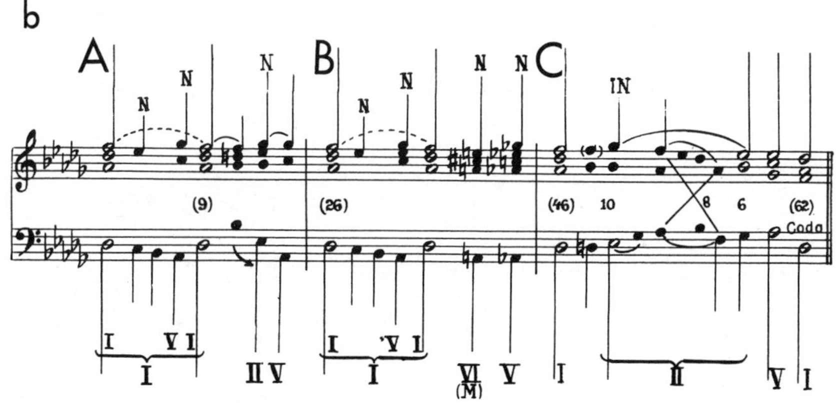
A
B
C
N
N
N
N
N
N
N
IN
(9)
(26)
(46)
10
8
6
(62)
Coda
I
V I
I
II V
I
V I
I
VI
(M)
V
I
II
V
I

507 MOZART Fantasia, C minor, K. 475

a

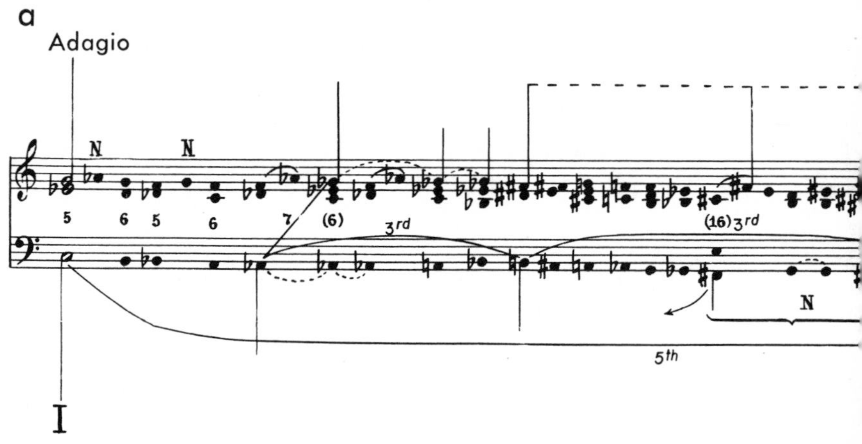

a cont'd

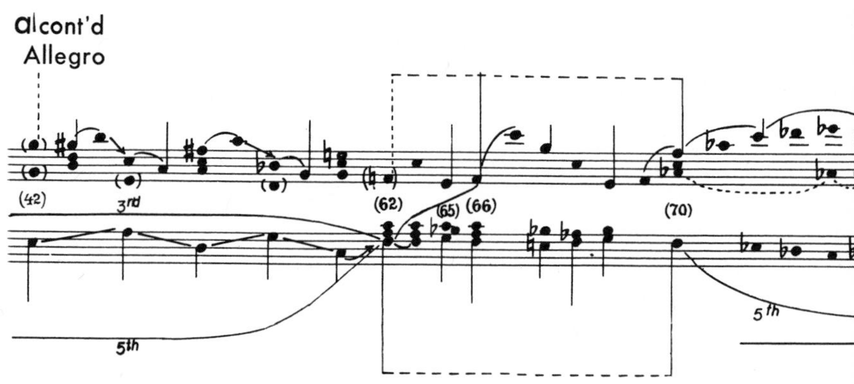

a cont'd

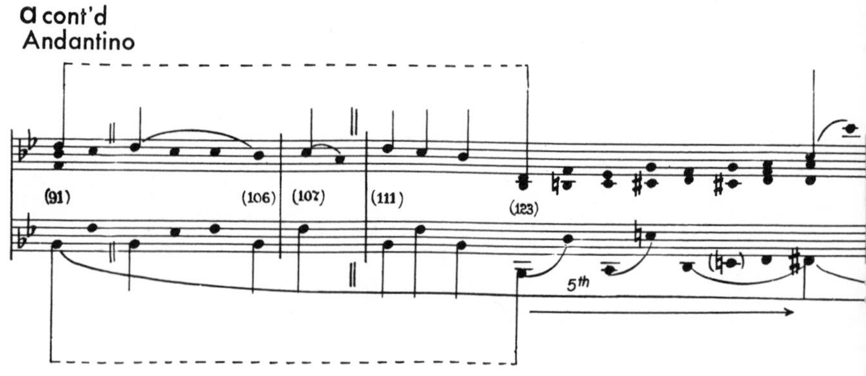

507 cont'd

cont'd

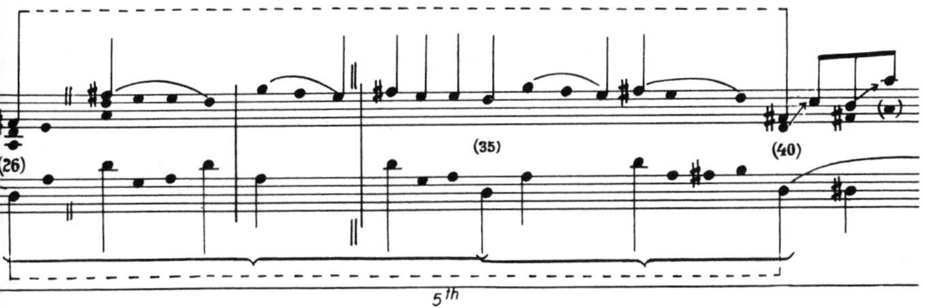

cont'd

cont'd
Più Allegro

507 cont'd

a cont'd

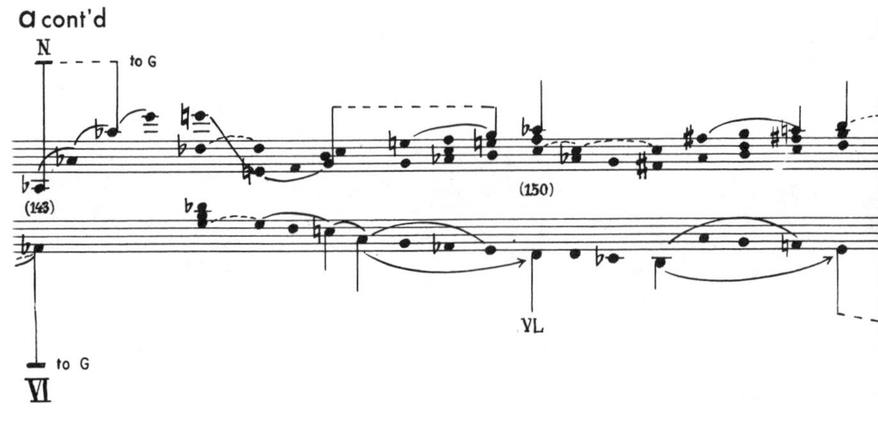

b

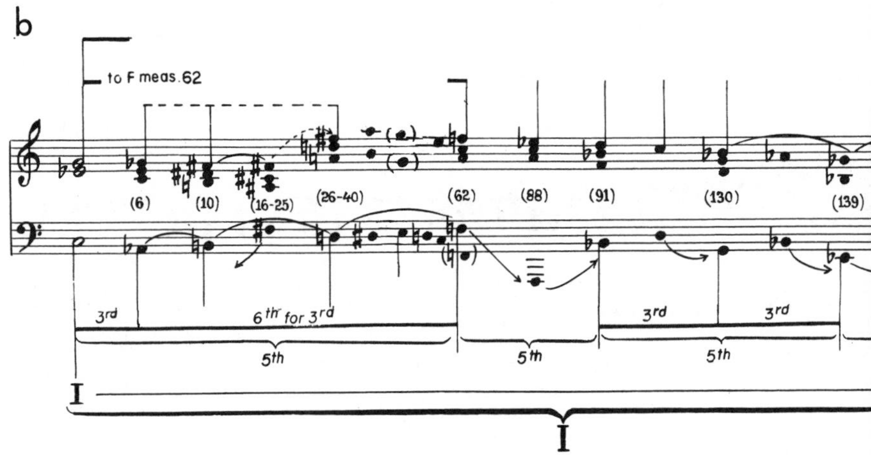

c

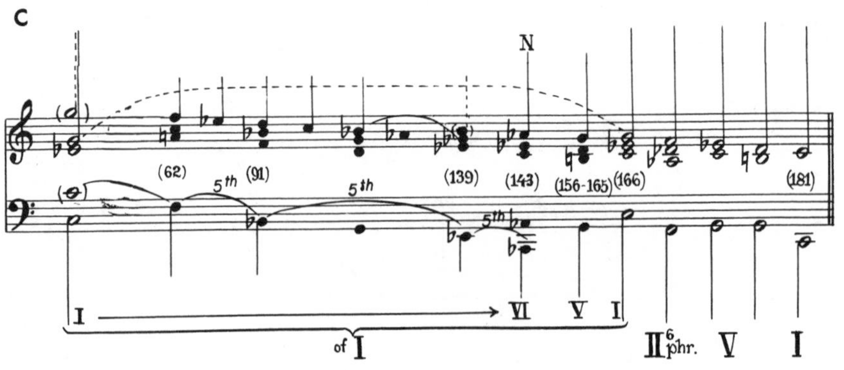

507 cont'd

a cont'd

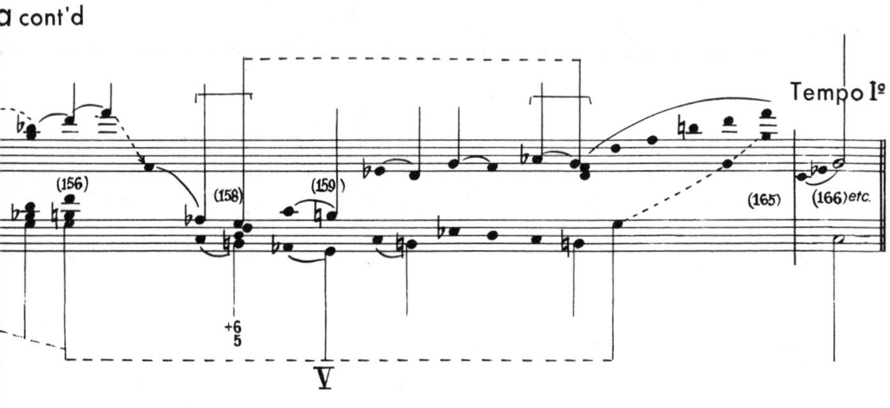

b cont'd

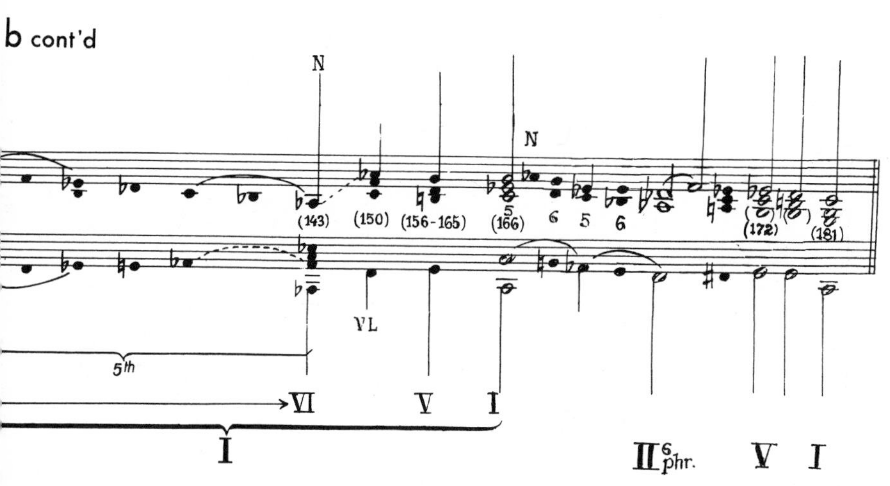

508 CHOPIN Nocturne, Op 37, No. 2

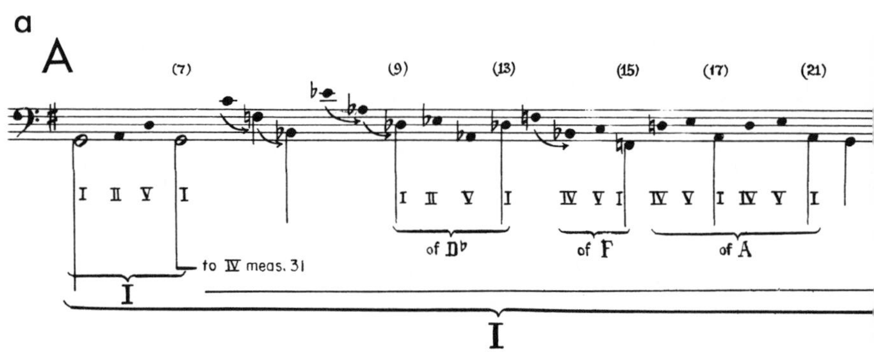

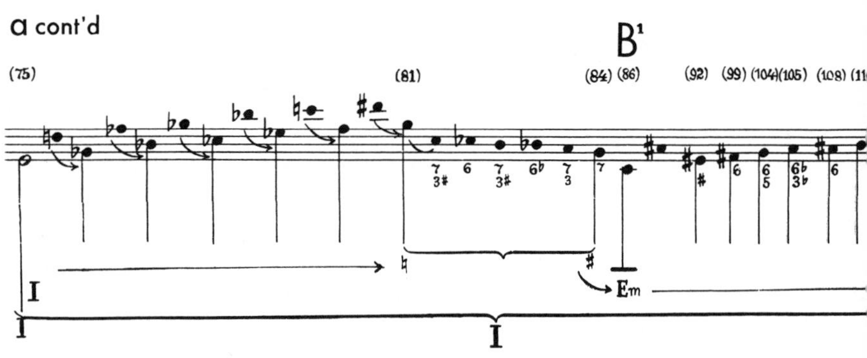

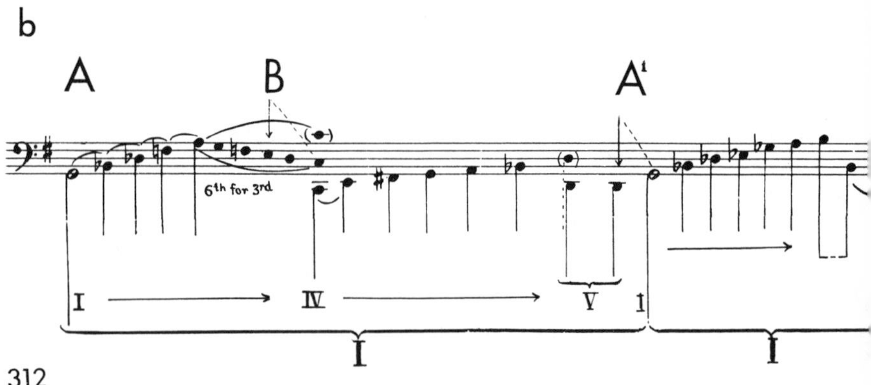

508 cont'd

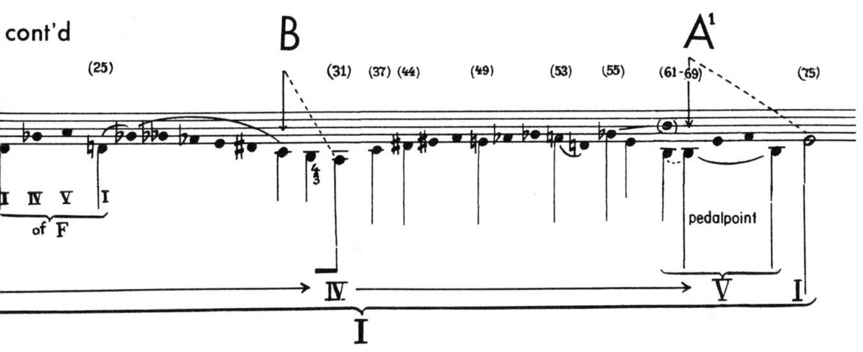
cont'd
B
A1
(25)
(31) (37) (44)
(49)
(53)
(55)
(61-69)
(75)
I IV V I
of F
pedalpoint
IV
V
I
I

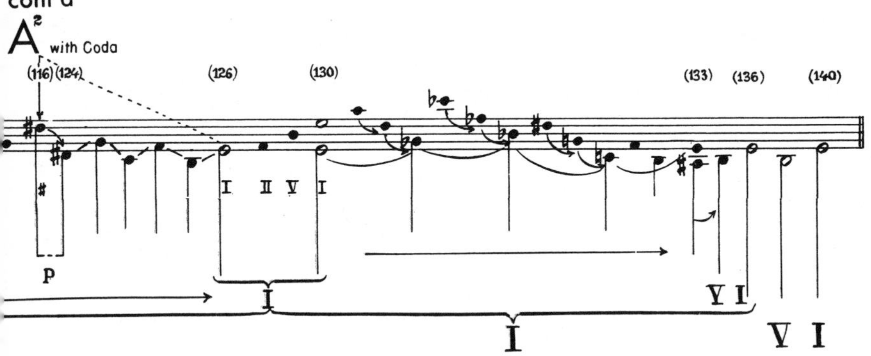
cont'd
A2 with Coda
(116) (124)
(126)
(130)
(133) (136)
(140)
P
I II V I
I
V I
I
V I

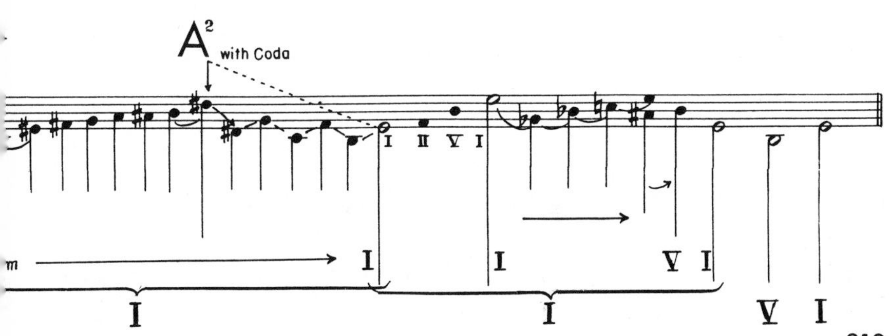
cont'd
A2 with Coda
I II V I
I
I
V I
I
I
V I

509 LASSO Christe Dei soboles

[From *HDM*, Vol. I, P. 333]

Part III Chapter Two

510 ALLELUIA ANGELUS DOMINI

510 cont'd

[From *HAM*, Vol. I, No. 26c]

511 BENEDICAMUS DOMINO (School of St. Martial)

[From *HDM*, Vol. I, P. 179]

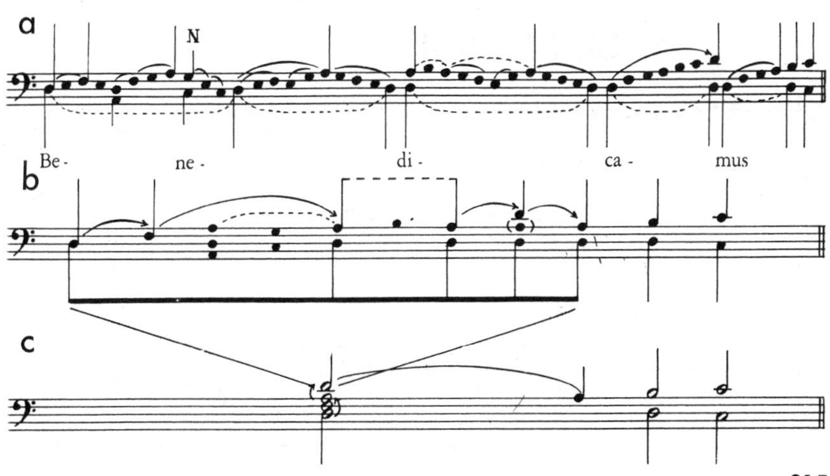

512 BENEDICAT ERGO (School of Compostela)

[From *HDM*, Vol. I, P. 182]

a

513 VIDERUNT HEMANUEL (School of St. Martial)

[From *HAM*, Vol. I, No. 27a]

a

514 LEONINUS Alleluia Pascha

[From AUDM, PP. 94-95]

a

(4) (8) (12) (15)

N N N

C G

515 ORGANUM (Style of Perotinus)

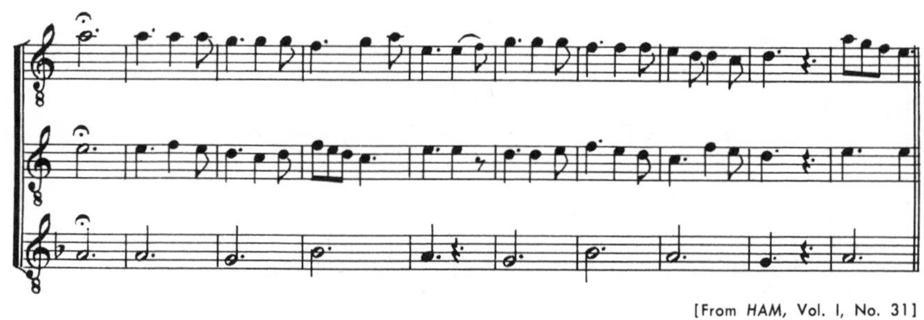

[From *HAM*, Vol. I, No. 31]

a

b

A G A

516 PEROTINUS Organum Triplum

[From *HDM*, Vol. I, P. 226]

516 cont'd

a

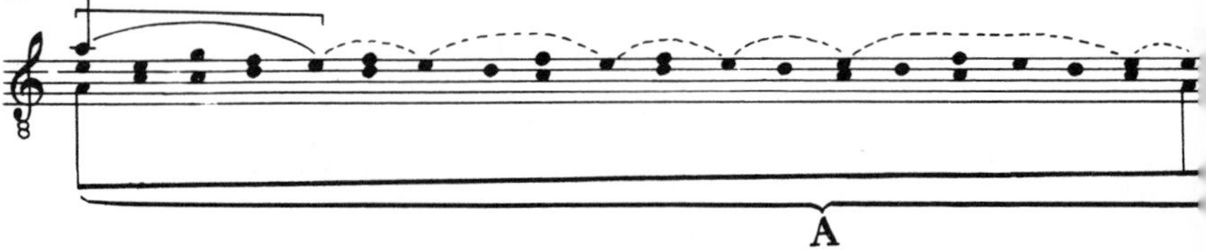

A

a cont'd

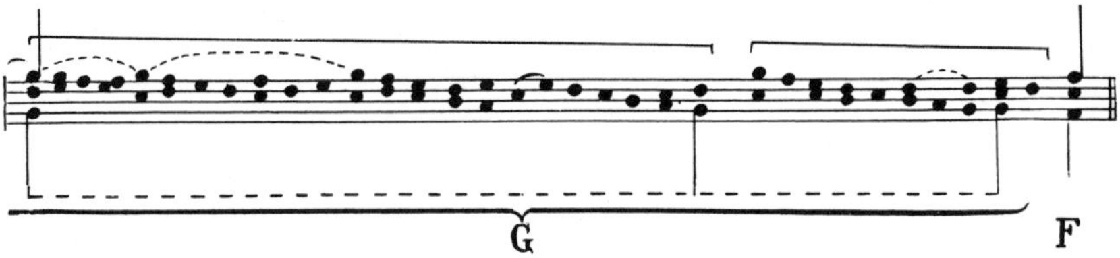

G
F

517 MOTET

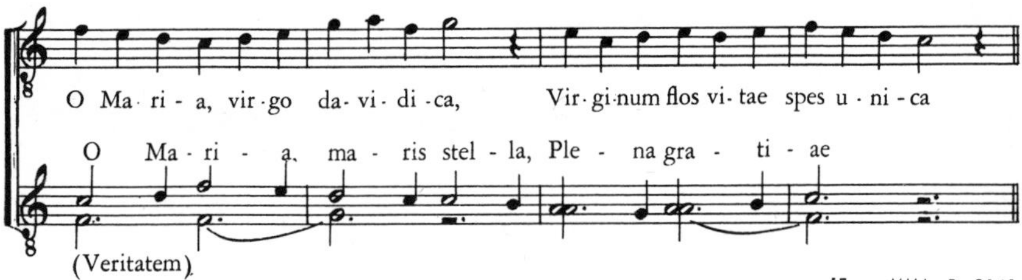

O Ma-ri-a, vir-go da-vi-di-ca, Vir-gi-num flos vi-tae spes u-ni-ca
O Ma-ri-a, ma-ris stel-la, Ple-na gra-ti-ae
(Veritatem)

[From MMA, P. 316]

a

UN
LN
F

b

F

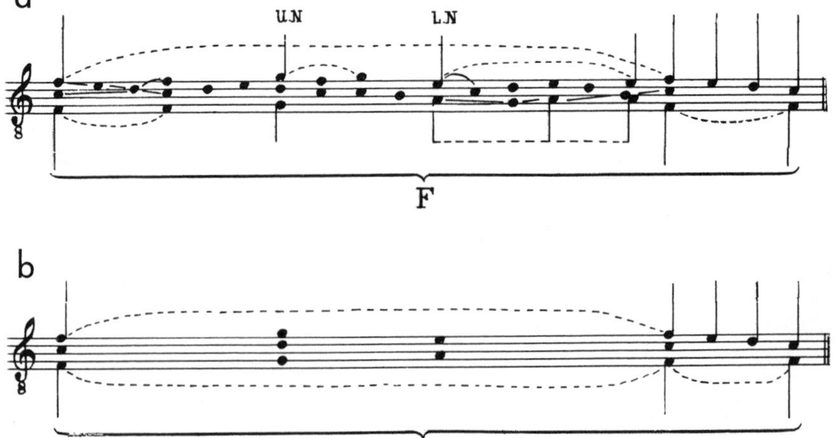

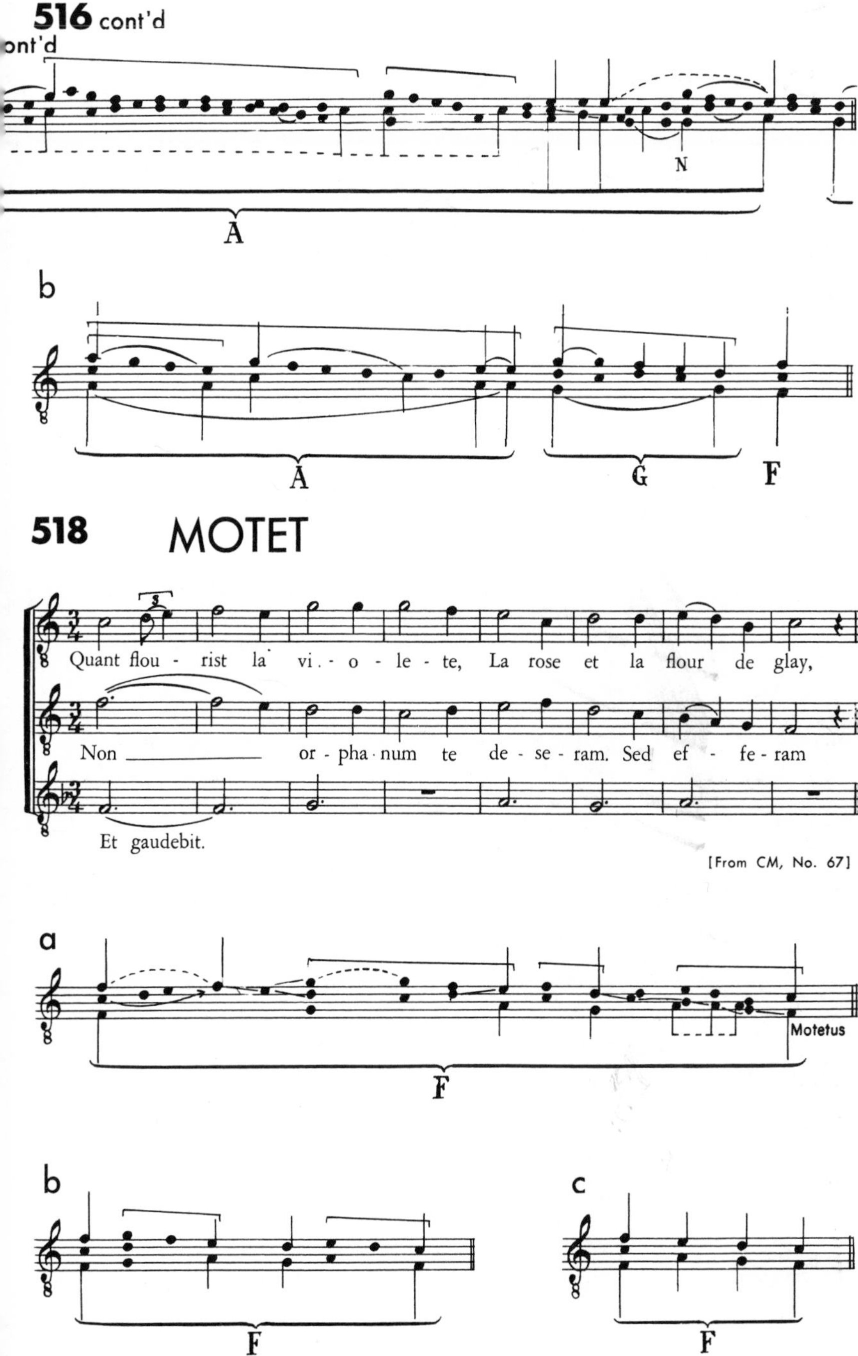
516 cont'd
ont'd
N
A
b
A
G
F
518
MOTET
Quant flou - rist la vi - o - le - te, La rose et la flour de glay,
Non ___ or - pha - num te de - se - ram. Sed ef - fe - ram
Et gaudebit.
[From CM, No. 67]
a
Motetus
F
b
F
c
F

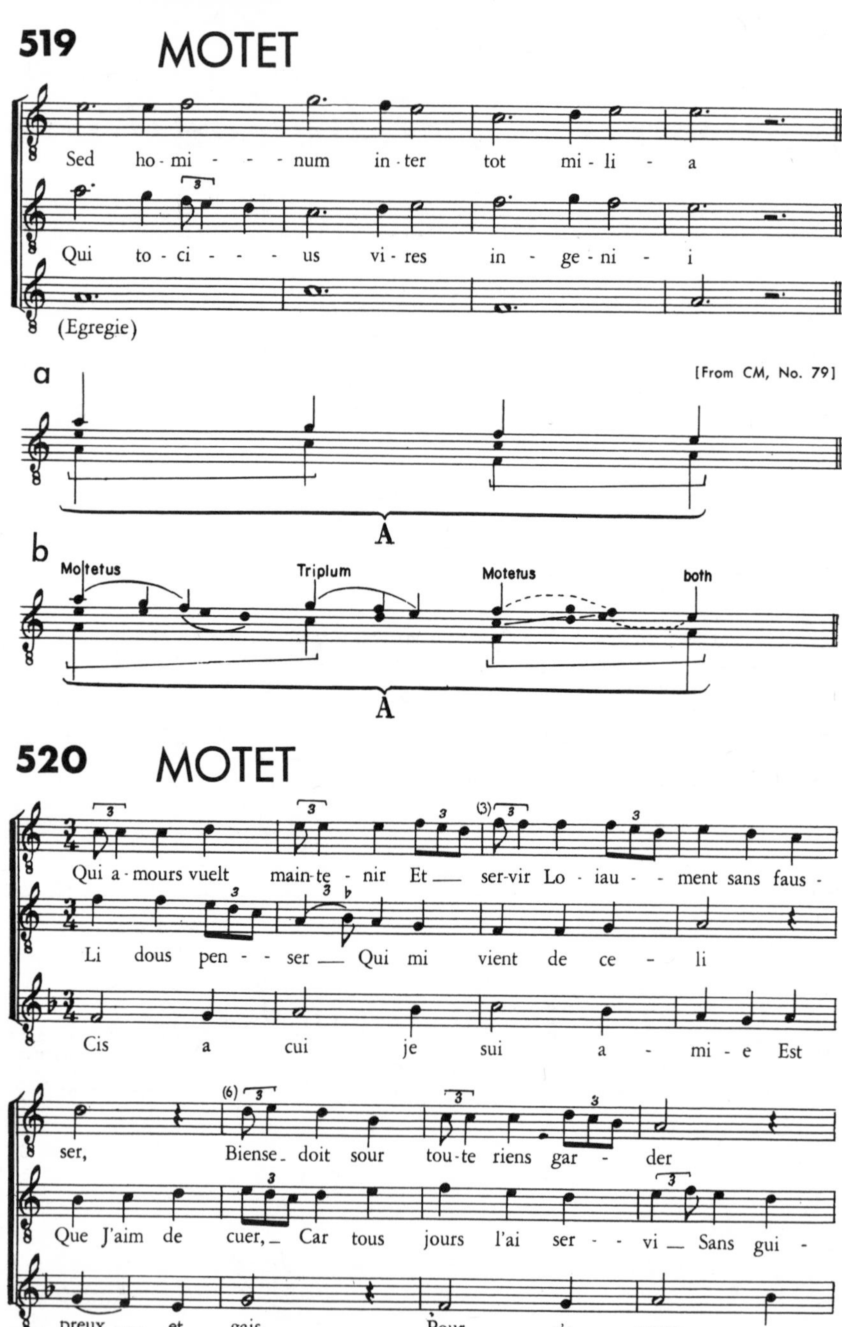
519 MOTET
Sed ho-mi - - - num in-ter tot mi-li - a
Qui to-ci - - - us vi-res in - ge-ni - i
(Egregie)
a
[From CM, No. 79]
A
b
Motetus
Triplum
Motetus
both
A
520 MOTET
Qui a-mours vuelt main-te - nir Et — ser-vir Lo - iau - - ment sans faus - ser, Bien se - doit sour tou-te riens gar - der
Li dous pen - - ser — Qui mi vient de ce - li Que J'aim de cuer, — Car tous jours l'ai ser - - vi — Sans gui -
Cis a cui je sui a - mi - e Est preux — et gais, Pour s'a - mour se -

520 cont'd

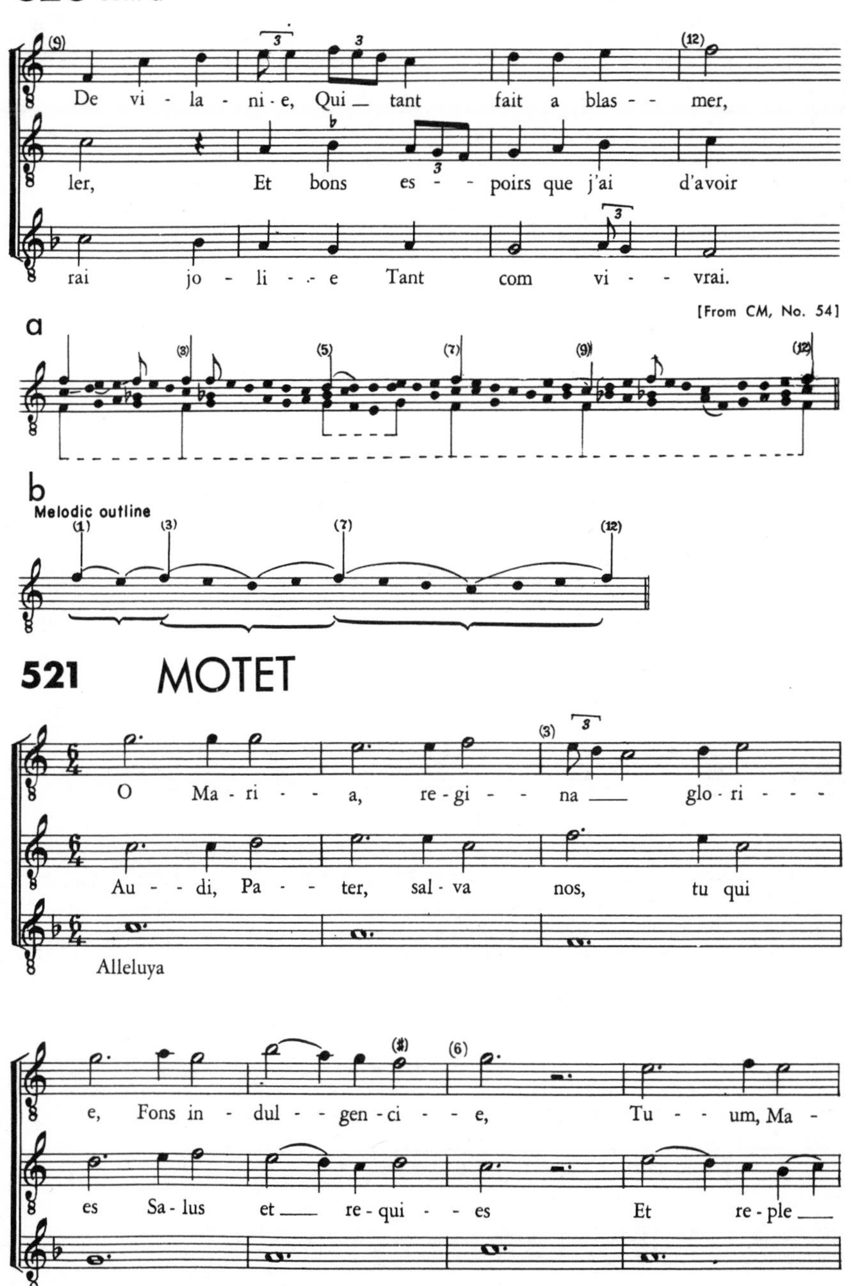
De vi - la - ni - e, Qui tant fait a blas - - mer,
ler, Et bons es - - poirs que j'ai d'avoir
rai jo - li - - e Tant com vi - - vrai.
[From CM, No. 54]
a
b
Melodic outline
521 MOTET
O Ma - ri - - - a, re - gi - - - na glo - ri - - -
Au - - di, Pa - - - ter, sal - va nos, tu qui
Alleluya
e, Fons in - dul - - gen - ci - - - e, Tu - - - um, Ma -
es Sa - lus et re - qui - - es Et re - ple

521 cont'd

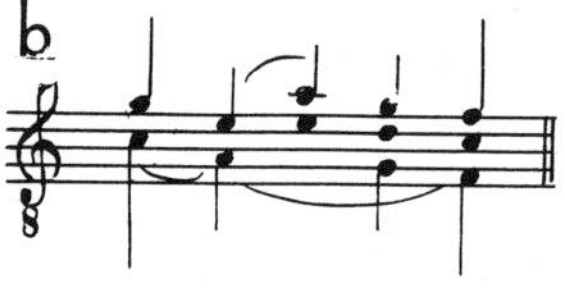

522 MOTET

[From CM, No. 40]

521 cont'd

[From CM, No. 9]

cont'd

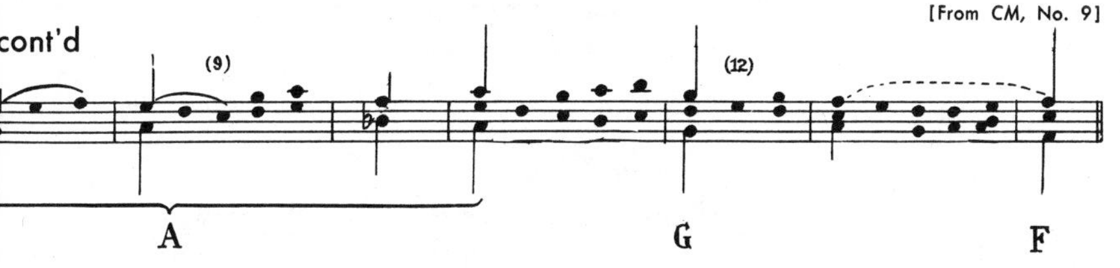

522 cont'd

a

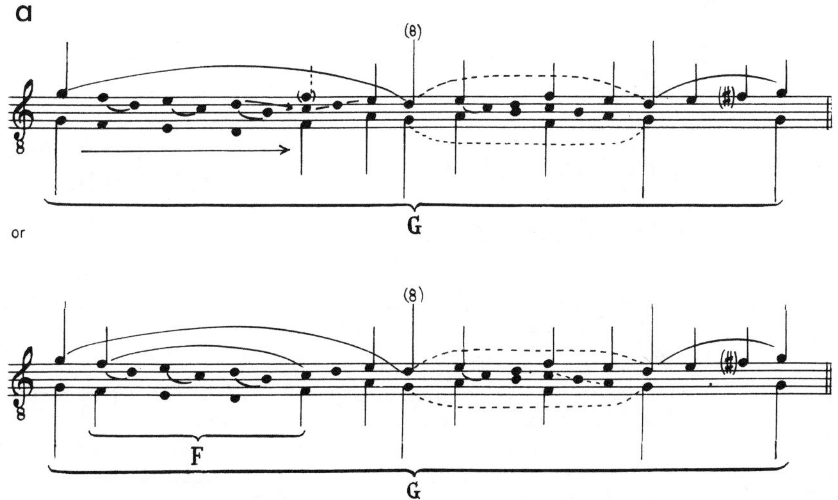

523 RONDEAU: Amours et ma dame aussi

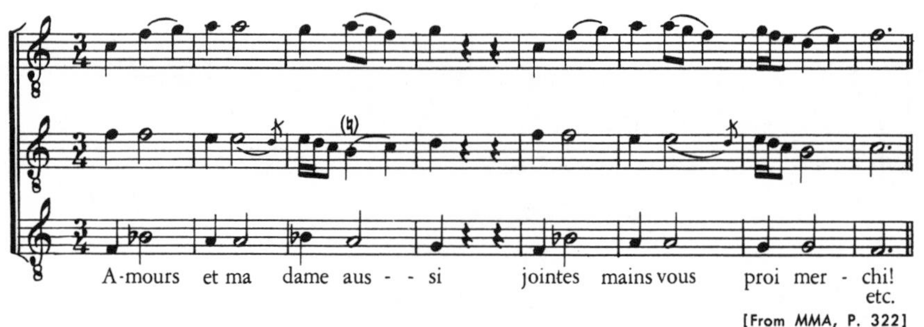

[From MMA, P. 322]

a

524 ADAM DE LA HALLE Li maus d'amer (1st part)

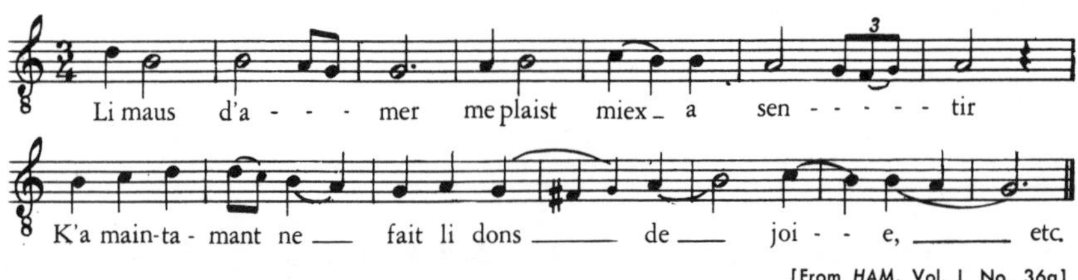

[From HAM, Vol. I, No. 36a]

525 ADAM DE LA HALLE Rondeau: Tant con je vivrai

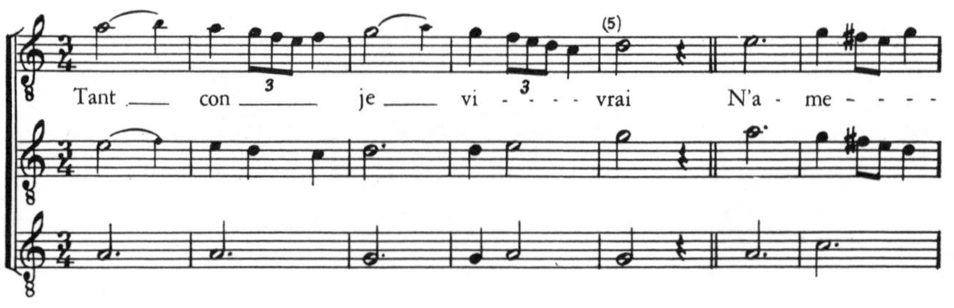

525 cont'd

a

[From *HAM*, Vol. I, No. 36b]

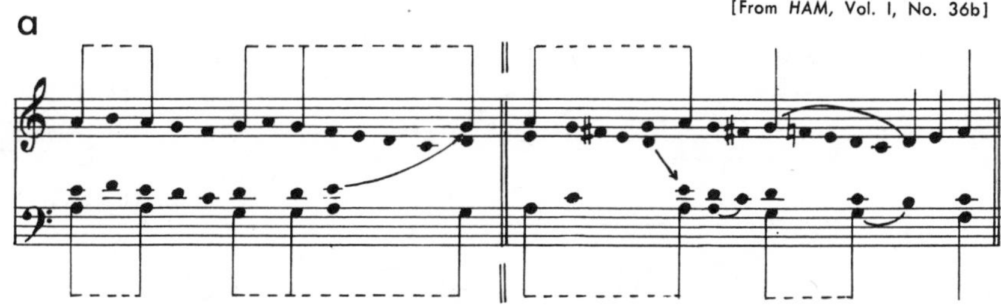

526 MOTET

527 MOTET
(♯)
(♯)
3
Au dous, etc.
3
Biaus, etc.
Manere
[From CM, No. 18]
a
I
V
I
528 MACHAUT Virelai (No. 38)
De _ tout - sui si con - for - - - te - e
[From MW, Vol. I]
a
I
V
I
529 MACHAUT Virelai (No. 32)
Da - me mon _ cuer em - por - - tes
[From MW, Vol. I]
a
I V I V I
I

530 MACHAUT Ballade (No. 3)

[From MW, Vol. I]

531 cont'd

a

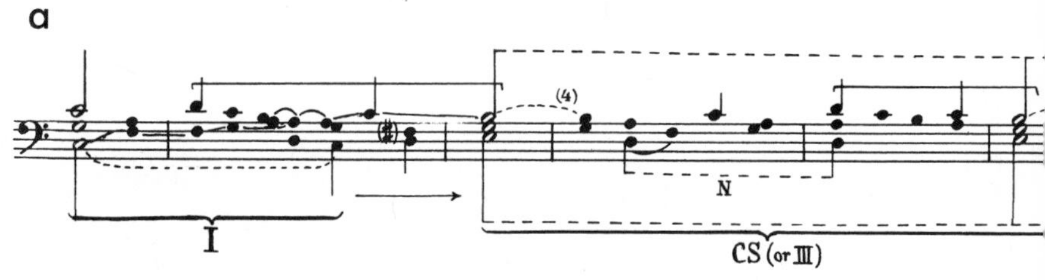

b

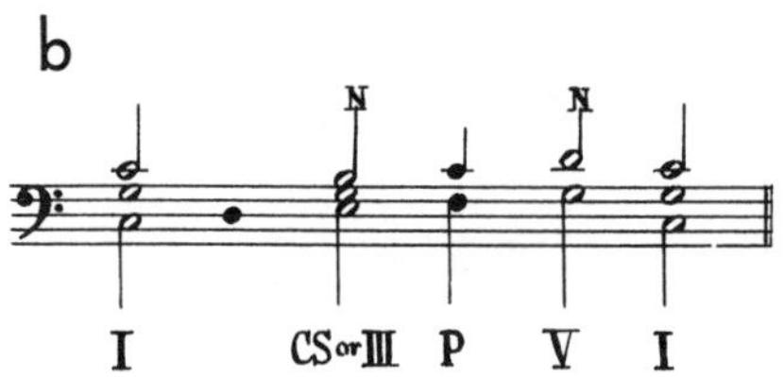

532 MACHAUT Virelai (No. 31)

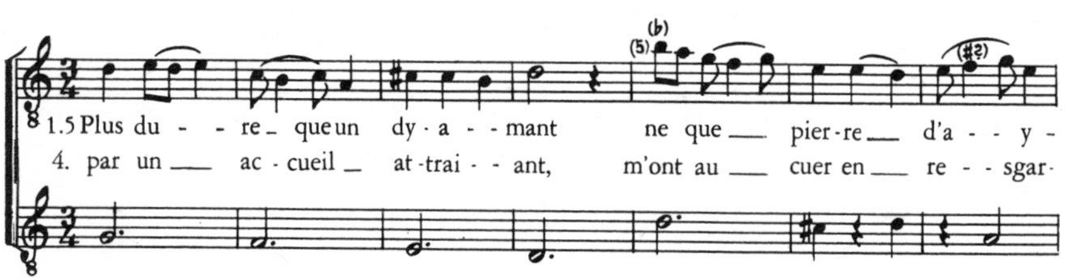

531 cont'd

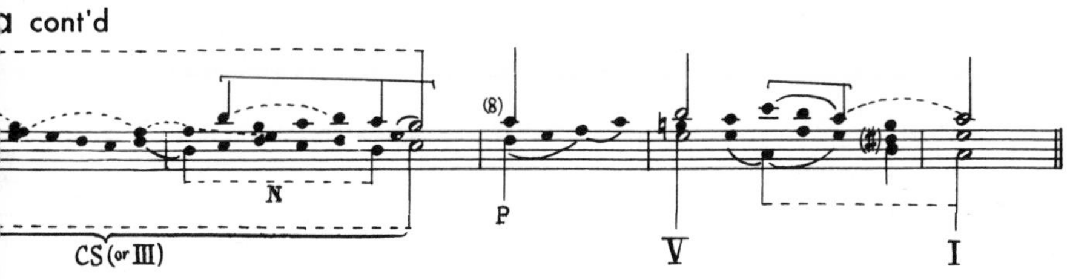

a cont'd

(8)
N
P
CS (or III)
V
I

532 cont'd

vostre a - - mant qu'o ci - - - es en _ de - - si - rant vostre _ a - mi - - tié.
sques a - - tant que vo ___ gra - ce _ quil ___ a - tant m'au - - res don - - né.
2. Da - me, _ vo pu - - re _ biau - té qui _ tou - tes ___ passe, _
3. simple et _ plein d'u - - mi - - li - - té, de _ dou - ceur _ fi - -
a _ mon - gré, et ___ vo _ sam - blant
ne _ pa - ré, en ___ sous - ri - - - ant,
1.
2.

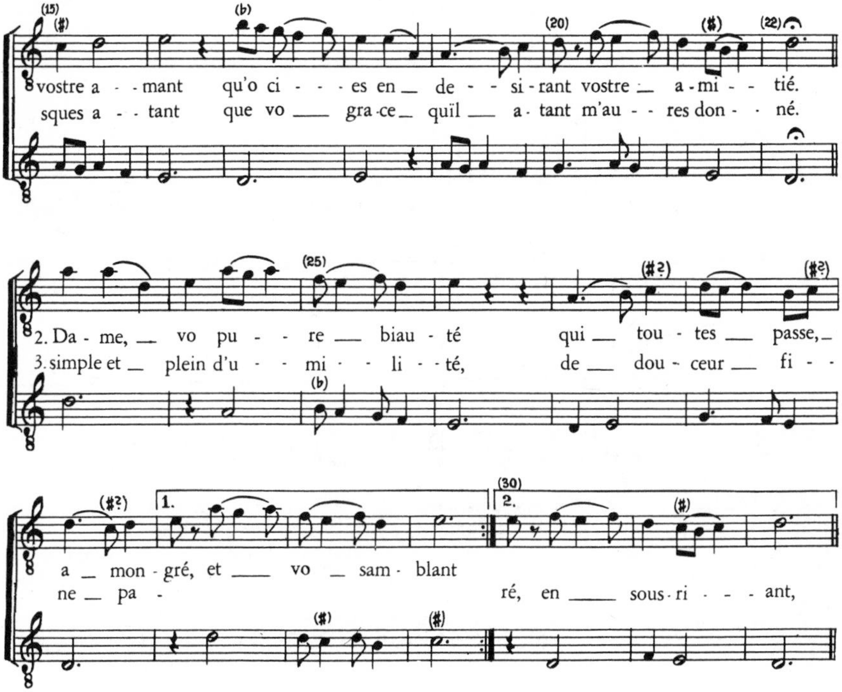

[From MW, Vol. I]

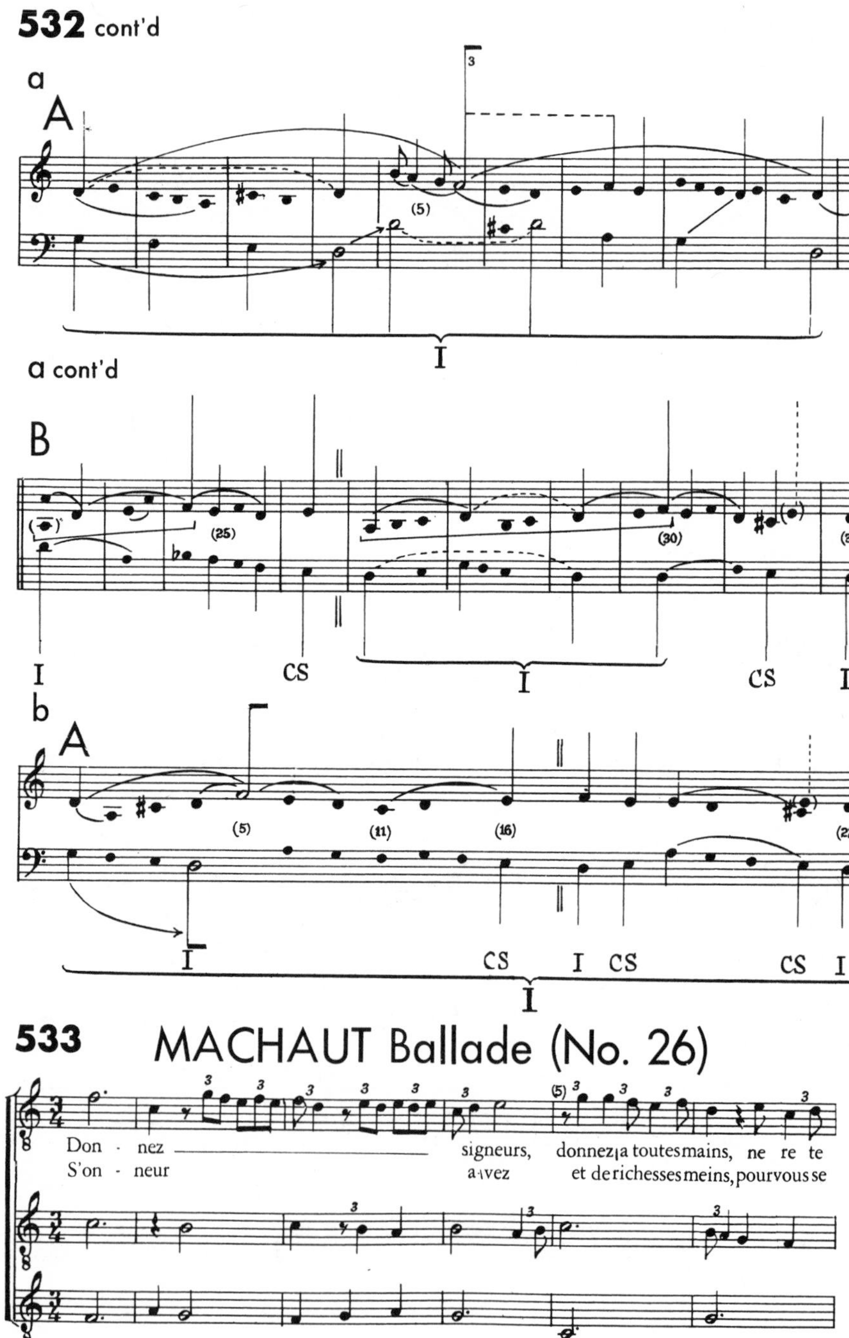
532 cont'd
a
A
I
a cont'd
B
I
CS
I
CS
I
b
A
I
CS
I
CS
CS
I
I
533 MACHAUT Ballade (No. 26)
Don - nez signeurs, donnez a toutes mains, ne re te
S'on - neur a - vez et de richesses meins, pour vous se

532 cont'd

a cont'd
N
(15)
(20)
(22)
CS I CS CS I
a cont'd
A¹
repetition of meas. 1 - 22.
CS I CS CS I
b cont'd
B
A¹
(25)
(30)
(32)
repetition of meas. 1 - 22.
I CS I CS I
I
CS I CS I
533 cont'd
(10)
nez seu - le - ment fors
ront li grant et li

533 cont'd

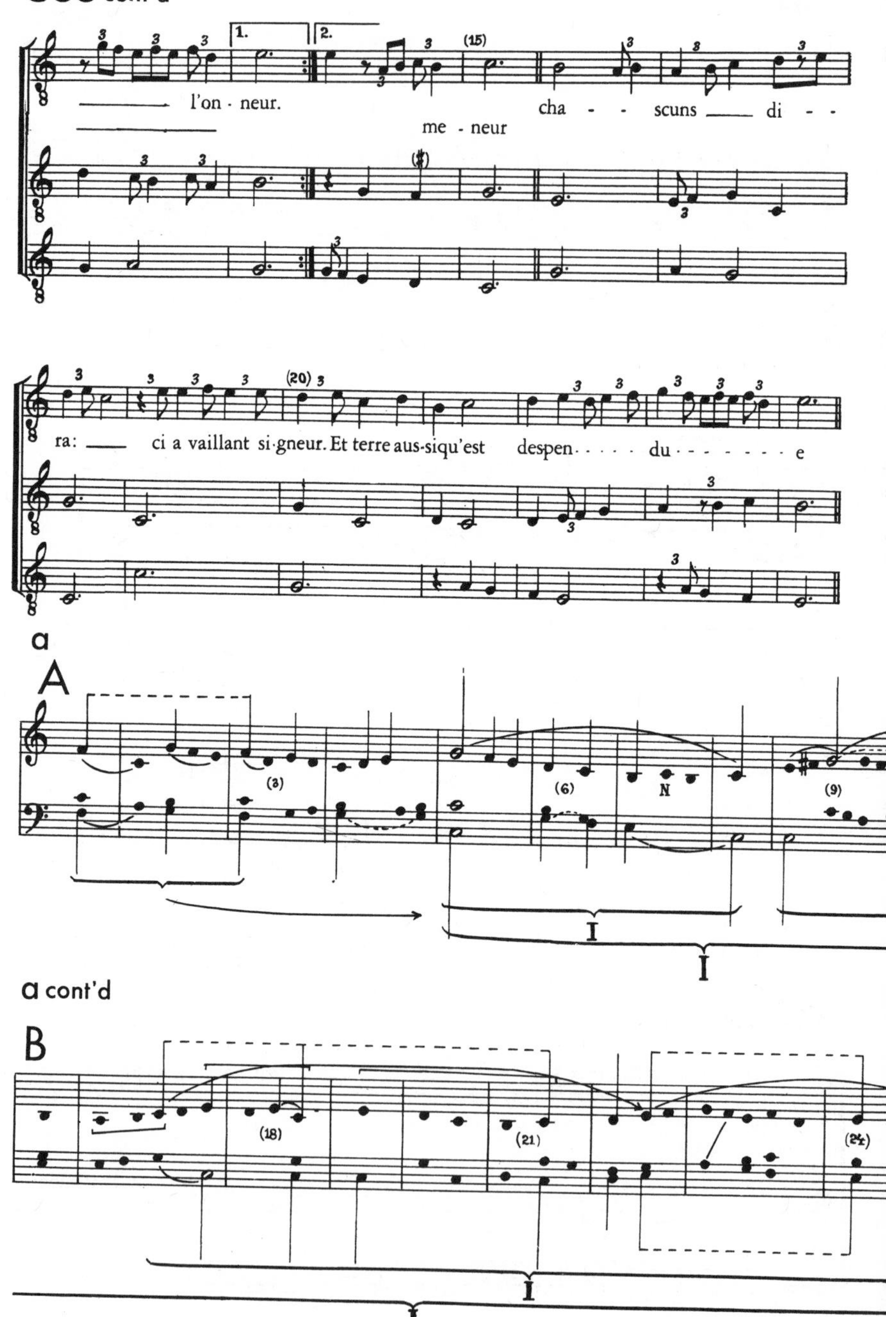

1.
2.
(15)
l'on - neur.
cha - - scuns — di - -
me - neur
(20)
ra: — ci a vaillant si-gneur. Et terre aus-siqu'est despen- - - - - du - - - - - - - e
a
A
(3)
(6)
N
(9)
I
I
a cont'd
B
(18)
(21)
(24)
I
I

[From MW, Vol. I]

a cont'd

(12)
(15)
8 8 6
I
I

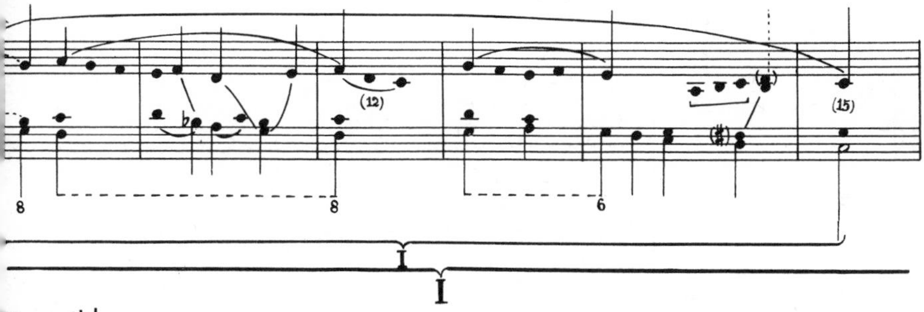

a cont'd

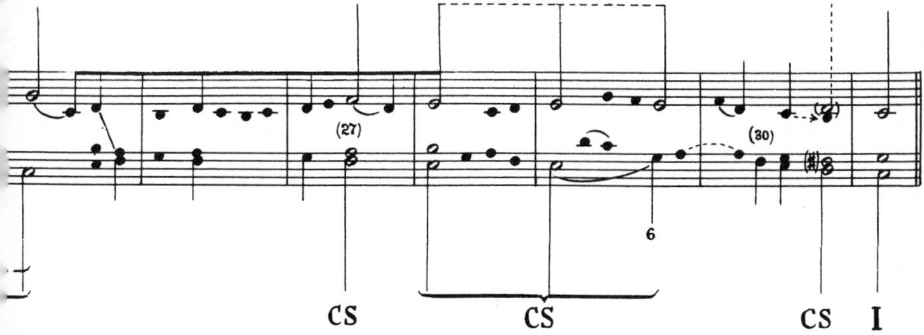

(27)
(30)
6
CS CS CS I

533 cont'd

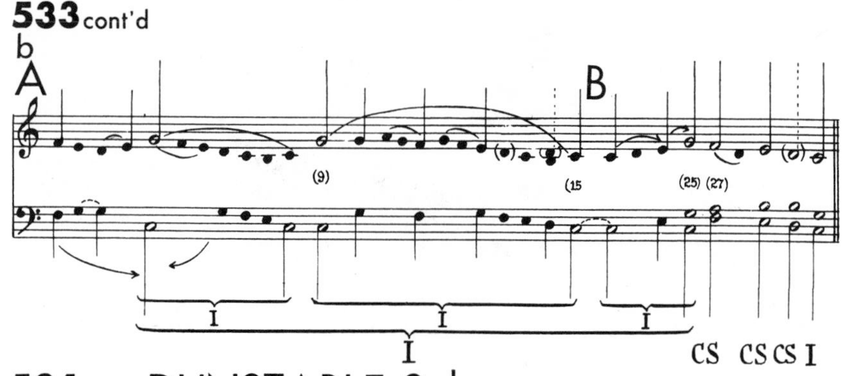

534 DUNSTABLE Sub tuam protectionem

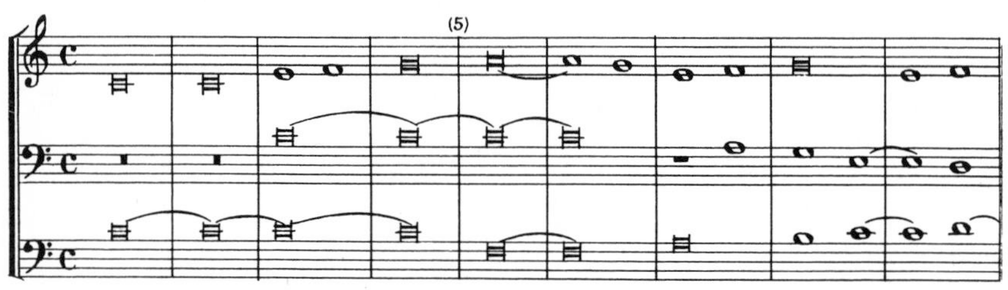

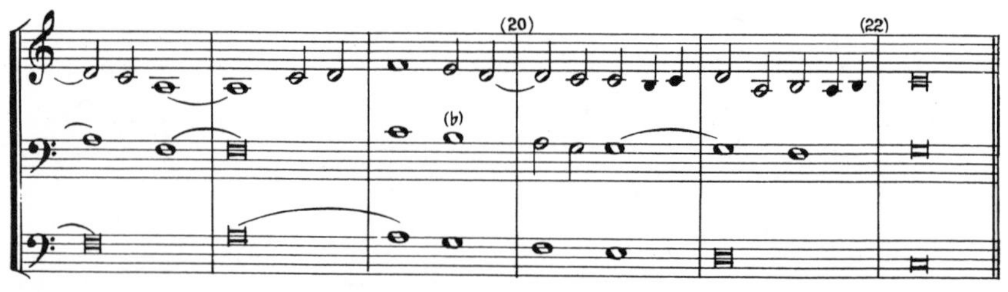

[From *TC*, Vol. I, P. 198]

[From *TC*, Vol. I. P. 254]

535 cont'd

a

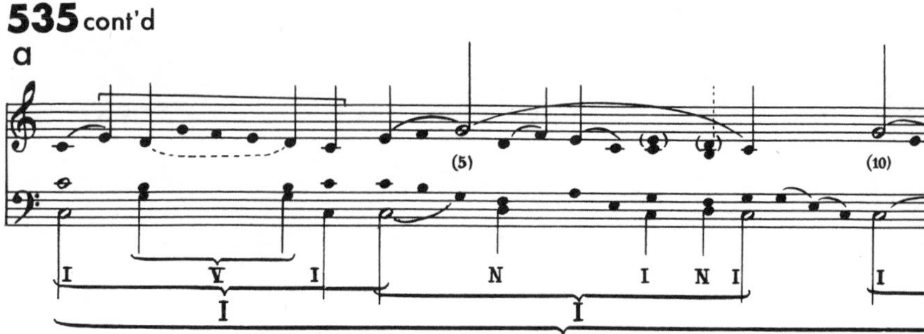

536 DUFAY Adieu m'amour

535 cont'd

a cont'd

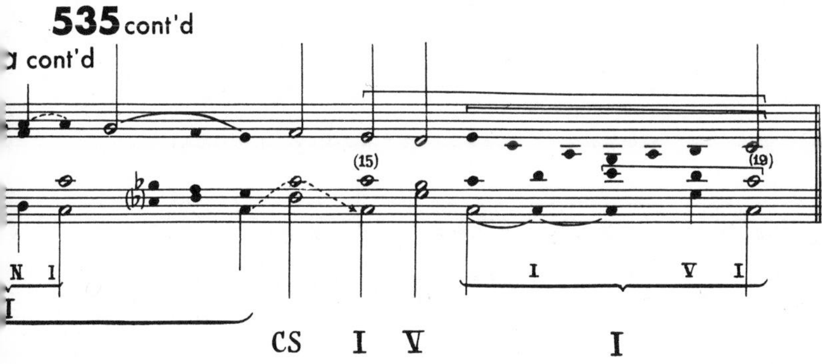

536 cont'd

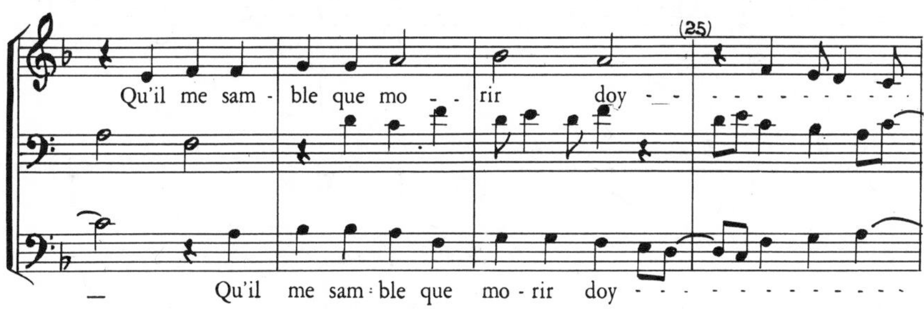

[From *DAS CHORWERK*, Vol. XIX]

536 cont'd

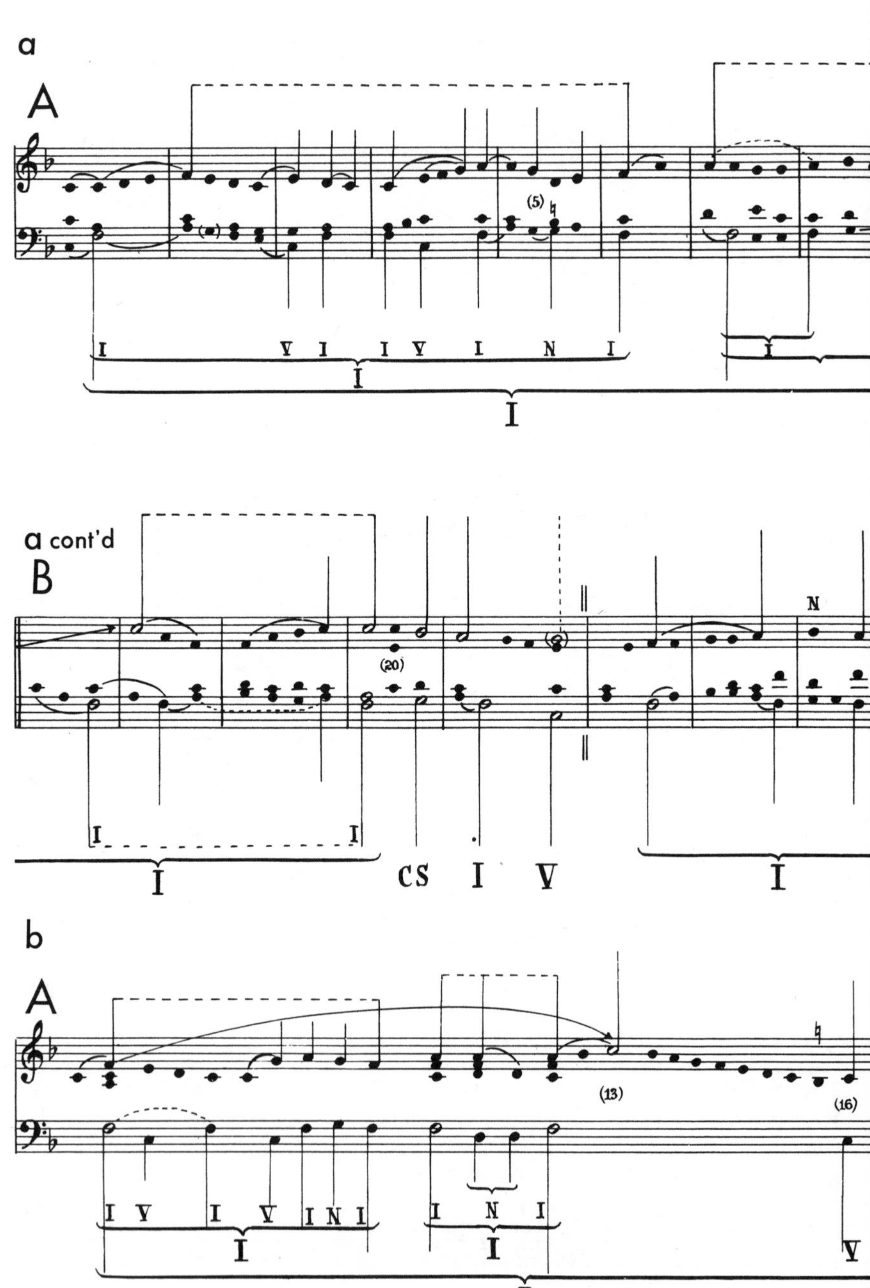

a
A
(5)
I V I I V I N I
I
I
I
a cont'd
B
(20)
N
I I
I
CS I V
I
b
A
(13)
(16)
I V I V I N I
I
I N I
I
V
I

cont'd
N
(10)
(#) (#)
N
(15)
N I
I
V
I
cont'd
(25)
N
I
CS CS CS I
cont'd
(21) (22) (27) (29)
CS I V I CS CS CS I

537 OBRECHT Osanna (Missa: Je ne demande)

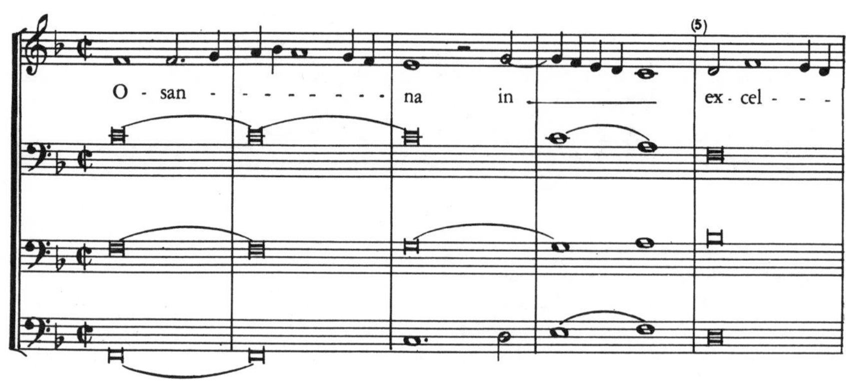

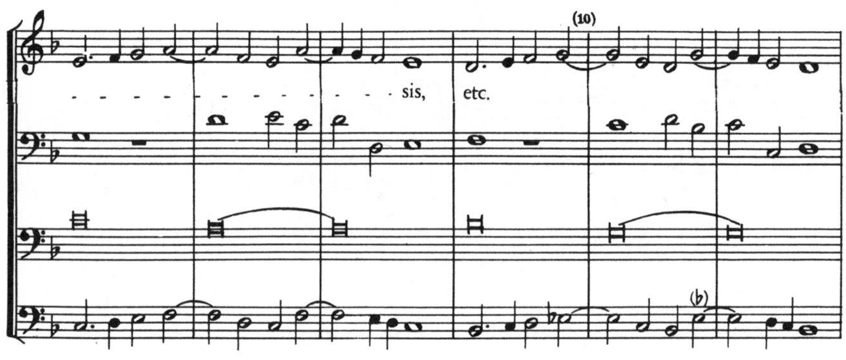

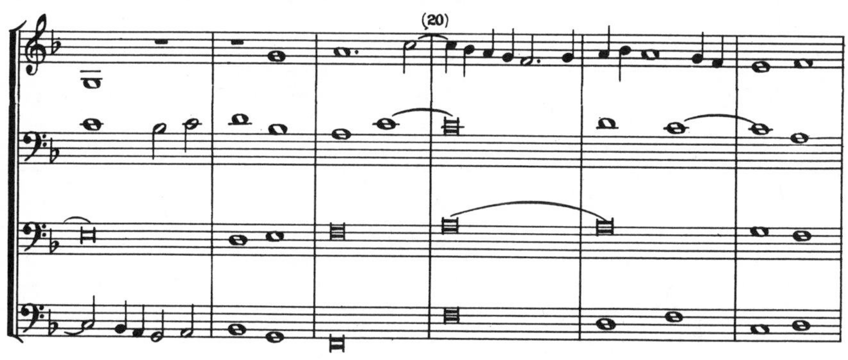

[From *WJO*, *Missen*, Vol. I, No. 1]

537 cont'd

a

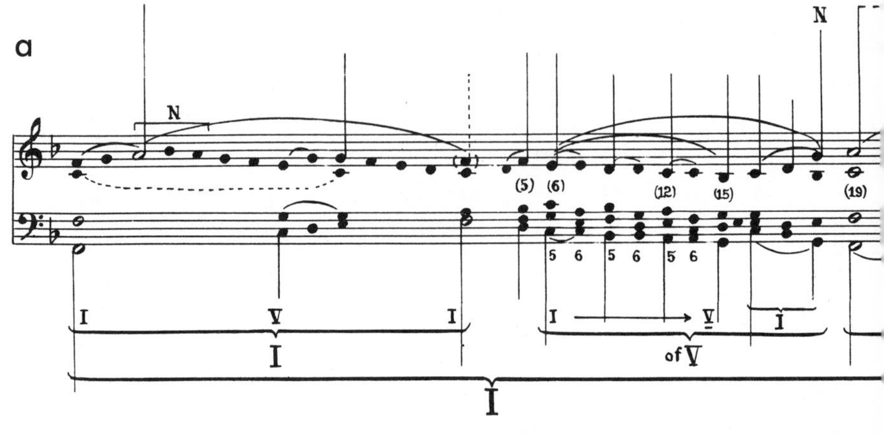

b

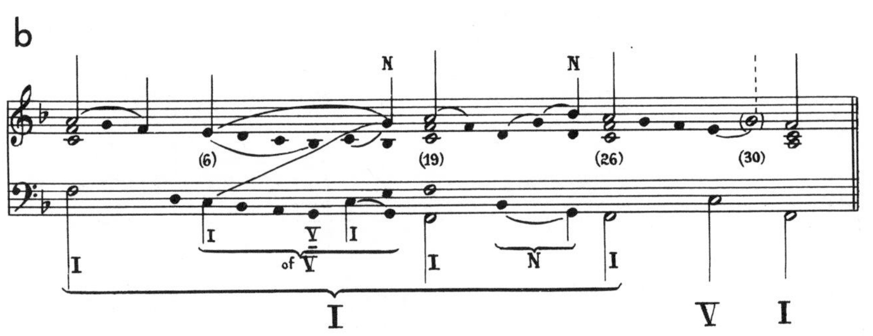

538 ISAAC Kyrie (Missa Carminum)

537 cont'd

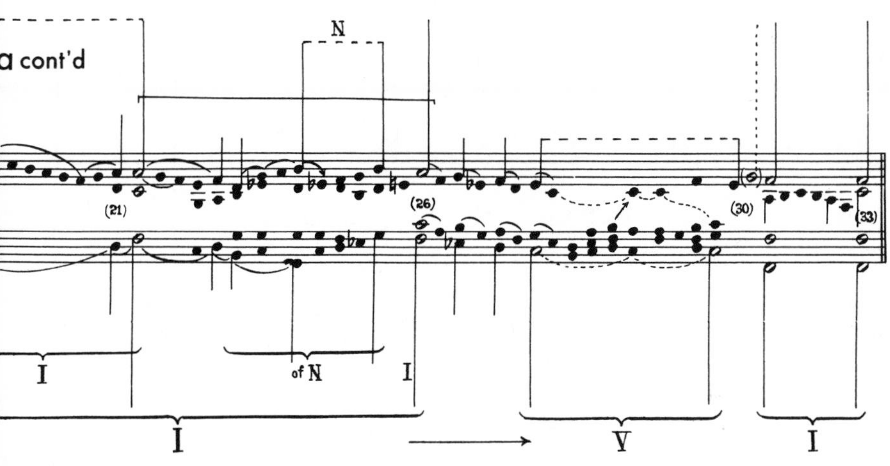

538 cont'd

[From *DAS CHORWERK*, Vol. VII]

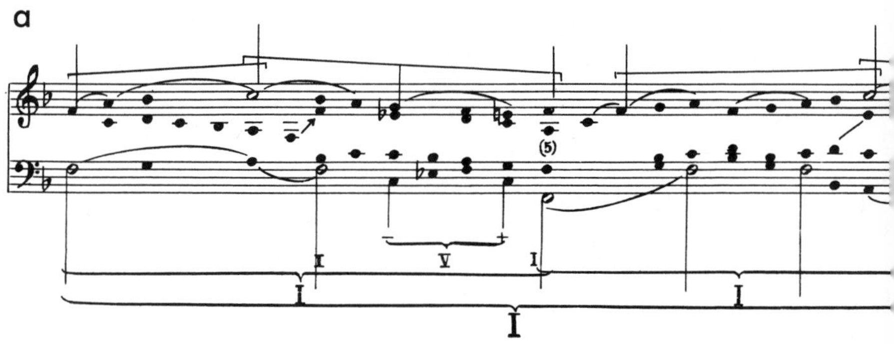

539 JOSQUIN Motet: O Domine Jesu Christe (1st part)

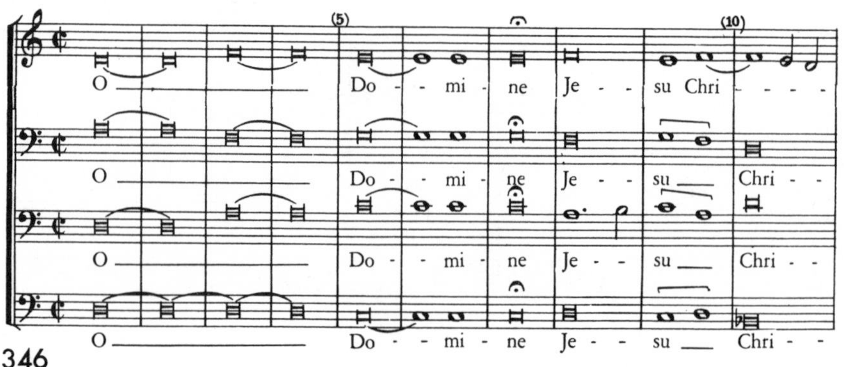

538 cont'd

a cont'd

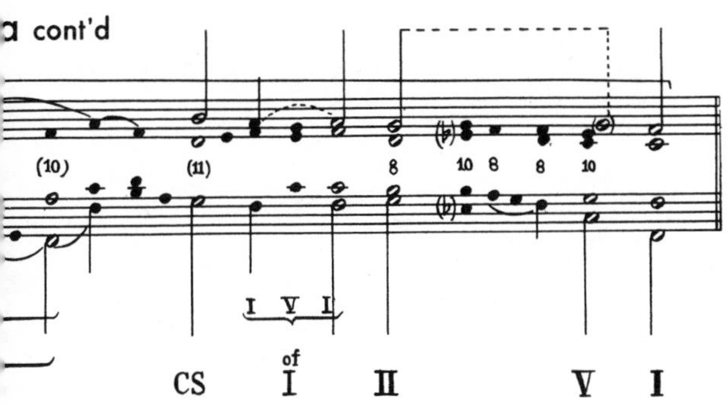

539 cont'd

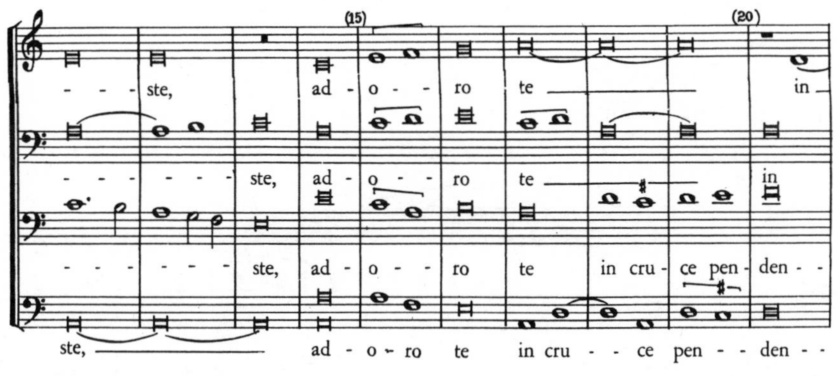

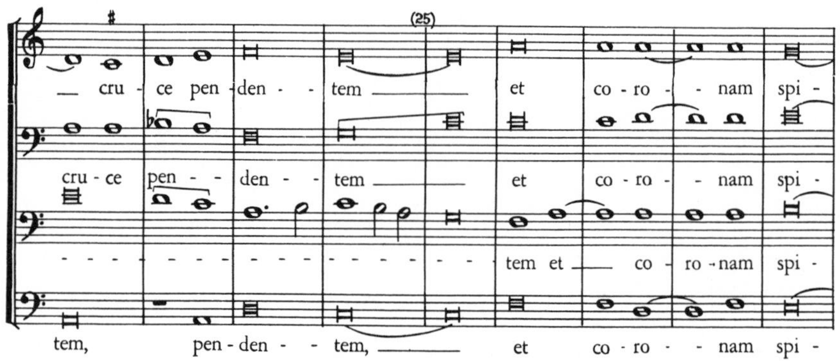
(25)
cru - ce pen - den - - tem et co - ro - - nam spi -
cru - ce pen - - den - - tem et co - ro - - nam spi -
tem et co - ro - nam spi -
tem, pen - den - - tem, et co - ro - - nam spi -

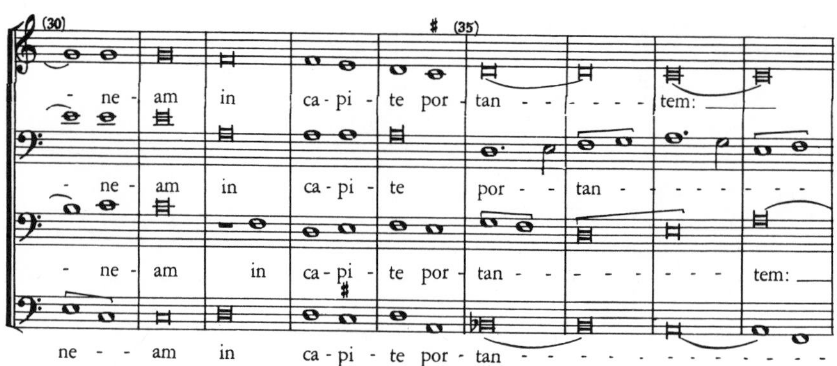
(30)
(35)
- ne - am in ca - pi - te por - tan - - tem:
- ne - am in ca - pi - te por - - tan -
- ne - am in ca - pi - te por - tan - tem:
ne - - am in ca - pi - te por - tan -

a

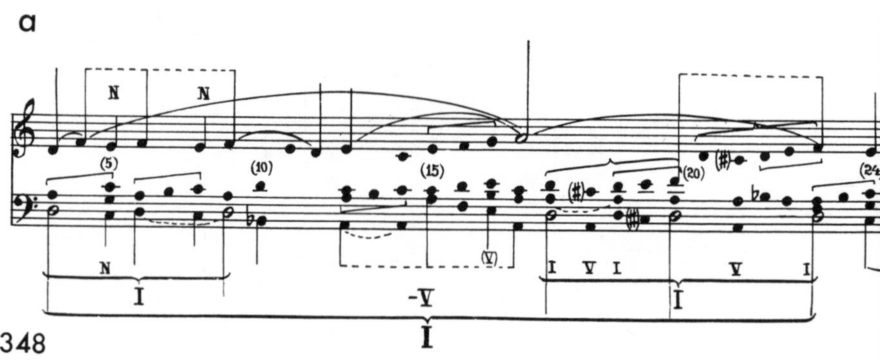
N
N
(5)
(10)
(15)
(20)
N
I
-V
I
I V I
I
V I

539 cont'd

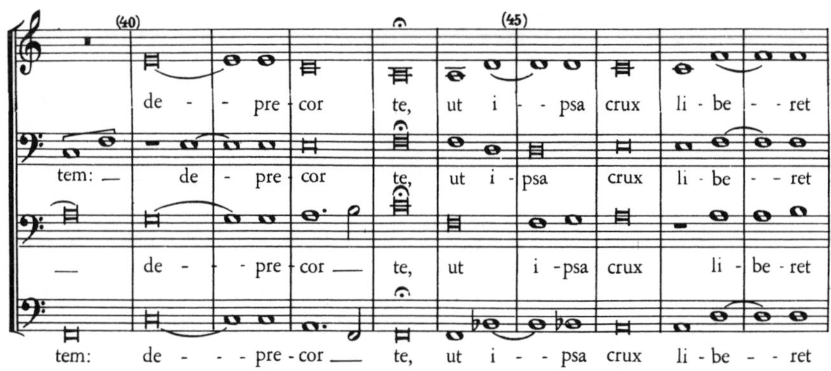

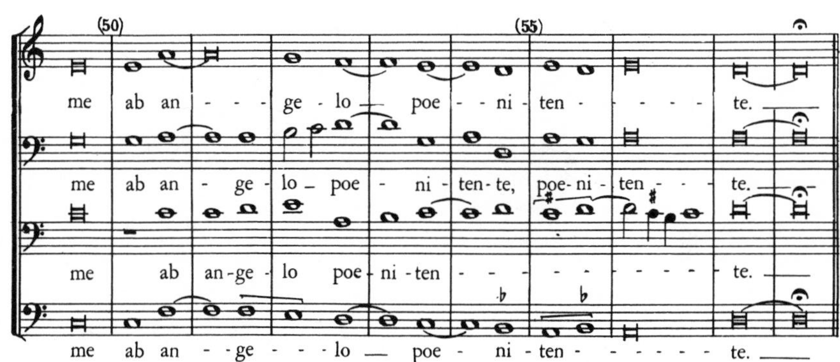

[From *WJP, Motetten*, Vol. II, P. 35]

a cont'd

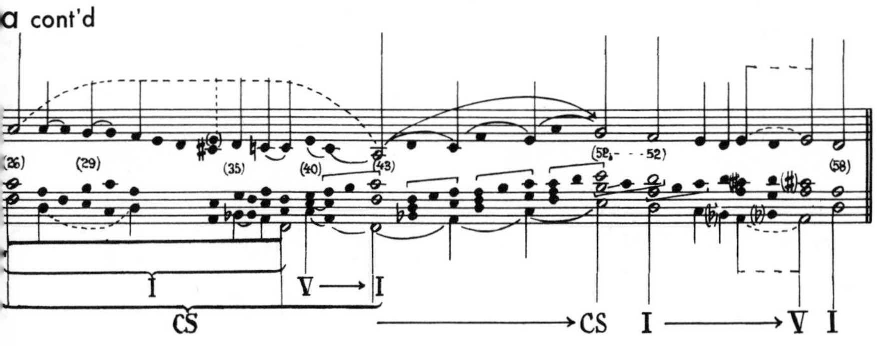